Over the Line

Over the Line

North Korea's Negotiating Strategy

Chuck Downs

The AEI Press

Publisher for the American Enterprise Institute

WASHINGTON, D.C.

1999

The American Enterprise Institute thanks the Korea Foundation for support for this project.

Available in the United States from the AEI Press, c/o Publisher Resources Inc., 1224 Heil Quaker Blvd., P.O. Box 7001, La Vergne, TN 37086-7001. To order: 1-800-269-6267. Distributed outside the United States by arrangement with Eurospan, 3 Henrietta Street, London WC2E 8LU England.

Library of Congress Cataloging in Publication Data

Downs, Chuck.
    Over the line : North Korea's negotiating strategy /
Chuck Downs.
      p. cm.
    Includes bibliographical references and index.
    ISBN 0-8447-4028-4 (cloth : alk. paper). — ISBN 0-8447-4029-1
(pbk. : alk. paper).
    1. Korea (North) — Foreign relations. 2. Negotiation. I. Title.
DS935.65.D69   1999
327.5193—dc21   99-12372
                                       CIP

3 5 7 9 10 8 6 4

The AEI Press
Publisher for the American Enterprise Institute
1150 17th Street, N.W., Washington, D.C. 20036

Printed in the United States of America

Contents

Foreword

Dealing with North Korea is a tough proposition. There are no quick fixes. The North Koreans pursue every tactic in the book and they are especially adept at brinkmanship. They have a reputation for being hard nosed, unyielding, and uncompromising. By simply refusing to come to terms, they force tensions to a breaking point, leaving their cliff-hanging opponents biting their nails. They threaten war, engage in terrorism and infiltration, mobilize their public, call up their reserves, execute counter-revolutionaries, put their oversized military on full alert, and appeal to humanitarianism. They make a show that convinces us they mean business. They are at once pathetic and pathological. Then they extract their price and celebrate. They take from the negotiating table what they are unable to win in any direct conflict. They survive not just to fight another day, but to create a new crisis when they are better equipped and stronger.

But they have not always won. They back down when they encounter skill and tough resistance. After the axe murders at the Joint Security Area in 1976, General Richard Stilwell had B-52s fired up and flying. Fighter aircraft were called in from bases in Japan. U.S. and ROK forces went to heightened alert. Knowing North Korean actions had alienated even his Communist allies, Kim Il Sung requested private meetings with the United States, issued what passed for an apology, deflected blame to the armistice arrangements, and pulled back his troops. Again, in 1981, the North Koreans fired a missile at an SR-71 "Blackbird" reconnaissance plane. The United States issued a stern warning that it would take out the missile site the next time they tried that, and it never happened again. Those are only two examples.

On many occasions, firm resolve, intelligence, and wisdom foiled North Korean schemes at the bargaining table. In hundreds of instances where words and not lives were at stake, North Korea demanded everything but actually took whatever it could get.

Failing to see what motivates the North Korean regime's agile shifts of tactics, many analysts find them bizarre, illogical, and puzzling. More myths than explanations have arisen from North Korean negotiating behavior. More anecdotes than serious studies have been used to instruct officials who have the task of dealing with North Korea. All too often, intelligence agencies and scholars alike are allowed to shrug their shoulders and say no one really knows what North Korea is trying to do. The long negotiating record has not been mastered and historical precedents have been ignored.

What is worse, policy toward North Korea is based on preconceived notions and Western logic that have little relevance to the regime's unique character. And to support policy objectives, American diplomats and analysts come up with explanations about North Korean behavior that support whatever arrangement they're trying to deliver. They persuade the American people to support policy outcomes that are little more than concoctions of how things *should* work out with North Korea. Analyses and interpretations of why North Korea does what it does are distorted to give weight to immediate policy objectives. Even the North Koreans are happy to play this game— they are more than willing to subscribe to deception if it means they benefit—so they temper or escalate their actions to lend credence to misconceptions that serve their purposes.

The stakes in negotiating with North Korea are too high to build policy on misconception. These stakes include an immediate threat to 37,000 American military personnel assigned to South Korea to defend democracy and American interests there. They include the lives of more than 46 million South Koreans who live under constant danger of a repeat of the Korean War. And if North Korea is able to deploy the missiles it is developing, the stakes include the security of the East Asian region, with the potential for widespread international conflict. For these reasons, we must have a clear understanding of what motivates North Korea, how the regime pursues its objectives, and what will condition its behavior.

It is not a new idea that the answers to these questions can be found in North Korea's negotiating record. When American negotiators first encountered North Koreans across the table, they assiduously recorded their observations. Admiral Joy, Herbert Goldhamer, Arthur Dean, and William Vatcher, conscious of the danger North Korean negotiating behavior posed, left us a detailed record of the proceedings they witnessed. The Republic of Korea has trained generations of its diplomats with compilations of the progress and pitfalls of South-North dialogue. But for more than a generation of American scholars, these rigorous analyses of how North Korea accomplished its objectives have been ignored as too cumbersome and as relics of the cold war.

This book is the first effort since the 1950s to take an objective and more thorough look at North Korea's pattern of behavior, across the entire spectrum of its negotiations. It includes material from obscure, out-of-print sources, and military records that have never before been exposed to the public. Chuck Downs, a former deputy director of the Pentagon's Asia and Pacific office, has written a single volume that puts North Korea's five decades of negotiations within readers' reach. His insightful analysis of the material, well-reasoned arguments, and well-substantiated conclusions are right on target. James M. Lee, a bilingual Korean-American and a former adviser to the commander of the United Nations Command, provided AEI with an excellent, thorough research draft covering the military negotiations, the highlights of which Mr. Downs condensed for this book. The result is a comprehensive study of North Korea's entire negotiating record from the truce talks at Panmunjom to the four-party talks in Geneva.

The world needs to deal with North Korea from an objective perspective informed by the accumulated experience of its negotiators. We have to open our eyes to what North Korea tries to do, and how it tries to do it. First, we have to read North Korea's negotiating record closely. This book represents a very careful effort at describing the motives and objectives of North Korea's regime. It seeks to clarify the regime's negotiating strategy in a way that has not been done before.

With North Korea on the verge of developing nuclear weapons and long-range missile delivery systems, this book cannot be read a second too late.

JAMES R. LILLEY
American Enterprise Institute and
former U.S. ambassador to Korea and to
the People's Republic of China

Acknowledgments

The book benefits immeasurably from the contributions of James M. Lee, a Korean-born American patriot. During the Korean War, Mr. Lee graduated from Seoul National University and volunteered to work with UN forces, serving in the Pusan perimeter and the Inchon landing with the U.S. First Marine Division. He went on to devote twenty-eight years of his life to dealing with North Korea as a principal adviser to the commander of the United Nations Command, Military Armistice Commission (UNCMAC). In that role, he attended every significant meeting of the Military Armistice Commission, including a number of secret meetings, during the crucially important years 1966–1994. For that service to his adopted country, Mr. Lee was awarded the president's award for Distinguished Federal Civilian Service in 1997, becoming the first American citizen born in Korea to receive that high commendation.

No other individual has devoted so long a period of his life and so much of his talent, at such a consistently high level of responsibility, to the task of understanding negotiations with North Korea. Recognizing his unique contributions to the field, the American Enterprise Institute, on the initiative of Ambassador James R. Lilley, then director of Asian Studies, hired Mr. Lee to put together a history of the military negotiations with North Korea. Diplomatic negotiations with North Korea have received substantial study, but military negotiations have received little attention, in spite of their fundamental importance to understanding the regime's strategy and objectives. Researching UNC-MAC documents is difficult; access can be obtained only through military channels, and filing procedures have been inconsistent. It is almost impossible to approach the task without first knowing what to look for, and that is why Mr. Lee's role was especially valuable. Mr. Lee's research in these obscure documents constitutes the first full-scale investigation of the UNCMAC proceedings; and it is comprehensive—the material condensed in chapters 6 and 7 of this book represents only a fraction of his extensive research and observations. Mr. Lee's fine work on the research draft that formed the basis of these chapters and his advice and comments throughout the book are very gratefully acknowledged, as is the role of the American Enterprise Institute in hiring Mr. Lee to conduct the research.

Jim Lilley of the American Enterprise Institute originated the idea for the study and guided the project to completion. He not only assigned the project to me, but also provided constant encouragement and advice. At Jim Lilley's invitation, the project was launched in a seminar attended by the nation's foremost experts on negotiations with Korea—including Ambassador Robert M. Gallucci, Admiral William Pendley, Dr. Henry Sokolski, Colonel James Young, Mr. Rinn Supp-Shinn, and representatives of intelligence agencies. Their counsel was appreciated whether or not this book reflects their views.

I am deeply appreciative of the unwavering support of the leadership of the American Enterprise Institute, President Christopher DeMuth, Executive Vice President David Gerson, and Senior Vice President John Bolton. The American Enterprise Institute is an intellectual gold mine that could not be better suited to promoting significant foreign policy research. I found enthusiastic interest, insightful comments, research leads, and excellent ideas in frequent discussions with Jim Lilley, John Bolton, Jeane Kirkpatrick, Nicholas Eberstadt, Lynne Cheney, John Fonte, and Jeff Gedmin. The project benefited immensely from the publishing experience of Dana Lane, Virginia Bryant, Leigh Tripoli, Alice Anne English, and Mary Catherine English, my superb editor; from the research advice of Dan Foster, Gene Hosey, Andy Olson, and Jonathan Tombes; and from the assistance of researchers and interns including Yoshiko Tanaka, Jed Stremel, Jane Dokko, and David Nemecek, whose persistence was essential to finding the original of the Kaesong document referred to in chapter 4.

I appreciate the willingness of a number of experts and former government officials to answer my calls, letters, and inquiries regarding the events surrounding the Kaesong negotiations: David Rees, Brian Crozier, Lord Greenhill of Harrow (who is the last surviving participant in the Rusk meeting with British embassy personnel on July 3, 1951), Ambassador David Popper, and Dr. Lincoln Bloomfield. None of them was in a position to substantiate, but each of them agreed it was possible, that the choice of Kaesong for the opening negotiations was influenced by Kim Philby.

A number of experts on Korean matters kindly reviewed drafts and offered highly valuable suggestions. They included Spence Richardson, Colonel Ashton H. Ormes, Wallace O. Knowles, Colonel Donald W. Boose, Jr., Guy Arrigoni, and David E. Reuther. Because I wrote the book while on a career rotational detail from my position in the Pentagon's office of International Security Affairs, I am grateful to a number of people who facilitated that detail: Joseph S. Nye, Franklin D. Kramer, Kurt M. Campbell, Frederick C. Smith, and Franklin C. Miller. In order to guarantee that all material used in this book was properly releasable, I was required by regulation to submit the draft to the Pentagon's office of security review. I am grateful to that office for carrying out its responsibilities expeditiously. I am compelled to point out that the views expressed in this book are those of the author and do not reflect the official policy or position of the Department of Defense or the U.S. government. While I am grateful to a number of officials at the Department of Defense for their kind encouragement, they bear no responsibility for this book's content.

Finally, I proudly acknowledge the patient support of my wife, Jill, and our children, who have grown used to having me descend to my "dungeon" to work on this book every evening and every weekend. Writing this book took much longer than anyone expected, more than a year beyond my time at AEI. I would probably not have had the tenacity to stay with the project had it not been for their understanding, and the inspiring enthusiasm my father showed for the project during the final year of his life.

CHUCK DOWNS
McLean, Virginia
November 11, 1998

1

★

Understanding North Korea's Negotiating Strategy

In the Korean War, almost half a million Americans, South Koreans, and other allied soldiers[1] lost their lives in one of history's noblest replies to totalitarian aggression. More than 10 million South Koreans, more than a million Americans, and tens of thousands of allied personnel put their lives on the line for freedom on the Korean peninsula.[2] Despite this demonstration of resolve, the war in Korea was a limited one. The forces of freedom accepted a zone for tyranny, ignoring Benjamin Franklin's admonition that those who "give up essential liberty to obtain a little temporary safety deserve neither liberty nor safety."[3]

The end of the war marked a partial victory for freedom, but safety was not assured. Since the 1953 armistice, 221 American troops and 496 South Korean troops have been killed or wounded trying to preserve the fragile truce that emerged from the Korean War. Many of them have died along the line that transects the peninsula and divides freedom from tyranny. In South Korea 302 civilians have been killed or wounded by North Korean agents who crossed over the line with orders to kill.

Those who have lived under North Korean tyranny have borne even greater sacrifices. Pierre Rigolo, a French scholar who wrote about North Korea in *Le livre noir du communisme*, calculated that 100,000 North Koreans have been killed in Workers Party purges,

1.5 million in detention camps, 500,000 in famine, and 100,000 thus far in the 1990s food shortages.[4] Within the year 1996 alone, more than 500 North Korean citizens who had offended the North Korean regime were executed.[5] An estimated 2 million to 5 million face starvation today because of the regime's stewardship of the northern zone of the peninsula.[6] Kim Jong Il's Marxist regime is willing to sacrifice the welfare of its own people in the interest of maintaining the regime's control and extending its own survival. No matter how much the rest of the world might try to ease the collapsing regime's transition and facilitate normal diplomatic relations within the international system, we must not forget the regime's disregard for its own people. Yet some concessions Western negotiators have made have facilitated the regime's oppression of its people.

North Korea's aggressive behavior was not extinguished by its defeat in the Korean War nor by its pledges in the armistice agreement. From 1966 through 1969, North Korea instigated 241 armed attacks on U.S. and South Korean military personnel. These included sinking ships and shooting down aircraft, bombings, assaults on the South Korean presidential mansion, the seizure of the USS *Pueblo*, and commando landings in South Korea. North Korea has engaged in terrorism, attempting to assassinate South Korea's presidents, and killing innocent civilians traveling on commercial airliners. It has identified its nuclear energy production facilities as military secrets and refused to account for the plutonium produced in those facilities. Even while facing famine, it invests scarce resources in offensive military capabilities—long-range missiles—so that it can threaten to deliver weapons of mass destruction. North Korea continues to defy with impunity international commitments that limit its military buildup. Despite international efforts to modify its behavior with inducements at the negotiating table, North Korea's military advantages may yet be turned on Western forces in a war. Yet some concessions Western negotiators have made have strengthened the North's military might.

How this small, relatively powerless nation uses negotiation to advance domestic oppression and foreign intimidation deserves careful scrutiny. Although North Korea brings very little to the negotiating table, it has consistently won benefits that strengthen the regime's political control and improve its military capabilities. The consequences of this phenomenon are crucial to the security and prosperity of people around the world. Were it not for the regime's careful and clever management of the process of negotiation, few people outside the Korean peninsula would have had any reason at all to concern themselves with North Korea. The negotiating process, and North Korea's manipulation of it, is what makes North Korea matter at all.

Negotiations with North Korea are widely recognized as difficult and unpleasant. Many who read this book will learn the process has been even more unpleasant than they suspected. Secretary of State Dean Rusk referred to the ten months of negotiations with North Korea after the seizure of the USS *Pueblo* as the most frustrating episode in his career. Kenneth T. Young, a career diplomat who directed preparatory talks for the Korean peace conference, wrote that "the shrill echo and cold image of Panmunjom" cast a pall over U.S. relations with North Korea's ally China for over a decade.[7] Calling the negotiations "trying indeed," Korean War commander General Matthew B. Ridgway commented, "Sometimes the repetition of points already made, the oratorical flourishes, the tiresome vituperation were nearly enough to make men welcome a return to battle."[8]

The first American negotiator to confront the North Koreans wrote, "Discussion between Nam Il and me flowed with all the speed of stiff concrete mix."[9] A subsequent American negotiator complained, "No individual could speak personally to anyone on the other side. There could be no exchange even of ordinary amenities at the start or end of a meeting. . . . There was no way in which the normal tensions of difficult diplomatic negotiations could be relieved."[10]

When Americans first found themselves across the table from North Koreans, they were perplexed by the extreme rigidity of North Korean behavior. The negotiating records are sprinkled with fascinating reflections on cultural differences, such as this description Colonel Andrew J. Kinney wrote of North Korean negotiator General Lee Sang Cho:

> Four black flies were very much at home crawling over North Korean General Lee Sang Cho's face. The tough Communist negotiator made no move to flick them off.
>
> I watched, fascinated. Not a facial muscle twitched as one fly wandered over a bushy eyebrow and another paced down the bridge of his nose. He remained perfectly motionless, his face expressionless.
>
> I wondered: "What's he trying to prove? That flies don't bother him? That American DDT, used to spray the Korean Armistice tent, is worthless? Is he entertaining us with Oriental muscle control?"[11]

Kinney's superior, Admiral C. Turner Joy, also noted Lee's stoic behavior: "It fascinated all of us to watch Lee Sang Cho permit flies to crawl across his face without brushing them away." Admiral Joy considered Lee's behavior a psychological tactic that had little effect. "I concluded," Joy wrote, "he was simply accustomed to having flies on his person."[12]

For many years, the most undiplomatic insults and rudeness characterized the North Korean negotiating style. One American negotiator had to endure being called "a capitalist crook, rapist, thief, robber of pennies from the eyes of the dead, mongrel of uncertain origin," a "murderer lying in the gutter with filthy garbage," a "war monger," and a consort of rams.[13] In the first sessions the United Nations Command held with North Korea, Admiral Joy, a man of uncommon dignity and patience, countered such invectives with the following lecture:

> Military men are expected to be sufficiently mature to realize that bluster and bombast phrased in intemperate language do not and cannot affect the facts of any military situation. No amount of such vituperation as was indulged in by you this morning . . . will sway the concentration of the UNC [UN Command] delegation on the serious problems before this conference. No amount of discourtesy will tempt the UNC delegation to utilize similar tactics.[14]

North Korean verbal assaults continued unabated for decades. After Americans walked out of a particularly abusive meeting, the chief North Korean representative shouted after them, "Get out of South Korea with your troops like that! Get out quickly, Son of a bitch!"[15] Threats of war have also marked North Korean negotiating tactics. Even though North Korean verbal assaults have abated since 1991, one North Korean official threatened in 1994 that his South Korean counterpart would burn in "a sea of fire," and on December 3, 1998, the vice minister of North Korea's People's Armed Forces threatened to "blow up the territory of the United States as a whole."[16]

South Koreans, often critical of American negotiating techniques, are quick to point out that the rudeness shown by the Communist North Koreans is a matter of tactics, not culture. A South Korean who participated in North-South talks, Song Jong Hwan, observed that North Koreans exploit a Western cultural tendency toward objective self-doubt. "It is quite possible to exploit this tendency to self-accusation," Song noted, "by setting into motion a steady barrage of hostile actions accompanied by expressions of hatred. The natural reaction of the victims, if they are Americans, can be and often is bewilderment, followed by guilt." He concludes that this creates "an atmosphere conducive to concessions whose purpose is to propitiate the alleged injured party."[17]

For years North Korea has won concessions from the West because of its reputation for ill temper. To this day, North Korea escapes being called to task for infractions of international agreements because those who wish to see them stay at a negotiating table strive to maintain a commodious environment. Western negotiators avoid raising some issues that might irritate the North Koreans and cause them to call off the talks. The North Koreans, accordingly, benefit from merely entering into negotiations, regardless of the outcome.

Whatever tactical benefit North Korean discourtesy has had, however, it has also reinforced a Western tendency to view the negotiations as a moral confrontation. Any negotiation with North Korea is a confrontation between two distinct value systems. Whether the indignities suffered fortify resolve or weaken it depends a great deal on the character of the negotiators. Generally, Western negotiators have been frustrated by their own inability to deal effectively with what they have considered North Korea's immoral and underhanded tactics.

Herbert Goldhamer, a RAND scholar with an appreciation for Machiavellian realpolitik, was asked to assess United Nations negotiators' performance during the Korean armistice negotiations in 1951. At that time, Western optimism about the United Nations was fresh and untarnished, and the negotiators were particularly proud to represent the high ideals of the newly created international organization. The international coalition demanded the highest standards of professional diplomatic behavior. Goldhamer observed that the Western negotiators suffered precisely because of self-imposed requirements for maintaining the moral high ground:

- UN negotiators tolerated insults and disadvantageous arrangements because they believed "the only matters of real consequence were the actual discussions in the conference room."
- Reasonable and gracious behavior was expected to demonstrate the good faith of Western negotiators and "induce by a process of gratitude similar courteous behavior from the Communists."
- The Communists were expected not to take unfair advantage of concessions or opportunities that Western negotiators had graciously extended to them.

- Western negotiators, who avoided the tactic of bluffing, took Communist demands at face value, assuming similar restraint by the Communists.
- UN standards of diplomatic courtesy meant that complaints against the Communists were delivered in a soft and plaintive manner.[18]

According to Goldhamer, "the belief that one should or could only ask for those things which were ethically justified was quite strong" among UN negotiators. Their reaction to his clever tactical advice was "sufficient shock to make me feel slightly uncomfortable, as if I were some sort of immoral monster associating with persons of a finer and more spiritual character." [19]

Although Admiral Joy believed the moral underpinnings of his team were certainly to their credit, he became painfully aware that North Korea took advantage of some Western attitudes. For example, he surmised that North Korea used the West's impatient desire for progress to its own advantage. He lamented that Americans were especially weakened by impatience:

> We are taught by word and example throughout our lives that once we tackle a job, the point is to finish it successfully as soon as possible. It is probably true that this same quality of impatience made America the greatest nation on earth. It is certainly true, however, that the Communist negotiating method recognizes and seeks to gain advantage by aggravating our American tendency to impatience through the imposition of endless delays.[20]

Joy believed that North Korea found Western negotiators especially pliable "if delays meant greatly increased human suffering and loss of life."[21] Joy had in mind "war and its attendant horrors," but by the end of the twentieth century, North Korea would use the suffering of its own starving people as leverage to pry concessions from the West.

Fred C. Iklé, who wrote a seminal study of diplomatic negotiations, observed that Americans have frequently exercised self-restraint to their detriment. Disavowing a constructive ability to employ threats, he noted, had particularly unfortunate consequences in Korea:

> The Korean Armistice negotiations might have ended faster or on terms more favorable to the West had Peking been left

in greater doubt whether or not the Chinese mainland (then exceedingly vulnerable) might be attacked from the air or the sea. At least the threat should have been kept alive that the United Nations forces would try to regain part of North Korea. On February 3, 1951, months before the armistice talks had even started, the State Department declared (according to the *New York Times*) "that the restoration of peace in Korea would not be helped by 'speculation' about whether UN forces would or would not cross the 38th parallel if they reached it in a new offensive." The restoration of peace might indeed have been helped if just such speculation had been encouraged very loudly in Washington![22]

The fact that Western negotiators are distinguished from their North Korean counterparts by a difference in moral values, self-restraint, and a higher standard of diplomatic behavior ought to equip them with, at minimum, righteous indignation. Yet the opposite is true. American negotiators have frequently given North Korea the benefit of the doubt when none was deserved. Such naiveté in the face of the nature of North Korean strategy has naturally been exploited by North Koreans.

In the first months of the armistice negotiations, North Korea claimed that UN forces had violated the neutrality of the negotiating conference and had killed a Communist leader who supported the Kim Il Sung faction. For all the UN forces knew, Yao Ching Hsiang was killed by a competing Communist faction in the strife-ridden environment of North Korean politics at that time. For reasons of his own, Kim Il Sung wanted to make Yao an heroic martyr, and "spontaneously" orchestrated an elaborate memorial service for him. At the negotiating table, North Korea found an opportunity to make a speech extolling Yao's virtues and invited the United Nations delegation to attend Yao's memorial service. Because the request was made with apparent sincerity, the UN delegation, who had been called Yao's murderers not long before, actually considered attending the Communist service.[23]

Seventeen years later, North Korea seized an American vessel in international waters and incarcerated its crew more than ten months until the United States rendered a humiliating apology. An American colonel, probably without thinking, pocketed the pen his superior had used to sign the apology. When the colonel walked away from the table to meet the crew members of the *Pueblo*, a staff member of the North Korean secretariat ran after him. The North Korean asked to have the pen back, and the American, whose options ranged from denying that he had it to smashing it into the ground, chose to hand it over politely. The gratified North Korean soldier delivered the pen to his superiors, and it has been on display in North Korea's Panmunjom museum ever since.

Why the West has not been more creative, more demanding, or more unyielding in its dealings with North Korea is difficult to assess. Part of the reason is a lack of vigilance, and part a lack of resolve. But part of it is a certain optimism and a desire to avoid human suffering. The colonel who returned the pen wanted to avoid a complication that could send the *Pueblo*'s commander and his men back across the Bridge of No Return. He was more concerned about his fellow Americans' safety than about North Korea's propaganda. The negotiators who wondered whether they should attend the funeral of a Communist henchman thought that perhaps they could improve the negotiating environment. They were much more concerned about concluding an agreement than they were about the regime's political intrigues.

This deferential sensitivity to North Korea's wishes has often been rationalized as an effort to permit the Communist regime to save face. The concept of "face" deserves special attention in any study of negotiations with Asians because it is so widely believed to play an important role. Innumerable benefits have been bestowed on North Korea to help it save face, although the evidence indicates that North Korean negotiators are not at all embarrassed when their leadership orders them to portray themselves as hapless victims or settle for less than they previously sought. As Lucien Pye has pointed out, the preoccupation of Western negotiators with Asian face-saving is "greatly exaggerated." In a study of Chinese behavior, Pye pointed out, "The Chinese manipulate such solicitous attitudes to their own advantage."[24]

At the time of the armistice negotiations, Goldhamer detected a more complex phenomenon relating to notions of face. The Americans, not the Chinese or North Koreans, were the most concerned about being embarrassed. The American negotiating team, he observed, worried that they would be undermined by abrupt changes in policy in Washington:

> . . . while during the negotiations there was constant talk of the Communists being concerned to "save face," this psychological consideration was in fact probably much more important in the UN delegation than for the Communists.

We thus have the curious spectacle of the UN delegation assuming that Orientals in negotiation are concerned greatly with "saving face" whereas they themselves, that is, the UN, were the primary consumers of this particular psychological tendency."[25]

Goldhamer concluded that the desire to avoid subsequent embarrassment made the UN negotiators present their demands tentatively; they perceived that a position "must be stated in a way as to permit retreat to be graceful and not to cause a loss of face."[26]

A question that has for decades plagued analysts of negotiations with North Korea is whether a change in attitude and behavior on the Western side of the table would necessarily change the nature of the process and improve outcomes. Goldhamer clearly believed it would. He tried to persuade the UN to meet every challenge with a firm response:

I am confident that prompt action on completely trivial matters would have had real consequences of an advantageous character, that is, such a UN reaction would have diminished Communist confidence in how much they could get away with in the way of psychological warfare and other attempts to bring pressure on the UN delegation. Prompt reaction would also probably have given the Communist delegation a greater sense of the ultimate intransigence of the UN position.[27]

As the history of the negotiations makes clear, however, Western negotiators are not always at liberty to take unyielding stands. Despite Goldhamer's advice, Washington might not have supported the negotiators if they picked fights over trivial matters. Western negotiators must be responsive to the wide range of opinion that is generated in free societies. Repeatedly the policymakers to whom the negotiators report have avoided well-defined positions and have sometimes discarded positions at the last minute in the interest of peace. But when negotiators have been able to hold firm and back up their words with military action, North Korea has always yielded.

North Korea negotiates from a position of understanding these and other weaknesses that plague representatives of democracies at the negotiating table. This understanding, in turn, makes the process of negotiation a fundamentally different process for North Korea. An American participant in the 1951–1953 armistice negotiations,

William H. Vatcher, described the disappointing but valuable lesson the United Nations began to grasp in its first sessions across the table from North Korea:

> It learned that the basic premises of the delegations for wanting a conference differed. To the Communists, negotiation is a technique in their broad strategy. What they cannot accomplish by one method, they attempt by another. Having been unsuccessful in attaining their objectives on the Korean field of battle, they turned to the conference table as a means of achieving their ends. Their use of the conference table was obvious indeed: to gain precious time while they rebuilt and strengthened their forces, to obtain every possible benefit from the UNC, and to serve as a sounding board for their propaganda.[28]

North Korea enters into negotiations for its own reasons. It does not generally participate in negotiations because it seeks an agreement. Its objective is to gain concessions and benefits merely in the process of agreeing to talk, or as a consequence of participating in talks. North Korea's opponents pursue negotiation as a means of reaching an agreement, and they expect that agreement to represent a bargain North Korea will honor. Neither their expectations of reaching an agreement nor their faith in North Korean adherence to the terms of its agreements is justified by North Korea's record.

There are also differences in the notion of give-and-take in the bargaining process. Song Jong Hwan has observed that the "Western, especially American, view of negotiation is based on a commercial tradition which is inherently predisposed toward compromise: each trading transaction, after all, must hold some profit for both parties. Negotiation is over the division of profits."[29] Americans consider concessions a normal part of the bargaining process.

North Korea claims a distinctly different view. In its official dictionary, the word "concession" is described as "giving up one's right or privilege to others." So that the onerous meaning of the term is fully understood, the North Korean dictionary expounds, "In our class struggle, a concession means a surrender."[30] But like so many other things written in North Korea, that definition is more fiction than reality, more propaganda than fact. The North pursues concessions cleverly when it serves the state's purposes. Nevertheless, the notion that something can be generously conveyed to the opposing side without recompense is clearly considered treasonous.[31]

North Korea's negotiating practices are neither flawless nor overwhelmingly successful. But they are devious. As South Korean negotiator Lee Dong Bok has cautioned, "North Korea has continued to remain committed to its own rules of the game, turning every opportunity to talk its opponents into an arena where it put all the negotiating techniques that it had at its disposal to their best use."[32]

Like many countries, North Korea has a repertoire of skillful negotiating techniques. Many of them are not attributable to North Korea's unique ideological foundation, its strong central leadership system, or its cultural characteristics. They are methods any negotiator might pursue to win the greatest advantage. They include the following widely used techniques:

- Making threats and insults
- Using obsequiousness and flattery
- Stalling and delaying
- Demanding faster action
- Portraying itself as strong, with victor's prerogatives
- Portraying itself as the victim, seeking to right old wrongs
- Waiting for opponents to reveal objectives, claims, or accusations
- Insisting on being first to present demands, claims, or accusations
- Playing adversaries against each other
- Pretending there are internal differences over negotiating authority

In addition to these techniques, however, North Korea has developed tactics that are hallmarks of a unique negotiating style. Some of these include:

- Setting preconditions for talks
- Creating incidents that redirect the attention of the negotiating parties
- Setting the stage to put its opponents on the defensive
- Loading the agenda with foregone conclusions
- Negotiating North Korean objectives first
- Perceiving concessions as a sign of weakness

- Introducing spurious issues as bargaining chips
- Reversing charges by claiming the other party committed the grievance
- Incorporating a North Korean veto on enforcement of agreements
- Demanding renegotiation of previously negotiated provisions

What differentiates North Korea's negotiating strategy from other countries' is that it derives from the fundamental difference that distinguishes North Korea from all other countries. Its negotiators are bound by strict discipline to the objectives of a single decisionmaker. North Korean negotiators, along with all other subjects of the regime, adhere to a pledge: "They absolutize, defend, and safeguard the Leader ideologically, they carry out the Leader's teachings unconditionally to the last, and they dedicate their entire being to the Leader to ease the worries of the Leader."[33] North Korean negotiators have seldom been troubled with consistency, logic, or arguments over "rights"; their task has been to implement a strategy dictated in Pyongyang.

The degree to which North Korea's peculiar totalitarian form of government would influence its negotiating style was noticeable from the very beginning. In 1951, when liaison officers were sent to work out arrangements before the official negotiations started, American Colonel Kinney asked a straightforward question: "Is your delegation agreeable to meeting on July 10?" Whatever authority Soviet-trained North Korean Colonel Chang had been given by his superiors, he had not been given the authority to set a date, and was not about to interpret his instructions creatively. Chang replied that the time of the meeting had been arranged by the commanders. Kinney in turn pointed out that the agreement merely specified "between the tenth and the fifteenth," and he had been ordered to fix the date for the start of the talks. Chang replied that the date "shall be as the commanders have agreed." "But when?" asked Kinney, "Shall it be the tenth, eleventh, twelfth?" Chang insisted the matter was not for negotiation by liaison officers. At that point, a Marine colonel advised Kinney to try a different approach. Kinney then announced, "The United Nations Command delegation will arrive in Kaesong at 1100 hours on July 10." Chang replied, "The commanders have agreed and it shall be so."[34]

Systemic differences continue to shape the negotiating process. North Korea's negotiating strategy is rooted in its unique brand of Communist ideology, which it calls *Juche*. The word is often translated into English as "self-reliance," but that translation gives it a connotation that, to American minds, is incorrectly laden with images of valiant frontiersmen battling the elements. Nicholas Eberstadt more accurately defines *Juche* as "Take Charge-ism."[35] An ideology of self-reliance could never rationalize the mendicant policies North Korea has pursued in the 1990s; but an ideology that sees such policies as merely another way for the state to "take charge," subvert external interests, and strengthen its grip on its own population would certainly adopt such policies. The negotiating record set out in this book clarifies that in every instance North Korea strives to take charge of the process. Whether by intimidation, deceptive acquiescence, or the creation of incidents that determine the course of the negotiations, North Korea does what it can to direct or terminate the course of any negotiation.

As a consequence of "take charge-ism," North Korea has certain unmistakable advantages at the negotiating table. North Korea has made a science out of the Chinese notion that a crisis has two attributes—danger and opportunity.[36] Managing both aspects of crisis requires a high level of discipline. A nation that must accommodate many voices cannot adhere to a perilous negotiating course that might bring the nation to the brink of annihilation. That strategy, which North Korea mastered so well under the leadership of Kim Il Sung, requires iron-fisted control by one side of the negotiating table and clever manipulation of the other. In pursuing such brinkmanship, tyranny is a strategic imperative.

Studying the systemic differences between North Korean tyranny and Western liberty can yield important lessons. Gyula Szilassy, a nineteenth-century Austrian-Hungarian diplomat, said, "The best diplomat is he who, inspired solely by cold reason, asks himself only what he can obtain and how he will arrive at it."[37] This book attempts to reverse the process: to reveal North Korea's negotiating strategy by asking what diplomats in North Korea think they can obtain and how they think they can obtain it.

North Korea's strategy emerges from the broad sweep of its negotiating record—from the armistice negotiations, the talks that were incidental to the implementation of the armistice, the discussions that defused crises instigated by North Korea, the dialogue between South Korea and North Korea, and the international efforts to force North Korea to abide by its nuclear agreements. Patterns emerge, and the strategy they expose is intriguingly consistent and well designed.

Those who remember that vigilance is the price of liberty will notice a pattern in North Korea's behavior and be alarmed. Tyranny continues to threaten liberty on the Korean peninsula. In the current series of talks with North Korea, the West still needs to hold ground in the war of nerves that has been played out in face-to-face confrontations with North Korea for almost half a century. The starting point is understanding the nature of the struggle.

Dealing with North Korea since the terrible sacrifices of 1950–1953 has been a contest convened at negotiating tables where freedom and tyranny have vied for advantage, with human lives at stake. Every success in this process, for either side, has been attributable to resolve.

2

Securing Korean Democracy

At the end of World War II, the victorious allies perceived that the people of Korea were unprepared for independence because they lacked political maturity and stable institutions. The people of Korea, however, believed they had been prepared by decades of suffering under Japanese rule to take their rightful place among the independent nations of the world.[1] Roosevelt and Stalin began to discuss Korea's status at the conferences in Cairo, Teheran, Yalta, and Potsdam as the war came to a close, but in these meetings Korea was far from the most pressing topic. Roosevelt advocated a trusteeship for Korea, reasoning that four great powers—the United States, the USSR, Great Britain, and China—should administer the country until it could develop stable political institutions. That objective made considerable good sense internationally, but showed little comprehension of the forces at work inside Korea.

The United States perceived a need to buy time for Korea's political development. But time was short. Japanese troops in Korea had been scattered to operations elsewhere in the closing months of the Pacific war, and those who remained in Korea could not keep order. The lights had been turned off in most Japanese-run factories, and the economy of Korea was in ruin. On August 10, 1945, Japan offered to surrender Korea and by that date 120,000 Soviet troops had already entered North Korea.[2] Among them were some 30,000 Russian-trained troops of Korean ethnic extraction, including an individual who called himself Kim Il Sung.[3]

In Washington, two young Army colonels serving in the Pentagon were assisting in a late-night meeting hurriedly called to decide how to proceed to accept the surrender. A future secretary of state, Colonel Dean Rusk (soon to figure prominently in discussions of Korea as assistant secretary of state for east Asia), and a future commander of U.S. forces in the Far East, Colonel Charles Bonesteel, were asked on short notice "to come up with a proposal which would harmonize the political desire to have U.S. forces receive the surrender as far north as possible and the obvious limitations on the ability of the U.S. forces to reach the area."[4] The two picked the 38th parallel, a line clearly marked on available maps.[5]

"It was intended to be no more than a temporary and facilitative demarcation line, simply for the purpose of accepting the surrender of Japanese troops," historian Richard Whelan aptly observed, "and not in any sense a political boundary."[6] Yet as Kim Joungwon pointed out in *Divided Korea*, "The division would have an immediate impact on internal politics . . . [and would be] even more damaging to the value of remaining Korean economic enterprise, for the two areas had been totally interdependent, both in agriculture and in industry."[7] The line would be seen as authorizing the division of Korea into an industrialized northern area of some 48,000 square miles and a predominantly agricultural area of approximately 37,000 square miles, including Korea's capital city of Seoul, in the south. Although well marked on political maps, the 38th parallel cut across topographical features, mountains and valleys, and provincial boundaries in a way that mocked military requirements and blocked political objectives. That it had been given little thought even in terms of the strategic assets conveyed was evident from the fact that the decision transferred Japan's nuclear weapons research center near Hamhung to Communist control.[8]

The line would, however, serve to protect half of Korea from being subsumed into the Soviet bloc. American policymakers had substantial cause for concern over the way the Soviet Union had rushed into Eastern Europe and established Communist dictatorships where it held military control. Having seen these consequences in Eastern Europe, the United States was eager to avoid the same results in the Far East. To establish order and provide a counterweight to Soviet influence in the southern part of the peninsula, the United States dispatched American troops, who arrived in Korea a full month after the Soviets. Lieutenant General John Reed Hodge was ordered to establish a military government,[9] accepting the surrender from the Japanese governor general on September 9, 1945.

For the next four years, the United States military sought to establish a single, unified Korea under a freely elected, non-Communist government. Establishing free political institutions in the complex political milieu of the emerging nation was, however, no easy task. Participation in political processes had been denied Koreans for decades (some would argue, centuries). Competition for political leadership was fierce between diverse local interests and a group of returning foreign-trained exiled nationalists. Some prominent figures were assassinated as they sought to consolidate their influence. There were frequent attempts at coup d'état. As many as 2 million refugees from the North surged south. The restive population demanded independence and reviled the notion of trusteeship. Even American-educated Korean leaders who had strong influence in the American Military Government proved to be uncompromising advocates of political resolutions the United States could not support. Sessions aimed at establishing trusteeship broke down when only the Soviet-trained Communists could muster sufficient internal party discipline to pretend to be supportive of that objective. They demanded that any party opposed to trusteeship should be disenfranchised.[10]

By September of 1947 many in Washington doubted that Korea was worth the trouble. The Joint Chiefs of Staff concluded that "the United States has little strategic interest in maintaining the present troops and bases in Korea."[11] Accordingly, the United States sought to pull out gracefully. It would not do so, however, without an attempt to determine the will of the Korean people themselves. The United States proposed a draft UN General Assembly resolution calling for elections throughout Korea by March 31, 1948. UN observers would guarantee that the elections held by both occupying powers were fair. Representation in the National Assembly would be proportionate to population. Proportionate representation, however, was unacceptable to the Soviets because the populous South would have twice the voting power in the National Assembly. The Soviets countered with a proposal for the simultaneous withdrawal of Soviet and American troops, leaving the people of Korea to sort out their disarray. That would have guaranteed violence the deciding role.

On this issue the line in Korea was actually drawn. The United States and the United Nations sought to avoid the bloodshed that the

Soviet approach would have guaranteed. The United Nations General Assembly (UNGA) voted on November 14, 1947, to establish a special commission to go to Korea, look into developments there, and arrange for free elections throughout the entire country prior to independence. Because the United Nations recognized the Nationalist government of China as the legitimate representative of China (rather than the Communists who were fighting for control of Beijing), the Soviets refused to participate in UN meetings and argued that UN resolutions on Korea were illegal. When commission members arrived at the 38th parallel, Soviet military authorities refused to let them cross into the North. UN-supervised elections could thereafter proceed only in the American zone, and were set for May 10, 1948.

A legitimately elected majoritarian government was established by the vote of May 10, although 100 of the 300 seats in the National Assembly were left vacant because North Koreans did not vote.[12] When the National Assembly convened, a coalition of those who advocated gradual moves toward independence[13] elected American-educated anti-Communist Syngman Rhee as its president; he took office on July 20, 1948. On August 15, 1948, the U.S. military government turned over its powers to President Rhee and the National Assembly. The United Nations General Assembly, in its resolution 293 of October 21, 1949, declared that the "Government of the Republic of Korea is a lawfully established government," "the only such Government in Korea," and that the elections of May 10, 1948, were "a valid expression of the free will of the electorate."[14]

U.S. occupation troops began to leave; by June 1949, only 500 American troops remained in Korea. They formed the Korean Military Advisory Group, whose mission was to help train the new Republic of Korea (ROK) Army. The United States, fearing that Rhee might attempt to attack the North in an effort to reunify his country, decided not to provide offensive weapons. The Communists were not so constrained. The Soviets sent North Korea fighter planes and tanks, and after China fell to the Communists, Mao sent 30,000 soldiers, primarily ethnic Koreans living in China, across the Yalu to join North Korean Army regulars.[15]

Unable to stop the May vote, Communists in the North retaliated by cutting off the flow of electricity from power plants in the North soon after the election. In July, the North Korean People's Assembly announced its own plans to hold an election on August 25 to elect representatives to a "Supreme People's Assembly." That assembly, convened in September, claimed to have participation from all of Korea, declaring that 360 of the 572 unelected members actually represented the South. The government of the Democratic People's Republic of Korea (DPRK) was proclaimed on September 9, 1949, with Kim Il Sung as its premier. Born Kim Song Chu in 1912, Kim had spent his youth in Manchuria and four years in the Soviet Union. While living in Manchuria, he adopted the well-known name of a legendary hero of the anti-Japanese resistance.[16] His own accession to power was not without competition and dissent, especially from a faction of Korean Communists trained in China, but, as Kim Joungwon points out, "By 1948, a more viable political base had been established in the North than in the South, largely because the Russians had followed a single-minded policy in backing up the consolidation of a political regime."[17]

Two distinct, hostile governments now claimed sovereignty over Korea, and their rivalry would confound international security for the rest of the twentieth century.

By 1950, the government of Syngman Rhee appeared to the North to be weak and fraught with internal disunity. Having seen that the United States had not intervened while mainland China fell to the Communists and Chiang Kai-shek retreated to Taiwan, Communists became convinced that the United States would also hesitate to support Syngman Rhee with troops. Believing that to be the case, Beijing and Moscow gave in to Kim Il Sung's persistent pleas to permit him to seize South Korea.[18] North Korea amassed and trained an army of at least 100,000 at the 38th parallel by late spring, 1950.[19] North Korea further initiated a series of deceptive peace offensives, including calls for peaceful unification, to distract the South's attention from the North's preparations for war.[20] On June 8, 1950, the central committee of the DPRK called for new Korea-wide elections and a new government to be established *in Seoul* by August 15, 1950. The significance of the North Korean statement was discounted by American officials.

On June 25, 1950, North Korea's army crossed over the line and surged toward Seoul. Inadequately equipped South Korean soldiers fought off the assault of Soviet tanks. Their numbers dwindled from 98,000 to 22,000 within three days of fighting.[21]

When word of the Communist invasion reached the United Nations, the Security Council acted swiftly to pass a resolution condemning the invasion, calling for the immediate end of fighting and demanding that "the authorities in North Korea" withdraw north of the 38th parallel "forthwith." Passed at a time when Nationalist China held the UN seat and the Soviet Union was boycotting UN participation, this resolution called upon all UN members to refrain from assisting North Korea.[22]

Just five months earlier, in a speech before Washington's National Press Club, Secretary of State Acheson had described a "defensive perimeter of the Pacific" encompassing countries like Japan and the Philippines which the United States would be compelled to defend. Korea, he said, was an area of "lesser" interest, susceptible to "subversion and penetration" that "cannot be stopped by military means."[23] His remarks were issued publicly. The Joint Staff's earlier conclusion that the United States had "little strategic interest" in its bases in Korea was classified, but may well have been provided to Moscow by the Soviet spy Kim Philby and his cohort. Together, these indications of U.S. disinterest may have given weight to Kim Il Sung's arguments in Moscow and Beijing.

Such statements by American policymakers before the start of the Korean War show the perils of appeasement, conflicting diplomatic signals, and isolationism. The invasion that followed proved that public indications of America's desire to exit a quagmire do not facilitate such an exit. Those who would challenge American interests, however, should also learn from what happened. Indications of lack of interest on the part of the United States cannot be taken as an endorsement of aggression. Even when there is strong evidence that American officials discount the strategic importance of some parts of the globe, America cannot be expected to sit idle while aggressive powers take actions inimical to American objectives. As other aggressors have done before and since, the North Koreans underestimated the American potential to respond strongly to clear acts of aggression against innocent people.

President Truman immediately convened a meeting with his advisers in Blair House and designed the course of American intervention to save the Republic of Korea. MacArthur, then commander in chief of American forces in the Far East, headquartered in Tokyo, was ordered to assist the ROK efforts. The U.S. Seventh Fleet was ordered to Sasebo, Japan, the nearest naval base to Korea. American airplanes flew over South Korea in preparation for evacuation of American civilians; the air war began when one of these was fired upon. In addition to taking out a number of Russian-supplied aircraft, American planes targeted and destroyed North Korean airfields. Airfields in

North Korea, as Admiral C. Turner Joy pointed out after the war, were not "combat effective" during any significant period of the Korean War.[24]

A second United Nations resolution on June 27, 1950, called for UN members "to provide such assistance to the Republic of Korea as may be necessary to repel the armed attack and to restore international peace and security in the area."[25] Fortified by the two UN resolutions, President Truman ordered American forces to turn back the North's aggression.

Early engagements demonstrated that a substantial commitment of troops and resources would be required. On July 1, 1950, a battalion at less than full strength was flown to Korea to undertake a holding action against the assault from the North. Task Force Smith, under the command of Lieutenant Colonel Brad Smith, could delay but not halt the North Korean advance. In the meantime, American troops from two divisions poured into Korea. MacArthur requested four divisions, was turned down, and increased his request. Americans began to comprehend the fierce strength and discipline that characterized the North Korean troops. Before he was taken prisoner, General William F. Dean advised MacArthur: "I am convinced the North Korean army and the North Korean soldier and his status of training and equipment have been underestimated."[26]

On July 7, 1950, the Security Council adopted Resolution 84 (1950) outlining the organization and management of UN troops in Korea as follows:

> *The Security Council,*
>   *Having determined* that the armed attack upon the Republic of Korea by forces from North Korea constitutes a breach of the peace,
>   *Having recommended* that members of the United Nations furnish such assistance to the Republic of Korea as may be necessary to repel the armed attack and to restore international peace and security in the area,
>   *Welcomes* the prompt and vigorous support which Governments and peoples of the United Nations have given to its resolutions 82 (1950) and 83 (1950) of 25 June and 27 June 1950 to assist the Republic of Korea in defending itself against armed attack and thus to restore international peace and security in the area;

Notes that members of the United Nations have transmitted to the United Nations offers of assistance for the Republic of Korea;

Recommends that all Members of the United Nations
make such forces and other assistance available to a unified
command under the United States of America;

Requests the United States to designate the commander
of such forces;

Authorizes the unified command at its discretion to use
the United Nations flag in the course of operations against
North Korean forces concurrently with the flags of the various nations participating;

Requests the United States to provide the Security
Council with reports as appropriate on the course of action
taken under the unified command.[27]

The United Nations Command was accordingly established under the
leadership of the United States and headed by a U.S.-appointed commander, General Douglas MacArthur. As the United Nations Command official history notes, "The establishment of the UNC in Tokyo
on 24 July 1950 marked the first time in history that free nations of
the world united under the UN flag to repel aggression."[28]

By mid-September, sixteen nations had contributed ground forces
to the UNC.[29] The contribution from the United States accounted for
50.3 percent of all ground forces (the ROK contributed 40.1 percent;
other UN members, 9.6) and 93.4 percent of UNC air forces (the ROK
contributed 5.6 percent).[30]

The North Koreans steadily advanced south and east across the
peninsula, while U.S. forces concentrated in and held a quadrangle
formed by a bend in the Naktong River surrounding the southern port
city of Pusan; this area became known as the Pusan perimeter. Fighting along the Pusan perimeter and throughout the ROK was intense.
The North Koreans lost no time consolidating their power, fortifying
Kimpo airport near Seoul for anticipated shipments of advanced aircraft from China and the USSR, and holding tribunals where South
Korean anti-Communist civilians were tried and executed.[31]

Their plans, however, were in vain. MacArthur ordered an am-
phibious landing at Inchon, the port west of Seoul, far behind North
Korean lines, and at the same time reinforced UN forces attacked
north from Pusan. This successful strategy cut off the North's commu-

nications and supply lines, and squeezed North Korean troops into a northward retreat.

The Republic's government was restored in its capital on September 29, 1950. MacArthur, in turning over control of the city to President Rhee, said,

> By the grace of a merciful Providence our forces fighting under the standard of that greatest hope and inspiration of mankind, the United Nations, have liberated this ancient capital of Korea. It has been freed from the despotism of Communist rule and its citizens once more have the opportunity for that immutable concept of life which holds invincibly to the primacy of individual liberty and personal dignity.[32]

Calling MacArthur "the savior of our race," Rhee accepted "the discharge of the civil responsibility," and, looking at the surrounding soldiers, asked, "How can I ever explain to you my own undying gratitude and that of the Korean people?"[33] By October 1, UN forces from Pusan and Seoul had pushed North Koreans back across the line.

There were obvious reasons for the UNC to continue fighting after the 38th parallel had been reclaimed. Korea was generally viewed as a single polity, the weakened North Korean forces were in retreat, Americans wanted a resolution of the Korean question, and many believed that North Korea should suffer the consequences of its aggression. At the United Nations, the United States sponsored a calling for all necessary steps "to ensure conditions of stability throughout Korea." But the logic of moral equivalency that would divide Korea so severely for so long was already beginning to emerge. The president of the UN Security Council, India's representative Benegal Rau, argued that "it would impair faith in the UN if we were even to appear to authorize the unification of Korea by the use of force against North Korea, after we had resisted the attempt of North Korea to reunify the country by force against South Korea."[34] Rau's argument did not carry the day, but set a marker for future positions taken by "neutral," "nonaligned" nations at the United Nations.

The United Nations Command was authorized to cross the line into North Korea by language specifying that UN forces "should not remain in any part of Korea otherwise than so far as was necessary for achieving [UN] objectives."[35] When the resolution passed on October

7, 1950, ROK forces had already advanced north of the 38th parallel. U.S. and other UN troops marched beyond the parallel that day. Victory seemed certain; the coalition fought well and captured the North Korean capital of Pyongyang on October 19, 1950.

American military leaders believed that allied air superiority would deter China from entering the war on the side of the North.[36] Having just assumed power after a long and difficult civil war with the Kuomintang, Chinese Communist leaders were expected to shy away from a foreign conflict. Instead, Chinese military planners believed that war with the United States was inevitable, and advised that it should be fought on the peninsula rather than in the Chinese homeland.[37] When North Korea's fortunes changed so drastically, China may have concluded it had no alternative but to enter the war.[38] Partly in a bid to buy time, Chinese Foreign Minister Chou En-lai stated that China would attack if UN or U.S. forces crossed the 38th parallel. Those warnings were dismissed as bluster.

From recently released records, we now know that China's decision to enter the war had been made before its warnings were given.[39] Nevertheless, China waited until U.S. troops marched north of the parallel and ordered its troops to cross the border on the next day. The fortunes of war soon changed again. The two American divisions that had been chasing a retreating force of demoralized North Korean Army regulars back into the mountains of the North now found themselves facing an advance of fresh Chinese forces. The United Nations Command's 500,000 troops were outnumbered by a combined Communist force of about 750,000.[40] The Communist forces pushed the front line some fifty miles south of Seoul by late January 1951. Freezing weather conditions during the winter of 1950–1951 sent bleak images of the war into American homes. Concerns were raised at the United Nations that the situation would give rise to a World War III. A resolution sponsored by future members of the nonaligned movement, calling for an immediate cease-fire, was approved by the UN General Assembly. In response, the United States initiated a resolution identifying the People's Republic of China as the aggressor and authorizing continued fighting to defend the Republic of Korea. Although the resolution passed, the goals fell considerably short of earlier American objectives; there was no mention of reunifying Korea or punishing the aggressors.

The policy debate in America was polarized between those who sought an honorable means of resolving the conflict, restoring the status quo ante bellum, and those who believed the full force of American military might should be brought to bear to force the Communists out of the North and to unify the country. The divergent views were personified in the struggle between General MacArthur and President Truman. Almost fifty years later, MacArthur's objectives can still inspire sympathy, since reunifying the country at that time might well have precluded the suffering and sacrifices that came with two additional years of war in Korea and that have accompanied Korea's division. In America, however, the issue is more often seen in its Constitutional context. Truman is credited with strongly enforcing the principle of civilian control of the military. He dismissed MacArthur for openly challenging presidential decisions not to extend American attacks into China.

Upon MacArthur's dismissal, Matthew B. Ridgway was given command of the United Nations forces. He was able to articulate the notion of limited war, bringing military doctrine in line with political realities. His strategy was to force the Communists into vulnerable locations, then hit them hard with American artillery and air power. UN forces again fought their way to the 38th parallel by March 31, 1951.[41]

UN forces continued to drive Communist forces northward, and by late spring held a line north of the 38th parallel in the east and south of the parallel, along the Imjin River, in the west. By June 1, 1951, UN Secretary General Trygve Lie stated that he believed the objectives of the June 25 and June 27, 1950, United Nations resolutions had been carried out.[42]

3

Seeking the Truce

Having achieved a military stalemate that approximated the Soviet and American political zones before the war, American policymakers reviewed their options. On May 17, 1951, a top-secret (now declassified) National Security Council document discussed American policy objectives:

> The United States has consistently sought as an ultimate political objective the establishment of a unified, independent, and democratic Korea . . . . The intervention of the Chinese forces in Korea has so changed the situation that it appears militarily impossible now to bring about a situation under which a unified, non-Communist Korea could be achieved by political means. Therefore, while in no way renouncing the ultimate political objective which we hold for Korea, the present task should be to bring about a settlement of the Korean problem which at the minimum will deny to Communist control that part of Korea south of the 38th parallel."[1]

What was "militarily possible"? Combat historian Robert Leckie summarized the condition of the Communist forces in mid-June 1951 as follows:

> In one year of warfare, the North Korean Army had suffered an estimated 600,000 casualties (including 100,000 men

who had surrendered) and was virtually destroyed. In only eight months, the Chinese Communists had lost an estimated half million men. The April and May offensives had subjected the Red Army to a frightful pounding and the May assault had clearly revealed its inability to support large bodies of men moving against modern firepower. Communist Korea was in shambles, its railroads ruined, its communications crippled, its industry close to nonexistent . . . . All Communist supply now came from the Soviet Union and Russia had already shown, in the disastrous May offensive, how she could fail to deliver the goods."[2]

Eager to avoid a second full-scale UN assault north of the parallel, Communist forces appeared ready to cease the hostilities.

The view in Washington was less optimistic about additional successful military action to reunify Korea than the view on the battlefield. Lieutenant General James Van Fleet designed a strategy for taking North Korea from his strong position in the east, but the Joint Chiefs of Staff did not approve his proposal. Ridgway authorized Van Fleet to make local advances merely in the interest of seizing better ground.[3]

Ridgway himself believed that the UN forces could have fought successfully to the Yalu, as he said in his memoirs:

Military men, and statesmen too, will long debate the wisdom of stopping that proud Army in its tracks at the first whisper that the Reds might be ready to sue for peace. To my mind it is fruitless to speculate on what might have been. If we had been ordered to fight our way to the Yalu, we could have done it—if our government had been willing to pay the price in dead and wounded that action would have cost. From the purely military standpoint the effort, to my mind, would not have been worth the cost. A drive to the line of the Yalu and the Tumen would have cleared Korea of the Chinese enemy. But he would have still been facing us in great strength beyond those rivers. The seizure of the land between the truce line and the Yalu would have merely meant the seizure of more real estate. It would have greatly lengthened our own supply routes, and widened our battlefront from 110 miles to 420. Would the American people have been willing to support the great army that would have been required to hold that line? Would they have approved

our attacking on into Manchuria? On into the heart of the
great mainland of Asia, a bottomless pit into which all the
armies of the whole free world could be drawn and be
ground to bits and destroyed? I doubt it."[4]

Ridgway's logic was based on a sound understanding of the limited objectives of American and allied policy, and certainly took into account
the views of his superiors in Washington.

For Koreans, however, the UNC decision not to advance to the
Yalu involved more than real estate. They recognized that negotiating
with the Communists was likely to mean the division of their country
on a lasting basis. President Syngman Rhee accordingly issued his
own conditions for peace: withdrawal of Chinese Communist forces
north of the Yalu, the termination of arms shipments by China and the
Soviet Union, and the disarmament of the North Korean People's
Army; no peace settlement without ROK participation; and no terms
contrary to the sovereignty of the Republic of Korea.[5]

The Republic of Korea, however, could not enforce that position
in 1951. The objectives of the United Nations Command, on which
South Korea depended for its national survival, no longer included
Korean unification. Peace had become the objective of the United Nations; negotiation had become an objective of the Communists.

American officials undertook a lengthy diplomatic offensive to
test the waters for truce talks. In this process, an overriding concern
emerged: the question of how to allow China to save face. In early May,
a Chinese interlocutor told a member of the State Department's policy
planning staff, "If the United States and its allies should crow about
the matter as if it were a victory, it would be difficult, perhaps out of
the question" for China to end the war.[6] Similarly, when George Kennan was asked to explore the topic "unofficially" with Soviet diplomat
Jacob Malik, he reported that Malik "repeatedly turned the talk to the
problem of the Chinese Communists and our relations with them,
going into the usual propaganda line about how sensitive they were,
how we had offended them, etc."[7] Yugoslavian permanent representative to the United Nations, Dr. Ales Bebler, also emphasized that the
other side should "be allowed to save some face."[8] It was with these
thoughts in mind that the American commander in the Far East, General Matthew B. Ridgway, gave his views of negotiating with Asians on
the eve of the armistice negotiations. "In dealing with Orientals," he

said, "great care had to be taken not to cause them to 'lose face.'" He perceived that providing a "golden bridge" to allow the Communists to back out of difficult circumstances was of great importance.[9]

The initiation of truce talks followed months of give-and-take in Washington, New York, Moscow, and other cities where representatives of the concerned countries could be found. In this long, drawnout process, American diplomats disposed of Communist efforts to link the truce to political determinations regarding Korea, UN membership for the People's Republic of China, and the status of the Republic of China on Taiwan.[10] American diplomats generally avoided making concessions just to get to the table; nevertheless, a notion had sneaked silently into American thinking about the truce talks: Asian Communists needed to save face. That notion, mixed with the victors' genuine inclination toward magnanimity, undermined the American posture in the negotiations even before they began.

UN Secretary General Lie was eager to see truce talks initiated. From his perspective, such talks would bring to a seemingly successful end the difficult Korean problem that had taxed the institutions of the United Nations in their infancy. He publicly urged the Soviets, as leaders of the Communist world, "to say the one word the world is waiting for."[11] In a radio broadcast on June 23, the Soviet delegate to the UN, Jacob Malik, having twice discussed the matter with George Kennan informally, gave the first public indication that talks could end the fighting. He said, "The Soviet peoples believe that as a first step discussions should be started between the belligerents for a cease-fire and an armistice providing for the mutual withdrawal of forces from the 38th parallel."[12]

President Truman instructed the American ambassador in Moscow, Alan Kirk, to explore with Soviet Foreign Minister Andrei Gromyko what Malik meant. "Gromyko indicated he considered cease-fire as part of what he terms an 'interim military armistice,'" Kirk reported of his meeting on June 27. "By this he said he meant that the parties fighting in Korea would meet and conclude a military armistice which would include a cease-fire, and which would be limited strictly to military questions and would not involve any political or territorial matters." Kirk added, "As to assurance against resumption of hostilities, Gromyko said that this would be subject of discussion between Commands in formulating terms of military armistice."[13] Many in the United States government perceived that the Gromyko proposal coincided with key American objectives: avoiding political issues, developing armistice terms that addressed military concerns, and establishing a commission to monitor compliance with the truce.

The American ambassador in Moscow was accordingly asked his views on why the Soviets had developed such a reasonable approach. He suggested that the Communists might want "to call off war in Korea as a bad job which can be renewed under more favorable circumstances" and might hope to use "a fairly short period of cease-fire for improvement in their military situation." He reasoned that the Communists saw a clear advantage in retaining control of North Korea and anticipated that they "would hope through subversion in the ROK to make some progress." Finally, he surmised, "They would also hope that with cessation of Korean hostilities the unity of UN states which have supported collective action in Korea would degenerate; . . . the expense of keeping large UN forces in ROK would be expected to prove unattractive as time goes on."[14]

On the subject of Chinese attitudes toward truce talks, the Soviets were cunningly vague. The Soviets had already decided to keep a distance from the peace talks, a position the British spy Donald Maclean claimed they took on his advice.[15] Gromyko curtly told Kirk that the Soviet government did not know the view of the Chinese government and urged the United States to ask the Chinese.[16]

Some U.S. officials were troubled by the Soviet deferral on the issue. As difficult as cold war relations were, the Americans still found it easier to discuss international issues with the Soviets than with the Chinese. The Soviet government, as Kennan told Malik in his second unofficial meeting with Malik, could be trusted to take "a serious and responsible attitude toward their own interests. . . ." "The Chinese Communists, on the contrary," he said, "seemed to us to be excited, irresponsible people on the consistency of whose reactions there could be no reliance."[17]

The Soviet deferral considerably strengthened the hand of the Communist Chinese, who, defeated on the battlefield, would nevertheless emerge as a major regional power, capable of challenging the power of the United States. In his study of Chinese negotiating behavior, Alfred Wilhelm made the following observation about the practical consequences of the Soviet hand-off:

> U.S. leaders were momentarily confused when the Soviets passed their lead by recommending . . . that the two sides

in the Korean War seek a cease-fire and an armistice. . . .
It was a maneuver designed to elicit a substantive proposal
from the United States to which the Chinese could respond.
. . . A direct overture by the United States, from the Chinese
vantage, was an important element for setting the stage psy-
chologically.[18]

In Washington, some resisted having the United States initiate
the truce. In an atmosphere still charged with the residual static between Truman and MacArthur, dissenting views from high-ranking
military leaders needed to be heard in confidence and dealt with qui-
etly. It is not uncommon in such situations for officials at the State Department to shore up their political support and convene a meeting to
engage in a little arm-twisting, to resolve the debate and get a consensus on a course of action. Nor is it uncommon in such meetings to mix
major issues with seemingly insignificant details, conveying an impression of high-level approval on matters that are in fact given little
attention. That is how policy is made.

On June 28, 1951, Assistant Secretary of State Dean Rusk, accompanied by U. Alexis Johnson, his director of the office of northeast
Asian affairs, went to the Pentagon for a top-secret meeting of historic
proportions. At Rusk's request, Chairman of the Joint Chiefs of Staff
General Omar Bradley called together the chiefs of the military services to iron out a consensus on the Korean truce offer.[19] According
to the official notes from this meeting, Air Force Chief of Staff General Vandenberg was "unalterably opposed" to the State Department
proposal to have the U.S. commander in the Far East, General Ridgway, initiate a message to the opposing command. "He felt that the
U.S. should use the Soviet proposal as a springboard to place the onus
on the North Koreans and the Chinese, and that any message from
Ridgway would in effect mean that we are asking for peace, instead of
the Communists."[20] Vandenberg argued "that the drain of hostilities
was now beginning to tell on the Communist forces and that we should
in no sense be put in the position of suing for peace at this point or
stopping the fighting just when it was beginning to hurt the other
side."[21]

The notes of the meeting demonstrate that some of the chiefs believed that an armistice, if necessary, should establish a "commission of
some type to observe whether the Communists introduced additional
personnel and materiel into North Korea." General J. Lawton Collins,

the Army chief of staff, shared Vandenberg's concerns about U.S. initiation of truce talks, but focused his arguments on verification of Communist forces' compliance with an armistice. He said there was "no hope" for an armistice if it did not include observation teams, which, he anticipated, should be stationed along the Yalu River. When Rusk tentatively suggested that a UN Peace Observation Committee, including Soviet representation, could perform the task, he encountered strenuous objections from Vandenberg and Collins. "Any respite given them by an armistice would only permit them to build up to start fighting again," Vandenberg argued. Rusk countered that "the build-up of Communist forces was a permanent part of the problem, whether the end of the fighting came within Korea or on the northern borders," but he eventually had to give in on this question. The requirement for a military armistice commission was later written into the American negotiating instructions, and became a critical feature of the armistice talks.[22]

Arguments against the United States' first contacting the enemy, however, did not persuade Rusk or Chairman of the Joint Chiefs of Staff Bradley. White House support for an American effort to initiate the truce was already clear, and everyone present knew the State Department had devoted months of diplomatic efforts to that end. General Bradley, sensitive to political exigencies, argued that public support for the war effort, both in America and among the allies, would be harmed if the JCS "turned down what appeared to be an opportunity to end the hostilities."[23]

In response, General Vandenberg cautioned that the UNC stood to lose more than it would gain. General Bradley, however, believed the Soviets had set up the approach to Beijing and Pyongyang in good faith and that Gromyko had been careful to design the approach "to give China a chance to save face." Bradley ended the discussion by directly contravening Vandenberg's argument, making it clear who was chairman. He said, "A simple statement from our side to the opposing side to the effect that if they agree with the proposals made by the Soviets, let us know and we will arrange a meeting did not in any sense mean that we were suing for peace."[24] Rusk's notetaker observed there was consensus and that a working group should draft the message for further consideration by the Joint Chiefs of Staff.

In a meeting of the JCS on the next afternoon, Major General White repeated the U.S. Air Force's "grave doubts with regard to the policy that was being followed concerning an armistice and questioned whether it was to our advantage." General Collins, however, interjected that the decision to proceed had already been made the previous day "with the concurrence of all the Chiefs and it was far too late to reopen the question." When Air Force Vice Chief of Staff General Nathan F. Twining arrived, he stated his concern over "entering into an armistice without adequate guarantees as to what the other side would do." To this, General Collins responded that no armistice would be signed unless it "would include provision for adequate observation of North Korea." Notes from this second meeting conclude, "With that, General Twining entered no further objection."[25]

Accordingly, the United Nations Command was instructed to take the initiative to contact the parties to the truce. After presidential approval, the following order was sent to General Ridgway:

> The President has directed that at 0800 Saturday (the 30th) Tokyo Daylight Saving Time you send following message by radio in the clear addressed to Commander in Chief Communist Forces in Korea and simultaneously release to press:
> "As Commander in Chief of the United Nations Command I have been instructed to communicate to you the following:
> "I am informed that you may wish a meeting to discuss an armistice providing for the cessation of hostilities and all acts of armed force in Korea, with adequate guarantees for the maintenance of such armistice.
> "Upon the receipt of word from you that such a meeting is desired I shall be prepared to name my representative. I propose that such a meeting could take place aboard a Danish hospital ship (*Jutlandia*) in Wonsan Harbor."[26]

Ridgway broadcast that message at 8 A.M., June 30, Tokyo time. On July 2 he reported that Kim Il Sung, as commander in chief of the Korean People's Army, and Peng Teh Huai, as commander in chief of the Chinese People's Volunteers, had responded:

> Your broadcast message of June 30, regarding peace talks, has been received. We are authorized to tell you that we agree to suspend military activities and to hold peace negotiations, and that our delegates will meet with yours.
> We suggest, in regard to the place for holding talks, that such talks be held at Kaesong, on the 38th parallel.
> If you agree to this, our delegates will be prepared to meet your delegates between July 10 and 15, 1951.[27]

Ridgway named Vice Admiral Charles Turner Joy to head the United Nations delegation; the Republic of Korea named Major General Paik Sun Yup; North Korea named Lieutenant General Nam Il, the chief of staff of the North Korean People's Army; and China named General Hsieh Fang, chief of staff of the Chinese People's Volunteer Army.

The course of the negotiation of the truce, and the lasting division of Korea that emerged from it, had been determined primarily by UN self-restraint. Having decided not to pursue Van Fleet's proposal for conquest in the North, the United Nations accepted the notion of a stalemate before its terms were defined. Limited war led to limited objectives and produced limited results. For the United Nations Command, self-restraint did not invite reciprocity from the other side.

4

★

Beginning at Kaesong

"At the very start we made a concession that we early had cause to regret," General Ridgway reflected fifteen years after the United States accepted the Communist proposal for talks to begin at Kaesong.

"When I first offered to open the discussion," Ridgway recalled, "the suggested meeting place was the *Jutlandia,* a hospital ship under the Danish flag, to be anchored in Wonsan harbor."[1] Ridgway expected "that 'neutral ground' of this sort, yet under the enemy's guns as well as our own, would invoke the spirit of compromise at once." The chief negotiator Ridgway named to deal with the Communists saw it in the same light. "The *Jutlandia,*" Admiral C. Turner Joy reasoned, was "a hospital ship, internationally recognized as a nonbelligerent facility, a ship provided by a government (Denmark) which had not participated in the Korean fighting. This neutral, noncombative ship was to be placed in waters controlled by Communist guns and mine fields. This seemed as reasonable an arrangement as could be conceived."[2]

The Communists, however, had their own views on what would constitute an appropriate site for the commencement of a truce. They wanted the talks to be held in Kaesong, an ancient Korean capital near the west coast. In addition to its historical significance, Kaesong was an important trading city with a large merchant class.[3] It had been part of the Republic of Korea before the war, and its population was defiantly anti-Communist. Indeed, freedom fighters in Kaesong challenged Kim Il Sung's iron rule into the 1960s.[4] Kim Il Sung may have recognized that holding talks there would indicate to the anti-Communists the degree to which the Western world had abandoned them. Moreover, Kaesong was south of the 38th parallel, thirty-five miles northwest of Seoul, and these factors alone seemed evidence of the North's victory in the war. Kaesong was the perfect location from the Communists' point of view and they had taken steps Ridgway and Joy would never know to determine that Washington accepted the site.

Washington policymakers accepted the Communist suggestion and ordered the UN Command to agree to Kaesong. The UNC accordingly exchanged radio broadcasts to set up an advance meeting of liaison officers to work out the details for the military delegations' meeting. On July 8, 1951, the liaison team's helicopter circled "enemy-held Kaesong," noting that it had been leveled during the war and seemed to be vacant. The helicopter landed in a marked open space on the north side of the town, at a place called Kwangmun Dong. The advance team, led by Colonel Andrew J. Kinney, USAF, and Colonel James C. Murray, USMC, was met by "Red soldiers" who ringed the landing site. The soldiers escorted the team in captured American jeeps to Nae Bong Jang, a private mansion the Communists appear to have expropriated from a wealthy landowner, Mr. Yi Hee Cho.[5] The United Nations team was offered an Italianate mansion nearby to use as its residence, but, recognizing that it could not operate effectively under constant enemy surveillance, it set up a base camp in territory under UNC military control at Munsan-ni, about ten miles south on the road to Seoul.[6]

The advance team was shown the facilities that would be used for the truce talks, including the table covered with green felt that would become a hallmark of United Nations–North Korean talks for decades. But the Communist liaison officers were apparently not authorized to arrange details; they stonewalled even on the critical question of the date the talks would begin.[7] On the key issues Ridgway asked the advance team to resolve—"time, place, routes and procedures for movement, size of delegations, safe conduct for representatives and necessary safety zones"[8]—Kinney was unable to move beyond what little had been agreed in exchanges of radio broadcasts. The North Koreans reserved such matters for high-level attention.

The degree to which the Communists wanted to control the negotiating environment became apparent when Kinney's team walked into the meeting place and, without meaning to give offense, took seats on the northern side of the table. As early as 1835, there are records of

British dealings with the Chinese in which Chinese protocol dictated that Mandarins were seated on the north side of the table, while supplicant Cantonese were seated on the south.[9] The UN team had taken the victors' side of the table and the reaction from the Communists in Kaesong was consternation. "The Communists were flustered and dismayed by this development," Joy said Kinney noticed, "so much so that the Communist liaison officer actually stuttered in replying to Kinney's opening remarks."[10] It could certainly be argued that the inadvertent UN action was appropriate and that the UNC should have insisted on retaining the north side of the table. On July 10, however, the Communist side took their own seats first, and Admiral Joy's delegation accepted seats on the south side. The Americans generally viewed the seating arrangement as one of those face-saving measures that could be extended to their Asian opponents.

The Americans paid closer attention to security concerns. When Ridgway first proposed the meeting of liaison officers, he said that if the group traveled by convoy "each vehicle will bear a white flag."[11] Kim Il Sung and Peng Teh Huai in return advised Ridgway of the route their liaison officers would take to Kaesong. Seemingly because of concern for the safety of their officers, the Communists specified that each motor vehicle "will have a white flag set on top of it" and emphasized, "Please take note of this information."[12] Ridgway assured them, "This convoy will be immune from attack by my forces during its travel from Pyongyang to Kaesong. In addition, the area within a 5-mile radius from the center of Kaesong will be observed by me as a neutral zone from the time of arrival of your delegates in Kaesong."[13] Through this generous gesture, the UNC forfeited its fight for possession of an important trading city that had been part of the Republic of Korea a little more than a year earlier.

The opposing side made no such gestures. Admiral Joy was alarmed by the menacing treatment his advance team received. He reported, "Kinney and his party, though completely without arms, were surrounded by troops of armed Communist soldiers brandishing hand machine guns threateningly." Joy and his negotiating team did not seem to fear capture or murder, but the large number of armed personnel heightened the potential for accidents. More importantly from the negotiating perspective, it provided an unacceptable environment of hostility that would eventually have to be dealt with. For the short term, however, the Americans tolerated the threatening behavior, primarily because it seemed like a harmless public relations stunt. As

Joy noted, "Communist photographers and press representatives did not fail to make the most of this [threatening behavior], in line with their thesis that the United Nations Command, not the Communists, needed and sought a truce."[14]

The commanders in the field did not anticipate the media debacle that was about to unfold when the truce talks actually started. In Washington, the Joint Chiefs of Staff cabled Ridgway almost literally at the eleventh hour, directing, "We consider it essential that the press of the United Nations have representation at Kaesong as to pictures and news coverage at least equal to that assumed by the Communists."[15] Their message (sent at 3:09 P.M., July 9, Washington time) was received in the early hours of July 10. At that point, there was little Ridgway could do except disturb Joy's sleep. Ridgway reported back to Washington that he had held a meeting the previous day in which he worked out arrangements for briefing newsmen at the UNC base camp on the delegation's return from Kaesong. He promised to raise the matter of on-scene press participation: "No information here at this time of Communist planned press coverage of Kaesong conference. Senior UN delegate will propose at first meeting 10 July that 16 representative correspondents be in Kaesong."[16]

The Communists had not been so nonchalant about press management. They had gathered public affairs officers from the far-flung parts of the Communist world, and some reliably leftist ones from the West. Alan Winnington, a correspondent for the London *Daily Worker*, an organ of the British Communist party, and Wilfred Burchett, an Australian Marxist working for the leftist French newspaper *Ce Soir*, lived in Kaesong as guests of North Korea and helped the Communists orchestrate media events. They were a constant presence during the talks, advising the Communists of media opportunities even during official negotiating sessions.[17] Winnington and Burchett later collaborated to edit the forced confessions of allied soldiers in North Korean prisoner of war camps,[18] and wrote books describing the West's "perfidy" during the negotiations.[19] With this one-sided array of press representatives gathered in Kaesong, the first truce talks between Communist forces and the West were launched. As Winnington bragged at the time: "This is the first time Oriental Communists have ever sat down at a conference table on terms of equality with Americans, and they intend to make the most of it."[20]

What the Communists intended to make of the start of the talks was visible to Admiral Joy as his helicopter landed at Kaesong. Joy could see that "as the UNC staff approached Kaesong by car, their white flags were clearly visible." He recalled that

> there was no atmosphere of neutrality at all. The city of Kae-song was in Communist hands. Their armed guards infested the area of the truce talks, and Red soldiers with tommy guns gruffly ordered our envoys about. The appearance of our delegates, in jeeps carrying the white flags of truce, was photographed for the Asian press as a scene of surrender.[21]

The view from the UNC staff convoy on the ground was even more dramatic:

> The motor convoy of the UNC delegation, bearing large white flags, was halted at the outpost of Panmunjom, on the morning of the 10th, while the Communists made "preparations" for their safe conduct. When the convoy reached Kaesong, the nature of these "preparations" became apparent. Three vehicles filled with Communist officers in full dress swung in front of the line and posed as victors as the procession drove through Kaesong. Communist photographers gave full picture coverage to this parade.[22]

If, as some have suggested, American officials accepted the Communist proposal to hold the talks in Kaesong in order to allow the enemy to save face, there is no indication that such sentiments were extended reciprocally. In fact, the Communists saw an advantage in embarrassing the United Nations Command, and because they controlled the setting of the talks, they had ample opportunity.

"At the first meeting of the delegates," Joy wrote, "I seated myself at the conference table and almost sank out of sight." His hosts had seen fit to give him a chair that was "considerably shorter than a standard chair" while North Korean General Nam Il had been given a chair "four inches higher than the surrounding ones." Joy was taller than his North Korean counterpart, but, he wrote in good humor, "General Nam Il protruded a good foot above my cagily diminished stature." Unembarrassed by this inhospitable treatment of his Western guest, Nam Il "puffed his cigarette in obvious satisfaction as he glowered down on me, an apparently torpedoed admiral." Joy simply exchanged his chair for a normal one, and seems not to have been troubled by the slight. He was bothered, however, that "Communist photographers had exposed reels of film" preserving his awkward moment.[23]

The UNC side had expected the negotiations to be conducted between two delegations, but at 4:15 in the afternoon of the first day, they learned the press was to be an active part of the process. The discussion over the agenda had been a major part of the first day's activities. The Communists wanted an agenda indicating that certain key issues, such as the truce line, had already been decided. The UNC intended to keep military pressure on the enemy until the truce agreement was actually signed. Accordingly, the UNC opposed the Communist proposal that the first item of the agenda would be setting the truce line at the 38th parallel, most of which was already under UNC control. The Communists asked for an adjournment to devise a response to the UNC agenda.

The Communists used their control of the media to apply pressure during the negotiations. When they "finally produced three smooth copies of their agenda in Korean, Chinese and English," Ridgway reported to the JCS, "a half dozen photographers dashed in and commenced taking pictures."[24] The UNC was negotiating with the other side of the table, but the Communists were negotiating with the other side of the world, and their connection to that world was through hand-picked, sympathetic media.

Joy and Ridgway realized that Western newsmen had to be admitted to the sessions to level the playing field. The UNC raised the problem in the first day and was encouraged by the North Korean general's initial agreement. Ridgway's report to the JCS stated simply:

> [At] 1620—UN Command stated proposed introduce 20 press subsequent meeting. Communists requested complete breakdown by newsreel, cameramen, photographers, etc. finally agreement on mutual basis for 20 press. This was a memorable agreement being the first.[25]

North Korea's first agreement with the UNC did not last twenty-four hours. General Nam Il retracted his concurrence the next morning, saying that the admission of Western press had to be referred to higher authorities. When no agreement on the topic was reached during the second day's talks, Joy read a note from Ridgway that threatened suspension: "It is requested that we be informed by 0730 hours tomorrow on what date it will be possible to resume the conference with newsmen present at the conference site."[26] The next day, whether in an attempt to preserve their advantage or to test the resolve of the UNC, the Communists turned back the newsmen in a UNC-sponsored convoy as it headed to Kaesong. Joy accordingly sent a note to Nam Il by messenger saying that the talks would be resumed only "upon notification from you that my convoy, bearing personnel of my own choosing, including such press representation as I consider necessary, will be cleared to the conference site."[27] The UNC proved its mettle on this question. "When our delegation failed to appear at Kaesong," Joy recorded, "the Communists hurriedly dispatched a message to the United Nations Command agreeing to equitable conditions."[28]

Ridgway and Joy were under pressure to live up to the unrealistic expectations of a war-weary world for a fast conclusion to the talks. Ridgway was repeatedly advised that if there was a breakdown in talks, it must be attributable to Communist unreasonableness.[29] Fussing over matters as insignificant as chairs and seating would not have been tolerated, and even taking a hard line on security measures might appear to delay an early truce. Insisting on attendance of Western newsmen, however, was naturally an issue the Western press could support, and Washington was already on board. Accordingly, Ridgway and Joy, having obtained JCS approval, seized the opportunity to seek other improvements in the negotiating environment, notably new security arrangements.

The threatening behavior of Communist soldiers, which Joy had noted in Kinney's description of the liaison officers' discussions, had worsened after the formal talks started. "Kaesong and the entire conference area is continually heavily guarded," Ridgway wrote to the JCS, "no freedom is given the United Nations Command delegation."[30] The extent of the security problem had been demonstrated during an adjournment when the UNC negotiators attempted to send a courier with a message to Ridgway. The courier was halted by a North Korean guard and delayed until it was too late to get the message transmitted. The UNC protested. The Communists must have realized they could not be permitted to block couriers, so they used the opportunity to obtain another arrangement that was still decidedly in their favor. They said they would safeguard the passage of couriers, but must be informed of their passage "well in advance of each trip," and they asked how many times couriers would be sent to the UNC camp at Munsan-ni. Rather than finding the Communist query completely unacceptable, the UNC took their bait and responded that "there would possibly be 5–6 courier trips daily."[31] The Communists were allowed to determine how many UN couriers assigned to the truce talks could transit a single road in "No Man's Land."

"No Man's Land" was beginning to look much like Communist-held territory. Therefore, as a condition for the resumption of talks on July 12, the UNC delegation insisted on the establishment of a neutral zone with a five-mile radius centered on the traffic circle in Kaesong, as Ridgway had originally proposed on July 3.[32] The two sides agreed to withdraw all forces except military police from this zone, and during daylight hours the UNC was given unrestricted use of the road from Kaesong to Panmunjom without advance notice.[33]

In spite of these commitments, the Communists sent forces south of Kaesong into the neutral zone. One was encountered on August 4 when the United Nations Command delegation was on its way to the sessions, and it made no effort to hide. "Our convoy of jeeps was halted in mid-course," Joy recorded, "while an entire company of about one hundred heavily armed Chinese, complete with machine guns and mortars, marched across our path and through the immediate conference area." Admiral Joy believed the patrol's timing was intentional. "The point of this demonstration," Joy perceived, "seemed to be that notwithstanding verbal agreements to keep the conference area free of armed men, no one would be allowed to forget the hard fact that Communist military forces actually surrounded and controlled the area."[34]

On arrival in Kaesong that morning, Joy protested to Nam Il that the UNC party had encountered a Chinese patrol. Nam Il dismissed Joy's protest and said the forces in question were "military police."[35] Joy had to suppress his pique at this response for the entire day. Other than couriers, the UNC delegation in Kaesong had no easy, secure communication system back to Ridgway and could not report to him until it returned to the UNC base camp at Munsan-ni each night. This was opposite to the advantage Kaesong afforded the Communists. According to interviews of Chinese participants decades later, the Chinese maintained telephone contact with the Foreign Ministry in Beijing throughout the negotiations.[36]

When Joy finally returned from Kaesong on the night of August 4, he reported the encounter with the Chinese soldiers to General Ridgway, pointing out that the show of Chinese muscle south of Kaesong must have been designed "to emphasize Communist military control of Kaesong."

"General Ridgway," Joy wrote, "reacted with characteristic vigor. Resorting again to open radio broadcast, he announced suspension of the negotiations with resumption contingent on the creation of a neutral zone around Kaesong into which no armed personnel of either side were to be introduced."[37] "To ask us to believe that Military Police had to go about armed with machine guns and 60-mm. mortars was rather too extreme," Ridgway himself recalled later, "I immediately broadcast an announcement that the talks had been suspended until we could have a satisfactory agreement concerning demilitarization. The Communists held out for five days, then finally asked us to resume the talks under proper safeguards."[38]

The five-day delay may have been yet another testing technique, and the Communists may have thought the pressure of world opinion would bring the UNC back to the table. But Joy believed that "those days of hesitation must have been a period of dead-end frustration for the Communists." The UNC had curtailed its military efforts while the talks proceeded. Joy reasoned, "If they *did not* accept General Ridgway's requirements, the military breathing spell they so badly needed would terminate. If they *did* accept General Ridgway's dictum, pretensions that Communists sat at Kaesong in the seat of victors would be difficult to believe."[39] Not surprisingly, the Communists chose the lesser of the two evils. They agreed to Ridgway's demands, and switched from portraying themselves as victors to portraying themselves as victimized underdogs.

North Korean negotiators try to glean some benefit even when the desired objective is elusive. In this case, they sought to obscure their giving in at all. "In replying to General Ridgway by radio broadcast in the English language, they politely accepted his requirements and requested the United Nations Command delegation to return to Kaesong as soon as possible," Joy recalled. "In Japanese and Chinese translations, however, they 'demanded' the return of the UNC 'at once.'" General Ridgway was informed of this subterfuge, and by that time had tired of giving the Communists the face-saving maneuver he called "the golden bridge." "Instead," Joy recorded, "he declared their reply evasive and demanded still further assurances of equity at Kaesong."[40] Ridgway himself commented, "This brought a more courteous request and specific agreement."[41]

Establishment of the neutral zone was a hard-won objective, but its creation in territory under control of the Communists and enforced primarily by Communists would afford the Communists a number of advantages. First, it gave them an opportunity to put white flags on their military vehicles and send them to the front to resupply their military forces. When UNC forces strafed one such truck on August 9, the Communists decried the action as a violation of the neutral zone. Joy had seen intelligence reports that the Communists were resupplying the front in precisely this way. He answered the protest by pointing out that vehicular movement was protected only when arranged in advance. No such notification had been provided, so he told them, "your complaint is totally without validity."[42]

The Communists were not interested in defining arrangements they could abide by. They were interested in taking full advantage of arrangements they were offered. Although they ran the risk that some of their supply vehicles would be hit, they took advantage of the neutral zone as an opportunity to resupply their front, and an opportunity to demand, when trucks were strafed, "that the violators be punished."[43] They were not embarrassed by Joy's concern over their apparent deceit. From their perspective, their supply missions would go to the front whether or not they were protected; they might as well equip them with white flags. They certainly would not give the UNC advance notice of such resupply efforts, since the UNC could easily surmise what trucks were on business relating to the truce. The official negotiating delegation itself, however, took care to file advance notices of its transit in order to guarantee its own safety.[44]

The neutral zone also meant that parts of Korean territory would not be contested by UNC forces. As a result, local Koreans fighting against the Communists found their villages turned over to the enemy. One such group of partisans of Songgong-ni decided to attack a Chinese military platoon patrolling near their village in the neutral zone. Their efforts on behalf of liberty not only went unsupported, but also became the subject of investigation by both Communists and the UNC. No UN or ROK units had been close to Songgong-ni at that time, and witnesses said members of the attacking force were wearing civilian clothes. The attackers had been seen in the area before. The UNC, for its part, concluded that the attack was carried out by "partisans friendly to the ROK but acting independently."[45] Although the Communists may have found it advantageous to be able to convene an international tribunal to look into a small group of freedom fighters' efforts in the neutral zone, they were not pleased by the UNC's conclusion.

After the incident with the Songgong-ni villagers, the Communists trumped up some serious-sounding allegations. Kim Il Sung and Peng Teh Huai themselves signed a complaint that on August 19 some thirty UNC personnel had entered the Kaesong conference site and killed one of their platoon leaders, Yao Ching Hsiang, and that on August 22, a UNC plane had bombed the conference site.[46]

The funeral for Yao may have been significant to Communist party efforts to suppress internal dissent, and it placed him among the North's revolutionary martyrs, but the alleged bombing was more significant in the negotiating process. On August 22, the UNC received an urgent message from Kaesong decrying a violation of the neutral zone. Colonel Kinney, as UNC chairman of an investigatory subcommittee, was awakened about midnight and sent to investigate. When he arrived at 1:45 A.M., Colonels Chang (North Korea) and Tsai (China) and their handpicked press corps were waiting on the porch. They demanded that Kinney immediately look into their allegation and drove him to the site of the alleged bombing.[47] A United States Army summary of this incident is worth quoting at some length:

> Despite the darkness and a driving rain, Kinney and his associates inspected the evidence. Although there were several small holes, the so-called bomb fragments appeared to be parts of an aircraft oil tank and an engine nacelle. The Communists claimed that one of the bombs had been napalm, but nowhere was there any badly scorched earth area that a napalm explosion would have caused. After viewing the evidence, Kinney termed the whole affair "nonsense." Whereupon Chang retorted that "all meetings from this time" were called off.
>
> As the UNC party drove to Panmunjom, the Communist liaison officers overtook them and urged them to return and complete the investigation. Kinney preferred to wait until daylight but Chang and Tsai insisted that new evidence had been uncovered. Reluctantly Kinney returned and was shown two more small holes, several small burned patches, and some pieces of aircraft metal. There was an odor of gasoline and a substance in one of the holes that might have been a low-grade napalm that had not been ignited. When the UN investigators requested that all the evidence remain in place until it could be inspected by daylight, the Communists refused. They intended to gather it all for analysis and considered the investigation over.[48]

"When Kinney reported the foregoing events to me," Admiral Joy recalled, "one fact stood out plainly. No individual Communist, not even their delegation, would have assumed the responsibility for terminating the armistice conference without checking such intentions with higher headquarters." "Yet Chang," Joy pointed out, "was able to make his announcement of termination *immediately* [emphasis in the original] upon hearing that Kinney refused to acknowledge responsibility for the 'bombing'." [49] The alleged bombing was used as a pretext for suspending the talks, and that in turn signaled the start of a Communist military offensive to reclaim territory lost to UNC forces above the 38th parallel in eastern Korea. This tactic proved ill advised, however. In new hostilities, the Communists, particularly the Chinese, lost tens of thousands of men in the fighting during months while the talks were suspended.

When the talks were eventually resumed, on October 25, 1951, Joy and Ridgway were able to correct the mistake that had been made, as Ridgway said, "at the very start." They insisted that the location of the talks be moved. The rest of the long, torturous armistice negotiations—almost two more years would be devoted to the effort—would take place in a more suitable environment, at a conference center built along the actual line of contact between North and South, in Panmunjom.

The Mistake of Holding Negotiations in Kaesong

Agreeing to hold the talks in Kaesong has been recorded as a major tactical mistake and strategic blunder, perhaps the most obvious such error in the history of American negotiations. The negotiators themselves, Admiral Joy in 1955 and General Ridgway in 1967, described it as a mistake, as have numerous historians and analysts. Among the latter group, Vatcher's criticism is particularly sharp, since it points out the strategic consequences of the decision. "Meeting at Kaesong, which stood in the route of advancing UNC forces," Vatcher wrote, "discouraged and impeded further UNC advances." He argued that the area in western Korea around Kaesong could easily have been taken, but UNC military efforts had to be focused on more difficult terrain in eastern Korea instead. If the talks had been held in the east, he reasoned, the UNC could have pushed the line closer to North Korea's capital of Pyongyang and farther from Seoul. The loss of lives the decision cost is not easy to estimate, but Vatcher believed that if it had been allowed to fight in the more strategic western area, "the UNC could have pushed forward, thereby making the Communists more receptive to agreeing to an armistice sooner."[50]

Expanding on Vatcher's observations, South Korean General Lee Suk Bok has pointed out that consenting to Kaesong was a strategic mistake that caused permanent adverse consequences for the Republic of Korea. Korea's capital city of Seoul, he points out, is "close to the Communist threat, in fact, within range of long-range artillery guns or rocket attack, very vulnerable in terms of security, politics, economy, and social stability" because the UNC permitted North Korea to retain the Kaesong area. Lee believes the UNC should have sought to hold the talks "off the sea coast, either aboard ship, or on a small island, not in the middle of the combat zone, since this prevented an ROK advance."[51] In fact, the U.S. Army had made the same point in a meeting chaired by Paul Nitze on June 28, 1951. The army proposed Yo-Do, an island near Wonsan, as the alternative site for talks if the North Koreans found the Danish ship unacceptable.[52]

In 1994, an American army colonel and sinologist, Alfred Wilhelm, interviewed Chinese negotiators who had participated in the Korean truce talks. He discovered that "the acceptance by the United States, without any further bargaining, of a site that so obviously favored the Chinese surprised them." Wilhelm saw the Chinese refusal of the Danish ship *Jutlandia* as understandable, because the Chinese feared the appearance of a shipboard surrender similar to that of the Japanese on the USS *Missouri*. "Kaesong, however," those he interviewed said, "favored Chinese interests just as the ship favored U.S. interests. A more neutral site would have been agreeable."[53]

How Did the UNC Make the Mistake?

How did the United States fall into an obviously disadvantageous situation? The record raises some interesting questions about the decision to hold talks in Kaesong.

In *The Korean War*, Ridgway wrote that "Washington directed me to accept this suggestion at once, in a further effort to expedite the end of the fighting and to prove our sincerity."[54] That explanation, shared by others in Panmunjom,[55] may represent a generous effort to give Washington undeserved credit. Dean Rusk, then assistant secretary of state, admitted to an interviewer years later that "the site was okayed rather quickly in Washington without intense evaluation, simply to expedite the beginning of talks."[56]

Ridgway had sent a message to the JCS on July 2, 1951, saying that unless he was directed otherwise, he planned "to answer the Communist commanders' message accepting Kaesong as the location, making provision for cessation of hostilities along the Munsan-Kaesong road and in the Kaesong area."[57] When that message was received in Washington, Rusk saw it as making the specific point that the talks should be held in the city of Kaesong itself. Official notes record that Rusk "pointed out that General Ridgway in his reply avoided the generality of 'in the area of Kaesong' by saying 'at Kaesong.'"[58] Washington may not have adequately absorbed Ridgway's point about "making provision for cessation of hostilities" in the Kaesong area. Ignoring that qualifying phrase, Rusk might have concluded that Ridgway found Kaesong acceptable.

Confusion regarding Kaesong is understandable. Having a Communist response at all, especially one signed by the principal military leadership of both Pyongyang and Beijing, caused some excitement in Washington. The State Department was disturbed by the Communist reference to the 38th parallel, and Ridgway was ordered not to mention it in his response, but no one was in the mood to quibble.

Ridgway might have thought Washington was directing him to accept Kaesong. The confusion, however, was no doubt compounded by the fact that Rusk had heard others in Washington suggest Kaesong earlier. In a briefing to discuss the Communist response with British and other allied representatives, Rusk is recorded to have said, "*we* [emphasis added] too had been thinking in terms of Kaesong as an alternative site for the meeting."[59]

For almost five decades, it has been assumed that Kaesong was first proposed by Pyongyang and Beijing, and that was the impression Joy and Ridgway had for the rest of their lives. Strangely, however, Kaesong had been identified as an acceptable location even before the Communists proposed it. Two locations, the *Jutlandia* and Kaesong, were specified in an attachment to a package of documents submitted by Dean Rusk and Alexis Johnson at the decisive meeting in the Pentagon on June 28, 1951. In that meeting (discussed in the previous chapter) Generals Vandenberg and Collins aired their concerns about approaching the Communists to suggest peace talks. Before official contact with the Communists was initiated—in fact, before the decision to contact the Communists had been taken—and well before the Communists proposed Kaesong in their response, Kaesong was identified.

Reference to Kaesong appeared in the top-secret (now declassified) "Check List on Action to Meet the Present Korean Situation," which covered many details of the proposed talks. Precisely as it appears in the original document under "Arrangements for a Meeting

Between the Military Commands in Korea," the reference to Kaesong is as follows:

> a. The first step would be a public announcement, as soon as
> possible, by General Ridgway as CINCUNC, inviting
> representatives of the communist command in Korea to
> meet with representatives of CINCUNC on board the
> Danish Hospital Ship JUTLANDIA at __(location)__
> at __(time)__; JUTLANDIA to be under the full operational
> control of the Danish Government which has undertaken to
> make this ship available on a neutralized basis for this
> purpose. NOTE: An alternative would be a suitable
> location ashore near the front, such as KAESONG.[60]

The reference to Kaesong seems to have been rejected out of hand at the Pentagon and was not made part of the outgoing message to the Communists. No one argued for it and no one seems to have cared where it originated.

Although its origin is difficult to discern almost five decades later, it is clear where it did not originate. It was not from the Korea desk in the State Department. The package of papers was assembled in the State Department, but while Rusk was presenting the document at the Pentagon, the Korea desk was preparing a dissenting memorandum excoriating the Rusk-Johnson approach.[61] The idea of holding talks in Kaesong did not originate in the Pentagon; the Pentagon's extensive review of potential contingency arrangements covered a number of alternative locations on the evening of June 28, but never considered Kaesong.[62]

The document in which Kaesong appeared seems to have been derived from consultations with the British. It contains many points that had been worked out in consultations with the British embassy, and shares phrases in common with other documents derived from those discussions.[63] The checklist probably was developed in the top-secret Inter-Allied Board, which discussed major policy issues arising from the Korean War, and in which Kim Philby and Guy Burgess served as British representatives.

It is difficult to imagine why the British would have suggested an obscure, ancient capital on Korea's western coast for any reason that advanced UNC objectives in Korea. It is more likely that the insertion of the idea constituted a compromise of the process. In other words, individuals who were *not* supportive of UNC objectives may purposefully have found an opportunity to set a course of action that would undermine UNC objectives.

Such a scheme is, unfortunately, all too possible. In the months while the approach to the Communists was under discussion in allied channels, the spy ring of British Communists headed by Kim Philby, Guy Burgess, and Donald Maclean operated out of Washington and London, in direct cooperation with the Soviets and the Communist Chinese. They had established a "Moscow-Peking-Pyongyang conduit" that caused MacArthur so much concern he delayed sending operational information about the Inchon landing plans to Washington, fearing that leaks of his intentions were occurring in the nation's capital.[64] Although the Philby-Burgess-Maclean troika left Washington before the offer of truce talks, they had ample opportunity to plant the Kaesong notion in the checklist Rusk took to the meeting in the Pentagon.

Harold Adrian (Kim) Philby had arrived in Washington in October 1949 to serve as first secretary at the British embassy. His duties included liaison with the Central Intelligence Agency, where CIA officials have said he was given access to anything he wanted to learn. He met with CIA Director Bedell Smith routinely to discuss Korea.[65] Guy Burgess arrived in Washington to serve as second secretary in August 1950. Burgess came from the Foreign Office's far eastern department, where, starting in 1947, he had specialized in Communist Chinese affairs, and had been given access to highly classified documents on Korea.[66] While assigned to Washington, Philby and Burgess represented the United Kingdom on the Inter-Allied Board.[67] In 1951, Maclean was head of the American department of the Foreign Office in London, a position he attained in November 1950, having previously been first secretary at the British embassy in Washington.

The activities of the Philby spy ring are legendary now, but it took decades for their work to be brought to light. Not until 1983 did Soviet sources cite Maclean's espionage efforts' "crucial role in determining the outcome of the Korean War."[68] By 1996, William Breuer, an historian of intelligence operations, was able to conclude, "Burgess and Maclean had been Soviet spies whose treachery had inflicted incalculable harm to the security of Great Britain's and UN forces in Korea."[69]

Philby could easily have instructed a subordinate at the embassy to suggest Kaesong, and no one would have suspected a treasonous motive. If the Soviet-controlled international network functioned well, and by all accounts it did, a requirement or recommendation could be made in North Korea, transmitted to Moscow or Beijing, and reemerge as instructions in Washington.

It would seem highly conjectural to suggest that the Philby espionage network had succeeded in compromising a top-secret decision document put before the Joint Chiefs of Staff. Before his death in Moscow, however, Maclean himself "boasted that he gave Stalin on a plate every significant secret decision on the war taken by President Truman."[70] The Kaesong decision may show the Philby espionage network was not only able to pass on a number of secrets but could also deliver a few foreign policy successes along the way.

The first two months of negotiations in Kaesong had revealed some disturbing indicators about the nature of negotiations with North Korea. The world learned that North Korea's tactics and objectives were not what they appeared to be, that negotiations were not limited to the conference table, and that incidents outside of the truce tent would be staged as a part of the negotiating process. The talks in Kaesong proved that dedicated ideologues serving centralized power structures can be uncannily deft and agile, and surprisingly effective. Many authors have concluded that the lesson learned from Kaesong is to assess carefully the setting for talks, and insist on neutral ground. As valid as that point is, the more fundamental lesson from Kaesong is that the capabilities and motives of the North Korean side are treacherously obscure.

5

Negotiating the Armistice

The UNC negotiators' experience at Kaesong and the two years of difficult truce negotiations that followed gave rise to a myth of Communist success at the negotiating table. American negotiators found the process frustrating, particularly since the lives of soldiers on the front and prisoners of war depended on the swift progress of the talks. Ridgway, Joy, Kinney, Murray, and others openly discussed their anxieties in news features and books that were widely read by an American and allied public eager to see an end to the war on the peninsula. In their analyses, UNC negotiators were generally dissatisfied with the course of the talks, displeased with the terms of the final armistice agreement, and pessimistic about future dealings with the Communists. In a story that has been recounted many times, Joy's successor in the talks, Lieutenant General William K. Harrison, United States Army, passed a one-word note when asked how to negotiate with Communists: "Don't."[1]

It is not surprising to us today that Communists at the truce table treated representatives of a superior military force with utter contempt. But the American military negotiators who first encountered such contempt were shocked.

The negotiators themselves often observed weaknesses in the West's approach and advantages in the Communists' approach. Recriminations volleyed between commanders in the field and officials in Washington. Aspects of the negotiators' approach have been criticized for decades,[2] and will doubtless be a subject for analysis for decades more.

Almost a half-century later, however, the UNC negotiators' conduct as well as their accomplishments command respect. Despite difficulties, they achieved the critical objectives demanded by their negotiating instructions, and defeated three key Communist objectives. They thwarted Communist efforts to establish an indefensible line between the opposing military forces, forced the Communists to set aside demands that foreign military forces withdraw from the Korean peninsula, and guaranteed that prisoners of war who sought refuge in the South were not turned over to North Korea. In 1953, as at any other time since the establishment of the Communist regime in North Korea, the Communists' key objectives would have guaranteed violence a decisive factor in Korean political development. The fact that half of Korea has had an opportunity to develop into a stable democracy attests to the UNC's fundamental success at the negotiating table.

Contrary to the impression they often left in their own writings, the military negotiators assigned to this task were effective, creative, and clever. William P. Vatcher, one of the first authors to compile a record of the negotiations, provided a summary of their contributions:

> The United Nations Command had mustered all its negotiatory weapons in an effort to effect what it considered would be an honorable settlement with the Communists over a war they had started. Of the sixty-two paragraphs [in] the final twenty-eight–page armistice document, sixty-one were originated by the UNC. It is true that each paragraph was written many times, with each side fighting over every word, phrase, and sentence before final agreement was reached. The UNC was instrumental in exploring every approach to resolve each impasse that arose.[3]

Another way to evaluate the negotiators' achievements is to compare negotiating instructions with the final agreement. The initial negotiating instructions were set out in a message from the Joint Chiefs of Staff to General Ridgway on June 30, 1951.[4] The message described the overarching goals of "a cessation of hostilities in Korea, an assurance against the resumption of fighting, and the protection of the security of United Nations forces."[5] It acknowledged that the agreements might have to endure for an extended period until new political arrangements in Korea could be devised, and emphasized that the talks were to be, as Soviet diplomats had originally suggested, strictly military in nature.

The instructions were precise about how these goals were to be achieved in the final negotiated document. The terms of the armistice agreement, the message said, "shall require the establishment of a demilitarized area across Korea; and shall require all ground forces in Korea to remain in position or be withdrawn to the rear . . . of the demilitarized area."[6] To enforce this truce, the instructions required the establishment of "a Military Armistice Commission . . . empowered to inspect to insure that the terms, conditions, and arrangements as agreed to are carried out by all armed forces."[7]

Agenda

Negotiations over the agenda were completed before the talks were broken off in Kaesong over the trumped-up bombing incident. Although the UNC was able to insist on coverage of all the issues of importance to the JCS, it found that it had to fight North Korea's efforts to word the agenda to prejudice the outcome of the talks. Joy discerned that a Communist tactic was to "seek an agenda composed of conclusions favorable to their basic objectives."[8] He advised that "if their rigged agenda is carelessly accepted by their opponents," the Communists are able to argue that the only questions left are procedural.[9] The UNC therefore firmly refused the Communists' agenda, and the one finally agreed to on July 26 contained merely topics, not conclusions.

The first item was, "Agreement on the agenda," followed by item 2, worded as the UNC insisted: "Fixing of military demarcation line between both sides so as to establish a demilitarized zone as a basic condition for the cessation of hostilities in Korea."[10] The Communists wanted to restore the status quo ante bellum, and accordingly advocated that the first item on the agenda read: "Establishment of the 38th parallel as the military demarcation line between both sides, and establishment of a demilitarized zone, as basic conditions for the cessation of hostilities in Korea." The negotiations on this matter did not conclude before the talks broke down in Kaesong, so the establishment of the military demarcation line became the first substantive item when the negotiations moved to Panmunjom. After that, the agenda would deal with the institutions to monitor the truce (item 3), the return of prisoners of war (item 4), and recommendations to the governments involved in the political resolution of the conflict (item 5).

After the breakdown of August 23, the talks were halted until October 25, 1951. Scholars continue to debate the reasons why the Communists chose to break off the negotiations using the trumped-up bombing as a pretext. Cables from Mao Tse-tung to the military commanders in North Korea suggest that the Communists may have hoped to launch a fall 1951 offensive after they broke off negotiations over the staged incident.[11] Communist strategists may also have hoped to detract from the San Francisco discussions of the U.S.-Japan peace treaty by portraying the United States as responsible for the breakdown in negotiations. Whatever the Communists' intentions, neither the combat offensive in Korea nor the peace offensive in San Francisco worked out as they had hoped. By September 20, the Communists agreed to a resumption of discussions between liaison officers.

Seizing the opportunity, Ridgway insisted that the liaison officers meet at Panmunjom, not Kaesong. At Panmunjom the front lines of the opposing forces met near the 38th parallel. The Communists initially accepted this site for liaison officers' meetings, but resisted moving the delegation talks there, not wishing to lose the advantages Kaesong offered them. They were especially resistant to Ridgway's proposal to narrow the neutral zone, insisting that Kaesong must continue to be immune from UNC attack (and liberation).

After a month of discussions and continued UNC military pressure in eastern Korea, however, they finally agreed to Panmunjom as the official conference site. Through unyielding persistence, Ridgway and Joy also forced the Communists to respect freedom of movement for each side in a clearly defined neutral zone around Panmunjom. Talks resumed in the new location on October 25, 1951, and Panmunjom has been the conference site for military talks between the United Nations Command and North Korea ever since.

Military Demarcation Line

To keep the pressure on the Communists to sign the armistice agreement, the initial negotiating instructions directed that the provisions of the agreement would not go into effect until signature. That meant UNC military forces would continue to push Communist forces northward in eastern Korea, a tactical approach that Admiral Joy believed played the major role in securing Communist agreement. Had the fortunes of war been reversed, of course, the tactic would have backfired. Policy-makers in Washington, sincerely desiring an early end to fighting, reversed the tactic, declaring temporary suspensions of hostilities, when they believed it might help the progress of the talks. In each instance, however, the Communists built up their forces to launch counteroffensives; Admiral Joy criticized Washington's approach for giving the Communists unwarranted opportunities and causing costly delays.

In keeping with the strategy of withholding benefits until the agreement was actually signed, the UNC sought to set the demarcation line as the point of contact between the military forces at the time the armistice agreement went into effect. For negotiating purposes, however, the UNC sought a line deeper into North Korea, composed of a demilitarized zone extending north of the front line of allied troops. The UNC argued that neutralization of that territory was "compensation" for existing military capabilities that would be withdrawn by the allies, including what was then unquestioned naval and air superiority over all of North Korea.[12]

Discussions about the military demarcation line, as mentioned previously, began in Kaesong. North Korea's negotiator, General Nam Il, argued that the 38th parallel was "recognized by the whole world" as the point at which the belligerence broke out, and should therefore be established as the line between North and South. He proposed a mutual withdrawal from the parallel to create a ten-kilometer demilitarized zone on both sides. The UNC, however, turned his argument around: aggressors had twice violated the 38th parallel, and that showed the indefensibility of the line. Admiral Joy also pointed out that had an armistice been concluded a year earlier, when UNC forces had retreated to the Pusan perimeter in southern Korea, Nam would hardly have argued that allied forces be restored to their earlier position along the 38th parallel.[13]

The Communist position benefited from Secretary of State Acheson's controversial statement before the Senate on June 2, 1951. In a widely reported comment, he agreed that there could be a settlement "at or near the 38th parallel," leading to the withdrawal of "both Chinese and UNC troops."[14] Anticipating that the Communists would use this statement to their advantage, the official negotiating instructions took the unusual step of advising: "If the Communist Commander refers to statements attributed to United States Government officials that the United States is prepared to accept a settlement on or around the 38th parallel, you should take the position that such statements are not applicable to an armistice in the field but are properly the subject for governmental negotiation as to a political settlement."[15] That approach was intended both to dispose of the issue in the armistice talks and to compel the Communists' interest in the full political negotiations that were expected to follow on the heels of the armistice.

Admiral Joy used that argument during the talks in Kaesong but felt uncomfortable about it.[16] He told the Communists, "The line and zone you have proposed fulfills none of the requirements we believe essential. Its only significance is a political one dating back to 1945 but violated in 1950. If it is discussed again at any time in the future it should not be by military commanders . . . but by heads of state."[17] Knowing that the line selected by Rusk and Bonesteel in that late night session at the Pentagon in 1945 was clearly intended not to be a political one, but merely a military convenience, Joy might well have been somewhat discomfited by his own argument. He was more effective with Nam Il when he argued on the basis of a military rationale. "There are no reasonably sound defensible positions near the 38th parallel and there is no reason why there should be due to the line," Joy argued. "The UNC is in a defensible position at present. It does not intend to jeopardize the security of its forces by relinquishing such a position."[18] Nam Il appears to have understood the logic of a commander's responsibility to the security of his troops, but had to refute the UNC position. He replied, "We cannot accept the line you propose as the demarcation line at all. . . . Our stand is absolutely immovable."[19]

A month into the talks, both sides remained intransigent on the question of the demarcation line. On August 10, after the opening statement by Admiral Joy, the Communist delegation sat silently for two hours and eleven minutes. The silence was broken when Admiral Joy proposed that the delegations move on to the next agenda item. The Communists refused the suggestion, and the silent glaring continued.

After five more days of intractability, Admiral Joy observed dryly, "our present manner of exchanging views is tedious and somewhat stilted." He proposed that the delegations name a subcommittee of one delegate from each side, supported by two assistants (including interpreters), "to make recommendations to the two delegations as to ways and means of emerging from the present deadlock." The next day, Nam Il subjected Joy to a sixty-minute harangue on the incorrectness of the UNC position on the line, and then said, "I agree . . . to your proposal of forming a subcommittee." This tactic of harangue followed by concession was one with which the UNC became familiar. The UNC suggestion of referring intractable issues to lower level subdelegations also became familiar; it proved to be the most effective method of resolving intransigence in the talks.[20]

The subcommittee met from August 17 to August 22 and made steady progress, with both sides describing their demands as "adjustable" and North Korean Major General Lee Sang Cho concluding, "I think we have reached a point where both sides have come much nearer."[21] That pending agreement, however, was set aside when the Communists broke off the Kaesong talks.

By the time the talks resumed, on October 25, 1951, the beatings Communist forces had suffered at Bloody Nose Ridge, the Punchbowl, and the Hwachon reservoir, well north of the 38th parallel, persuaded them to take a different tack on the question of the demarcation line. At Panmunjom, they set aside their insistence on the 38th parallel, to Washington's relief. The negotiations now would focus on how to define the line of contact between the forces.

Ridgway had learned to drive a hard bargain. The UNC accordingly sought to include Kaesong, then under full control of the North, in the demilitarized zone. General Hodes, chief UNC representative on a subcommittee of the negotiating team, was quite open about why the UNC sought this objective:

> We have asked for withdrawal in the Kaesong area for a number of reasons. First, whether you admit it or not, if there had been no armistice negotiations, the Kaesong area would have been occupied by UNC troops. The only reason UNC troops are not in the Kaesong area is because it was declared a neutral zone. . . . We desire the Kaesong area to give more adequate security to the capital of the Republic of Korea.[22]

Washington became apprehensive about Ridgway's hard-line tactics. Partly out of concern over allied impatience and partly out of a belief that the American public needed reassurance that the bloodshed would end, officials at the Departments of Defense and State became restive.[23] At a top-secret (now declassified) Pentagon meeting on November 12, Chairman of the Joint Chiefs of Staff Bradley complained, "I don't know why we are arguing about Kaesong." When General Collins pointed out that it was important for the security of

Seoul, Bradley replied it was "not worth taking a chance of a break-down in the talks."[24]

Ridgway's proposal on Kaesong could not have been better de-signed to provoke a response from the Communists. He correctly viewed it as "the crux of Communist objections."[25] It may be that when North Korean records are opened, the world will find that North Korean propagandists had used Kaesong as an example of Communist class warfare for domestic propaganda as well as an example of East-West conflict for international propaganda. They may have told their people the change in venue of the negotiations from Kaesong to Pan-munjom indicated a UNC retreat. For North Korea, losing Kaesong to the UNC or having it subsumed in a demilitarized zone would have been seen as a major embarrassment.

That the UNC had hit home was apparent from the outcry it elic-ited from the North Korean side. "Communist reaction," as Ridgway summarized it, "was strongly negative."[26] North Korean Major Gen-eral Lee Sang Cho fumed:

> Should the peace-loving people of the world see [your pro-posal] they will certainly say it is not just and reasonable. Should we publish our proposal which we presented here today, the righteous people will certainly see it as a just pro-posal based on the present contact line. If the righteous world public sees these two different proposals, the right-eous world public can see who is trying for the armistice and peace.[27]

China's Major General Hsieh Fang, in his more elegant style, also ap-pealed to world opinion:

> The Korean armistice negotiations have been going on for more than one hundred days and the hopes of the people of the world for peace have not been realized. The negotiations have been interrupted with many holdups and now that the negotiations have been resumed I believe it is imperative that we face the realities and try to solve the problem on the basis of realities. . . . In making our proposal, we have been seriously concerned with the interests of the Korean people and the hopes for peace of the people of the world.[28]

The Communists keenly felt the pressure to propose an alterna-tive, and therefore offered one they knew the UNC would find attractive. They gave up on regaining the 38th parallel. On October 31, 1951, General Lee proposed that "both sides withdraw two kilometers strictly from the existing contact line, with the area evacuated by both sides as the demilitarized zone."[29] The Communists had accepted the principle of the point of contact determining the line, and offered a suggestion of how far to withdraw from that line to create a demilitarized zone.

Having achieved this concession, the UNC was prepared to move on to the next agenda item. On November 2, Joy suggested "leaving the finalization of the agreement on Agenda Item Two until such time as it is possible to settle it definitely in order to reach an agreement in all questions related to an armistice in Korea at the earliest possible date."[30] The Communists cried foul; they wished to delineate the line before proceeding to the next agenda item.

The UNC negotiators perceived that drawing the line before negotiating the rest of the agreement would be a grave error. "The enemy," Admiral Joy argued, "wants all of the advantages of a de facto cease-fire so that he can prolong the armistice negotiations without cost to himself. He wants immediate relief from our inexorable military pressure—the pressure which would be an incentive to arrive quickly at agreement on other items."[31] Ridgway and Joy had witnessed the effectiveness of military pressure and firm negotiating, and believed both would be needed to encourage future concessions. "The course you are directing will lead step by step to sacrifice of our basic principles," Ridgway wrote to the Joint Chiefs of Staff. And as if that were not strong enough to make an impression, the general called the approach advocated by his military superiors "a repudiation of the cause for which so many gallant men have laid down their lives."[32]

Officials at both the State Department and the JCS had been encouraged by the resumption of talks at Panmunjom and sought to acknowledge the Communists' acceptance of the principle of establishing the line along the "present line of contact." Overlooking the fact that the Communists had no better choice than to offer the concessions they did, Washington felt grateful for the progress in the talks. In a gesture of compromise approved by the president, they instructed the UNC first to negotiate the actual line of contact on a map, and then to pursue the next item "as promptly as possible."[33] When the line had been determined, Washington instructed, it would become the final demarcation line under the armistice, if all other matters were resolved within thirty days. They thought the Communists would be encouraged to proceed. That was not how it worked out.

First, there was the task of drawing the line. For this purpose, staff officers—Colonels Kinney and Murray for the United Nations Command delegation—were once again assigned to work with Colonels Chang and Tsai. Joy recorded what happened:

> Kinney and Murray were promptly presented with a Communist map showing the battle line about twenty miles behind the front-line positions of the United States Eighth Army. Some points on the Communist "line of contact" were even behind the division headquarters of our front-line divisions. Our staff officers recognized the futility of debating with Communists who were deliberately choosing to deny facts. Accordingly, they proposed to Colonels Chang and Tsai that all four officers proceed by helicopter along the battle line, identifying by actual examination the location of key points held by one side or the other. . . . The Communists refused. They wanted no close contact with truth.[34]

A line was finally drawn, "mile by tortured mile" as Joy described it, across the map of Korea. "Each point on the line was disputed," Joy recalled, and even when the line was drawn, "Colonel Tsai turned to previously agreed sections of the map and announced that he could not accept the positions marked thereon. The first point he disputed was in a section of the line that he himself had marked in with a red pencil." Colonel Murray, "a formidable-looking Marine," pounded the table at one point and called his Communist counterpart a "damned buffoon" and scolded, "You deny agreements you entered into not an hour ago, in fact you yourself offered!" Tsai retreated from the map table "muttering that he could not be bullied."[35] The staff officers reached agreement on the line on November 26, a full month after talks had resumed. In the first plenary session since the resumption of talks at Panmunjom a month earlier, the staff officers' recommendations were accepted by both sides.[36]

Although this seems to represent a successful point in the negotiations, Joy later reflected that the UNC had fallen into a trap:

> We failed to foresee the use that the Communists would make of the chronological order of the agenda items. By allowing the item on "Establishment of a Demarcation Line" to precede all others, we opened for the Communists a road to a de facto cease fire *prior* [emphasis in original] to agreement on other substantive questions. By agreeing to discuss

the position of the truce line first, we permitted the Communists to insist that this question had to be settled before other agenda items were explored.[37]

The Communists now had UNC recognition of a type of boundary. The JCS took pains to claim that Washington's offer of a quiet thirty-day period for completing the agreement did not constitute a truce. Fighting would continue if instigated by the other side, in which case any ground gained would be held, but turned over to the enemy when the armistice was concluded.[38] In theory, this sounded fine, and the interagency logic is certainly clear. In practice, however, these are not circumstances under which American commanders choose to risk their men's lives. General Van Fleet felt justified in ordering those under his command to limit operations "to the minimum essential to maintain present positions."[39] The thirty-day period, later extended for an additional fifteen days, was in fact, as men in the trenches called it, a "little armistice."

The JCS was guided by a logic the Communists did not share and by the naive belief that a temporary cease-fire would somehow encourage the Communists to accomplish the remainder of the agenda.[40] The Communists instead saw an opportunity to fortify their military position and prolong the negotiations.

Taking full advantage of the lull in fighting, the Communists set about making their now officially recognized line impregnable.[41] In messages cabled to his commanders, Mao ordered the construction of a defensive network of tunnels along the line.[42] "Into this mushrooming defensive line," the combat historian William Leckie observed, "the Chinese fed great numbers of well-equipped troops." "By the end of the year," he calculated, "Lieutenant General James Van Fleet found himself facing an enemy army of 850,000 men, rearmed, resupplied, and already receiving shipments of excellent Russian artillery with which to carry on trench warfare. Communist diplomacy, assisted by American naivete, had done Communist arms a great service."[43]

Joy called this "the turning point of the armistice conference."[44] It was in many ways the achievement of an objective the Communists had sought from the start of the negotiations—an agreement that implied recognition of Communist authority over the territory under Communist control.

Many have looked for lessons that should be learned from this experience. An important but often overlooked lesson is how effectively the North Korean–led negotiators made use of a concession. In negotiating with North Korea, the long hours of repetitive stonewalling seem impossible to surmount. When the Communists appear to make a major concession, relieved Western policymakers appreciate a break in a deadlock and feel a certain sense of accomplishment. Western negotiators have a tendency to lose sight of the fact that the Communists merely resolved a crisis they instigated. The lesson is certainly difficult to learn. It is important to keep in mind that North Koreans have repeatedly taken advantage of what appears to be a concession. Moreover, they know they have achieved major negotiating objectives through the creative use of false concessions on issues over which they had created the intransigence in the first place.

At times, perhaps, concessions should be met with unilateral acts of faith or generosity. In this case, however, the concession that the enemy made was motivated by fear rather than altruism. Ridgway and Joy recognized this; Washington appears not to have done so. As negotiations continued, Joy believed, the difference in Communist confidence was palpable: "we were confronted with Communist stalling and delaying tactics at every turn."[45] A recently released message from Mao Tse-tung to Peng Teh Huai shows this was in fact the Communists' strategy. "So long as we are not afraid of delaying and are not showing anxiety," Mao wrote to his chief negotiator, "the enemy cannot play any of its tricks."[46]

The United Nations Command had succeeded in achieving what the initial negotiating instructions demanded: "The demilitarized area shall be a zone . . . to be determined by the Commander in Chief of the United Nations command and the Commander in Chief of the Communist forces in Korea, based generally upon the positions of the opposing forces at the time the armistice arrangements are agreed upon."[47] But Washington's inclination to provide positive reinforcement for a North Korean concession undermined the ongoing negotiation process.

"It is my considered judgment," Admiral Joy lamented, "that this error in offering a concession to gain nothing more than apparent (and illusory) progress in the negotiations cost the United States a full year of war in Korea and armistice terms far more disadvantageous than otherwise could have been obtained. I hope our government learned a lesson."[48]

Foreign Forces

Compromises, as opposed to concessions, can succeed in moving negotiations with North Korea forward. This was the case with an important matter, the second item on the Communists' proposed agenda: "Withdrawal of all armed forces of foreign countries from Korea."

The debate over foreign forces occupied much of the first sixteen days of negotiation. The Communists asserted their "unshakable determination" to insist on the withdrawal of foreign forces from Korea after the armistice. "If the question of withdrawal of all foreign forces from Korea is not settled in this conference," Nam Il said, "a premise will be lacking for the forthcoming peace conference." Consistent with the long-standing Communist position, the North Korean general argued, "because foreign armed forces have been drawn into the Korean War, preventing the Korean people from settling their own affairs, it has not been possible to restore peace in Korea." Admiral Joy responded, "history demonstrates clearly that hostilities did occur in Korea in the absence of foreign forces. How, then, could absence of foreign forces be a guarantee against hostilities resuming in Korea?"[49]

The UNC was then treated to the mirror-image logic of North Korea's interpretation of history. It makes no more sense today than it did in 1951, but it is considerably more familiar, having been reiterated with consistency for almost fifty years:

> There were indeed no foreign forces in Korea on 25 June 1950, but the occurrence of the incident of 25 June and subsequent developments were inseparable from the fact that large numbers of foreign armed forces arrived in Korea on 27 June which prevented the peaceful settlement of the internal problem of Korea for which we have consistently stood, and converted the war into one involving many countries. It was only when the foreign troops participated and one side had penetrated deep into the interior of the Democratic People's Republic of Korea and directly threatened the security of the People's Republic of China, that the Chinese people were compelled to send volunteer units to assist the Korean people to fight against intervention by foreign armed forces.[50]

In other words, violence instigated by Korean Communists against those who disagreed with them was actually a peaceful effort to gain unchallenged possession of the Korean peninsula.

It became clear to the UNC that lengthy ideological polemics would not be worthwhile and efforts to straighten out differences in the interpretation of history would be fruitless. In the interest of speeding up the pace of negotiations,[51] UNC negotiators avoided defining "aggressors," and left unchallenged comments about how World War II had been resolved. Joy argued instead that the removal of foreign troops was a political question beyond the scope of a military armistice:

> The various governments with armed forces in Korea operating with the United Nations Command have authorized these armed forces to be in Korea. Therefore, the withdrawal of these armed forces from Korea must be approved by those same governments, as well as by the United Nations itself. The delegation of the United Nations Command can make arrangements only pertaining to the cessation of military action of these armed forces within Korea.[52]

By July 21, foreign troop withdrawal remained the only obstacle to conclusion of agreement on the agenda. China's representatives at the talks may have tired of the slow pace[53] or of the emphasis on "foreign troops." After a three-day recess in which China and North Korea mulled over their joint approach, Nam Il returned to the talks and proposed to add a fifth item to the four "Recommendations to the governments of the countries concerned on both sides." The fifth item provided "that within a definite time limit after the armistice agreement becomes effective a conference of their representatives of a higher level be convened to negotiate on the question of withdrawal, by stages, of all foreign armed forces in Korea."[54]

"Our delegation," Joy wrote, "considered the Communist proposal from the standpoint that, after all, it constituted no more than a *recommendation* [emphasis in original] to the governments involved in the Korean War. Those governments could accept or reject the recommendations as they saw fit. Therefore we promptly accepted the Communist proposal."[55]

So quick an acceptance of the proposal from the UNC threw the suspicious Communist delegation "into a state of confusion." Nam Il wondered how he had blundered. The North Korean general asked for a forty-minute recess, perhaps to contact superiors in Pyongyang and Beijing, then asked for an additional twenty-four–hour recess the next day. "When we met again," Joy noted, "Nam Il delivered a long statement full of escape clauses affecting his own proposal." But even that was not enough to reassure the head of the Communist delegation. He asked that staff officers be appointed to discuss his proposal further. Although the proposal had already been accepted by both sides, Joy agreed that staff officers could study the proposal, but he instructed Colonel Kinney not to permit any changes to the proposal. "Though they had submitted their proposal in writing and argued for it in a vigorous fashion," Joy summarized, "none of us in the United Nations Command delegation would have been at all surprised if they had denounced it utterly when our meetings were resumed."[56]

The obstacle over withdrawal of foreign forces was overcome in the armistice negotiations by deferral. The issue would be revisited frequently in the ensuing decades. Then as now, the North Koreans could not bring themselves to understand a simple fact: American troops are not in Korea because they want to be, not because the United States has an interest in maintaining an imperial presence, and not even because Korea is a militarily strategic location. American troops are in Korea because if they were not, violence itself would determine Korea's political future.

Armistice Commission

It is because of North Korea's policies that foreign forces have been required to play their important role in guaranteeing peace on the Korean peninsula. North Korean efforts in the negotiations undermined the monitoring institutions proposed by the UNC, making it imperative for the Republic of Korea and its allies to make extraordinary investments in deterrence throughout the decades of the armistice. Had the UNC won North Korean agreement to a mechanism that would genuinely monitor and restrict postwar military reconstruction efforts, so large a deterrent composed of foreign forces would not have been necessary. North Korean negotiators who eviscerated the inspection regime guaranteed that North Korean objectives regarding the withdrawal of foreign forces could not be achieved.

In its discussions before the truce talks and in messages to General Ridgway, the Joint Chiefs of Staff made it clear that establishment of a Military Armistice Commission to enforce the truce was mandatory. The UNC hoped that maintenance of the truce would require no fighting and fewer forces than the war itself, and that is what they sought from the agreement. The negotiating instructions directed Ridgway and

Joy to win agreement on a commission that would keep the opposing sides from "reinforcing air, ground or naval units or personnel during the armistice . . . and from increasing the level of war equipment and materiel existing in Korea at the time the armistice becomes effective." The objective was to freeze the level of capabilities. The Military Armistice Commission, the instructions said, "must be empowered to inspect to insure that the terms, conditions, and arrangements as agreed to are carried out by all armed forces." And in order to do that, Washington insisted, "the Commission and teams of observers appointed by the Commission shall have free and unlimited access to the whole of Korea and shall be given all possible assistance and cooperation in carrying out their functions."[57]

The UNC negotiators adhered to these objectives long after Washington discarded them. On October 26, 1951, before negotiations on UNC inspection proposals even began, Assistant Secretary of State Rusk told allied ambassadors in Washington, "More extensive inspection than absolutely necessary might create more difficulties for us than benefits, both in reaching agreement and in providing a source of incidents."[58] Washington's lack of resolve on inspections, however, was not revealed to the UNC negotiators for many months.

Ridgway tried to guard against possible moves in Washington that would pull the rug out from under the negotiators. In a message to the JCS, he pointed out some lessons the negotiators had learned in the field:

> Experience in dealing with agenda item 2 convinces me that lack of authorization to indicate or take an unyielding stand regarding a UNC proposal inevitably induces an aggressive attitude in the Communists. Actual UNC concessions, made without equivalent concessions by the Communists, result in an increased determination on the part of the enemy to press for further concessions. Moreover, lack of knowledge as to the ultimate national position on an agenda item produces uncertainty within the UNC delegation in its negotiatory processes. This further encourages the Communists to take adamant positions. These facts have been learned through experience.[59]

The negotiations over the commission and its responsibilities began on November 27, 1951, under agenda item 3, "Concrete arrangements for a Cease-fire." The Communists proposed that the two sides simply stay in their respective zones; the UNC insisted on the right of inspection in the Communist zone to determine compliance with the truce. As had become the customary process for starting talks on difficult issues, the sides exchanged a set of general principles for discussion. The UNC list specified there would be "no increase of military forces, supplies, equipment, and facilities" during the period of armistice, and proposed a supervisory organization, "equally and jointly manned by both sides," which "shall have free access to all parts of Korea, for itself and for the joint observation teams responsible to the Armistice Commission."[60]

Nam Il immediately reiterated his standard argument that foreign forces should be removed. "If all foreign forces are withdrawn from Korea," the Soviet-trained general stated, "there will be no practicable question of the military supplies, equipment, and facilities exceeding the level existing at the time of the signing of the Armistice Agreement."[61] He also struck out at the UNC position on inspections: "Your side maintains that the supervisory organ should have free access to all parts of Korea to carry out inspections. This is clearly a brazen interference in the internal affairs of the other side. This is unreasonable and impractical, and our side absolutely cannot agree to such a provision."[62]

The UNC argued that the provisions would cover only the period of the armistice, not the peace that would follow the anticipated government-to-government political discussions, and therefore should not be seen as a violation of sovereignty. The UNC's only interest was in guaranteeing compliance with the terms of the truce, adding that they would abide by the terms themselves.[63]

The proposed principles, as U.S. Air Force Major General Turner argued, would accordingly benefit the Communists as well as the UNC:

> [We] propose only that during the armistice you shall not gain a military capability which you do not now possess. . . . We agree to apply the same restrictions to ourselves, even though you lack the military capability today to implement these restrictions by force of arms. But you complain this is unfair—you who are unable to impose any of these military restrictions upon our side by your own strength. You complain it is unfair for us to insist on continuing restrictions through armistice terms which we are fully able to impose, and are imposing on you by military means during hostil-

ities. In short, you seek to gain, through negotiation, what you could not win through fighting. You seek to avoid, through negotiation, what you could not avoid through fighting.[64]

Having obtained clarification from the UNC on what inspection regimes were envisioned, the Communists pursued a clever negotiating stratagem. On December 3, they proposed "mutually agreed" inspections by a supervisory commission formed of neutral nations. Using the language "as mutually agreed" is a negotiating technique to cover over substantive differences with language that appears to resolve more than it does. It is a deferring tactic that works in negotiations characterized by good faith and fundamental agreement. The words are easy for two sides to agree to because the entire act of negotiation itself constitutes mutual agreement. By definition, it seems that language specifying "mutual agreement" can almost always be accepted. In this instance, however, mutual agreement would undermine the objective of inspection, giving a veto to the side that resisted inspection.

Rather than a concession, the change in the Communists' approach may more accurately be described as bringing their negotiating posture in line with Moscow. While avoiding specifics, the Soviets had given a nod to the convening of representatives of the concerned military commands to supervise the truce, even before the truce talks had begun.[65]

The North Korean proposal of December 3 gave flesh to this notion:

> invite representatives of nations neutral in the Korean War to form a supervisory organ to be responsible for conducting necessary inspection, beyond the demilitarized zone, of such ports of entry in the rear *as mutually agreed upon* [emphasis added] by both sides and to report to the joint Armistice Commission the result of the inspections.[66]

North Korea had nothing to lose; by insisting on mutual agreement for the inspection of ports of entry, they could block inspections they did not want. As Admiral Joy saw it, "They conceived that the neutral observers would be notified by the local authorities when a shipment was to enter Korea, and could then proceed to the railway station, dock, or airfield being used. The neutral observers could then, and *only* then, check the entry or exit involved."[67] At the same time, the Communists recognized that if the UNC did not object, the representatives of neutral nations would have an intelligence-gathering opportunity in the South.

The UNC saw North Korea's concurrence in the notion of a supervisory commission with some powers of inspection as a step forward. The Communists insisted on UNC withdrawal from coastal areas and waters of the North Korean side of the military demarcation line, but also supported the notions of the inviolability of the demilitarized zone, and of an armistice commission with equal representation from both sides. The questions of limiting military activities under the truce and conducting inspections of the other side were to become the sticking points. Joy proposed that the matter be referred to a subdelegation, and Nam Il agreed.

On December 7, the UNC proposed a revision relating to the withdrawal of forces from the demilitarized zone, and the Communists found it acceptable. In exchange, the UNC accepted (on December 12) North Korean demands that the UNC withdraw from certain islands off the coast of North Korea that had been taken by allied naval forces and had served as search and rescue centers during the war. The Communists continued to insist that a Military Armistice Commission should include observer teams from "neutral nations." The UNC moved toward agreement on two institutions: the Military Armistice Commission itself and a Neutral Nations Supervisory Commission (NNSC), which the UNC saw as subordinate to the Military Armistice Commission. As Admiral Joy described it, there were to be two cooperative institutions ensuring compliance with the terms of the truce:

> One, a Military Armistice Commission, was to supervise, among other things, proceedings in the narrow neutral strip between the two opposed armies after the cease-fire went into effect. The other, a Supervisory Commission, was to be charged with the inspection of activities of each side in the rear areas. This latter commission would conduct its inspection by means of a number of observer teams permanently located at ports of entry, and by another group of mobile observer teams which could be sent anywhere to investigate reported armistice violations.[68]

Winning agreement to establishment of a commission, however, is one thing. Empowering it to investigate violations of an agreement is something else. As the end of 1951 approached, the monitoring issues still to be resolved were how to implement—through aerial surveillance, ground inspections, and inspections in ports of entry—provisions limiting military personnel rotations and restrictions on the construction of airfields.

JCS instructions had required UNC negotiators to guarantee that the provisions prohibiting increases in military capabilities would not restrain the UNC from rotating new troops in to replace existing troops.[69] When Nam Il first heard the idea, he naturally questioned why new troops should be admitted. "If armistice is effected in Korea," he reasoned, "why should there be introduced fresh troops, military supplies, and equipment since there will be no shooting?"[70]

The rotation issue was raised by the UNC because the JCS sought to affirm the UNC's right to rotate troops, but it is difficult in hindsight to understand why UNC rotations were considered negotiable. In order to proceed on the issue, briefings had to be provided by American negotiators simply to explain to the Communists how the UNC system of personnel rotations worked. Possibly because the briefings on UNC force structure and deployments created an intelligence benefit, the Communists indicated a willingness to consider the question. The Communists also recognized the advantages inherent in the UNC's willingness to submit its own activities to the inspection regime. Although the UNC was in the militarily superior position, the negotiations gave North Korea an opportunity to engage in defining the terms that would apply to military rotations in the South.

Accordingly, on December 14, the Communists accepted the notion that forces could be replenished, and took the opportunity to limit such rotations to 5,000 monthly. "By holding personnel rotation allowances to a grossly insufficient figure," Joy discerned, "they hoped to accomplish the attrition of United Nations Command forces until none remained in Korea."[71] If only 5,000 UNC personnel per month could be rotated, each would have a tour of duty in Korea lasting seven years.[72] UNC forces came from distant democratic nations and could not be expected to serve in Korea indefinitely, so in practice the restriction applied only against the UNC. The provision applied legally to the Chinese as well, but had only a theoretical impact, since the China–North Korea border facilitated undetected movement of Chinese troops.

Prohibiting airfield reconstruction in North Korea was an intractable issue critical to UNC commanders. Airfields in North Korea had been bombed in the early days of fighting and, according to Admiral Joy, "had not been 'combat effective' during any significant period of the Korean War."[73] "We of the United Nations Command delegation," he wrote, "could see no reason why the Communists should be allowed to develop an important military capability during the period of truce."[74]

By January 31, when little apparent progress had been made on the inspection issues, Admiral Joy recommended a subdelegation be set up to skip to item 5 of the agenda—a process that led to the conclusion by February 17 of a set of recommendations, including the recommendation on foreign forces, discussed above. Joy hoped that the provisions agreed to on those questions would be attractive inducements to the Communists to faster action on the unfinished business of agenda items 3 and 4.[75]

The two sides were deadlocked on key issues surrounding inspections. On January 9, however, the UNC had consented to the establishment of a Neutral Nations Supervisory Commission, which the Communists had proposed to bear the responsibility for inspection on the ground, aerial surveillance, and port inspection. Each side was to nominate three countries "acceptable to both sides which have not participated in the Korean War."[76]

On February 16, however, North Korea put the negotiating process into a tailspin by nominating the Soviet Union, Poland, and Czechoslovakia as the "neutral nations" to serve as members of the NNSC. The nomination appears to have taken the UNC by complete surprise.

When the pertinent Communist archives are opened, it will be interesting to see whether the Communist nomination of the Soviet Union, pursued on the day before the resolution of item 5, had been decided in Moscow as much as a year earlier, or whether it was decided during the course of the negotiations. In the spirit of cooperation with the Soviets that had marked the original decision to start the truce talks, Dean Rusk had in June 1951 suggested a role for them on an inspection commission, but his idea had been discarded.[77] There is no reason Ridgway or Joy would have known that; the notes from the Washington meeting were probably not distributed to them and were not made public until 1983. The Soviets, however, were likely to have known of Rusk's views through the Philby-Maclean espionage network, and may have been surprised at the negative UNC reaction to their nomination.

The UNC reaction was indeed a strong one. When he wrote of it four years later, the Communist move still caused Admiral Joy's blood to boil. He perceived it as a prime example of a Communist tactic of introducing spurious issues in order to use them as bargaining points, and he called this one "the most absurd red herring it has ever been my misfortune to encounter."[78] From the start, he believed they used the nomination of the Soviet Union as a negotiating device that "would allow them to construct military airfields in North Korea after the armistice was put into effect."[79] "There is no doubt in my mind," Joy wrote, "that the Communists realized fully how unacceptable the Soviet Union was to the United Nations Command. They knew we would oppose their nomination . . . and they intended to withdraw it at a later date in return for favorable resolution of the airfield issue."[80]

The UNC nominated Norway, Sweden, and Switzerland in its response to the Communist proposal, and stated its refusal to accept the Soviet Union. A month later, the UNC, still stymied by the proposal, suggested reducing the membership of the NNSC to four, dropping Norway and the Soviet Union. As the issue dragged on, it was clear the North Koreans had found an opportunity to weaken UNC resolve on many peripheral issues as the UNC fought to get out from an issue that tended to undermine American prestige in the region. If the United States had been forced to accept the Soviet Union's membership in the NNSC, the horse laugh would have been heard across Asia.

Concessions were made to promote incremental progress on other issues. From January 29 to February 13, the UNC dropped its demand for monthly rotations of 75,000 troops to 60,000, then 40,000. The Communists raised their maximum allowance from 5,000 to 25,000 to 30,000. A week after the Communists introduced the issue of Soviet membership on the NNSC, the UNC accepted the number of 35,000—less than half of its desired number.

Discussions of numbers of ports of entry that would be open for inspection took much the same course. When the Communists finally agreed in principle that some ports could be opened to inspection, the UNC sought access to twelve ports. "The supplies for North Korea's war effort all came from outside the country," Admiral Joy explained; accordingly, "they sought to limit the number of ports of entry [subject to inspection], since by doing so they would reduce the number of neutral observers behind their lines, and thus gain greater freedom to violate the agreements regarding resupply." The Communists agreed to three, then four, then five. The UNC lowered its demand to eight, seven, six, and finally five on March 16.

On the other monitoring stumbling block, aerial surveillance, the UNC was initially unyielding. Aerial surveillance was clearly the most effective means available at the time to ascertain that the truce was not being used for a military buildup, especially given the uncertain diligence the NNSC would bring to ground and port inspections. Joy saw the Communist objection to aerial surveillance in this light:

> In order to facilitate the functions of these mobile neutral observers, we had proposed that the observers be afforded the right to reconnoiter by air any area of Korea. The Communists refused to agree. They insisted on a two-edged veto. First, they proposed that the activities of the supervisory bodies be contingent upon unanimous agreement of the members. A dissent by one of the Communist members would constitute a veto. Second, they refused to allow aerial reconnaissance. Thus, even if all Communist members of the supervisory organ voted in favor of investigation, the observer teams on the ground could be effectively frustrated through lack of aerial reconnaissance."[81]

The UNC persisted in its vision of putting in place an inspection regime that would guarantee the enemy's compliance. Washington, however, had begun to conclude that deterrence alone could be relied on to keep the truce. Advances in surveillance technology may also have strengthened the view that allied aerial surveillance capabilities would be sufficient to operate without agreement from the Communists. Such a reversal in negotiating strategy, however, was repugnant to Ridgway. "I cannot concur," Ridgway wrote to the JCS, "in your view that 'the only real assurance we have against a resumption of hostilities is the maintenance of sufficient and appropriate military power.'"[82] He continued to advocate a strong inspection regime.

Eventually, however, Washington ordered the UNC to concede on aerial surveillance in exchange for Communist concessions permitting majority calls for inspections by the NNSC. Joy was not pleased with the new instruction from Washington. "As a result," Joy wrote, "though we did eventually win grudging Communist agreement to procedures not contingent upon unanimity in the supervisory organizations, our victory was hollow."[83]

Contrary to Washington's expectations, the concession on aerial surveillance did not speed the negotiations. Joy observed, "No sooner did the Communists witness the United Nations Command concession on aerial observation of the truce than they stiffened noticeably in their opposition to the United Nations Command proposal on airfield rehabilitation."[84]

The UNC negotiators had stood firm against permitting the North to rehabilitate and reconstruct airfields, which the North firmly viewed as its sovereign right. From Washington's perspective, the process of whittling away each side's resistance was a way to sculpt an agreement, but UNC negotiators were worried about the North's reconstructing an offensive military capability. "When Washington decided, in a final effort to achieve an armistice, to allow the Communists to build airfields in North Korea during the truce period," Joy complained, "the basic premise upon which the armistice had been designed went up in a wisp of smoke. . . . [T]here was no longer any chance to prevent the military capabilities of Communist forces in Korea from increasing in a major degree during the truce."[85]

Washington's approach to resolving deadlocks in negotiations was to offer package deals—combinations of carrots and sticks to be considered as a whole. As a negotiating tactic, there are problems with this approach: first, there is never an effective way to insist on a take-it-or-leave-it proposal when the primary goal is to complete a negotiation, because any reasonable revision will naturally be accepted; and second, carrots can almost never be retrieved from the table, but sticks always can. Take-it-or-leave-it deals have a tendency to become take-some-and-leave-some deals.

Nevertheless, package deals can breathe new life into a stagnant situation, and stagnancy prevailed in the spring of 1952. The negotiations had labored on for almost a year. The subcommittee discussions of the return of prisoners of war were bogged down. A subdelegation appointed to deal with the questions of NNSC membership and reconstruction of airfields was deadlocked.

Therefore, on April 25, 1952, the UNC suggested more progress might be made in plenary session. After a hiatus of two months, a plenary session was scheduled for April 28.[86] At that session, Admiral Joy submitted the UNC package proposal:

> In the interest of reaching an early armistice agreement, we are willing to accede to your stand that no restriction be placed on the rehabilitation and construction of airfields. I

must make it absolutely clear, however, that our acceptance of your position regarding airfields is contingent upon your acceptance of our positions regarding prisoners of war [i.e., voluntary repatriation] and the composition of the Neutral Nations Supervisory Commission [i.e., omission of Norway and the USSR, thus leaving Poland, Czechoslovakia, Sweden, and Switzerland].[87]

It was not an offer Joy was pleased to make. Years later, he still regretted the move: "This concession utterly departed from the basic principle on which the United Nations Command delegation had been trying to arrange the armistice—the principle of freezing the military capabilities of both sides so that neither could add substantially to its strength during the period of truce."[88]

The UNC concession on airfields also failed to bring the talks to an end. The Communists agreed to drop one stumbling block they had positioned in the negotiations—the membership of the Soviet Union in the NNSC. In return they obtained UNC acquiescence that North Korea could reconstruct airfields, building up a military capability it had never had before. North Korea would emerge from the peace talks with stronger capabilities than it carried in. Nevertheless, despite this concession, offered on May 7, 1952, the negotiations went on for another year and two months, on the single issue of the repatriation of prisoners of war.

Prisoners of War

"The armistice document signed at Panmunjom on July 27, 1953, was practically identical to that which I tabled in April, 1952," Admiral Joy reflected in his memoirs, "in all but details relative to the mechanics of exchanging prisoners."[89]

The prisoner of war issue was not expected to be a difficult one to negotiate. Initial negotiating instructions consisted of two sentences: "Prisoners of war shall be exchanged on a one-for-one basis as expeditiously as possible. Until the exchange of prisoners is completed, representatives of the International Committee of the Red Cross shall be permitted to visit all POW camps to render such assistance as they can."[90] No one seems to have anticipated that this single issue could hold up the signing of the armistice for more than a year after all other issues had been resolved. In April 1952, when all the other issues seemed close to resolution, Secretary of State Acheson was confident the prisoner of war issue would be resolved within the month.[91]

Tremendous frustration accompanied the negotiation of the prisoner of war issue, and few of the elements of the final resolution resulted from progress made at the negotiating table. The issue was, in essence, taken out of the truce tent. In the course of its consideration, the issue was also removed from Panmunjom to Washington, Beijing, and Moscow. For a time, it appeared that even these capitals would refer the issue to a coalition of nonaligned UN members emerging to solve the problem in New York. When the stalemate finally ended, it was largely because of the death of Stalin and the rise of a more conciliatory group of leaders in Moscow, not because of negotiation. Negotiations on the final agenda item, nevertheless, provided a valuable lesson: not every issue lends itself to negotiation with North Korea. The prisoner of war issue was one on which the fundamental perspectives of the two sides were so different that no amount of discussion could paper over the differences. One side had to give, and the compromise eventually came from factors outside North Korea.

At the start of the negotiations, little was known about the POWs held by North Korea. North Korea had refused repeated Red Cross requests for information during the war, disallowed inspection visits, and gave only spotty information in the few North Korean radio broadcasts on the issue. After the negotiations began, 110 names of prisoners were passed to the Red Cross on August 15 and September 12,[92] but even the Communists acknowledged that the information was incomplete. As early as November 27, 1951, Admiral Joy raised the issue in plenary session and suggested an exchange of data by both sides, but the Communists refused. In an effort to bring focus to the issue, the UNC recommended simultaneous subdelegation meetings on agenda items 3 and 4 on December 4, 1951. The Communists finally agreed to proceed six days later. Accordingly, discussions on item 4 started on December 11, 1951, with Rear Admiral Ruthven E. Libby and Major General Lee Sang Cho leading their respective subdelegations.

General Lee Sang Cho summarized the Communist point of view on the issue. As on other issues, the Communists' opening remarks offered little by way of ideas for resolving the issue: "We have been insisting that as soon as the armistice agreement is signed the prisoners of war should be released and we should let them go home and enjoy a happy life."[93] Admiral Libby opened by demanding information:

> Your side has callously ignored the fundamental right of our
> side to receive POW data. What you expect to accomplish
> by holding out this information is not too clear to us. It may
> be that you think that our desire to achieve a speedy arm-
> istice has made us what we call "easy marks." We do hope
> for an early armistice but not at the price of giving every-
> thing for nothing. . . . It may be that you think you can wait
> us out and that by evasive and nonsensical replies to our
> questions, you will cause us by sheer frustration to negotiate
> without knowledge. . . . We refuse to negotiate blindly.[94]

"I want to ask you which is the important question," Lee retorted, "to release the POWs held by both sides or to exchange the data for it?[95] And so it continued.

In keeping with their negotiating instructions, the UNC immediately pressed North Korea to permit the International Red Cross to visit its prisoner of war camps. This brought a sarcastic reply from General Lee: "Does your delegation present here represent the military authorities or does it represent the Red Cross society?" [96]

When UNC representatives pointed out that the Geneva Convention required that POW camps be opened to neutral inspections, Lee said, "You time and again quote and talk of observing the Geneva Convention, but we must tell you that we not only observe the Geneva Convention, but, more than that, we treat the prisoners more humanely than is provided for in the Geneva Convention."[97] Neither the record of unanswered communications from the Red Cross nor the testimony of captives in Korea after their release substantiated that statement.[98] At the end of the century, given what the world knows of North Korea's behavior, it is baffling to imagine that the Communists once tried to portray their camps as idyllic refuges. Nevertheless, in a campaign that reached its zenith in two books co-written by Alan Winnington and Wilfred Burchett, the world was treated to pictures of Chinese guards toasting their prisoners on Christmas, and picnicking with them along the Yalu River.[99]

On December 18, the first lists of prisoners were finally exchanged, and a recess was declared to give both sides time to study the information. In propaganda broadcasts during the war, the North had claimed to have captured some 65,000 UNC soldiers. The world was shocked, and the American public outraged, to hear that North Korea now claimed to hold only 11,559 POWs—7,142 were identified as South Koreans, 3,198 were Americans, 919 were from the UK, and the rest were from other allied nations.[100]

Because the United States officially listed 11,224 as "missing in action," the figure of 3,198 meant that more than 8,000 Americans might have died after capture. For South Korea, the numbers were ten times worse; nearly 80,000 South Koreans were unaccounted for. The UNC list accounted for 132,474—95,531 were identified as North Korean POWs, 20,700 were Chinese, and 16,243 were South Koreans who were captured while fighting for the North Korean Army.

The notion of a "one for one" exchange had been specified in Admiral Joy's original negotiating instructions. Ridgway had hoped it could be used to return as few enemy military personnel to active service as the UNC wished to return.[101] Lee Sang Cho had made it clear on December 12 that the Communists would demand an all-for-all exchange and, given the disparity in numbers, a one-for-one exchange was no longer feasible.[102]

The UNC expressed its anguish over the North Korean figures on December 21. Its written complaint pointed out that the North Korean list did not even include names of prisoners who had been identified in North Korean radio broadcasts. Of the 110 names the Communists had provided earlier to the Red Cross, 66 did not appear on the December 18 list.[103] The UNC also argued that the Republic of Korea carried tens of thousands of soldiers as "missing in action," making it impossible to believe the North had captured only 7,142. The UNC specifically demanded an accounting of the some 50,000 prisoners North Korean radio broadcasts had said were captured during the war. The UNC had records that some captives had escaped at the front and returned to the South; they accounted for 177 of the 50,000.[104]

In response, General Lee chortled derisively while giving the following explanation:

> If we had, like you, detained all the persons we captured, it would be possible that we would have the 50,000 you mentioned. But we allowed those who wanted to go back home and who did not want to join a war against their country to go back and lead a peaceful life at home. And we directly released at the front those foreign prisoners of war who did not want to join the war against people who fight for their real independence, who fight for their own people. These measures of ours are perfectly right and I tell you that the

righteous people of the world praise this revolutionary policy of ours towards the prisoners of war.[105]

A number of ROK soldiers captured by the North had been pressed into service for North Korea's Army. Some of those who were subsequently recaptured by the South described the process: Captured South Korean soldiers were given a choice of "being turned over to the North Korean Security Police, to be tried for treason against the Korean people," or "volunteering to join the forces of the [North] Korean People's Army to drive out the American invaders and aid in the unification of Korea."[106] Lee Sang Cho admitted this was the case.

Prisoners in the South were not conscripted into military service, but many were willing to fight rather than return to the Communists. On December 23, the UNC started down a path from which it never returned when it pointed out that some prisoners did not wish to be repatriated.

That the UNC might not return those who feared to return infuriated the Communists. They claimed that Article 118 of the Geneva Convention of 1949 required "that all prisoners shall be repatriated whatever opinion they might seem to have, or that their captors might say they had."[107] They based their argument on a provision of the convention that states, "each of the detaining powers shall itself establish and execute without delay a plan of repatriation."[108] The United States, however, argued that the convention bestowed rights on individuals, not their country of origin.[109] Furthermore, the convention states, "Prisoners may in no circumstances renounce in part or in entirety the rights secured to them by the present Convention."[110]

General Nam made it clear how deeply North Korea detested the UNC suggestion that it could retain individual prisoners who wished not to return to North Korea. "That principle of 'voluntary repatriation,'" Nam said, "is, in effect, a principle of forced retention of the captured personnel of our side."[111]

In a session with the Communist subdelegation on January 2, 1952, Admiral Libby noted the general agreement of the two sides that all POWs should be released. "The UNC proposal differs from yours," he continued, "in that it expressly provides that all repatriation will be voluntary."[112] The UNC position on voluntary repatriation had therefore been put forward at the talks, but it was still being debated in American policy circles.

Admiral Joy himself had problems with the growing consensus

that the United States should insist on giving the prisoners the freedom to choose whether they would be returned. In the interest of a speedy resolution of the talks, Admiral Joy had some sympathy with the Communists' position, although not with their rationale. Joy saw the issue pragmatically:

> "Voluntary repatriation" placed the welfare of ex-Communist soldiers above that of our own United Nations Command personnel in Communist prison camps, and above that of our United Nations Command personnel still on the battle line in Korea. I wanted our own men back as soon as we could get them. Since we were not allowed to achieve a victory, I wanted the war halted. Voluntary repatriation cost us over a year of war, and cost our United Nations Command prisoners in Communist camps a year of captivity. The United Nations Command suffered at least 50,000 casualties in the continuing Korean War while we argued to protect a lesser number of ex-Communists who did not wish to return to Communism.[113]

Ridgway also argued some of these points in messages to Washington, but Washington would later compel an unyielding stance.[114]

In advancing voluntary repatriation, the UNC appears to have been so focused on its moral argument that it failed to recognize a sensitive and practical Chinese sore point. The UNC knew that many Chinese "volunteers" were Nationalists pressed into service for the Communists,[115] but it did not expect China to object when these soldiers were not returned home. The Chinese reaction, however, was vehement. Colonel Tsai accused the UNC of having as its primary objective turning over prisoners to Chiang Kai-shek, and Major General Lee picked up the charge: "You want to deliver a part of them to a certain friend of yours in South Korea and a part of them to a certain friend of yours in Formosa."[116]

Genuinely taken aback by the Communist charge, the UNC denied that its objective was to supplement the forces defending Taiwan. Believing it had merely erred in presentation, the UNC took the initiative to redraft its set of principles on repatriation repeatedly throughout the month of January. On February 3, the Communists submitted a counterproposal that was seen as encouraging. The next day, the UNC proposed turning the issue over to staff officers, and the Communists agreed.

In the meantime, the debate over forcible repatriation was also building steam in Washington. Ridgway had appealed to Secretary of Defense Robert A. Lovett that an intractable stand on voluntary repatriation could delay progress in the talks. Lovett was sympathetic, and sensitive to views on Capitol Hill that reflected Joy's on the harm that could be done to American captives and soldiers. At a meeting in the Pentagon on January 29, the majority concluded that the POW issue "was likely to become the major unresolved issue."[117] Secretary of State Acheson defended the view that the West had a responsibility to the prisoners of war "whose lives would be endangered if returned to the Communists," and tentatively suggested "immediately screening and releasing [those] POWs."[118] Screening is a process of interviewing to assess the validity of claims of political persecution or to discern preferences regarding repatriation. In ideal circumstances, it is followed up with investigations once refugees and former prisoners are returned to their homeland, to guarantee appropriate treatment after their return.

At a subsequent meeting on the matter, Secretary of Defense Lovett, reflecting the concerns of the UNC, called for greater ingenuity in pursuing a solution acceptable to both sides.[119] But the die was already being cast, and Washington was moving toward a confrontation with the Communists that would purposefully draw a clear ideological distinction. A decision was made *not* to bring the negotiators into this discussion. "It was concluded that as the decision involved a question of fundamental national policy," a notetaker at an interagency meeting recorded, "recommendations of the Departments of State and Defense should immediately be put to the President for his decision and the message should not therefore at this time be sent to General Ridgway pending that decision."[120]

Secretary of State Acheson drafted a memorandum to President Truman on February 4, 1952, describing the high purpose behind a U.S. policy insisting there be no forced repatriation of prisoners: "Any agreement which would require United States troops to use force to turn over to the Communists prisoners who believe they would face death if returned would be repugnant to our most fundamental moral and humanitarian principles, and would do much to jeopardize our moral position vis-à-vis the Communist world."[121] When the memo was finally sent to the president on February 8, the text had been supplemented with the phrase, "and would seriously jeopardize the psychological warfare position of the United States in its opposition to

Communist tyranny."[122] Whether that phrase was added to win support on Capitol Hill or the White House is not clear; it may actually have served to admonish the Department of Defense. The argument had not been a fundamentally military one; it was a humanitarian one, with Defense attempting to facilitate an early conclusion, and State trying to guarantee a fair one.

President Truman approved the memo on February 8, determining that the UNC would not force prisoners to return against their will. It was now necessary for the negotiators to win Communist approval of a means of determining who could be repatriated, and to what homeland. For a while that appeared possible.

In staff officer talks at Panmunjom, the UNC substituted "no forced repatriation" for "voluntary repatriation," distinguishing between POWs and civilian internees, and discussed joint Red Cross teams rather than the International Red Cross. There was extensive discussion of the meaning of "repatriate," and on February 11, the UNC dropped its previous proposal to send interview teams into North Korea after repatriation to monitor the return of displaced civilians. With these steps taken February 14–20, there were signs of progress as revised drafts were exchanged, and focus was on definition of the terms "no forced repatriation" and "voluntary repatriation." Both sides made constructive efforts to define the terms, although the process was a slow one.

When meetings of the staff officers could proceed no further, discussions were returned to the subdelegation on February 29. In a subdelegation meeting on March 5, the Communists proposed that the lists exchanged on December 18 could be used as the basis for return of prisoners; this meant the Communists would stop insisting on an accounting of what they claimed were the missing 44,000 and the UNC would drop its demand for an explanation of the missing 50,000. The subdelegation meeting, however, degenerated into an exchange of epithets, and staff officers were asked to resume their talks on March 16.

The commitment of the highest levels of government in Washington, and the general support of the allies, was abundantly clear to the Communist negotiators. Furthermore, the Communists stood to gain more from the outcome of the issue than the UNC side; a larger number of potential soldiers would be returned to the North under any conceivable outcome. Given these factors, the Communist side was inspired to find the means of compromise. On March 21, the Communists offered a "provision in principle":

> After the Armistice Agreement is signed and becomes ef-
> fective, the Korean People's Army and the Chinese People's
> Volunteers shall release and repatriate all of the 11,559
> prisoners of war in their custody and the United Nations
> Command shall release and repatriate all of the 132,474
> prisoners of war in its custody. The lists of the names of the
> prisoners of war above shall be finally checked by the staff
> officers of both sides.[123]

The next day, the Communists agreed that some "adjustments" might
be necessary, in cases where some "particular situations might arise."
The UNC found this an encouraging indication of flexibility on the
question of screening.[124] Meeting in executive session, the staff officers from the Communist side further allowed that while all Chinese
and North Korean POWs must be repatriated, South Korean POWs
(those resident in South Korea at the start of the war but who served
in the North Korean army) and civilian internees should have a choice
on repatriation. On March 28, the UNC agreed that the issue could be
resolved "within the framework of the Communist principle of 21
March."[125]

On April 1, 1952, the UNC proposed what eventually became the
POW provision of the final armistice agreement. It contained no numbers, and the UNC cautioned that there was a danger in trying to estimate numbers of returnees:

> We indicated at the beginning of our executive sessions that
> we considered that 132,000 failed to take into consideration
> all pertinent factors and, therefore, was likely to be too high
> a figure. We indicated that possibly 116,000 would more
> nearly indicate the magnitude of the exchange, but that we
> could not say that this number would reflect all considera-
> tions. In short, we did not want to mislead you or ourselves
> in attempting to guess at a figure, the development of which
> would require several days.[126]

Despite this cautionary statement, the UNC had made a tactical blunder. The Communists were looking for a number that could plausibly
be used to argue that a significant portion of the POWs had chosen to
return. Knowing that no progress was likely on the ideological argument over the principle of individual choice, the UNC negotiators
sought to give some reassurance that the Communists could anticipate
an acceptable number of returnees. Despite UNC efforts to qualify es-

timates given in executive session, the numbers raised expectations beyond what would be deliverable.

The UNC was, in a sense, forced into this mistake because it had not been authorized to conduct screening earlier. Joy and Ridgway had argued that despite the Communists' statements condemning screening, they would acquiesce if the UNC screened prisoners. Advice from negotiators on the scene was not heeded; Washington officials believed they had a better understanding of the likely Communist reaction, and the Communists had stated their objections vociferously. Washington had, however, misjudged the motives behind the Communists' stated opposition; UNC inaction allowed tensions to increase in the prisoner of war camps, and that was to the Communists' advantage. Washington's deferential attitude, trying to accommodate Communist sensitivities on this key issue, showed a lack of fortitude.

When screening was finally authorized on April 3, the Communists did not respond as Washington expected; instead, on April 6, they took advantage of the screening to deliver a declaration of amnesty enticing prisoners to return home:

> We wholeheartedly welcome the return of all of our captured personnel to the arms of the motherland; we have further guaranteed, in an agreement reached with the other side, that all captured personnel shall, after their repatriation, rejoin their families to participate in peaceful construction and live a peaceful life.[127]

On April 19, the results of the screening were presented. Knowing that the Communists would respond unfavorably to startlingly low numbers of voluntary repatriates, UNC representative Colonel Hickman calmly informed Colonel Tsai in a staff officers' meeting that only some 70,000 prisoners would be returned. That number was slightly over half of the figure provided by the UNC on December 18, and only 40 percent of the number the North Koreans believed the South actually held. North Korea indicated that about 12,000, essentially all of those held in captivity, would be returned.

The Communists could not tolerate the imbalance. "For once Tsai was speechless, overcome with emotion," Walter Hermes wrote in his history of the talks. "When he finally recovered himself enough to talk, he quickly requested a recess ostensibly to study the figures."[128] By the next day Tsai had been authorized to deliver the following angry response:

> It is completely impossible for us to consider your estimated number of 70,000 of our captured personnel. . . . Your side averred repeatedly that you were willing to settle the problem within the framework of our proposal of 21 March. Your side also indicated in the executive sessions that the number of our captured personnel whom your side was going to repatriate would be close to 116,000. The round number of 70,000 submitted by your side loses all connection both within the framework of 132,000, which you said you were willing to accept, and with the figure of 116,000, which you specifically indicated.[129]

In this instance, the Communist response was not merely bluster; they believed that they had been "deliberately deceived."[130] Their reaction demonstrated an ideological obstacle that plagues negotiations between free countries and totalitarian ones. Communists expect democratic governments to deliver results that are sometimes beyond the reach of democracies. In this instance, both parties at the table were startled by developments that were based on an expression of free will. The democratic governments that had sought to give the prisoners a voice were startled by the degree to which prisoners resisted repatriation to the North. The Communists, believing that power in the West actually resided with a "Wall Street clique," could not bring themselves to conclude that choices made by individuals might have precedence over policies of government. In their own system, the Communists had no trouble determining what decisions would be made about prisoners—the prisoners were at the mercy of the government—and the Communists did not believe that in the South the situation was really any different. They could only conclude the UNC had stacked the deck to determine a small number would return to North Korea. That they could not accept.

Despite Acheson's optimism, the Communists rejected the UNC package proposal of April 28. General Nam dismissed it with the simple conclusion: "our side fails to see how your proposal of this morning can really be of help to the overall settlement of the remaining issues."[131] He called for an indefinite recess. On May 2, the delegations met in executive session to hear the Communist side propose that it would withdraw the nomination of the Soviet Union to the NNSC if the UNC would return its 132,000 prisoners in exchange for North Korea's 12,000 prisoners. Admiral Joy naturally turned down this proposal; short, uneventful meetings occupied the next few days.

By May 7, both sides had concluded that the POW issue was the only issue on which there could be no agreement. General Ridgway sought a firm statement from Washington that, in his own words, "our position is one from which we cannot and shall not retreat."[132] President Truman accordingly issued a White House statement on what he labeled *Ridgway's* approach, affirming, "There shall not be a forced repatriation of prisoners of war. . . . We will not buy an armistice by turning over human beings for slaughter or slavery."[133]

Both sides of the table in Panmunjom sought to bring pressure by actions taken outside the negotiating tent. The UNC applied military pressure on the battlefield; the Communists were considerably more inventive. The two leaders of the North Korean negotiating team, General Nam Il and General Lee Sang Cho, had for years infiltrated saboteurs into the prisoner of war camps to incite riots.[134] Carefully selected combat-hardened soldiers were sent to the front purposefully to be captured by UNC forces. When they were in place in the camps, they terrorized other prisoners, organized opposition to screening, and incited violence against the UNC. For propaganda purposes, the Communists sought to show that the U.S. policy of no forced repatriation required a policy of forced screening.

On the very date that President Truman pledged not to turn over human beings to slaughter or slavery, the Communist negotiators' clandestine efforts bore fruit. Communist gang leaders at Koje-do lured the camp's commandant, Brigadier General Francis T. Dodd, into a meeting and took him hostage. The Communist negotiators now had a second table at which to negotiate.

Colonel William H. Craig was sent to take command at Koje-do with instructions to "talk them out."[135] Craig asked a seemingly cooperative senior North Korean officer from another compound, Colonel Lee Hak Koo, to persuade the prisoners to release Dodd, but when the cagey North Korean was inserted into the rebellious compound, he immediately took over as the spokesman for the group. Perceiving that the UNC would not immediately use force to gain Dodd's release, the Communists staged a war crimes trial, demanding that General Dodd answer charges of brutality.

Signaling that military force might be used to quell the disturbance, General Van Fleet sent a combat officer, Brigadier General Charles F. Colson, to take charge of the camp and win Dodd's release. Colson took obvious steps to prepare for an assault. This caused the Communists to produce a four-point paper listing their grievances.[136]

Colson had "only a sketchy acquaintance with the issues being discussed at Panmunjom."[137] Under his command, the UNC responded in writing to the prisoners' complaints, ignoring its own ultimatum for resolution of the confrontation. Colson negotiated long into the evening of May 10, revising the UNC statement three times to meet the Communists' demands. As finally drafted and signed by the American general, the UNC statement

- admitted "instances of bloodshed where many prisoners of war have been killed and wounded by UN forces"
- distanced the camp commanders from positions taken at Panmunjom, which was referred to as a "peace conference"
- pledged "no more forcible screening" would be conducted, and
- acknowledged the Communist saboteurs as the legitimate voice of the prisoners.[138]

The Communists knew exactly what they had achieved, but their army interlocutors seemed not to. When Washington learned of the statement in the ensuing weeks, Generals Colson and Dodd were reduced to the rank of colonel, and Brigadier General Paul F. Yount, who had helped review the statement, was given an administrative reprimand. Satisfied with the statement, the Communists under Colonel Lee had the audacity to propose holding General Dodd overnight, so that he could be released ceremoniously at daybreak. The request was turned down, and the prisoners released General Dodd in the late evening of May 10.[139]

Pro-Communist prisoners, emboldened by these events, increased their resistance. A month later, a battle between UNC forces and the prisoners at Koje-do broke out. It took tanks to end the fighting of the prisoners, who had fortified their position with trenches and were armed with 3,000 spears, 4,500 knives, 1,000 grenades, and hundreds of other hand-made weapons.[140] Thirty-one prisoners were killed in the fight and 139 were wounded. One American soldier was killed and fourteen were injured.[141]

The Communists had succeeded in focusing the world's attention on the treatment of prisoners in the UNC camps in South Korea rather than on the tens of thousands of captives missing, and presumed killed, in the North. Nam Il used the propaganda points gained from subversion of the POW camps at the continuing, though stalemated, talks at Panmunjom. On May 16, he reminded the delegations, "The commandant of your prisoner of war camp has already declared to the whole world the utter bankruptcy of your proposition."[142] And on May 20, he delivered the following statement:

> The unshakable fact is that public confessions of the commandant of your prisoner of war camp have killed and buried the myth that our captured personnel refuse to be repatriated. In spite of all your threats and violence, our captured personnel rose in heroic and just resistance against your forced screening.[143]

By May 22, 1952, Admiral Joy said there is "nothing more for me to do. There is nothing left to negotiate."[144] He was replaced by Major General William K. Harrison. The UNC gave the Communists until October 8, 1952, to accept the package proposal, and meetings continued on an irregular schedule, primarily to hear Communist protests of alleged UNC violations. The war once again intensified in the mountains of eastern Korea. When, on October 8, the Communists did not accept the package deal, talks were indefinitely suspended.

The talks did not resume until a new president occupied the White House, and new leadership occupied the Kremlin. President Eisenhower reaffirmed President Truman's stance on the prisoner of war issue, and took steps to enhance UNC military capabilities on the peninsula. Some historians have credited his administration's willingness to consider the use of nuclear weapons with motivating the Communists to resume talks in the spring of 1953.[145] The talk of nuclear war undoubtedly gave added impetus to a group of neutral nations led by India, which proposed face-saving methods whereby prisoners in Korea could be relocated to neutral countries, and then in stages repatriated to their homes.[146]

By the time of Stalin's death on March 5, 1953, a more conciliatory group of Soviet leaders vied for power. Faced with other concerns, they were eager to resolve the continuing war on the Korean peninsula. It is likely they made their position clear to Chinese Premier Chou En-lai when he visited Moscow for Stalin's funeral.[147] Soon thereafter, Chou proposed a compromise that immediately won new Foreign Minister Molotov's endorsement in Moscow[148] and Kim Il Sung's in Pyongyang:[149] "that both sides to the negotiations . . . undertake to repatriate immediately after the cessation of hostilities all those prisoners of war in their custody who insist upon repatriation and to hand over the remaining prisoners of war to a neutral state so as to insure a just solution to the question of their repatriation."[150]

On March 28, Kim Il Sung and Peng Teh Huai answered a February 22 letter from Ridgway's successor, Major General Mark Clark, suggesting a proposal for exchange of sick and wounded that, they hoped, "would lead to smooth settlement of the entire question of prisoners of war."[151] Liaison officers met at Panmunjom on April 6 and reached an agreement on exchange of sick and wounded five days later. Dubbed "little switch," this limited repatriation began on April 20.[152]

Plenary negotiations resumed on April 26, 1953. Nam Il, who continued to hold the leading position on the Communist team, presented their proposal for resolving the POW issue. In his first point, he conceded that "both sides would repatriate all the prisoners desiring to return home," but in five additional points he outlined a lengthy process for a neutral state to determine the status of the remaining prisoners. General Harrison turned down the proposal, arguing that sixty days, not six months, should be enough time to accomplish the task, and that the neutral nation could carry out its function in Korea, rather than having the prisoners relocated abroad.

In an effort to force the Communists to identify which neutral nation they would propose to perform the function, Harrison specifically mentioned Switzerland, which the Communist side rejected. Harrison thought there was considerable room for negotiation on procedural matters, but his superiors recalled the nomination of the USSR as a neutral nation, and insisted on a tactic of smoking out the Communists on this question. On April 29, Nam indicated the Communists' preference for an Asian neutral, and, on May 2, offered the names of India, Burma, Indonesia, and Pakistan. On May 4, the UNC indicated it preferred Pakistan. On May 7, the Communists conceded many of the points the UNC objected to, but proposed the establishment of a Neutral Nations Repatriation Commission (NNRC) with five members— Poland, Czechoslovakia, Switzerland, Sweden, and India—operating on the basis of majority rule, to carry out the repatriation.

Washington was encouraged by these developments and by the apparent spirit of compromise in which they were offered. A problem remained, however, that persuaded the UNC to press harder for a more attractive arrangement. Many of the prisoners in the South were South Koreans who had been forced into service for the North, and subsequently surrendered to the UNC. They were considered genuinely loyal to the Republic of Korea and decidedly anti-Communist. President Rhee was not about to turn these "nonrepatriates" over to neutral nations, some of whom he did not consider neutral. When the UNC responded to the Communist proposal on May 13, it included a provision for the release of these individuals. Nam responded with an attack on the UNC's lack of cooperation and called the counterproposal "a backward step." Harrison waited, and Clark prepared plans for an air offensive against the North, including the lifting of neutrality that had been afforded to Kaesong.[153]

Harrison's tenure as chief negotiator for the UNC was much shorter than Joy's and focused on the details of only one issue, but he nevertheless demonstrated considerable cleverness in his negotiating tactics. He refused to demonstrate impatience or haste, and forced North Korea to push for action at the negotiating table. Even after the Communists tried to wear him down with repeated delays, Harrison demanded that the meeting on May 25 be held as an executive session, closed to press, "to reinforce the solemn, nonpropaganda character of the proceedings."[154] The Communists hesitated, then consented.

Taking a page from the Communist book of tactics, Harrison first declared what the UNC found nonnegotiable. After sufficient emphasis was given to the principle of no forced repatriation, he then set out the four concessions the UNC was willing to make regarding treatment of the nonrepatriates and length of time afforded the commission to do its work. He followed with areas of dispute, insisting on no use of force or threat of force against the prisoners; assumption by India, as the leading member of the Neutral Nations Repatriation Commission, of certain financial and managerial responsibilities; and a maximum time period for completion of the task.

General Nam had some immediate objections to the UNC presentation, and suggested a recess of four days. Harrison insisted the Communists take even more time to study the proposal, proposing a resumption of meetings on June 1. Nam Il agreed. The UNC then put its proposal in writing and sent it directly to Kim Il Sung and Peng Teh Huai.[155]

The Communists considered the UNC proposal until June 4, then made small enough changes to guarantee its acceptability to both sides. On June 8, Generals Harrison and Nam signed the terms of reference for the POW exchange. The negotiating process between the UNC and the Communists had been concluded, but at the expense of some terms the Republic of Korea found unacceptable, particularly those provisions pertaining to nonrepatriates. On June 18, therefore, President Rhee on his own authority ordered the release of the nonrepatriates. Some 27,000 anti-Communist prisoners were set free in

South Korea by ROK guards who reported to the republic's constabulary rather than to the republic's army, which was under the authority of the UNC. The UNC commander was understandably furious at this end run.[156]

The UNC fully expected Rhee's action to influence the Communists' "willingness to proceed with armistice negotiations."[157] Not surprisingly, the Communists broke off talks, with an objective of winning a price for their resumption. They said they would return when the United States had brought Rhee under control. Rhee, no stranger to the notion of leverage, threatened to withdraw ROK forces from the UNC and announced the ROK would not sign the armistice.[158]

American officials viewed Rhee's actions with deep concern, thinking his release of the nonrepatriate prisoners and his refusal to sign the armistice would imperil the agreement itself. Once again, North Korea's perspective was misjudged; by being the only Korean signatory to the armistice, its claims to national sovereignty and victory against outside powers were, from its perspective, enhanced. By getting assurances that the UNC would not support South Korea in any effort to violate the armistice, the North strengthened its ability to portray the Rhee government as a puppet of the West. In later years, North Korea repeatedly used its signature of the armistice, and the South's refusal to sign, to argue that South Korea should be excluded from peace talks.

The UNC issued an apology for the South's action and assured the North of South Korea's cooperation on July 8. But North Korea would not readily let go of the opportunity to force a harder UNC stand on South Korean adherence, and raised the issue repeatedly when parties returned to the negotiating table on July 10, two years after the negotiations had begun in Kaesong. General Harrison was instructed to state in response to these taunts, "I told you that we had received suitable assurances from ROK that will enable us to carry out this obligation. Form and content of such assurances are not properly matters for concern by your side."[159] Nam and Harrison reached agreement on July 19, 1953, after the UNC gave the combined Communist forces the guarantee that the Republic of Korea would not upset the terms of the truce.[160]

At long last, "The Agreement between the Commander-in-Chief, United Nations Command, and the Supreme Commander, Korean People's Army, and the Commander of the Chinese People's Volunteers, Concerning a Military Armistice in Korea"[161] was signed by Generals

Harrison and Nam on July 27, 1953, at 10:00 A.M. in Panmunjom. Nine copies were transported to the UNC base camp at Munsan-ni where they were signed by the commander in chief of the United Nations Command, General Mark Clark, and another nine sent to Kaesong where they were signed by Marshal Kim Il Sung and General Peng Teh Huai. The signing ceremonies put an end to two years and seventeen days of this phase of negotiations with North Korea.

6

★

Implementing the Armistice

lthough the 538 negotiating sessions conducted over a period of two years and seventeen days produced a lengthy and seemingly comprehensive armistice agreement, many issues were left unresolved. The difficult political questions—including the withdrawal of all foreign forces from Korea and the peaceful settlement of the Korean question—had been deferred to "a political conference of a higher level," which both sides agreed would be held within three months after the armistice was signed.[1] Numerous daily operational issues that would arise in implementing the armistice were also left to be worked out by mutual agreement as circumstances dictated.

The Collapse of the Political Talks

The armistice agreement had produced a truce, but not a peace, and President Rhee doubted publicly it would ever lead to a permanent peace. As he warned in a letter to President Eisenhower on the day the armistice was signed:

> With the signing of the truce, one phase of our problem ends and another begins. . . . We will have many trials in the future and there is much to be accomplished. You have labored with great patience and great skill to bring about the

signing of the truce. I pray with all my soul that your hopes from it may be fulfilled and your statesmanlike objective of the unification of Korea may be obtained in peace. Never in all my life have I hoped so much that my own judgment should prove to be wrong."[2]

The task of the negotiators at Panmunjom was completed, but Panmunjom continued to serve as the headquarters for the institutions established by the armistice agreement. After initial resistance from North Korea, a new Military Armistice Commission (MAC) conference building was built to straddle the line, and both sides constructed adjacent buildings to serve as their headquarters. Panmunjom was to become the seat of the armistice and a safe haven for authorized contact, a single opening along the long barrier that separates the former combatants. In its unique role as a portal for history, it was to serve as the point of transit for repatriated military personnel, displaced relatives, Soviet spies, North-South negotiators, and President and Mrs. Jimmy Carter.

The new conference center was completed in mid-October 1953, permitting its use on October 26, 1953, for Ambassador Dean's first planning sessions for the peace conference envisaged by article IV of the armistice agreement. Arthur H. Dean, an American attorney appointed by the secretary of state, had studied the lessons of Kaesong, was suspicious of the North's preparations for the talks, and inspected the facilities in Panmunjom "to be sure there is no propaganda value to them."[3]

In the planning talks, China was represented by Huang Hua and North Korea by Ki Sok Bok, both from their foreign ministries. Chinese predominance in these sessions was more apparent than it had been in the armistice negotiations. Dean recorded that everything Ki said had to be written out in advance and approved by the Chinese.[4] The negotiators met daily except on Sundays, and the negotiating sessions lasted as long as six hours. They proceeded much like the armistice negotiations.

As Dean's deputy described them, however, the sessions were even more hostile than the armistice negotiations had been:

No individual ever spoke personally to anyone on the other side. There was never an exchange of greetings or amenities on starting or ending a meeting. . . . This was negotiation without contact, a contradiction in terms. It expressed the

ruptured relations of the two sides and the bisected compound—two worlds apart, divided by a metal strip and men-
tal segregation. . . . The quonset hut for the talks, located in
this demilitarized neutral zone, lay exactly at right angles
athwart the military demarcation line whose metal bands bisected the zone and separated North and South Korea for
some 150 miles from east to west. In turn, the negotiating
table bisected the building from side to side. The straight
crease along the middle of the table's green cover ran directly above the military demarcation line underneath. As a
matter of practice, Communist officials never went into the
United Nations half of the hut, and vice versa. . . . This total
separation between the two sides was carried to such ex-
tremes that ash trays were always "stationed" on top of the
crease when not in use so that they too were evenly bisected
by the military demarcation line![5]

Dean decried the lack of collegiality. "The Chinese stared ahead,
frozen-faced, ignoring our presence," Dean wrote. "There was no way
in which the normal tensions of difficult diplomatic negotiations could
be relieved."[6]

Taking a page from Admiral Joy's lessons at Kaesong, Dean resisted the Communists' initial effort to load the agenda. "People unfamiliar with negotiations with the Communists," he noted, "often ask,
'What difference does it make which item you take up first?'" The answer, he said, is that once you agree to the order, you cannot move on
to the next item "until you have yielded to Communist wishes on the
first."[7] Taking the lesson a step further than Joy, Dean tried to avoid
negotiation of an agenda at all, hoping to move directly into substantive discussions.[8] He was not successful; he got bogged down on the
first topic the Communists were willing to discuss.

Dean also followed the tactic of referring seemingly insurmount-
able obstacles to "second-level meetings" where they could be resolved "in secret, without propaganda or provocation, in a pragmatic
and businesslike way with some give and take."[9] Nevertheless, more
than four weeks were spent in lengthy talks that failed to resolve three
basic questions: the date, location, and composition of the political
conference.

It may be, as an Indian diplomat reported to Dean, that China
never intended to conclude a political agreement.[10] The Communists'
approach seemed to be one of trying to push the UNC negotiators to

the point of walking out of the talks. Huang Hua's use of insult and in-vective brought the Communist tactic to a new nadir, seemingly em-barrassing even his own translator. He called Dean a "capitalist crook, rapist, thief, robber of pennies from the eyes of the dead, mongrel of uncertain origin," a "murderer lying in the gutter with filthy garbage," a "war monger," and a consort of rams.[11] Personal attacks did not seem to bother Dean, but when the Communists devoted the sessions of December 11 and 12 to harangues against the "treacherous de-signs" and "perfidious actions" of the United States, Dean warned Huang that he would have to treat the remarks "as a notification that you wish these talks recessed indefinitely."[12] "Huang's tirade in-creased," Dean wrote, "So I picked up my papers, walked out and thus unilaterally recessed the talks."[13] Ambassador Dean's deputy, Ken-neth T. Young, kept the second-level meetings going, describing them as "a distinctive paradox, virtually empty of results but full of conse-quences."[14]

A month later, prisoners of war had been released in accordance with the armistice agreement; a Pyongyang-Beijing and a Seoul-Washington security pact had both been concluded;[15] the threat of unilateral action by the ROK to resume military action against the North had diminished; the United States had withdrawn two divisions; and some reductions in force among the Chinese in North Korea had also been noted. Young concluded that these developments lessened Chinese enthusiasm for the political conference and recommended that even the second-level meetings be indefinitely recessed, leaving open the MAC channel in the event the Communists made "some new and constructive proposal."[16]

In February 1954, expectations rose when the Soviets consented to a conference to consider a number of Far East matters. That meeting, however, dealt the final blow to hopes for a Korean peace conference in the near term. Convened in Geneva on April 26, this conference ar-gued inconclusively about Korea for nearly two months. General Nam, the familiar North Korean chief delegate to the armistice negotiations, speaking in his new capacity as foreign minister, presented a three-point proposal for national unification: (1) establishment of an "all-Korean committee" consisting of representatives from the North and South to supervise a general election throughout Korea and develop ec-onomic exchanges; (2) withdrawal of all foreign forces from Korea within six months; and (3) the holding of a general election without for-eign interference.[17]

However reasonable the North Korean plan might have sounded in the abstract to optimists unfamiliar with the tortuous history of Korean developments after 1945, North Korea showed its real intentions by its refusal to permit UN supervision of the election. The sixteen member nations of the UNC involved in the Geneva conference signed a declaration on June 15, 1954, reiterating their position that the UN had been rightfully empowered to take collective action to repel aggression and seek a peaceful settlement in Korea, and that UN supervision would be essential to guaranteeing genuinely free elections. "So long as the Communist delegations reject the two fundamental principles which we consider indispensible [sic]," the declaration concluded, "[further discussion at] the conference would serve no useful purpose."[18] The Geneva conference failed to yield an agreement on Korea, and turned its focus to the partitioning of Vietnam.

As Young had suggested, the MAC channel alone would remain as a means of addressing issues that arose from time to time between North Korea and the United Nations Command. No one at the time suspected, however, that half a century later a political resolution of the irreconcilable systems governing Korea would still be elusive. Nor did anyone anticipate that the institutions created by the armistice negotiations would serve for five decades as the primary means of contact between North Korea and the non-Communist world. They had not been designed for that role; their responsibility was strictly confined to purely military matters, and their authority extended only as far as authorized by the armistice agreement.

Establishment of the Military Armistice Commission

Certain aspects of the composition, functions, and authority of the Military Armistice Commission were spelled out in great detail in article II of the armistice agreement. The location of the MAC headquarters, for example, had been specified (at 37 57′29″N. 126 40′00″E.); daily meetings were dictated, and recesses were to be limited unless mutually agreed.[19] The agreement not only specified that there would be five members from each side, serving without a chairman; it also specified their rank.[20] It provided for creation of ten joint observer teams to assist the MAC in carrying out its functions in the demilitarized zone (DMZ) and Han River estuary. It also set out the reporting arrangements from the Neutral Nations Supervisory Commission to the MAC.

The MAC's functions were defined as follows:

- Supervise the armistice agreement
- Settle through negotiations any violations of the armistice agreement
- Transmit to the opposing sides reports of investigations of violations
- Provide supervision and direction to the procedures for repatriation of prisoners of war and displaced civilians
- Transmit communications between the commanders, who could at their discretion pursue other means of communicating as well
- Provide credentials and identification for MAC staff, joint observer teams, and equipment used in performance of MAC missions
- Dispatch joint observer teams to investigate violations or request the Neutral Nations Supervisory Commission to conduct observations and inspections
- Report corrections of violations

Both sides created a structure to manage their dealings with the MAC. To fill the five UNC positions on the MAC, the UNC commander in chief appointed two members from the Republic of Korea, one from the United Kingdom, one from the United States, and, on a rotational basis, one from the other UN member nations represented in the UNC. The UNC commission members are supported by an organization called the United Nations Command Military Armistice Commission (UNCMAC). The armistice agreement provided for the creation of a joint secretariat for the MAC, responsible for developing, translating, and recording all formal communications between the two sides. The UNC has generally been represented in the secretariat by a U.S. Army colonel, and until 1994, the Communists maintained a similar organizational structure.[21]

The armistice agreement left many aspects of the commission's functions undefined, but both sides agreed early on that they would generally continue customs established during the armistice negotiations. That facilitated operations of the commission considerably, but difficulties arose where precedents had not been established.

Scheduling Meetings. As Ambassador Dean's planning sessions bogged down, MAC activities seemed to warrant fewer than the daily meetings dictated by the armistice agreement. Both sides saw a need to define a less time-consuming approach. On January 4, 1954, the North Korean MAC secretary proposed that MAC meetings be recessed until either side requested a meeting; the UNC agreed. Albeit a minor modification, this action constituted an amendment of paragraph 31 of the armistice agreement; yet it was accomplished merely by the mutual agreement of the commanders at the time.

Agendas. On August 8, 1953, a set of mutually agreed procedures further modified the implementation of the agreement. The procedures stipulated the number of accredited members of the MAC necessary to conduct business, and determined that after the adjournment of each meeting, "the Senior Member from each side *may* [emphasis added] supply to the Secretariat a list of items which he proposes for discussion at the next meeting."[22]

Both sides consistently provided specific agenda items for MAC meetings in accordance with these "Rules of Procedures for the MAC" until February 1955. For the February 9, 1955, meeting, however, the North Koreans chose not to provide advance agenda topics. Their MAC secretary's note merely stated, "I am instructed by the Senior Member of our side to inform your side that among the matters to be discussed at today's MAC meeting are the questions pertaining to the serious violations by your side of the Armistice Agreement."[23] The UNC made the mistake of not only accepting the North Korean procedure, but also adopting it. In calling the MAC meeting for February 21, 1955, the UNC informed the North Koreans, "The subjects to be discussed are violations of the Armistice Agreement by your side."[24]

Giving the North Koreans a taste of their own medicine seldom yields a cure. Since that time, the UNC has generally provided specific agenda items for discussion, finding it useful to meet with North Koreans who are prepared to discuss the topic at hand. North Korea, however, has consistently refused to provide specific agenda items. The UNC had not anticipated the difficulties that would accompany North Korean resistance to providing specific agenda items. Having no advance notice of the topics deprived the UNC of the ability to reject meetings called merely to serve the North's propaganda objectives. This afforded the North an opportunity to level unexpected charges against the UNC at public MAC meetings, then exploit the UNC's bewildered reaction, which often appeared to be a blustering unwillingness to respond. UNC hesitation or confusion tended to give undue credence to the allegation.

Once the UNC realized its mistake, it tried to devise methods to work around the difficulties it had helped create. The UNC pressed the North Koreans to provide specific agenda items when they called a MAC meeting, but generally attended meetings even without an agenda, in the interest of hearing the concern. To smoke out North Korean objectives, the UNC would occasionally try to delay meetings. When North Korea proposed the meeting for May 22, 1959, for example, the UNC asked for an agenda, saying there had been no violation of the armistice agreement and, therefore, no reason for holding the meeting. The North Koreans cited provisions of the armistice agreement and demanded the UNC come to the table. In a counterproposal, the UNC asked that the meeting be postponed for a day for "administrative reasons," a tactic both sides had used during the armistice negotiations. The North Koreans yielded.

The UNC also tried to insist on fewer meetings. On October 28, 1964, the UNC proposed that unless one side presented the other with a proposed agenda, the MAC would meet no more than once a month and no less than once every six months. The North Koreans declined to agree with the procedure.

The UNC nevertheless pursued that approach to the agenda for a number of MAC meetings in 1967, increasing North Korean frustration, with attendant risks. North Korea called a MAC meeting on August 16, 1967, to unleash one of its most vituperative propaganda tirades against the United States, consonant with a North Korean Workers party campaign at the time. It requested another meeting immediately afterward, to dish out more propaganda. With no serious violation of the armistice agreement alleged, however, the UNC delayed the meeting for a week, demanding an agenda.

The North Koreans responded to the apparent delaying tactic with a show of force. They sent armed infiltrators across the DMZ in broad daylight to attack the 76th U.S. Army Engineer Battalion at the UNCMAC advance camp. They killed one American and two Korean soldiers and wounded twelve American and nine Korean soldiers.

The attack was designed to force the UNC to come to the table. When they came to the table, the UNC demanded an investigation by a joint observer team (JOT), the investigative mechanism of the Military Armistice Commission. This resulted in a show of force of another kind. The North Koreans refused to agree to a JOT investigation on grounds JOTs had no authority outside the DMZ itself. The UNC's call for an NNSC investigation was also turned down. Even though the NNSC had specific responsibility for violations alleged to have occurred outside the DMZ, the Czechoslovakian and Polish delegates to the NNSC refused to permit an investigation. The ratcheting up of tensions held severe risks, both in terms of human life and in terms of establishing unfortunate procedural precedents for future incidents.

Types of Meetings. The armistice agreement provides for four types of official meetings: MAC plenary meetings, MAC secretaries' meetings, duty officers' meetings, and security officers' meetings.[25] In practice, however, many layers of meetings developed.

MAC plenary meetings were sometimes attended by all ten members and almost always attended by both senior MAC members and their staffs. They had three purposes: to settle violations of the armistice agreement, to discuss and negotiate significant military tension-reducing measures, and to facilitate a channel of communication between the two sides. The crowded meeting room was generally closed to press, but during open sessions, reporters could use cameras and recorders through the windows, filming and recording the sessions. Such meetings were media events, and often had a staged quality.

The senior members, however, could also meet in executive or private sessions at their discretion. Private sessions permitted the senior members to complete their business without indulging in propaganda. Some North Korean negotiators who engaged in endless harangues about the evils of the United States, and hurled insults at their counterparts in the plenary sessions, were polite diplomats in the executive sessions. In addition to the sobering effect of meeting one's counterpart eye-to-eye, the private sessions seemed to afford the North Korean representatives an opportunity to react rationally, without fear of revealing flexibility in public or conciliation in front of their compatriots.

MAC secretaries' meetings were called to iron out administrative issues before the commission and to handle issues delegated by the commanders. The meetings followed the tradition of the liaison officers' meetings during the armistice negotiations. Under a mutually agreed provision,[26] the secretaries were vested with a special role in the repatriation of human remains, including those of military personnel killed during the Korean War.

A joint duty office was established to maintain 24-hour telephone links between the commands. To coordinate its activities, the UNC and North Korean joint duty officers were authorized to meet on a daily basis to receive and transmit messages, reports, and other correspondence between the commanders.

Security officers' meetings were convened specifically to handle alleged infractions by security guards and other matters regarding the security of personnel within the joint security area. Joint observer teams met as authorized. Language personnel from each side met weekly to discuss official translations of records and correspondence.

Investigating Alleged Violations of the Armistice

MAC meetings allow each side to air grievances, allege violations, and manage investigations of charges levied against the other side. Although the record of North Korean disregard for and abuse of the provisions of the armistice agreement could not be clearer, the North Koreans claim they have committed only one minor violation of the agreement. It occurred in 1953. A North Korean soldier carried a pistol into the camp of India's contingent of the custodian forces. No weapons were allowed in the camp, and it was difficult for North Korea to deny the violation.[27]

Over the years the North Koreans have expressed regret over certain incidents. Kim Il Sung personally expressed regret after the August 18, 1976, axe murder of two U.S. Army security officers in the joint security area, and a negotiated text of an apologetic statement was issued after the 1996 submarine incursion into South Korea.[28]

Otherwise, the North has denied all UNC charges of armistice agreement violations, calling them "fabrications," the result of *South* Korean revolutionary activity, or matters in which they had no role. When the facts regarding the occurrence of an incident have been indisputable, the North Korean response has generally been to claim that the UNC actually instigated the incidents and the North's retaliation consisted merely of "self-defense measures."

The Joint Observation Teams

Under the terms of the armistice agreement, joint observer teams were to conduct thorough investigations of any incident, through mutual agreement. Requiring mutual agreement for a JOT to conduct its work, however, rendered the team ineffective. Moral suasion seldom brought North Korea to the conclusion that a JOT should proceed. When North Korea did not wish to be subjected to an investigation by a JOT, it simply refused to authorize the investigation.

The inadequacy of the joint observation team provision was clear to the armistice negotiators even while it was being drafted. As Major General H. M. Turner, USAF, said during the talks, "It is difficult for us to conceive how your side can insist upon a fair, reasonable, and effective armistice and then contradict your implication of this sincerity by refusing to accept measures which will make it effective."[29] Admiral Joy noted that Communists as a rule "aspire to reduce the scope of investigations which may arise from their premeditated violations of agreements."[30]

These fears were borne out in implementation of the armistice agreement. By 1967, JOT meetings had become infrequent because the North Koreans tended not to consent to investigations of UNC allegations.[31] The April 6, 1967, JOT meeting was one of the last, and it occurred almost two years after the previous one. It was held because North Korea demanded an investigation of the "diabolical atrocities" the UNC had allegedly committed on the previous day. The JOT's task was to establish the facts behind an incident in which three North Korean guards had been killed in the UNC side of the demilitarized zone.

The UNC JOT stated what happened:

> (1) Three North Korean Army soldiers crossed the line and proceeded to a point 20 meters south;
> (2) An alert UNC work party fired on the North Korean Army soldiers and killed them;
> (3) From concealed positions along the line North Korean Army soldiers fired automatic weapons at the UNC work party as it attempted to withdraw to its assigned guard post;
> (4) North Korean Army soldiers retrieved one of three North Korean soldiers killed south of the line and dragged him to a point 7–8 meters north of the line; and
> (5) A fourth North Korean soldier was killed in the ensuing firefight.[32]

The North Korean JOT could not accept the UNC version. The UNC JOT senior member said he would be willing to meet his North Korean counterpart at a mutually agreeable time to work on a joint report. He added, however, that the UNC would file its report with the MAC unilaterally if the North Koreans did not wish to meet again. The North Korean member proposed to discuss the matter the next day.

On April 7, the North Korean JOT senior member presented his version. He charged that the UNC fired on and killed North Korean

Army "civil police" engaged on a routine patrol north of the line and claimed the UNC subsequently removed the bodies from the north side to the south in an attempt to prove that North Korean Army personnel had intruded across the line. He demanded that the UNC agree to the North Korean version of the report.

The UNC rejected the North Korean version and said it would submit its evidence to the Military Armistice Commission unilaterally. The North Korean side stated it would do the same.

The UNC permitted a North Korean work party to cross the line to retrieve the bodies of the soldiers. The North Korean JOT was allowed to supervise the retrieval. A few days later, North Korea held a state funeral in Pyongyang for the North Korean soldiers, and North Korean media accused U.S. forces of "murdering" North Korean DMZ "civil police."

This was a perplexing level of attention to be given to a few North Korean intruders. The North's infiltrators were almost always specially trained commandos. It was standard practice for North Korea to deny these forces' identity once they had crossed the line, so that it could claim the infiltrators were actually revolutionary South Koreans. The attention given the so-called civil military police who crossed the line in April 1967 tended to indicate they were not special forces but merely regular soldiers, and the UNC conjectured they might have had a special connection to prominent party members. It was also possible the soldiers had sought to defect to the South. In either case, North Korea needed a cover story. The North's agreement to convene a JOT may well have been motivated by the need to develop an explanation and make it stick.

With but two exceptions, this April 1967 JOT investigation was the final one authorized in the DMZ. The first exception came in September 1976, after brutal axe murders, when an inspection was needed of the newly installed markers dividing the two security guard forces in the conference area of Panmunjom. In that situation, it was in the North's interest to participate fully in designating new security limitations within the joint security area. The second exception did not occur until 1997, when two acorn gatherers may have strayed across the line.

The Neutral Nations Supervisory Commission

The other major investigative mechanism of the MAC was similarly to be rendered ineffective. The NNSC was the monitoring and inspection regime set up at the Communists' behest in lieu of UNC arms control proposals. Under the terms of the armistice agreement, the NNSC, formed of four senior representatives from Sweden, Switzerland, Poland, and Czechoslovakia, was to field twenty inspection teams, called Neutral Nations Inspection Teams. Each NNIT of at least four officers was "to properly insure that reinforcing combat aircraft, armored vehicles, weapons, and ammunition are not being introduced into Korea." Five teams were to be located in specified ports of entry in the South; five in specified ports of entry in the North; and ten additional teams were to be stationed near the NNSC headquarters at Panmunjom to reinforce or stand in for other teams as necessary. The teams were to file reports with the NNSC, which in turn reported to the MAC.[33]

The purpose of this system was to "cease the introduction into Korea of reinforcing combat aircraft, armored vehicles, weapons and ammunition" except for that "destroyed, damaged, worn out, or used up" which could be "replaced on the basis of piece-for-piece of the same effectiveness and the same type."[34]

How the parties of the armistice agreement brought themselves to believe such a system might actually work is, in hindsight, a mystery. They must have had a great deal more faith in the other side than history concludes was justified. They certainly did not expect the NNSC to last for many decades, but it could not even perform its task for a year.

Between November 29, 1953, and February 12, 1954, UNC requests for NNSC mobile inspections in North Korea were denied on six occasions by the Czech and Polish delegations. This caused the Swedish member of the NNSC, General Mohn, to ask:

> Under what circumstances will the NNSC be allowed to send Mobile Inspection Teams to the territory controlled by the North Korean and Chinese side? Am I to understand that the side itself has to acknowledge the violation before a Mobile Inspection Team is allowed to go out? Should that be the case, I think that both sides could scrap Paragraph 28 of the Armistice Agreement right away.[35]

Not surprisingly, the inspection teams that were dispatched produced conflicting reports of what was discovered during the investigations.

North Korea not only refused to allow the investigation teams access to port records, shipping manifests, and other data necessary for valid inspections, but it also refused to allow spot checks at designated ports of entry in North Korea.[36] There was strong intelligence that North Korea had smuggled illegal weapons and equipment into North Korea,[37] but North Korea was able to block investigations by NNITs. As UNC senior member Rear Admiral Walter E. Moore, USN, concluded, "the evidence accumulated by our side over a period of more than 29 months indicates clearly, and without dispute, that the value of the NNITs and the Mobile Inspection Teams has been completely, willfully, and systematically destroyed by the tactics employed by your side."[38]

The NNSC record in the South, however, was completely different. As General Mohn commented dryly, "I am under the impression that we apply one system in North Korea and another in South Korea."[39] The UNC, as signatory to the armistice, enforced inspections in the South and therefore found itself in the position of forcing compliance from an unwilling and resentful Republic of Korea.

The commander in chief of the UNC, General John E. Hull, recommended to the Joint Chiefs of Staff that the NNSC be abolished because it was being used by the Polish and Czech members "to compile detailed intelligence data" and was harassing the UNC with "unfounded accusations and Communist propaganda exercises."[40] The Swiss member of the NNSC observed that the Czechs and Poles "were all too eager to inspect all sorts of goods which did not even remotely have any connection with combat materials." They requested "timetables, manifests, and other documents relating not only to combat materiel, but to all shipments in the South." He concluded the NNSC gave the Communists "an insight into the movement of all cargo in the South's ports of entry."[41]

The Swiss and Swedish delegations to the NNSC became disenchanted with the NNSC, and the United States tried to persuade them to withdraw from it.[42] But the United States did not wish to be seen as calling for the NNSC's termination, and, for the same reasons, the Swiss and Swedish resisted advocating termination. Accordingly, the level of frustration increased.

No party recognized the implications of the unbalanced predicament more than the Republic of Korea. On September 2, 1954, South Korea's Prime Minister Pyun wrote to General Hull, then commander in chief of the United Nations Command:

We expected Chinese Communists to withdraw from Korea in advance of UN forces, but what is actually happening is the reverse: U.S. divisions departing from Korea are leaving a huge gap hardly to be filled by ROK units which, in fact, do not exist even in paper-planning. While North Korea is bristling with airfields that did not either exist or operate during hostilities, but are now in full trim with jet fighters and bombers, ready on them, the few airfields in South Korea will soon go to weeds if they fail to get proper attention.[43]

The ROK government demanded that the NNSC be disbanded and the NNITs be forced to leave ROK territory. The National Assembly unanimously passed a resolution supporting that position.[44]

Partly to relieve the South's increasing anger, the Swiss and Swedish governments in January 1955 issued an *aide-memoire* suggesting abolishing or reducing the size of the NNSC. China replied on March 5 that only a reduction of the Commission's staff would be acceptable.[45] Weakening the inspection regime was always an acceptable Communist objective.

In July 1955, the South Korean Chiefs of Staff demanded the NNSC be disbanded and the ROK be permitted to develop military strength equivalent to the North's.[46] They threatened to take military action against North Korea before the imbalance became worse. On August 5, 1955, the ROK acting foreign minister gave to the NNSC and the UNC an ultimatum: the members of the NNSC would have to withdraw from the territory of the ROK by midnight August 13.

Large, violent demonstrations against the NNSC took place in the five South Korean ports of entry. The commander in chief of the UNC was forced to warn that he would protect the NNSC teams in accordance with the armistice agreement. Clashes between demonstrators and UNC guards protecting the NNSC members resulted in numerous injuries.

In October, the Swedish member proposed that all Neutral Nations Inspection Teams be withdrawn from ports of entry to camps in the DMZ. The proposal was supported by the Swiss delegation, but the Czechs and Poles would not accept it. The standoff was not resolved until seven months later. On May 31, 1956, the UNC took the dramatic step at a MAC meeting of announcing a unilateral suspension of the articles of the armistice agreement covering the operations of the NNITs, and called for immediate withdrawal of all NNITs from South Korea. Eager to preserve a small advantage when facing the loss of a larger one, the Communists agreed to withdrawal of

NNITs to the NNSC camps in the DMZ.[48] All NNIT personnel were withdrawn from South Korea by June 9 and from North Korea by June 12 to their respective camps within the MAC headquarters area at Panmunjom.

Since the withdrawal of the NNITs from the ports of entry, no inspections have been conducted by the NNITs in either North or South Korea. On several occasions, however, both sides have requested such inspections, fully aware that the NNSC was no longer able to carry out its mission. Such requests have been noted and filed without further action.

The functions of the NNSC came to be limited to evaluation of the "arrival and departure of personnel" reports submitted by both sides and the falsified combat materiel reports submitted only by North Korea. By mid-1957, North Korea had made a mockery of the provisions of the NNIT article by introducing a range of new weapons. Accordingly the UNC announced on June 21, 1957, that it would no longer consider itself bound by this article.[49]

North Korea complained, and Radio Pyongyang broadcast anti-U.S. propaganda tirades. For its part, North Korea continued to submit bogus reports on combat materiel, claiming it had not introduced any modern, reinforcing weapons since the signing of the armistice agreement in 1953. The North Koreans vociferously accused the UNC of "wrecking the armistice agreement and incapacitating the NNSC and its inspection regime."

Although the missions of the NNSC had been abandoned, the UNC maintained that the presence of "neutral" representatives was still potentially useful. The NNSC's presence in Panmunjom seemed to provide a stabilizing influence in this sensitive area, if not, as had been initially hoped, throughout the Korean peninsula.

With the collapse of communism in Eastern Europe, North Korea found itself in an ironic predicament. Czechoslovakia and Poland had become genuinely neutral and increasingly at odds with North Korean views. Since the NNSC no longer served the North's objectives, North Korea at that point openly sought its disestablishment.

North Korea found a pretext for dismantling the NNSC in March 1991 when Major General Hwang Won Tak became the first ROK general to be appointed senior member of UNCMAC. North Korea refused to come to the MAC meeting and began a campaign of harassment against the Czech and Polish delegations. It denied permission for the Czech Republic to succeed Czechoslovakia on the NNSC, and restricted the travel and access of the Czech delegation. The Czech Republic's delegation accordingly withdrew from North Korea on April 10, 1993. Subsequently, the Polish delegation was also forced to leave its camp in North Korea near Panmunjom, but it continues to play a role in the NNSC. The Polish delegation returns to Panmunjom via South Korea a few times each year to meet with other NNSC members.

Repatriating Military Personnel Who Crossed the Line

A major oversight during the armistice negotiations was the lack of attention to establishing a procedure for repatriation of military personnel who found themselves in enemy custody. Given the attention devoted to the repatriation of prisoners of war, it seems peculiar that post-armistice abductions, accidental trespassing, organized infiltration, and defection got no attention. The negotiators were aware of North Korea's behavior during the war, impressing civilians into their service and meting out "people's justice" against non-Communist prisoners, yet these matters were not addressed. Defections could be dismissed as a political matter beyond the purview of the commanders, but the opposing side's treatment of military personnel in their custody was very much a military matter. This important matter was left to the arbitrary development of precedent on a case-by-case basis. Not surprisingly, the status of personnel who had gone over the line became a major problem in the implementation of the armistice. It brought the opposing sides to the brink of war more frequently than any other matter of contention.

There had been an instructive detention while the armistice agreement was being negotiated, but it did not alert the negotiators to the need for specific repatriation procedures. On September 19, 1951, four unarmed members of a Red Cross medical team lost their way while on an antimalarial work detail. They inadvertently crossed a bridge into the North in their truck loaded with DDT. The bewildered team was surrounded by North Korean Army officers who detained them on suspicion of engaging in biological warfare. They were soon released, however, when UNC liaison officers signed a receipt for their return.[50]

The precedent for the return of military personnel under the armistice was first established at a MAC meeting on October 6, 1954, when the North Koreans repatriated U.S. Marine Lieutenant Colonel Herbert A. Peters with his light aircraft. North Korea did not in this instance ask for a receipt. The entire situation took the UNC by surprise because it had listed Peters as "killed in action." His return estab-lished a precedent that both sides could repatriate military personnel through the MAC channel.

After the first incident, and consistently for the first nine years of the armistice, North Korea returned military personnel who inad-vertently crossed the line within days. In some cases, the North Kore-ans did not ask for a receipt for the returnee, but in most cases the UNC tendered a simple receipt or a letter admitting crossing the line.[51] The UNC also returned North Korean military personnel rou-tinely for simple receipts, without demanding an admission of viola-tions.

This system was in place on August 17, 1955, when a USAF T-6 aircraft flew over the DMZ and was shot down by North Korea. Captain Charles W. Brown was killed, and Second Lieutenant Guy Hartwell Bumpas survived the crash. The North Koreans returned Lieutenant Bumpas and the remains of Captain Brown with the aircraft wreckage four days later without asking for a receipt.

When receipts were required during this period, they were rela-tively straightforward. The receipt for Captain Leon K. Pfeiffer, USA, shot down in North Korea on March 6, 1958, and returned on March 17, states:

> I duly received from the Korean People's Army/Chinese People's Volunteers side together with his personal belong-ings the following pilot of the United Nations Command side who crossed the Military Demarcation Line in violation of the Armistice Agreement to intrude into the air above the territory under the military control of the KPA/CPV side and was shot down on March 6, 1958.[52]

The matter became considerably more complicated after Septem-ber 5, 1962, when a fight broke out during a *Chusok* (the Korean fall harvest holiday) celebration. Six North Korean soldiers approached ROK soldiers at the demarcation line and asked the ROK soldiers to join them. The experiment in fraternal commemoration led to an ex-change of gunfire in which three North Koreans were killed and two wounded.

North Korea requested the return of the two wounded officers and the remains of the three soldiers. The UNC returned the remains but informed North Korea that the two officers chose to remain in the

ROK. At the MAC meeting of October 5, 1962, the North Korean senior member, Major General Chang Chung Hwan, angrily issued the following warning:

> I declare to you that if your side continues to behave in such a manner instead of returning our personnel at an early date, such lenient treatment as was given to 2nd Lt. Bumpas who could go back to your side after being shot down through our self-defense measures when he intruded into our territorial airspace will no longer be accorded to your side which incessantly commits provocative acts in violation of the Armistice Agreement. Our side will call your side to account for [those two North Korean officers] until your side returns our personnel.[53]

North Korea made good on this threat. On May 17, 1963, Captain Ben W. Stutts and Captain Carleton W. Voltz, flying a U.S. Army helicopter OH-23, became disoriented, flew over the Han River estuary, and were forced down in North Korea. At the next MAC meeting, General Chang hinted at a possible trial of the pilots as "criminals," and refused to discuss the incident further.

On November 6, 1963, General Hamilton H. Howze, the UNC commander in chief, wrote to Kim Il Sung asking him to cooperate in the early settlement of the incident. Three months later, Kim answered the letter.[54] He alleged that the pilots were engaged in "military espionage," and said that to obtain North Korea's leniency, the UNC would have to (1) admit the "grave criminal acts," (2) guarantee that no such "criminal acts" would be perpetrated by the UNC in the future, and (3) strictly abide by the armistice agreement. On March 5, 1964, General Howze sent a letter to Kim Il Sung formally apologizing for the helicopter incident, guaranteeing that the UNC would take measures to prevent a recurrence of such incidents, and promising to adhere to the terms of the armistice agreement.

After a delay of a few weeks, Kim noted Howze's apology and designated his senior member at the MAC to settle the matter. By May 5, no further action had been taken, so the UNC senior member proposed a private meeting to be held in Panmunjom.

The first private MAC meeting, held on May 8, failed to achieve any positive result. General Chang merely repeated Kim Il Sung's conditions for the release of the crew. At the second private meeting held a week later, the North Korean general insisted that Major General

Cecil E. Combs, USAF, the UNC senior member, sign a "receipt document" before discussing procedures for the release of the pilots to the UNC, and proffered a receipt that had been prepared by North Korea in Korean and English. Major General Combs signed both versions. The receipt for Captains Stutts and Voltz was a confession:

> Admitting the crimes of espionage and illegal intrusion by Captain Ben Weakley Stutts and Captain Carleton William Voltz, the U.S. pilots, who were captured by the self-defense measure of the Korean People's Army while they were committing espionage act, after illegally intruding into the air over the northern part of the Democratic Republic of Korea across the Military Demarcation Line in violation of the Armistice Agreement upon the orders of the 8th U.S. Army headquarters on May 17, 1963, and guaranteeing that it will not commit such criminal acts and will strictly abide by the Korean Armistice Agreement in the future, the United Nations Command hereby receives Captain Ben Weakley Stutts and Captain Carleton William Voltz, U.S. Army pilots, from the Korean People's Army side.[55]

The pilots were released at the meeting of the MAC secretaries on May 16, 1964, one day short of a full year after crossing the line.

The North Koreans had taken retaliatory action against the "detention" of two of their officers who were wounded in the fight in the DMZ on September 5, 1962. Their retaliation, however, was not limited to one counterpunch. A new precedent had been established. From then on, the North Koreans returned UNC personnel only after obtaining a signed "letter of apology" they prescribed, in which the UNC generally admitted "criminal acts" or "espionage."

The 1962 precedent became a factor in the protracted and difficult negotiations for the return of the USS *Pueblo* six years later.

On December 3, 1970, a North Korean MiG-15 crash landed on an east coast beach in South Korea. Soon after the incident, the ROK ministry of national defense announced that the MiG-15 pilot, North Korean Air Force Major Pak Sung Kuk, had defected to South Korea.

The North Koreans requested the MAC meeting held on December 5, and demanded the return of the pilot and aircraft. The North Korean senior member asserted that the pilot must have left Wonsan Air Base for high-altitude flight training, become disoriented "in thick clouds," and made an emergency landing. In reply, the UNC repeated the ROK position that the pilot had defected, and pledged that the North Koreans would "be advised accordingly after our side has had an opportunity to study the total evidence."[56]

Not until June 2, 1971, did the UNC officially inform the North Koreans that Major Pak Sung Kuk, the MiG-15 pilot, had decided to remain in the ROK. At that time the UNC stated that because the matter was a political not a military question, the UNC would "disassociate itself from the case."[57] Throughout four subsequent closed-door sessions requested by the North Koreans, the UNC maintained a position that "the issue would be settled based on the freely expressed desire of the pilot concerning his choice of residence and the pilot should be turned over to a disinterested third party to verify his choice."[58]

At the final private meeting, North Korea's senior member, Major General Han Ju Kyong, angrily warned:

> If your side persistently keeps on forcibly detaining our pilot and aircraft that made an emergency landing instead of returning them, it will bring about disadvantageous results to you. You must clearly keep in your mind that our just warning is not an empty talk.[59]

No UNC personnel fell into North Korean custody for six years after that threat. Despite North Korea's stern warning, the next time a U.S. Army CH-47 helicopter flew over the DMZ and landed in North Korea, North Korea quickly returned the survivor and the remains of the three crew members.

North Korea had its reasons for not following up on its threat in 1977. President Jimmy Carter had made an election year pledge to withdraw American troops from Korea, and Kim Il Sung refrained from taking action that would undermine Carter's determination to deliver on that pledge.

Communicating with the Other Side

Major General Gilbert H. Woodward, USA, who served as the UNC senior member during one of the most difficult periods, frequently mused, "I put on my best uniform and go up to Panmunjom to listen to the North Korean propaganda garbage for the sole purpose of maintaining communication between the Commanders."[60]

The MAC has performed a vital role as a channel for communication, one of the functions specified in the armistice agreement. Despite the ad hoc procedures that were developed for convening MAC meetings, the process of calling meetings routinely served a number of valuable tension-reducing purposes. MAC meetings and the MAC hotline have provided the opposing sides an opportunity to explain their positions and their concerns. This has inevitably precluded some misunderstandings and miscalculations.

The MAC process has, on occasion, checked North Korean military adventurism. North Korea has occasionally been warned in MAC meetings that UNC intelligence had discovered that the North was planning military actions. The MAC served as a channel for letting North Korea know that the UNC knew what was under way and was well prepared to counter such actions. This type of deterrent warning is facilitated when meetings are routine; when hostile parties do not meet regularly, an attempt to call a special meeting can itself increase tension.

The MAC channel sometimes provided North Korea with information about its own forces. In 1982, the North Korean senior member telephoned the UNC senior member asking for the return of any "bodies" that might be found along the east coast. He claimed some North Korean military personnel were unaccounted for after a training exercise on the evening of May 14. By the time of the meeting, the South Korean media had already reported that a team of three armed North Korean infiltrators had been intercepted on an east coast beach, that one was killed in ensuing gunfire, and that the other two fled. Some speculated that the three North Koreans had in fact become lost during training and crossed the line. The UNC returned the remains of the dead soldier; the other two were believed to have escaped back to North Korea. The MAC played a useful role by allowing North Korea to explain that the trainees were not the vanguard of an invasion force.

The armistice institutions have had definite flaws, and they have had, at best, a borderline ability to resolve the tensions on the peninsula. Even when the MAC functioned well, it could only air the grievances of two irreconcilable viewpoints. But that has been a valuable achievement, especially in the bleak climate of irresolution that has characterized Korea since 1951.

The implementation of the terms of the armistice by these institutions has, despite shortcomings, proved of value. Even North Korea has used the MAC channel when its interests compel direct communication. Although American officials periodically address the question of dispensing with its frustrating and often ineffectual processes, the MAC cannot be discarded without first establishing alternatives for dealing with the continuing dangers inherent in the armistice.

As the next chapter explains, the MAC managed a series of crises, any one of which might have brought other proud nations, at different periods in history, to war. The armistice institutions, because of necessity if not effectiveness, deserve to be maintained. The MAC also provides an intangible benefit that should not be undervalued: it is a constant reminder of allied resolve.

7

★

Managing the Years of Crisis

During the first decade of the armistice, the North Korean regime concentrated on consolidating control over its population,
increasing industrial production, and building up a powerful
military. As noted in the previous chapter, North Korea was able to by-
pass armistice restrictions on its military buildup and escape accountability for armistice violations. Facing a strong military deterrent,
however, North Korea cautiously avoided steps that might provoke a
war during the decade after the agreement was signed.

When viewed in retrospect, with the knowledge of the attacks the
North launched in the late 1960s, its violations of the armistice before
1966 seem benign. They included not wearing proper identification
armbands, carrying automatic weapons where only pistols were allowed, and arguably accidental discharging of weapons in the demilitarized zone (DMZ).

By the mid-1960s, the West's attention had shifted away from
Kim Il Sung to Ho Chi Minh. Faced with evidence of North Vietnam's
revolutionary vigor, North Korea recognized that its own efforts to foment revolution in South Korea and force a withdrawal of U.S. forces
had failed miserably. In an attempt to attain its objectives, North
Korea undertook a systematic escalation of violent acts against the
United Nations Command and the Republic of Korea. Kim Il Sung literally fought for attention.

With the United States increasingly devoting its attention to the war effort in Southeast Asia, North Korea felt compelled to provoke American attention and show its Marxist-Leninist fervor; at the same time, it correctly perceived it had greater space in which to operate without provoking American military retaliation. Distracted by the difficulties in Vietnam and student protests at home, United States policymakers sought to avoid conflicts in Korea.

Almost overnight, the pattern of North Korean armistice infractions accelerated to include acts of armed terror. North Korea infiltrated commandos over the line, created incidents that would bring the United States to the negotiating table, and used the resulting negotiations and MAC meetings for propaganda. In incidents like the seizure of the USS *Pueblo*, the North Korean negotiating objective ostensibly was to obtain an official "letter of apology" from the United States government, but the actual objective was more complex: to create friction between the ROK and the United States; to find a platform for inciting South Koreans to bring down their own government; and to humiliate the United States, garnering respect from Socialist nations and spreading fear among Western democracies. The United States was compelled to enter into negotiations with North Korea not only to respond to the incidents, but also to reaffirm the validity of the armistice agreement, restore security along the DMZ, and win the release of American personnel held by North Korea.

Simply winning American attention during the Vietnam years enhanced North Korea's international prestige. The Military Armistice Commission, as the only channel of communication available for dealing with North Korea's hostility, necessarily played a major role. The MAC could not avoid becoming an instrument of North Korea's objectives; it provided the means for North Korea to force direct discussions on the incidents of violence that were in so many cases staged specifically to initiate contact with the United States. At the same time, however, it served as a unique mechanism for managing the years of crisis.

At the height of America's engagement in Vietnam, North Korea waged armed attacks against U.S. and ROK forces in and near the DMZ on more than 280 occasions. Their major attacks included:

- sinking an ROK Navy patrol craft (PCE-56) in the Sea of Japan (the Eastern Sea) on January 19, 1967
- infiltrating North Korean commandos across the line into South Korea with orders to assassinate South Korea's President Park in January 1968

- seizing the naval vessel USS *Pueblo* on January 23, 1968
- attacking a UNC truck in Panmunjom on April 14, 1968
- landing more than 120 North Korean commandos on the east coast of South Korea on October 30–November 1, 1968
- shooting down a U.S. Navy EC-121 reconnaissance craft over the Eastern Sea on April 15, 1969

During the four years between January 1966 and December 1969, 75 U.S. and 299 ROK military personnel, 80 South Korean civilians, and 647 North Korean infiltrators were killed, and 111 U.S. and 550 ROK military personnel as well as 91 South Korean civilians were wounded in these North Korean actions. Any one of the actions instigated by North Korea might have cost more in terms of human lives and regional instability had it not been for the existence of the Military Armistice Commission.

The 1967 Patrol Craft Sinking

In the armistice agreement, the UNC negotiators had sought to create an enforceable truce by establishing a line of military demarcation across the peninsula—a line that would protect the people of South Korea from attack. The line could not, however, have been extended reasonably beyond the width of the peninsula itself. The armistice agreement did not address the question of ownership of the seas, and it would have been foolhardy to try to do so. Both North and South Korea would have claimed a right extending from the other's coast, since each claimed to be the legitimate government of the entire peninsula.

As it was, both governments asserted different territorial sea claims. North Korea claimed to have exclusive rights to fish in a territorial sea that extended twelve nautical miles from its shores; South Korea claimed three nautical miles.

A major fishing ground is situated more than three miles from North Korea's shore, just north of where the military demarcation line would be if it were extended beyond the eastern coast of Korea. Enterprising South Korean, Japanese, and other fishermen were attracted to these rich fishing grounds. Seeing their fishing as an infringement of its jurisdiction over the fishing grounds, North Korea sent patrol boats and occasionally fired shore batteries to harass the fishermen, who were frequently lost at sea or abducted. To protect the fishermen, the ROK decided to send its naval vessels to escort fishing boats to the northern fishing ground. Confrontations were inevitable. Especially during the pollock fishing season in the winter months, MAC meetings received numerous North Korean charges that South Korean naval vessels and "armed spy boats" had intruded into their waters.

At about 1:50 P.M., January 19, 1967, a South Korean naval patrol escort boat, PCE-56, with a crew of forty, was fired upon by North Korean shore batteries and sunk at a location 3.5 to 5.1 miles off the North Korean coast. The UNC called for a MAC meeting, which was convened on January 21, and charged the North Koreans with firing on and sinking a naval vessel on "peaceful, non-hostile duty." The UNC requested an investigation by the Neutral Nations Supervisory Commission in accordance with paragraph 28 of the armistice agreement.[1]

The North Korean senior member to the commission, Major General Pak Chung Kuk, charged that the patrol boat had "illegally intruded into our coastal waters . . . and overtly committed a vicious hostile act of suddenly opening gun-fire and showering scores of shells upon our coastal area." Pak claimed that North Korean shore batteries took "due self-defense measures," and warned against similar naval or air intrusions into the North Korean coastal waters or airspace.[2]

In the interest of maintaining peace, the South Korean government revised its policy toward fishing boat escort operations and transferred the escort mission from its navy to its maritime police.

Nevertheless, at MAC meetings between October 1967 and January 20, 1968, North Korea continued to charge the UNC with alleged intrusions by "armed vessels, spy boats and fishing boats," and threatened the UNC with retaliation. At the MAC meeting of November 7, 1967, for example, the North Korean senior member claimed that "your side has used South Korean fishing boats as a shield to cover up your espionage activities . . . and to find a pretext for unleashing another war in Korea," and demanded the UNC immediately stop sending "military spy vessels."[3]

The North Koreans had achieved a victory of sorts by causing a policy change in the South, with its attendant implication that the ROK Navy would not operate north of where the DMZ would be if it were extended. The victory, however, did not resolve tensions; it emboldened the North. Between December 23, 1967, and January 20, 1968, North Korea increased its charges that the UNC infiltrated numerous South Korean fishing boats and "various naval craft and armed spy boats" into their coastal waters.

The Raid on the Blue House to Assassinate President Park

On January 18, 1968, thirty-one North Korean commandos infiltrated across the military demarcation line into the United Nations Command portion of the DMZ. They cut a hole in the newly erected barrier fence along the southern boundary of the DMZ and penetrated deep into the territory of the Republic of Korea. The commandos' mission was to attack the Blue House—Chong Wa Dae, the presidential mansion in Seoul—to kill South Korea's President Park Chung Hee.

At about two o'clock in the afternoon, the commandos encountered four South Korean woodcutters on a hill near Popwon-ni, a village about four miles south of the DMZ. The infiltrators detained the woodcutters, asked them about South Korea, and told them they were "members of a group which would unify the country." The commandos held the woodcutters for five hours, then released them with the threat of execution if they told anyone about their encounter.

Despite the commandos' threat, the woodcutters reported the incident to the ROK national police when they returned to their village about two hours later. That so large a group of commandos could cross the DMZ unnoticed was hard for South Korean police to believe. They dismissed the woodcutters' story. By the time the woodcutters' report was relayed and police units had begun to search for the commandos where the woodcutters first encountered them, the commandos were fast approaching Seoul.

The North Koreans moved swiftly toward Seoul under cover of darkness, and began their final advance toward the Blue House at about nine o'clock on the evening of January 21. They encountered no ROK national police until they were about 800 meters from the presidential mansion. At that point, they came under police fire. The North Korean commandos split into smaller groups, fanned out, and retreated north.

Over the next three days, firefights between commandos and ROK police broke out in and around Seoul. Some of the North Koreans committed suicide rather than surrender. One hid a hand grenade in his clothing and blew himself up in the national police headquarters.[4] Thirty of the commandos died; only one was captured. In the firefights on the streets of Seoul, thirty-one South Koreans, including women and children, were killed and forty-four were wounded.[5]

The lone North Korean commando apprehended by the ROK national police took a UNC investigative team to the southern boundary barrier fence and showed where the North Korean commandos had cut the hole through the DMZ. He also confirmed that the commandos had been ordered to proceed to the Blue House to kill President Park.

Seizure of the USS *Pueblo*

On January 22, 1968, the UNC requested that a meeting of the MAC be held the next day. The North Koreans asked for a day's delay, and the UNC accepted.[6] No one at UNCMAC anticipated that in the intervening day, January 23, 1968, a North Korean Navy patrol craft would forcibly board and illegally seize an American military vessel in international waters off Wonsan, North Korea. It was, however, a cunning move. The North Korean action shifted attention from its treacherous attempt to assassinate a head of state and focused it instead on a superpower's efforts to spy on the North. America's attention was suddenly riveted on the *Pueblo*'s seizure and diverted from the Blue House raid. To illustrate the degree to which Washington's attention was focused on the *Pueblo*, it is useful to note that in Admiral Gallery's controversial book on the *Pueblo* incident, he makes no mention of the raid on the Blue House, even though he goes into depth on the question of whether the Pentagon might have ignored warning signs that the *Pueblo* could be in danger.[7]

On the afternoon of January 23, 1968, a North Korean PT (patrol torpedo) boat approached the American intelligence vessel, the USS *Pueblo*, more than sixteen nautical miles from the North Korean coast.[8] Using international signal flags, the North Koreans asked the *Pueblo*'s nationality. When she identified herself as American, the North Korean vessel signaled: "Heave to or I will open fire." The *Pueblo* replied: "I am in international waters." An hour later, three more North Korean patrol craft approached the *Pueblo*. One of the small vessels signaled, "Follow in my wake." North Korean boats took up positions alongside the *Pueblo*. Armed North Korean sailors boarded the *Pueblo*, and at 1:45 P.M., the *Pueblo* radioed Yokosuka naval base that North Koreans were on board. Twenty-five minutes later, the *Pueblo* reported that she was "requested" to steam into Wonsan. At 2:32 P.M., Commander Bucher, captain of the *Pueblo*, reported that he was going off the air.[9]

North Korea released a photo showing the ship's officers and crew in a forced march with their hands in the air.[10] The American re-action was anguished, but few advocated an immediate return to war in Korea. The seizure of the *Pueblo* raised the specter of a second war in Asia—one the United States, hard pressed in Vietnam, could ill afford; North Korea sought to exploit this weakness. North Korea also sought to exploit tensions the crisis would cause between the United States and South Korea.

The South Korean public was irritated that American concern for the *Pueblo*'s crew overshadowed the attempted assassination of their president and deaths of innocent civilians in their capital city.

The United States government was deeply concerned about the commando attack and made this clear in the MAC meeting of January 24, 1968. The UNC senior member, Rear Admiral John V. Smith, USN, opened the January 24 meeting by focusing on the attempted assassination of the ROK president. He charged North Korea with killing and wounding civilians and ROK national police officers in Seoul and displayed a photograph of a busload of women and children who had suffered a grenade attack. The UNC also showed the filmed confession of the apprehended commando.

Rear Admiral Smith emphasized that North Korea bore official responsibility for the attack on the Blue House, pointing out that Kim Il Sung himself had called for acts of violence in the South in a speech on December 16, 1967.[11] Kim had said:

> We must accomplish the South Korean revolution, unify the fatherland in our generation, and hand down a unified fatherland to the coming generations. We must quickly make all conditions ripe for the realization of the unification of the fatherland. [12]

The UNC then turned to the question of the *Pueblo*. It charged North Korea with an illegal seizure of the ship in international waters. The UNC demanded an immediate return of the ship and its crew, and an apology for North Korea's illegal seizure. Rear Admiral Smith then delivered an official message to North Korea from the U.S. government:

> The events of last year, and especially the last few days, have put a new complexion on the situation in Korea. The North Korean regime has embarked on a campaign of provocation, sabotage, and assassination in violation of the Ar-

mistice Agreement and international law. The Republic of Korea and the U.S. threaten no one. If the North Korean regime persists in this campaign, which can only endanger the peace in this area, the responsibility of the consequences will rest with the North Korean regime.[13]

North Korean senior member Major General Pak Chung Kuk, a member of the North Korean Workers party central committee, flatly denied the UNC charges, saying that the perpetrators were in fact "South Korean people who are rising up against the U.S. imperialist aggressors." The "South Korean people, who have risen up in the anti-U.S. patriotic struggle," he dissembled, "are carrying the fight to the Blue House located in the heart of Seoul." He claimed that the "patriotic struggle of the South Korean people" had nothing to do with the armistice agreement. Calling it the "unanimous desire" of the 40 million Korean people "to wipe out you U.S. imperialist aggressors," he said the North could unify the country in a generation.

General Pak charged that U.S. President Lyndon Johnson had visited South Korea in October 1966 to provoke a new war. He claimed UNC military provocations against North Korea had been more frequent, more extensive, and more vicious with each passing day. He charged, "U.S. imperialist aggressors are massacring South Korea people who are out for the anti-U.S. patriotic struggle for the unification of the country and nation."[14] Using a technique that had characterized public negotiations with North Korea, Pak turned to insults. He called his UNC counterpart a "mad dog" and, aiming at a raw nerve of Americans in the 1960s, asserted that Johnson would "meet the same fate as that of Kennedy."

That was all prelude to the charges he would level against the *Pueblo*. Accusing the United States of the "most overt and serious aggressive act of infiltrating an armed spy ship of the U.S. imperialist aggressor navy into our coastal waters on January 23," Pak elaborated that

> around 1215 hours, your side committed crude aggressive act of illegally infiltrating the armed spy ship of the U.S. imperialist aggressor navy equipped with various weapons and all kinds of equipment necessary for espionage activities into our coastal waters off Wonsan in the vicinity of 39 degrees 17 minutes North, 127 degrees 46 minutes East. The armed spy ship . . . intruded further deep into our coastal

waters and committed intolerable provocation against our side. Our naval vessels which were carrying out their routine patrol duty in our coastal waters returned the fire of the piratical group which intruded deep into our coastal waters and insolently made resistance, thus, killing and wounding several soldiers of the U.S. imperialist navy and capturing 80-odd of them alive.[15]

General Pak finally demanded that the UNC admit the "aggressive act" committed by the U.S. Navy "armed spy ship," apologize for it, severely punish those who were responsible for it, and give assurance that it would not commit such provocation again. North Korea reiterated the same demand in public and private sessions of the MAC senior members throughout the *Pueblo* negotiations.[16]

Admiral Smith responded that North Korea's wild statement and distorted version of North Korea's piracy against the USS *Pueblo* were obviously intended to divert attention from the North Korean regime's attempt to assassinate the president of the Republic of Korea and its seizure of the USS *Pueblo* in international waters. He said North Korea's charges were not the matters that had been proposed for MAC consideration, and the UNC would not be distracted from the proposed agenda.

General Pak responded that the UNC could not evade discussion of the *Pueblo*'s espionage attempts and demanded that the UNC senior member return with a UNC answer to the North's charges at the next meeting. Admiral Smith reminded his North Korean counterpart that an official communication from the U.S. government had already been presented, and it was intended for immediate transmission to Kim Il Sung.[17]

Initial Posturing. North Korea took swift action to maximize its propaganda advantage. Only two days after the seizure of the *Pueblo*, Radio Pyongyang announced that Commander Lloyd M. Bucher had presented a written confession that his ship "spied on various military installations . . . along the east coast areas and sailed up to the point 7.6 miles off Yo-do . . . intruded deep into the territorial waters of the Democratic People's Republic of Korea and was captured by the naval patrol craft of the Korean People's Army in their self-defense action . . . and we only hope . . . that we will be forgiven leniently by the Government of the DPRK."[18]

The *Pueblo*, as Admiral Gallery described it for the American public, was an electronic intelligence vessel whose mission was "to snoop as close as the law allows to an adversary's coast and gather data on radar and radio transmissions."[19] In the absence of North Korean cooperation in the inspections that had been envisioned by the armistice agreement, such intelligence activities were vital to the security of UNC forces and to peace on the peninsula.

Despite a general willingness to give diplomacy a chance to work, pressure mounted swiftly in America for retaliatory action. Presidential candidate Richard M. Nixon criticized the *Pueblo* affair as a "tactical blunder" of the Johnson administration. Americans and South Koreans alike were uncomfortable with American powerlessness against a third-rate power.

South Korean Premier Chung Il Kwon urged a massive retaliatory response, warning that a lukewarm U.S. attitude would encourage North Korea to mount another war in Korea. But President Johnson was cautious; his carefully measured response took into account American priorities in the war in Vietnam. His first step was to ask Moscow to put pressure on North Korea for the release of the *Pueblo* and its crew, but Moscow declined.

Johnson decided to increase military pressure with a limited call-up of air units and to increase diplomatic pressure by presenting the American case before the United Nations. He delivered a nationally televised speech moments before the United Nations Security Council began its emergency debate. In it, he pledged that he was pressing for a diplomatic solution but at the same time preparing militarily for "any contingency that might arise in Korea." He called North Korea's piracy a "wanton and aggressive act."[20]

U.S. Ambassador Arthur Goldberg called on the UN Security Council to act immediately lest the United States be forced to seek "other courses which the UN charter reserves to Member States," an implicit reference to military action. In his statement in the Security Council, Goldberg pointed out that the USS *Pueblo* had stayed at least thirteen nautical miles from the North Korean coast at all times—well clear of the twelve-mile territorial limit North Korea claimed. He provided evidence and charts showing the *Pueblo*'s position as 39 degrees 25.2 minutes North, 127 degrees 55.0 minutes East when it was approached by the first North Korean patrol craft. This location was 16.3 nautical miles from the nearest point of the North Korean mainland on the peninsula of Hodo and 15.3 nautical miles from the island of Ung-Do. Goldberg asserted that a North Korean submarine chaser that had intercepted the *Pueblo* had reported the *Pueblo*'s location as 39 degrees 25 minutes North, 127 degrees 56 minutes East, clearly in international waters. He recommended that the Security Council promptly call for the safe return of the *Pueblo* and her crew.[21]

The Soviet ambassador responded on behalf of North Korea that the dispatch of a spy ship into North Korean territorial waters was a violation of DPRK sovereignty and of international law; therefore, the detention of the vessel was within the jurisdiction of North Korea and not under the purview of the Security Council. He used the opportunity to argue that only the withdrawal of U.S. forces from South Korea could lead to peace in the Far East.[22]

In the meantime, the nuclear-powered aircraft carrier *Enterprise* was ordered into Korea's Eastern Sea, although no immediate military action was ordered against North Korea. This had a sobering effect on North Korea. Three days after the *Enterprise* steamed north, North Korean MiGs scrambled from the port of Wonsan trying to locate the aircraft carrier and its auxiliary vessels.[23]

The deployment of the *Enterprise* battle group unnerved Pyongyang; its deployment meant the United States was capable of massive retaliation with little warning. Throughout February 1968, North Korean General Pak frequently threatened to terminate the private meetings of the MAC senior members—the most promising discussions for the release and return of the *Pueblo* crew—unless the USS *Enterprise* and its escort vessels were removed from "Korean waters." He argued that the presence of the *Enterprise* posed a major threat and indicated a lack of American interest in solving the *Pueblo* issue through "peaceful means."[24] Despite his words, however, the carrier's presence helped to keep North Korea's attention focused on the negotiating process.

General Pak sent an informal message to UNCMAC, expressing North Korea's willingness to settle the incident through dialogue if the United States would negotiate rather than threaten North Korea through a show of force. The message also threatened that the United States would get "only bodies" if it used force in an attempt to free the crew. Admiral Smith responded that the United States would continue to pursue a prompt and peaceful solution to the problem, and requested an immediate meeting of the MAC to discuss resolving the problem.[25]

The U.S. proposal to deal with the *Pueblo* in the MAC struck a responsive chord among the North Koreans. At a January 31 dinner party in Pyongyang for a visiting Romanian Communist party delegation, Minister Kim Kwang Hyop complained that the United States had "illegally" brought the *Pueblo* case to the United Nations Security Council despite past precedents for handling similar cases through the MAC.[26] North Korea clearly interpreted President Johnson's dual approach—preparing militarily while pursuing diplomatic efforts at the United Nations—as alarming to its interests. It perceived that the United States was laying the multilateral diplomatic foundation for military retaliation. As an alternative, North Korea was eager to pursue a solution in the MAC.

On February 1, a State Department spokesman announced in Washington that the U.S. government accepted the North Korean proposal that the *Pueblo* crisis be handled through the MAC.[27] The process would involve two-way U.S.–North Korean talks, held under MAC auspices.

Confident that they had achieved their objective of bilateral U.S.–North Korean talks, the North Koreans put the United States on the defensive. Having received a level of reassurance from the previous week's give and take on the issue, North Korea could afford to do something offensive that might irritate the United States, but would not likely incite an attack.

On February 2, 1968, Kim Il Sung sent a laudatory letter to the North Korean Navy unit that had seized the *Pueblo*. Thanking the "men, noncommissioned officers and officers of the 661st Unit of the Korean People's Army" for achieving "brilliant results in the struggle to extend the military line of self-defense," he cited their capture of an "armed spy boat" and their assistance to "the armed guerrilla struggle of South Korean revolutionaries."[28] At a celebration of the twentieth anniversary of the founding of the Korean People's Army, Kim repeated that if the United States continued to try to solve the *Pueblo* incident by threats, "it would get nothing but corpses." He added that while North Korea did not want war, it was never afraid of it.[29]

Private Session Negotiations. In an atmosphere of bellicosity, the first U.S.-DPRK private meeting was convened on February 2, 1968. The two MAC senior members—Rear Admiral John V. Smith, U.S. Navy, and Major General Pak Chung Kuk, Korean People's Army—met in the Neutral Nations Supervisory Commission conference room at Panmunjom. Both senior members were accompanied only by a staff officer and a translator.

Admiral Smith stated the U.S. position that the *Pueblo* had not entered North Korean territorial waters and that the crew had committed no illegal act. He requested the immediate return of the ship and crew, in the interests of both sides. North Korean senior member General Pak assumed a listening mode. He attempted to draw out the complete UNC position on the issue by politely and repeatedly asking, "Please, tell me all that you want to tell me."

The UNC senior member reiterated that the *Pueblo* was in international waters all the time, offered no resistance, and violated no law. The *Pueblo* did not belong to the United Nations Command, Smith said, but he added that it was not really necessary to discuss whether or not the USS *Pueblo* belonged to the UNC when both sides had already agreed to negotiate for the return of crew "through the MAC channel in accordance with the past precedent."

Admiral Smith may have overlooked an important aspect of North Korea's reasoning. The question was no longer a matter of what forum would discuss the return of the crew; the point North Korea wanted to establish was that bilateral discussions between the United States and a country it claimed not to recognize were under way to obtain the release of the crew. Smith's remark that the *Pueblo* did not belong to the UNC was exploited by North Koreans who later insisted that these private talks on the *Pueblo* were in fact U.S.-DPRK bilateral negotiations rather than talks between MAC senior members. The hairline distinction between American military officers serving their nation as negotiators on behalf of the United States government and negotiating in their capacity as representatives of the United Nations Command is a significant one, requiring precision and intellectual discipline to maintain.

When Admiral Smith asked for the names of dead and wounded, General Pak declined, saying that "I have not yet been instructed to inform your side of it." Pak took the opportunity to urge the UNC to admit the intrusion and tender an apology. Despite the apparent stalemate, however, the closed-door session was both more casual and more businesslike than open meetings. The discussion was devoid of the usual propaganda.

When the second private meeting was held on February 4, General Pak complained that the United States not only failed to apologize for the intrusion by the *Pueblo* but also threatened North Korea by deploying "warships, fighters and bombers in the East Sea [the Sea of Japan]." He brought up Admiral Smith's remark at the previous meeting—that the *Pueblo* did not belong to the UNC—claiming that

Smith acknowledged that the *Pueblo* case should have been handled directly between the governments of the DPRK and the United States rather than through the MAC machinery. Pak suggested that the two governments should appoint appropriate representatives to bilateral talks rather than the MAC senior members. Admiral Smith asserted that although he was the senior member of the UNC side on the MAC, he also represented the U.S. government and had full authority to discuss the *Pueblo* case within the MAC. Again, no progress was made at this meeting.

A day later, newspapers across South Korea reported that North Korea had agreed to return the *Pueblo* crew upon receipt of an official "letter of apology" which the United States had agreed to sign, admitting the *Pueblo*'s intrusion into North Korean territorial waters. At a fourth private meeting, General Pak proposed formal closed meetings in which he would represent the government of the DPRK.

The ROK government had by now requested "open" MAC sessions with ROK representation, concerned that Admiral Smith and General Pak were appearing to negotiate bilaterally as equals. The ROK lodged a strong protest with the United States government for having held the fourth private meeting while the ROK government was still awaiting a U.S. response to its earlier demand for participation.[30]

The Republic of Korea's major concern was a possible misuse of this bilateral channel by the North Koreans to obtain de facto recognition of the Pyongyang regime or to enhance its prestige in the international community. The ROK feared the United States might play into North Korean hands, seeking a pragmatic solution to the problem at hand, at the expense of maintaining the legalistic structure that served less tangible interests of the wider alliance.

In response to the South Korean concern, President Johnson sent President Park a letter pledging U.S. continuing assistance for the security and defense of Korea. Johnson also dispatched special envoy Cyrus R. Vance to Seoul to ask for President Park's understanding of his efforts to have the *Pueblo* crew returned from North Korean custody.[31] Park and Vance met on February 12 and 15 and issued a joint communiqué. Their agreement to hold annual security conferences at the minister level to consult on defense and security matters of mutual interest and common concern marked the beginning of annual meetings referred to as Security Consultative Meetings, or SCMs. President Johnson further requested the Congress to approve an additional $100 million in U.S. military assistance for the ROK. The ROK government, in turn, toned down its criticism of the bilateral U.S.–North Korea negotiations behind closed doors at Panmunjom.

Several more private sessions were held at Panmunjom between the United States and North Korea throughout February 1968, with no result. The United States suggested convening an impartial inquiry into the *Pueblo* case after the return of the ship and crew, followed by a public announcement of its results, but the North Koreans refused. North Korea maintained its initial demand, presented at the January 24 MAC meeting, that the United States must tender a "letter of apology" for the return of the *Pueblo* crew.

Both sides maintained their respective positions throughout February and March, although the UNC made an unreciprocated concession, offering to provide an assurance to respect North Korea's claim for twelve-nautical-mile territorial waters. North Korea naturally accepted the assurance, but maintained its demand for an apology, seeing no reason to make a concession in return.

Starting in late January, North Korea kept American attention focused on the *Pueblo* crisis by periodically issuing crew members' "confessions." Following Commander Bucher's "confession, admitting the intrusion and espionage," Pyongyang Radio Service also broadcast one from the ship's "research officer," Lieutenant Stephen Robert Harris. Harris was reported to have stated, "I admit the crime committed by the armed espionage ship *Pueblo* and myself in conducting intelligence activities after having entered deep into the coastal waters of the Democratic People's Republic of Korea. I apologize for my crime." [32] Bucher and Harris were followed by many other crew members who made similar "confessions," almost daily, that the *Pueblo* "intruded deep into North Korean coastal waters and committed criminal acts of conducting espionage activities," apologizing and begging for leniency. From time to time, North Korea held press conferences to draw public attention to these so-called confessions.

In the private talks, North Koreans proposed to show the film of the alleged confessions by the *Pueblo* crew and threatened a trial of the crew members in accordance with North Korean law. Outside the MAC conference room during a February 14, 1968, meeting, with more than a hundred domestic and international newsmen in attendance, the North Koreans displayed photocopies of "confessions" by five officers of the *Pueblo* crew, including Commander Bucher.

The UNC had called the February 14 meeting to charge North Korea with twenty-one serious violations along the DMZ between January 23 and February 13, 1968, including four major armed attacks along the western sector of the DMZ. In the same session, the UNC again condemned the attempted assassination of President Park and offered to return the bodies of the North Korean Army commandos killed in the futile attempt.[33] The North declined. Reality was to conform with propaganda; in practice as well as theory, the commandos would be considered to be South Koreans the moment they went over the line.

North Korean senior member General Pak dropped his businesslike demeanor when the press was watching. He returned to delivering propaganda tirades:

> You are the sworn enemy of the Korean people that has been forcing the national split for as long as more than 20 years. We have never occupied your country the United States even for a single day, to say nothing of 20 years. However, you U.S. imperialist aggressors have been illegally occupying half of our country and committing all conceivable ruthless atrocities for more than 20 years, insisting upon the burglarious allegation that you have to occupy Korea because Koreans commit aggressive acts in Korea. . . . This is not the place to argue about the struggle of the South Korean people who are waging against you U.S. imperialist aggressors and your stooges . . . but a place to discuss matters relating to the implementation of the Armistice Agreement."[34]

Pak reiterated North Korea's now routine answer to UNC charges about the attempted assassination of President Park, saying that the incident had nothing to do with the armistice agreement. General Pak attempted to justify North Korea's seizure of the ship as a "resolute self-defense measure." He also claimed that the United States was taking advantage of the seizure of the *Pueblo* to make "full preparation for another war" and create a climate in which hostilities could be touched off "at any moment."[35]

During the February 14 MAC meeting, North Korea also took steps to outline the solution it sought to the crisis it had created. It displayed photographs of American aircraft that had been forced down in North Korea on March 6, 1958, and May 17, 1963, when they inadvertently flew into North Korean airspace. Their pilots had been returned after the United States provided receipts and letters of apology. These documents were displayed alongside photocopies of the "confessions" by the *Pueblo* crew. This was an unsubtle suggestion that the return of the *Pueblo* crew would be possible if the UNC followed these past precedents. The past precedents, however, involved unwitting intrusions over the line; the *Pueblo* had been forcibly seized in international waters. The distinction mattered considerably more to the Americans than to the North Koreans.

North Korea knew it had something substantial to bargain with—the lives of eighty-two innocent American servicemen. Absent military retaliation from the United States, which by mid-February seemed less likely, the North could count on receiving many benefits. It had distracted attention from its own treachery. It had embarrassed South Korea by showing how much more concerned Americans were about a small ship's crew than they were about attacks against civilians in South Korea's capital and an assassination attempt aimed at South Korea's president. The North stood in a position to persuade the strongest nation on Earth to apologize for a "crime" that both countries knew it had not committed. And it had created circumstances that might force bilateral ties with a superpower whose long-standing claim had been that the ROK was the only legitimate government on the peninsula, a point for which that superpower had sacrificed 40,000 lives in combat.

North Korea stood to achieve a great deal, and it had few real risks. Provoking military action, overplaying its hand, imperiling the health of the captives through a long delay, or losing diplomatic support from its friends and allies at the UN were potential pitfalls. Suggesting a means to resolve the crisis was therefore the logical next step.

At a private session held on the day after the highly publicized MAC meeting, the North Korean senior member presented the North's conditions for the release of the *Pueblo* crew. He said, "We will consider returning the crew only when your side apologizes and assures us that it will not commit such criminal acts again." North Korea wanted something similar to that of the May 15, 1964, letter of apology signed by the commander in chief, UNC, for the return of two U.S. Army helicopter pilots.

When he returned to the next private session, Admiral Smith told General Pak that the UNC would welcome resolution of the disagreement by an impartial international fact-finding organization, perhaps one named by the International Court, and that there could be no impartial inquiry while the crew was still being held by North Korea.

North Korea continued to demand a "letter of apology" since it was not in a hurry and did not fear retaliation. General Pak dismissed the third-party inquiry at the next meeting. He repeated the demand that North Korea would consider the return of the crew only if the proper apology and assurances were tendered on the basis of the "confessions" by the crew. General Pak played tapes of more "confessions" of the crew and said, "Don't expect the crew for nothing. Accept our proposal so that we can discuss concrete business-like matters for the return of crew." The UNC senior member maintained his position that no apology would be tendered.

One Carrot, Increasing Sticks. Within a week, Radio Pyongyang domestic service in Korean carried a *Rodong Sinmun* (North Korean Workers Party newspaper) commentary on "How the *Pueblo* case should be resolved." It made the following key points:

> The crewmen of the armed spy ship Pueblo are criminals caught in the act of committing a grave crime against our country. Therefore, they should be duly punished by the law of the DPRK. At present the crewmen . . . are repeatedly imploring the DPRK Government to pardon them leniently, while confessing and apologizing for their crimes. Recently, they [the U.S.] have even been spreading "public opinion" that they would investigate the true facts of the incident after the crewmen are returned, or that some international organization, for instance, the international tribunal, should be delegated to conduct such an investigation . . . . If the U.S. imperialists should refuse to abandon their present attitude, we will have no alternative but to take some other measures against their crewmen.[36]

On March 22, 1968, both Radio Pyongyang domestic service and the North Korean Central News Agency (KCNA) international service reported that the *Pueblo* crew under North Korean detention sent letters that "unanimously expressed thanks for the leniency of the DPRK government, said their health is good and they are receiving humanitarian treatment from the DPRK government," and stated that their confessions were "from the bottom of their hearts." The broadcast claimed that the crew asked the U.S. government to "admit the intrusion of the *Pueblo* into DPRK territorial waters and its espionage acts, . . . openly apologize to the DPRK government for this, and guarantee there will be no repetition of such hostile and aggressive acts." It closed by offering that the DPRK government "may deal leniently" should the U.S. government "tender an apology and give an assurance that it would not repeat similar acts."[37]

The DPRK pursued a two-track approach to increase pressure on American negotiators. In private sessions, they were unyielding: no progress was made throughout the month of March. At regular MAC meetings, with media present, the North Koreans claimed that the United States was using the *Pueblo* as a pretext to provoke another war in Korea. This approach ignored the fact that the North created the incident and held the key to its resolution. Nevertheless, the strategy restrained the United States from using force and compelled the United States to accept the North's terms.

North Korea Increases Tension. The North found additional ways to pressure the United States to accept its terms, increasing tensions along the DMZ and inciting hostilities that could not be resolved by the MAC. North Korea charged the UNC with four armed attacks and infiltrating well-trained "armed agents" across the military demarcation line during the latter half of March. They displayed what they claimed was captured equipment and played a "taped confession" of one of the agents allegedly captured by the North Koreans.[38] In reply, the UNC complained that North Korea failed to provide an agenda for that meeting, and said that if the alleged attacks had actually occurred, a joint observer team should investigate it in accordance with the armistice agreement. The North Koreans refused to participate in a joint observer team.

On April 13, 1968, North Korea demanded that a MAC meeting be held on April 17, again without providing an agenda. The next day, at about 11 P.M., on the eve of Kim Il Sung's birthday, North Korean infiltrators crossed into the UNC headquarters area and ambushed a truck carrying six UNC security guards. The UNC security guards were carrying only pistols, as prescribed by the armistice agreement. The North Koreans attacked them with hand grenades and machine guns. Two U.S. and two ROK security guards were killed; two others were wounded.

Immediately following this ambush, the UNC requested an investigation be conducted by a joint observer team, but the North Koreans retorted, "No provision of the armistice agreement permits that either side shall misuse the joint observer team in an attempt to cover up its criminal acts."[39] In his response to a UNC message protesting the North's refusal to conduct a joint investigation of this serious incident in the "heart of the Korean armistice," General Pak said, "it has nothing to do with our side."[40] General Smith stormed, "What I do not want from you is a tirade of loud, irrelevant North Korean Communist double-talk such as you are accustomed to dispense when you are backed into a corner."[41]

A period of trading allegations followed. North Korea charged the UNC with launching five major armed attacks across the military demarcation line between April 1 and 17, 1968, to preempt UNC charges against the North's attack on the UNC security guard truck in the MAC headquarters area. North Korean senior member General Pak brushed aside the UNC charge, explaining the attack as the "various guerrilla fights against the aggressors in South Korea by the patriotic people . . . [who] will burn you to death."[42] In an attempt to block the UNC's final statement, Pak threatened a walkout if the UNC made a long and "improper" final statement. The UNC closed the meeting by condemning North Korea's increasing violence, especially the North's April 14 ambush.

This MAC meeting lasted seven hours and twenty-two minutes, without a break—one of the longest MAC meetings. The North Koreans heard the UNC point, but had made a stronger one of their own. They could kill two Americans and two Korean security guards in the MAC headquarters area, only 1,000 meters from the conference hall, and not be called to account. To punctuate that point, and perhaps to remind the UNC that the fate of the *Pueblo* crew lay in their hands, North Korea's armed intrusions increased at every lull in discussions of the *Pueblo*.

On April 30, 1968, Army Major General Gilbert H. Woodward replaced Rear Admiral John V. Smith as the UNCMAC senior member and U.S. representative to the continuing private talks on the *Pueblo*. As his credentials were passed to the North Korean side, North Korea proposed that a MAC meeting be held on May 2, 1968, and the UNC accepted.

North Korea opened the meeting, saying that it had proposed the meeting to protest a UNC armed attack in the eastern sector of the DMZ on April 29. North Korean senior member Major General Pak warned that this type of incident might cause a "rapid chain reaction and cause the resumption of overall hostilities in Korea." General Woodward responded that it takes the efforts of both sides to make the armistice agreement work and protested against the North Korean acts of violence that had continued to increase in seriousness and number since October 1966.

For its part, the UNC charged North Korea with nine intrusions across the demarcation line and six incidents in which UNC forces were fired upon by North Korean automatic weapons between April 21 and May 1, 1968. The UNC also charged North Korea with ambushing a UNC patrol on April 27, 1968, killing one UNC guard and wounding two. General Pak stated that the armistice agreement had nothing to do with whether the U.S. "den of aggression" in South Korea was completely blown up, and that the "South Korean people" would wage a fiercer struggle against the United States in the future. This was more than ideological posturing; five months later, North Korean commandos infiltrated the Ulchin-Samchok area on the east coast of South Korea, about fifty miles south of the DMZ.

General Woodward attended his first private meeting with North Korean senior member General Pak on May 8, 1968. Woodward told Pak: "I am the senior member and represent the U.S. government [on the matter of the *Pueblo*] with full authority." General Pak presented a North Korean draft in which the U.S. government would: (1) acknowledge the validity of the confessions by the *Pueblo* crew and the evidence produced by the DPRK government that showed the *Pueblo* was seized by the Korean People's Army naval vessels in self-defense in the territorial waters of the DPRK, while conducting espionage against the DPRK, (2) apologize for espionage, (3) offer assurance that there would be no more intrusions by U.S. naval vessels, and (4) request the DPRK government's leniency for the crew.

There had been no retreat from the North's demands since the *Pueblo* was seized. Woodward, however, suggested subtle movement on the part of the United States. He noted Pak's demand, and repeated that the United States would note "confessions" by the crew, respect North Korea's twelve-nautical-mile territorial waters, and admit that the *Pueblo* was on an intelligence-gathering mission. Woodward offered to express regret if a third-party investigation proved that the *Pueblo* had entered North Korean waters.

The two met again twenty days later, but little progress was made because the UNC would not agree to the "document of apology and assurance" dictated by North Korea.

Pressuring North Korea in Return. In the meantime, MAC meetings were held as North Korea increased its incursions into South Korea while making blistering accusations against the United States. On May 17, North Koreans claimed they had apprehended four South Korean armed agents who crossed over the line, and charged the UNC with the alleged infiltration of "102 armed spy boats and fishing boats" into North Korean coastal waters since the previous MAC meeting. Line-crossing incidents increased throughout the spring and summer, with no less than eighty-four incursions reported that resulted in no less than eighty-six deaths.[43]

In the midst of the allegations, two stand out because, despite their similarity to the *Pueblo* circumstances, their relevance was never fully exploited. North Korea claimed that an ROK surveillance vessel had violated its territorial waters in the Western Sea (Yellow Sea),[44] and the UNC claimed that a North Korean intelligence vessel had became disabled while on an espionage mission near Cheju Island in South Korea. The UNC displayed photographs of the disabled seventy-ton espionage vessel, the dead and captured North Koreans, their equipment, and their weapons, including an 82mm recoilless rifle, a 40mm rocket launcher, and several anti-aircraft machine guns. The North Korean "agent boat" was carrying the flags of Japan, North Korea, China, and the ROK to provide cover for its true identity.[45]

The North deflected charges of espionage by showing no interest in the return of its own vessel or crew. It found it harder to assess UNC responses to the North's own charges. The North was probably troubled that ROK vessels had been listening in on North Korea. If the North actually believed what it charged—that the UNC was monitoring the North off shore, despite the difficulties the North had generated with the *Pueblo*—this showed a degree of allied resolve that the North had to find troubling.

Working toward Resolution. Major General Woodward and Major General Pak met in private session again on September 17, 1968. Pak repeated the North's demand that the U.S. government accept the May 8 draft statement. Signaling some flexibility, but at the same time requiring a modification from North Korea, Woodward asked whether North Korea would simultaneously release the *Pueblo* crew if he acknowledged "receipt" on the document prepared by North Korea. He insisted on "simultaneous release" of the crew, he said, and would be prepared to "acknowledge receipt" on the document with simultaneous release of the crew. General Pak understood a new possibility had been raised, but was probably perplexed by Woodward's insistence on simultaneity. Clearly irritated, Pak declared, "I already told you . . . sign the document for the crew."

Woodward complained that the May 8 draft did not say what would happen if it were signed. Pak responded that he would discuss specific arrangements for the return of crew if and when Woodward signed the document. General Woodward cautiously repeated that he would acknowledge "receipt" on the document, but he did not agree to sign the document. Accordingly, no agreement was reached at that meeting.

The two senior members met privately again on September 30. General Pak agreed to the "simultaneous release" that General Woodward had proposed, but reiterated the conditions for the release of crew and presented for General Woodward's signature a written document identical to the May 8 draft. General Woodward welcomed the North Korean agreement on simultaneity and asked how soon North Korea could release the *Pueblo* crew if he agreed to "acknowledge receipt on the document."

Woodward and Pak met again on October 10, 1968, to discuss further the "receipt" to be signed as well as the details involving the release of crew. General Pak noted General Woodward's agreement to sign the document prepared by North Korea, and proposed that: (1) the document be signed at the Neutral Nations Supervisory Commission conference room where the private meetings had been held, at 11:00 A.M., on the day crew was returned; (2) the document be signed in General Pak's presence with three photographers taking pictures of the event; (3) the crew must walk across the "Bridge of No Return" (Sach'on Bridge) two hours after the signing of the document; and (4) the whole operation would be conducted before the press. General Woodward replied that he would refer the procedures for the return of crew to his superiors, pointing out he planned to "acknowledge the receipt of the crew on the document prepared by North Korea, but not sign the document itself."

General Pak became agitated and exclaimed, "Whom are you fooling? No apology and no assurance—and no crew!" The meeting ended.

Two weeks later, North Korea proposed a MAC meeting, held on October 21. The North Koreans charged the UNC with launching armed attacks against North Korea across the demarcation line on three occasions and dispatching "armed spies" into North Korea on October 17. They also complained that the UNC had delayed the meeting for five days.[46]

The UNC in return charged North Korea with sixty-three separate armed intrusions since the previous MAC meeting and stated that thirty-eight North Korean intruders had been killed by the UNC forces since then. The UNC specifically protested the two most recent incidents in the joint security area and warned that the deliberate and hostile conduct of North Korean guards at Panmunjom had reached an unacceptable level. General Woodward stressed that steps must be taken to restore the proper conference environment.[47] The North Korean senior member, as usual, insisted that the UNC charges were all "fabrications to cover up the UNC's own guilt."

The two MAC senior members met privately on October 23, 1968, to continue discussion of the draft document. General Pak reiterated the North's demands and his strong objection to the U.S. proposal to "acknowledge the receipt of crew" on the draft document. General Woodward indicated his distaste for the document prepared by North Korea and urged Pak to reconsider the U.S. proposal. Pak questioned why Woodward wanted to write additional words on the document when everything was "already written on it." He held up the document and asked where the additional words would be placed. Woodward said he would write "acknowledge" on the face of the document, diagonally across the text. Pak angrily told him to come back to the meeting when he was ready to sign the document.

The UNC called for another private meeting, held on October 31, 1968, and asked General Pak if North Korea still objected to UNC procedures. The North Korean general asked his UNC counterpart if he had called the meeting "to waste time," and added, "If you don't sign, crew will pay. No alternatives." The meeting concluded in fifteen minutes. No private meetings were held throughout the month of November and the first half of December 1968.

In the meantime, North Korean armed intrusions and attacks across the demarcation line continued. The UNC charged North Korea with fifteen separate armed attacks against UNC personnel and guard posts in the DMZ and infiltration of armed intruders on twenty-five occasions between October 20 and November 3, 1968. Ten North Korean armed intruders had been killed in ensuing firefights.[48]

For its part, on November 5, North Korea charged the UNC with armed attacks on seven occasions between October 21 and November 3.[49] North Korea claimed, as usual, that the infiltration and armed attacks charged by the UNC were all fabrications to cover up the UNC's own crimes. They also charged the UNC with infiltrating some "1,550 armed spy boats and fishing boats" into North Korean coastal waters on eleven occasions since the previous MAC meeting and infiltrating two F-5A "fighter-bombers" into North Korean airspace on October

23, 1968.[50] It may be that North Korea's leaders concluded their seizure of the *Pueblo* had resulted in increased intelligence activities, not a reduction. This conclusion seems to have prompted their eagerness to settle the issue.

The elements of a resolution had been worked out between the two senior members, but the agreement was not brought to closure until the North thought it had gained all the advantages the situation might afford. That would include a more ambitious North Korean effort to foment revolution in the South.

The Ulchin-Samchok Commando Raid

On October 30, 1968, at about 2:00 P.M., North Korean commandos boarded an armed North Korean speedboat in Wonsan harbor and headed for South Korea. At about 11:30 P.M. that same day they landed on South Korea's eastern shoreline, in the Ulchin-Samchok area. By November 2, some 120 North Korean commandos, organized into fifteen-man teams, had landed in the vicinity of Ulchin and Samchok.

In the early morning of November 3, a group of the commandos entered the remote farming village of Kosu-dong and assembled all the villagers, about forty people, on the pretext of taking photographs. Instead of being photographed, however, the villagers were subjected to propaganda speeches exhorting them to support the North Korean Communist cause. The commandos handed out counterfeit South Korean currency and forced the villagers to sign application forms for membership in Communist organizations. While this was happening, a farmer returning home observed the unusual activity and tried to escape. The commandos caught him and killed him in front of the village, warning the other villagers that anyone who failed to cooperate would suffer his fate.

Despite this threat, a young villager wrote a message reporting the commando invasion and handed it to a woman who was selling eggs in the village. She in turn delivered the message to police about four miles away. Army and police units immediately took action; on their arrival at the village a gun battle broke out and three North Korean commandos were killed.

Two North Korean commandos were apprehended and provided useful information about the North's infiltration methods. They said a large number of young North Korean officers from their unit had received special insurgency training in techniques of ambush, night raids, and Tae kwon-do for about three months before being dispatched across the line. The commandos were all members of the 124th North Korean Army Unit, the same unit as the commandos sent to Seoul in January of that year to assassinate President Park.

The UNC requested a MAC meeting, held four days later, and opened the meeting by charging North Korea with infiltrating commandos into the Ulchin-Samchok area "to murder, torture, and kidnap in a 'suicidal' attempt to coerce South Korean citizens to support North Korean communism." The UNC described the subversion, terrorism, kidnapping, theft, and murder that were committed by North Korean commandos against innocent South Korean civilians in the area. General Woodward provided photographic and film evidence showing the infiltration area, testimony of local civilians, the atrocities committed, and the bodies of North Korean commandos. The film showed the two captured North Korean commandos describing their training in detail. Of 120 infiltrators, 107 were killed and seven were apprehended.[51]

True to form, the North Korean senior member stated that the North Korean commandos described by the UNC were an "uprising of South Korean patriots and revolutionary guerrilla units" and asserted that such UNC accusations had nothing to do with the Korean armistice agreement.[52]

The UNC replied that there was no support in South Korea for the North Korean cause, as demonstrated again by the conduct of South Korean civilians in the Ulchin-Samchok area, and warned against a serious miscalculation by the North Korean leaders in Pyongyang.

The Settlement. On December 17, 1968, a week after the MAC meeting in which Major General Woodward charged North Korea with the largest armed incursion of North Korean forces into South Korea in the history of the armistice, he met his North Korean counterpart privately to present a new UNC proposal. The crew of the *Pueblo* had been in captivity for almost eleven months. General Woodward proposed: (1) a receipt clause to read, "Simultaneously with the signing of this document, the undersigned acknowledges receipt of 82 former crew members of the *Pueblo* and one corpse" be inserted at the end of the document solely dictated by the North Korean government; and (2) the following statement be read into the record before the signing of the document to repudiate its contents and clarify that the document was signed for the sole purpose of freeing the crew:

The position of the United States Government with regard to the *Pueblo*, as consistently expressed in the negotiations at Panmunjom and in public, has been that the ship was not engaged in illegal activity, that there was no convincing evidence that the ship at any time intruded into the territorial waters claimed by North Korea, and that we could not apologize for actions which we did not believe took place. The document which I am going to sign was prepared by the North Koreans and is at variance with the above position, but my signature will not and cannot alter the facts. I will sign the document to free the crew and only to free the crew.[53]

General Pak asked for an hour's recess to report this new U.S. proposal to Pyongyang and receive further guidance. He must have thought there was a chance the offer could be accepted. He returned to the meeting soon thereafter and proposed the next meeting two days later.

When they met again on December 19, North Korea agreed to the procedure for the signing of the document as proposed by General Woodward, but General Pak argued that the U.S. statement (to be read into the record before the signing) could in no way alter the facts described in the document. General Woodward, he said, must affix his signature immediately above his signature block, not across the text of the document as he proposed earlier. North Koreans could live with a verbal U.S. repudiation of the document at a private session without the press so long as it was signed by the U.S. government representative for the world to see. A peculiar type of reciprocity had been devised wherein the United States and North Korea both asserted that the actions of signing the document and issuing the statement did not change the facts. That might well serve as a basis for agreement in any contentious negotiation.

The document signed by General Woodward on December 23, 1968, which was verbally repudiated before the signing, read:

TO THE GOVERNMENT OF THE DEMOCRATIC PEOPLE'S REPUBLIC OF KOREA

The Government of the United States of America,

Acknowledging the validity of the confessions of the crew of the USS *Pueblo* and of the documents of evidence produced by the Representative of the Government of the

Democratic People's Republic of Korea to the effect that the ship, which was seized by the self-defense measures of the naval vessels of the Korean People's Army in the territorial waters of the Democratic People's Republic of Korea on January 23, 1968, had illegally intruded into the territorial waters of the Democratic People's Republic of Korea,

Shoulders full responsibility and solemnly apologizes for the grave acts of espionage committed by the U.S. ship against the Democratic People's Republic of Korea after having intruded into the territorial waters of the Democratic People's Republic of Korea,

And gives firm assurance that no U.S. ships will intrude again in future into the territorial waters of the Democratic People's Republic of Korea.

Meanwhile, the Government of the United States of America earnestly requests the Government of the Democratic People's Republic of Korea to deal leniently with the former crew members of the USS *Pueblo* confiscated by the Democratic People's Republic of Korea side, taking into consideration the fact that these crew members have confessed honestly to their crimes and petitioned the Government of the Democratic People's Republic of Korea for leniency.

Simultaneously with the signing of this document, the undersigned acknowledges receipt of 82 former crew members of the *Pueblo* and one corpse.

> On Behalf of the Government of
> the United States of America
>
> Gilbert H. Woodward,
> Major General, United States Army
> 23 December 1968.[54]

General Woodward also signed the Korean version of the document. As had been agreed, on December 23, 1968, eighty-two *Pueblo* crew members led by Commander Bucher, and the remains of Seaman Hodges, were returned across the "Bridge of No Return."

The North Koreans believed they had won a clear victory. The North Korean Foreign Ministry spokesman said, "This means the ignominious defeat of the U.S. imperialist aggressors and constitutes another great victory for the Korean people." North Korea's Central News

Agency explained, "Today in Panmunjom, the historical place where the U.S. imperialist aggressors sustained a miserable defeat in the war against the Korean people fifteen years ago and, bending the knee before the Korean people, signed an instrument of surrender, focusing the attention of the people the world over once again as the U.S. imperialists knelt to the Korean people and apologized for the incident of the armed spy ship *Pueblo*."[55] The newspaper included the full text of the document signed by General Woodward *without* the receipt clause he insisted on inserting at the end of the document.

Washington could not have been satisfied with the way the issue had been resolved, but was relieved that it had, in fact, been resolved. Secretary of State Rusk pointed out that after the United States had "made every sort of reasonable offer, all of which were harshly rejected, we had come squarely up against a most painful problem: how to obtain the release of the crew without having this Government seem to attest to a statement which simply is not true." Rusk described the Woodward agreement as a "strange procedure. . . . Apparently the North Koreans believe there is propaganda value even in a worthless document which General Woodward publicly labeled false before he signed it," he commented. "If you ask me why these two contradictory statements proved to be the key to effect the release of our men," the American Secretary of State concluded, "the North Koreans would have to explain it."[56]

Nevertheless, Major General Woodward's agreement was welcomed with relief. Rusk commented, "There have been a few among us who counseled either violent reprisals, which could not save the men, or abject surrender to North Korea's demands. But the great majority of our people have kept their heads. And the crew has now been released in time to have Christmas with their loved ones." President Johnson said Woodward "carried out his difficult and successful assignment with distinction and has preserved the integrity of the United States while obtaining the release of the men of the *Pueblo*."[57]

Several years later, a Neutral Nations Supervisory Commission officer visiting the North Korean War Memorial Museum in Pyongyang saw on display an enlarged picture of the signed document, with a photo of General Woodward signing it. He made the interesting discovery that the North Koreans doctored the document by removing the last paragraph of the document—the "receipt clause" they had finally allowed General Woodward to insert at the end of the document.[58]

In the relatively peaceful month that followed the return of the

Pueblo crew, General Woodward and his North Korean counterpart were both given new assignments. Their final meeting on January 28, 1969, was a rare occasion for an exchange of reflections between negotiators of the two sides. Woodward told Pak he hoped Kim Il Sung had learned that he could not achieve his goals through violence, pointing out that North Korea's leaders had caused the deaths of more than 290 of their young people during the last seven months of 1968.[59]

A country that would sacrifice 290 young people merely to increase the negotiating stakes for a country that sought the safe return of eighty-two could not expect to win world admiration. Yet North Korea had ample reason to believe that seizure of the *Pueblo* had helped to refocus world attention on the Korean peninsula and to embarrass the United States. And they soon exploited another opportunity to pursue the same tactic.

The 1969 Shoot-down of a Naval Reconnaissance Aircraft

On April 14, 1969, North Korea proposed that a MAC meeting be scheduled for April 18. On Kim Il Sung's birthday, April 15, it shot down an unarmed U.S. Navy EC-121 reconnaissance flight, killing its crew of thirty Navy personnel and one marine. Like hundreds of planes before it, the EC-121 had been flying a routine reconnaissance track parallel to North Korea over the Sea of Japan. It was reported missing at about 2:00 P.M. At 3:55 P.M., Radio Pyongyang claimed that North Korea had shot down a U.S. aircraft that had intruded into North Korean airspace. The plane had been tracked at all times by U.S. radar and was never closer to the North Korean coast than forty-eight miles. When it was shot down it was ninety miles from shore.

The UNC sought guidance from Washington on how to proceed. After consideration of the options, Washington set aside the possibility of military retaliation. A similar decision had been taken in the case of the *Pueblo*, with the justification that retaliation might have endangered the crew. In the case of the EC-121, however, all thirty-one U.S. military personnel aboard had already been killed. The decision not to retaliate reassured, and emboldened, North Korea.

Washington instructed the UNC to proceed with the MAC meeting proposed by North Korea, and cautioned UNC representatives to be "calm, reasonable, and restrained." Washington also instructed the UNC to walk out of the meeting if the North Koreans seemed unresponsive to UNC protests of the shoot-down.[60] Especially given their behavior the year before, it is likely that the North Koreans called the April meeting knowing that they would shoot down the EC-121 on Kim Il Sung's birthday. Having requested the meeting, they had the prerogative to set the agenda for the meeting and to speak first.

The North Korean senior member, Major General Ri Choon Sun, opened the meeting by alleging routine armistice violations within the DMZ, making no reference to the EC-121 shoot-down. When it was his turn to speak, the American senior member, Major General James B. Knapp, USAF, charged North Korea with shooting down the unarmed U.S. aircraft while it had been flying a routine reconnaissance track over international waters. That flight path, he pointed out, was ninety miles from the North Korean coast and similar to the flight path of innumerable missions since 1950. He advised Ri that the proper course was to admit that North Korea had shot down the U.S. aircraft over international waters and to reassure the UNC that it would take appropriate measures to prevent similar incidents in the future.[61]

Major General Ri responded:

> You have just referred to a brigandish aggressive act of the U.S. Government which illegally dispatched a large-sized reconnaissance airplane on 15 April last for the purpose of conducting reconnaissance of the interior of our country. I, first of all, ask you: What country owns the EC-121 large reconnaissance airplane you have talked about?[62]

At that point, General Knapp and his party walked out of the conference room.[63] Ri had hoped to hear Knapp say the EC-121 belonged to the U.S. Navy, in which case he could argue the shoot-down was a bilateral issue between the United States and the DPRK.

In compliance with Washington's instruction, the UNC protest at Panmunjom had been mild and nonconfrontational. Although President Nixon had vociferously criticized President Johnson's earlier handling of the *Pueblo* incident, in this instance he pursued a similar approach. North Korea had tested the new administration and learned that there would be no retaliation for a direct attack on U.S. servicemen performing their duty in international airspace. President Nixon, however, in a clear show of resolve, ordered two aircraft carriers into the Sea of Japan and additional F-4s into the ROK—to protect U.S. reconnaissance flights that continued unabated, and unchallenged.[64]

Deprived by the American walk-out of an opportunity to use a

MAC meeting for a propaganda barrage, North Korea issued a "DPRK Government Statement" on April 23, 1969. It charged the United States intruded "deep into the territorial air of the DPRK to conduct hostile acts of espionage."[65] It objected, "On April 18, Nixon described it as if it were their right or a matter of course to conduct reconnaissance activities against our country, and said that reconnaissance flights against our country would continue in the future too." Finally, it warned, "If the reconnaissance planes of the U.S. imperialists intrude into the territorial air of our country, we will not sit with folded arms, but will take resolute measures for safeguarding our sovereignty."[66]

No MAC meetings were called by either side for four months after the UNC walk-out from the meeting on April 18, 1969. On August 14, a new UNC senior member, Major General Arthur H. Adams, USMC, met with North Korean Major General Ri. At that meeting the UNC complained North Korea had attacked UNC personnel and guard posts in the DMZ on four occasions since the April meeting. Twelve North Koreans had been killed in those attacks. The UNC also charged North Korea with infiltrations by sea on four occasions in June 1969, during which fourteen North Korean armed agents were killed and three more captured by the ROK defense forces.[67]

Major General Ri in turn criticized the UNC for walking out of the April 18 MAC meeting and said the EC-121 incident had nothing to do with the "main subject" of the meeting North Korea had called. The North Korean senior member went on to charge that the UNC had used the interval since the EC-121 incident to continue military efforts to provoke another war in Korea and reinforce its military hardware.[68]

The North Koreans had struck, ridiculed the UNC for flinching, and then complained that the UNC was shielding itself from the next blow.

The 1969 Shoot-down of an Army Helicopter

About 10:45 A.M. on August 17, 1969, an *unarmed* American observation helicopter (OH-23) on a routine training mission, with three U.S. personnel on board, crossed the Han River estuary (the western end of the DMZ) and entered North Korean airspace, where it was shot down. The UNC called for a MAC meeting that was held on August 21. The UNC senior member said he requested the meeting to discuss this "accidental, inadvertent, and purely unintentional" armistice violation and to make arrangements for the return of the personnel and helicopter. The UNC offered to study any proposal that North Korea might have to effect the release of the U.S. personnel involved in the accident.[69]

The North Korean senior member, Major General Ri, accused the UNC of distorting the facts concerning the helicopter incident. Ri said that the UNC illegally infringed upon North Korean sovereignty and infiltrated a military aircraft deep into North Korea's territorial airspace, where it was shot down by North Korean forces in self-defense. He criticized the UNC for its "failure to apologize" to North Korea for this "criminal act." When the UNC reiterated its position on the helicopter incident, Ri scolded, "Go back, consult with your commander and come back to this table when you get unmistakable instructions to make a clear-cut answer."[70]

About a week later, the UNC asked North Korea to provide information about the physical condition of the three U.S. personnel aboard the helicopter that had been shot down. Ri reported that Captain Crawford and Specialist 4 Hofstatter were "heavily wounded," that Warrant Officer Loepke was "lightly wounded," and that all three were receiving medical treatment.

The UNC senior member repeated that he was ready to consider any reasonable proposal the North Koreans might have for the return of the three wounded men. Although he had ignored the UNC request earlier, Ri now responded with points that closely paralleled those made by the DPRK after the capture of the *Pueblo* and its crew. In his closing statement regarding the return of helicopter crew, Ri said:

> Your side should state its real aim for having flown the military aircraft into our territorial air, frankly admit the criminal act of having dispatched the military aircraft into our side and seriously violated our sovereignty in flagrant violation of the Armistice Agreement, apologize to our side for it, and submit a document guaranteeing in a responsible manner that you will not commit such violations of the Agreement again. If your side writes and submits such a document, following the past practice, we will be ready to consider your request as far as the return of your pilots who are in our hands is concerned.[71]

The UNC on September 2 transmitted the following message, through the hotline at Panmunjom, in response to the North Korean demand:

> [We] are prepared to submit the document to your side simultaneous with release to us of the three crew members of the H-23 helicopter.[72] The document would accord with the facts as we have stated them. It would declare that the helicopter was on a military mission, and that it became lost and therefore flew into your territory. It would acknowledge the helicopter violated the airspace under the control of the Korean People's Army and violated the Armistice Agreement. It would contain an expression of regret and a statement that measures will be taken to prevent a recurrence of an incident of this kind.

The UNC argued:

> It is preposterous to think that a three-man, unarmed helicopter would have flown into your territory willfully or with any hostile intent. We know this, you know it, and the whole world knows it. If you wish to propose the language of a statement which accords with the facts as we have stated them, we will be prepared to consider a written proposal from your side. In the meantime, if you continue to detain the crew members and if there is a deterioration in the condition of the wounded, the responsibility in the eyes of the American public and the world is yours. We await your reply.[73]

In its opening statement at the next MAC meeting, the UNC complained that the North Koreans had not provided terms or conditions for the release of the three wounded U.S. personnel. The North Korean senior member reiterated that North Korea would consider the matter of returning three crew members upon receipt of a document. He stated: "Your side should frankly admit the criminal act of having dispatched the military aircraft into our territorial airspace, flagrantly violating the Armistice Agreement and seriously infringing upon our sovereignty, apologize to our side for it and write and submit a document guaranteeing in a responsible manner that it will not commit again such violations of the Agreement." He warned that "the UNC should not confuse this 'document' with the receipt to be written in the case of the receipt of the pilots." [74]

More than a month passed without resolution. In the meantime, on October 18, North Korean intruders ambushed a UNC police truck in the DMZ's U.S. second division sector, killing all four American soldiers aboard the vehicle. The UNC called the next MAC meeting and charged the North Koreans with the armed attack, committed in broad daylight. The UNC demanded that North Korea admit its crime, punish those responsible, and apologize to the UNC. The North Korean senior member ignored the charge by simply stating that the incident had nothing to do with North Korea.[75]

Six private meetings were held to negotiate the language of the document demanded by North Korea. At the fifth private meeting, on November 24, a final agreement was reached on a text. At the sixth private meeting, on December 3, 1969, the UNC senior member signed the "document of apology" demanded by North Korea, and the crew members were released.

North Korea exploited a lack of patience and a concern for U.S. lives whenever U.S. military personnel were in North Korean custody. By getting American officials of the UNC to accept humiliating language, they won propaganda advantages in their own society, suppressing those who might speak out for freedom, and they won some measure of peculiar admiration among the world's anti-American governments. This in turn undermined UN support for UNCMAC, and for the U.S.-ROK military alliance.

The Panmunjom Axe Murders

The world may never know whether the constant ratcheting up of violence against the UNC was planned in advance in Pyongyang and executed by North Korea's military in disciplined fashion; or whether the military creatively seized opportunities to implement tactics that had general approval in Pyongyang. Some of the incidents seemed unplanned, even driven by moments of ideological passion. But in the longer historical view, even emotional outbreaks seem to have fit into a series of ever-increasing steps to undermine the UNC and to press for the withdrawal of deterrent forces. Perhaps this was merely the North's astute ability to use opportunities when they arose; perhaps it was the execution of a well-formed plan.

At about 10:30 A.M., August 18, 1976, a UNC work party consisting of five South Korean workers, three UNC security officers, and a seven-man security force arrived in the vicinity of a UNC checkpoint east of the Sach'on Bridge, familiarly known as the Bridge of No Return. They intended to prune a poplar tree that obstructed observation between two UNC checkpoints. Shortly after the work began, two North Korean security officers and about nine North Korean security guards arrived. One of the North Korean security officers asked Captain Arthur G. Bonifas what he was doing. When Captain Bonifas explained that the work party was pruning the tree, the North Korean officer remarked "good." The work continued with some North Korean guards offering suggestions on how the tree should be pruned.

At about 10:50 A.M., the North Korean officer told Captain Bonifas to stop the work. An argument between the officers of the two sides followed, during which the North Korean officer threatened the UNC personnel. Bonifas ordered the South Korean workers to continue pruning the tree. The North Korean officer then tried to direct the South Korean workers to stop. When his instructions were ignored, the North Korean officer dispatched a guard across the Sach'on Bridge to the North Korean barracks.

Shortly thereafter, about twenty additional North Korean guards arrived at the scene. The North Korean officer took off his watch, wrapped it in a handkerchief, and placed it in his pocket. Bonifas was busy pruning the tree and did not notice this warning. The North Korean officer approached him, shouted "kill," struck him, and knocked him to the ground. Five other North Korean guards jumped on Bonifas while he was down, beating him. North Korean guards, retrieving clubs from the back of their vehicle, turned on the remaining UNC personnel. The UNC guards tried to disengage, but the North Korean guards continued their attack.

Some of the North Korean guards picked up axes that had been used by the South Korean workers and used them in the attack. As in previous North Korean attacks, individual UNC personnel were isolated from their main party and set upon by numerically superior North Korean forces. This unprovoked attack resulted in the deaths of two officers, Captain Arthur George Bonifas and First Lieutenant Mark Thomas Barrett. Their heads were brutalized beyond recognition. Ten other UNC personnel were wounded.[76] For the first time since the armistice agreement had been signed, security personnel had been killed in the joint security area. The savagery of the attack was also unparalleled.

The UNC proposed a MAC meeting to protest the murders. North Korea declined on grounds they had already asked for a meeting of security officers to discuss the incident. The UNC objected to North Korea's obvious attempt to delay the meeting and downgrade its significance by deferring the matter to a security officers' meeting, and demanded a MAC plenary meeting.

General Richard Stilwell, the UNC commander in chief, sent a message to Kim Il Sung saying that a delay was unacceptable. He said that in view of the "unprecedented murders of the UNC joint security force that morning," he and his representative, the UNCMAC senior member, would proceed to Panmunjom to attend the meeting on August 19, 1976, as proposed, and expected the North Korean senior member to be there.[77]

About eighteen minutes before the MAC meeting, the North Korean senior member, General Han Ju Kyong, proposed that an on-the-spot security officers' meeting be held at noon and the MAC meeting be held afterwards. The UNC senior member, Rear Admiral Mark P. Frudden, USN, counterproposed that the security officers' meeting and the 379th MAC meeting be held concurrently, and General Han accepted that arrangement.[78]

The UNC opened the August 19, 1976, MAC meeting by reading Stilwell's strongly worded protest addressed to Kim Il Sung. Admiral Frudden charged the North Koreans with "an unprovoked act of severe hostility," one of the most blatantly brutal acts ever committed under the armistice. He said,

> Never before in the twenty-three years since the cease-fire was formally signed has there been the outright and brutal murder of Joint Security Area security force personnel. This was not the eruption of an unplanned argument. It was a deliberate murder of two UNC personnel who, while engaged in routine maintenance functions of a type your personnel often perform, were attacked unmercifully by a numerically superior force, wielding axes and clubs. I ask your assurance that an incident such as this will not occur again.

With General Stilwell looking on, Frudden told his North Korean counterpart that the UNC commander in chief had personally ordered him to pass his formal protest to the supreme commander of the Korean People's Army, Kim Il Sung.[79] Admiral Frudden related the circumstances of the incident, using photographs showing the brutal acts committed by the North Korean guards, and warned that such belligerent acts could not be tolerated.[80]

General Han took the position that their security guards acted in self-defense "to protect themselves from a premeditated onslaught by an overwhelming force of your side." He also claimed that five North

Korean guards were injured, referring to some of them as "heavily wounded." He made the usual North Korean demand at the end of his statement that the UNC punish those who organized and commanded the latest "provocation," expel them from the joint security area, and make an assurance that the UNC would not commit such provocations in the future.[81]

The North Koreans did not seem to expect the United States to take strong action in response to the murders. But rather than simply calling a routine MAC meeting to protest the murder, General Stilwell argued the UNC needed to demonstrate that it saw the North Korean violation as a matter of grave concern. To do otherwise, he believed, would invite additional provocative behavior. Stilwell believed the North Koreans must especially be held to high standards in the joint security area, if only to indicate UNC respect for the armistice itself. He was determined to demonstrate resolve, and told his staff, "I want to cut the damn tree down."[82] He decided to use U.S. Army engineers, escorted by U.S. security forces and ROK special forces, to accomplish the task.

Stilwell's tree-cutting operation was dubbed Operation Paul Bunyan, after the mythical American lumberjack. During the operation, U.S. and ROK forces were put on increased readiness alert and the U.S. government deployed squadrons of F-111 and F-4 aircraft to South Korea for temporary stationing. B-52 flights were staged and the carrier USS *Midway* and her task group of auxiliary vessels weighed anchor for Korean waters. In the early morning of August 21, 1976, the UNC work force, consisting of U.S. Army engineers, escorted by U.S. soldiers and ROK special forces, entered the joint security area "to cut the damn tree down."[83]

The North Koreans were notified through the MAC hotline that the UNC work party would enter the joint security area (JSA) "peacefully" to complete the work left unfinished by the UNC work detail. The work party would remove the tree obstructing the field of vision between the two UNC checkpoints—and leave the JSA immediately upon completion of this task. The UNC message concluded, "As long as this UNC work party is not subjected to attack, there will be no violence."[84]

North Korea took Stilwell seriously. When the UNC work force entered the JSA, no North Korean security guards were in their guard posts along the road leading to the tree. About 25 to 30 North Korean guards watched from the east end of the Bridge of No Return, and 150 North Korean soldiers were seen fifty meters north of the bridge, but they stayed clear of the JSA. The North Koreans stayed away the entire time the UNC work force worked. Operation Paul Bunyan was completed in less than an hour.[85]

About two and a half hours later, at 11:00 A.M., August 21, the North Korean senior member sent a message to the UNC senior member asking for a meeting in the MAC conference room in the JSA at noon so that he could "quickly" deliver a reply from the North Korean supreme commander to the commander in chief of the UNC's protest message. The UNC agreed and held a MAC senior members' private meeting at noon on August 21, 1976. Upon opening the meeting, the North Korean senior member said that he was instructed by the supreme commander of the Korean People's Army to convey a message to the commander in chief of the United Nations Command:

> It was a good thing that no big incident occurred at Panmunjom for a long period. However, it is regretful that an incident occurred in the Joint Security Area, Panmunjom this time. An effort must be made so that such incidents may not recur in the future. For this purpose both sides should make efforts. We urge your side to prevent the provocation. Our side will never provoke first, but take self-defensive measures only when provocation occurs. This is our consistent stand.[86]

General Han requested that this reply be delivered to the commander in chief of the UNC "at the quickest possible time."

Having dutifully conveyed the message of regret from Kim Il Sung, the North Korean senior member could not keep from adding a complaint of his own about the "provocation which your side committed this morning" in the JSA, referring to Operation Paul Bunyan. He requested that such "provocation" would not recur. The UNC admonished him not to bring up anything other than the message from the North Korean supreme commander at this time. The meeting adjourned, having lasted merely thirteen minutes.[87] Until a North Korean submarine ran aground on September 19, 1996, and dispatched a team of commandos on a killing spree across South Korea, the axe murders were the only North Korean acts of violence that resulted in a statement from the North that could be described as apologetic.

It was also the first time that Kim Il Sung himself answered a protest made by the commander in chief of the UNC. This might indicate that the murders were not premeditated—that they resulted from a breakdown in discipline. The apology could conceivably indicate that North Korea felt a sense of shame over the savagery of the attack, but the decision to apologize was a good tactical move as well. In both the axe murders and the 1996 submarine incident, it was clear to the North Koreans that their own interests would be advanced by a statement of regret. In the case of the axe murders, they had reason to fear military retaliation; in the case of the submarine incident, they had reason to fear a cutoff of food aid. They needed to restore the status quo ante, and they took action to do so.

Doing so was not so easy as the North expected. At the MAC meeting of August 25, the UNC senior member remarked that the UNC considered the North Korean supreme commander's expression of "regret" and his remarks on a joint effort in the JSA to preclude future incidents a positive but insufficient step. He called for punishment of those North Korean guards responsible for the murders and demanded assurances of the safety of UNC personnel in the joint security area.[88]

The North Korean senior member replied that the North Korean position on the issue had been clearly expressed in Kim Il Sung's message of August 21 to the commander in chief of the UNC and repeated the key points of that message.[89] The UNC senior member continued to demand that North Korea punish those responsible for the axe murders.[90]

North Korea had a proposal at the ready. The North Korean senior member recommended changing the security arrangement in the JSA to separate all military personnel, including security guards (with the exception of the MAC members and their staff), by the military demarcation line. He added that the new security arrangement would force each side to have guard posts only in its respective portion of the JSA. He concluded by stating that detailed questions regarding this proposal could be referred to the MAC secretaries meeting.[91] In other words, the North was willing to improve security in the joint security area, but the North Korean senior member did not want a visible role in making such concessions.

An unquestionable show of force by the United Nations Command in response to North Korean provocation, the firm determination to take the requisite risks, the willingness to augment U.S. forces, and a reaffirmation of rights and prerogatives within the JSA were responsible for the North Koreans' more positive attitude. The UNC stand compelled North Korea to seek a negotiated settlement of the crisis rather than risk escalation of conflict.

The MAC secretaries held six sessions from August 31 to September 6, 1976. At these meetings, the North Koreans were business-like, straightforward, and eager to reach early agreement. At the sixth session, both MAC secretaries signed the "Supplement to the Agreement on the MAC Headquarters Area, Its Security and Its Construction." By September 11, the North Koreans had removed their four guard posts and barrier drop-gates in the UNC portion of the JSA. Because the famous Bridge of No Return now fell in the UNC side, the new arrangement also required the North Koreans to construct a new road into the JSA from the northwest, which they did. For the first time in two decades, the North Koreans agreed to have a joint observer team supervise a new survey of the military demarcation line and the placement of markers.

In an interview with the Japanese newspaper *Mainichi Shimbun* on November 27, 1976, President Kim Il Sung scrambled to regain some of the ground lost by the axe murders. He offered the following version of the incident:

> The tree had been standing at the same place for over 20 years. The security guards from each side stood guard, facing each other for many years, but the tree had not obstructed observation. The U.S. forces tried to cut down the tree, though our guards did not permit that. When our soldiers stopped them an American soldier took an axe from a South Korean worker and threw it at our soldiers. One of our men was hit by the axe thrown by the American soldier, and his nose started bleeding. Our soldier threw back the axe and it hit an American soldier and he fell down. "Confused fighting" then broke out between the two sides; the South Korean soldiers and workers all ran away. The fighting was between our four guard personnel and American soldiers. Two Americans were killed and several of our guard personnel were wounded, but no one, on our side, was killed.[92]

Following the axe murders, and perhaps because a new American president had been elected, North Korea refrained from inciting incidents along the DMZ. The MAC experienced the longest lull between meetings since the armistice was signed in July 1953. President Kim Il Sung welcomed President Jimmy Carter's campaign pledge of a unilateral withdrawal of U.S. ground forces from South Korea. Hoping to preserve an opportunity, North Korea maintained a far less hostile attitude toward the UNC and the United States in its media, and it pursued a generally more businesslike approach on armistice issues. But accidents happen.

The 1977 Helicopter Shoot-down

In the early morning of July 14, 1977, a U.S. Army CH-47 helicopter with four crew members left its base in P'yongtaek, south of Seoul. It headed east to provide transportation support for an ROK Army unit deployed along the eastern sector. On its way, the pilot became disoriented and flew over the northern boundary of the DMZ at 9:55 A.M. The pilot thought he heard the metallic sound of an engine malfunction and landed to check the engine. After he landed, turned the engine off, and let the crew out of the helicopter, he saw armed North Korean soldiers and civilians approaching. The crew returned to the helicopter as fast as possible, the pilot started the engine, and the helicopter started its ascent. North Korean soldiers fired on the helicopter. The pilot was hit and the helicopter crashed into the Nam-dae-ch'on River at about 10:10 A.M. Three crew members died and one was wounded.

At 1:40 P.M. that day, the UNC called for a MAC meeting to be held at 6:00 P.M. that evening. A little over an hour later, the UNC sent another message to the North Korean side, explaining that a UNC CH-47 helicopter had gone down north of the DMZ. The message said there were indications that it was forced down by North Korean fire during an "unintentional intrusion" of North Korea's airspace and requested that the crew and helicopter be returned immediately to UNC authorities. It also expressed the UNC's deep concern about the "regrettable incident."

While this message was being transmitted to North Korea, Radio Pyongyang ominously reported that a U.S. military helicopter "deeply intruded into North Korea across the DMZ on the eastern sector of the front." The report said the U.S. military helicopter had been shot down by Korean People's Army "artillery fire," and that three crewmen had died but one was captured alive. The report described the incident as an "illegal intrusion" in violation of the armistice agreement by an "armed" U.S. military helicopter."[93]

The White House immediately released a statement that the helicopter incident was "unintentional and regrettable." President Carter's spokesman explained, "We are trying to let [North Korea] know that we realize the mistake was made by the crew in going into the DMZ. . . . Our primary interest is in having the incident not escalate into a confrontation and to account for the crew members."[94] It was unprecedented for the president of the United States to tender an apology for a U.S. military aircraft's intrusion into North Korean airspace, especially in advance of discussions with the North Koreans. The routine practice would have been for the UNC senior member to explain the situation during a MAC meeting. North Korea readily understood the significance of the White House gesture. As an indication of its appreciation for the high-level attention the matter had received in Washington, Pyongyang responded swiftly. In less than twenty-four hours, the North Koreans provided full details of the "unfortunate incident."

North Korea also proposed that the MAC meeting proposed by the UNC for 6:00 P.M., July 14, be held two days later, at 11:00 A.M. Not knowing that North Korea was preparing to return the survivor and the bodies at this meeting, the UNC expected the worst, and asked twice for an earlier meeting. The UNC sought to discuss the incident and request an early return of the crew. North Korea responded to the UNC pressure by sending a message at midnight on July 14, informing the UNC that three crew members had died but one was wounded and receiving medical treatment.

On the next morning, the UNC again complained about the delay of the meeting, requested the return of the crew at the next meeting, and asked for the name of the survivor. North Korea provided the name of the survivor, Warrant Officer C. M. Schwanke.

The following day a North Korean guard asked a UNC guard if the UNC was prepared to receive the crew member on July 17, hinting that his release was imminent. North Korea followed with a statement on Radio Pyongyang:

At about 0955 hours, 14 July, a CH-47 helicopter belonging to the U.S. forces . . . intruded deep into North Korea airspace, crossing the MDL on the eastern sector. North Korean anti-aircraft gunners fired "warning fire" at the enemy helicopter which was compelled to land at a field in Kosong county [North Korea]. North Korean soldiers repeatedly made a signal to the enemy helicopter to stop there to be investigated, but the helicopter refused to do so and started to take off and fly. North Korean soldiers were compelled to fire again at the helicopter and it was brought down at about 10:08 A.M., 14 July. Two crew members were crushed while attempting to escape, another crew member in the helo died from shock, and another was wounded but survived, who is now being treated in a North Korean Army hospital. Whether it was an "intentional or unintentional" intrusion of the U.S. forces helicopter into the area of our side, if they had complied with the demand of our side and had not attempted to flee, after they landed in the area of our side at the warning firing of the anti-aircraft gunners of the Korean People's Army, such "unfortunate" incident would not have occurred. The "unfortunate" incident entirely resulted from the errors of the military personnel of the U.S. side. The U.S. side should take appropriate measures to ensure that such incidents would not occur again.[95]

At the MAC meeting of July 17, 1977, the North Korean senior member, Major General Han, said, "We are going to settle the incident leniently so that a complicated situation will not be created." "Taking into consideration your side's admission and expression of regret," Han concluded, "we declare that we are ready to deliver the survivor and the bodies of your side, proceeding from our humanitarian stand." The UNC senior member, Rear Admiral Warren C. Hamm, Jr., USN, responded that the UNC was prepared to receive the crew.

General Han pointed out that no condition had been attached to the return of the crew; the North simply asked for a receipt. Warrant Officer C. M. Schwanke and the remains of three deceased crew members were returned to the UNC through the secretaries meeting at about 7:20 P.M., July 16, 1977. Koreans involved in the transaction noticed that the remains were returned in very fine coffins, the best that some of them had ever seen.

Admiral Hamm made the following press statement after the return of the crew:

> We welcome the prompt North Korean response to our request for the return of the crew of our helicopter which unintentionally entered North Korean territory but we deplore the loss of life and the use of force against an unarmed and inadvertent intrusion. However, it is encouraging that the matter was handled by both sides in a manner consistent with the armistice agreement.[96]

In retrospect, North Korea's handling of the CH-47 intrusion is explained by Kim Il Sung's tenacious pursuit: the removal of U.S.

troops from the Korean peninsula. As long as there was hope that Carter might order the withdrawal, North Koreans at Panmunjom maintained quiet discipline. They abstained from delivering propaganda harangues at MAC meetings for 300 days. Harangues resumed, however, after President Carter announced in July 1978 that the withdrawal of U.S. ground forces from Korea would be held in abeyance. North Korea returned to familiar charges that the United States, as the main obstacle to Korea's "peaceful" reunification, had an obligation to negotiate directly with Pyongyang to replace the Korean armistice agreement with a peace treaty.

The Attempted Shoot-down of an Air Force Reconnaissance Plane

In the midst of this period of renewed anti-American rhetoric, another crisis occurred. At 4:34 P.M. on August 26, 1981, North Korea fired an SA-2 surface-to-air missile at an unarmed SR-71 "Blackbird" reconnaissance aircraft, from a North Korean missile site in the vicinity of Chokta-ri on North Korea's Ongjin peninsula. At the time, the SR-71 was in international airspace south of the Five Island Groups under UNC and ROK control in the Western Sea (Yellow Sea).

The UNC called for the MAC meeting held on September 1, 1981, and opened the meeting. The UNC senior member, Rear Admiral James G. Storms III, USN, said that he was directed by the commander in chief, United Nations Command, to charge North Korea "with a premeditated and unprovoked act of aggression against the UNC."

According to the UNC, North Korea, in June 1981, deliberately deployed an SA-2 missile launching site near Chokta-ri with the specific intent of attacking unarmed UNC reconnaissance flights, having full knowledge of both the flight path and the frequency of flights. Had North Korean SA-2 missiles shot down this unarmed UNC reconnaissance aircraft on a routine mission in international airspace, Admiral Storms said, the Korean peninsula would have been brought to the brink of a major confrontation—a confrontation that would have been precipitated by North Korea's hostile acts. He further warned, "the United Nations Command will take whatever measures are necessary to ensure the safety of our aircraft and crew and the UNC will react *against the source* [emphasis added] of any future such attacks if North Korea chooses to again attack any aircraft under UNC control in airspace in which UNC aircraft are entitled to fly." In his closing remarks, the UNC senior member demanded that North Korea conduct a thorough investigation of this unprovoked attack, punish those responsible, and ensure that such hostile acts would not recur in the future.[97]

General Han responded that the SR-71 "intruded into North Korean airspace to carry out espionage activities." He denied that North Korea had fired missiles at the aircraft, saying the UNC "fabricated the absurd incident" to slander and defame North Korea at the conference table.[98] The North Korean general further said, "In fact, it is your customary practice that you commit provocation against others first and charge others with provocation before the world public." His remark reflected a tactic the North Koreans had used during several incidents—using a counteraccusation to cover what North Korea itself had done.

In his closing statement, General Han complained again that the United States had revoked its plan to withdraw its troops from South Korea "to realize [its] wild design to invade the northern half of the Republic [North Korea]." He demanded that the UNC stop augmenting U.S. forces with up-to-date military equipment, cease military exercises of all kinds and aerial reconnaissance by SR-71s, and withdraw U.S. forces and nuclear weapons from South Korea. For its part, the UNC limited its presentation to a single topic: the North Korean missile firing at the SR-71 flight in international airspace over the Western Sea.

The Rangoon Bombing

Rangoon, Burma, was South Korean President Chun Doo Hwan's first stop on an eighteen-day visit to six Asian and Pacific capitals in 1983. On October 9, he planned to join members of his cabinet at the Burmese Martyrs' Mausoleum for a wreath-laying ceremony. His motorcade was behind schedule, however, partly because the Burmese foreign minister was delayed in traffic. The ROK's ambassador to Rangoon, however, made it through the traffic and arrived on time. When Ambassador Lee Kai Chul arrived at the shrine, three North Korean Army officers mistook him for President Chun. The terrorists triggered a remotely controlled device causing a massive explosion that destroyed the wooden pavilion built for the occasion and shook the mausoleum. Four South Korean cabinet ministers and thirteen other high ranking dignitaries were killed; forty-eight others were wounded.[99] In cities and towns across South Korea, tens of thousands of grieving and angry Korean citizens staged rallies to call for retaliation against North Korea.

An initial investigation conducted by the Burmese government concluded:

- Three North Koreans, whom Burmese authorities tried to arrest after the incident, attempted to commit suicide with hand grenades, a familiar tactic of North Korean infiltrators in the ROK.
- A North Korean delegation had previously attended a ceremony at the shrine to learn in advance where ROK officials would stand.
- The detonating device used and incriminating items captured from the suspects were manufactured in North Korea and similar to those carried by other North Korean infiltrators apprehended in the ROK.
- A North Korean vessel had docked in Rangoon days before the incident and was suspected of off-loading the terrorists.

The Burmese government concluded that there was strong circumstantial evidence that North Korea had been involved in the attempted assassination of ROK President Chun.

ROK government officials repeatedly requested that the UNC call a MAC meeting to lodge a strong protest against the Rangoon bombing. But conclusive evidence to prove North Korean responsibility was not yet available, and there was no precedent for MAC involvement in an incident off the peninsula. UNCMAC declined to ask for a meeting. North Korea accordingly seized the opportunity to call the MAC meeting itself, and UNCMAC sought a delay of a week in hopes that better evidence of North Korean responsibility might be available before then.[100] UNC strategy for the MAC meeting of October 31, 1983, was that if the North Koreans brought up the Rangoon incident at the meeting, the UNC would say that the incident was still under investigation but the weight of available evidence pointed toward North Korea's involvement.[101]

Such restraint provided North Korea with an opportunity. The North Koreans claimed that they called the meeting "to straighten out the situation created in Korea by the South Korean military fascist element that contrived the Rangoon explosion in an attempt to extricate itself from the crisis—to divert elsewhere the people's resentment and resistance." The North Koreans complained that ROK forces were placed on alert and South Koreans were openly talking about retaliation for the Rangoon incident. They warned that they were watching for any provocative acts by the ROK.[102]

North Korea was able to call the next meeting "in connection with your side's recent frenzied acceleration of nuclear war preparations in South Korea, which is straining the situation to the extreme." The North complained that the United States had deployed "an additional 248 nuclear bombs in South Korea," quoting the *Washington Post* as its source.[103] Finally, it demanded U.S. removal from South Korea of all the "illegally introduced" weapons including a total of "1,000 nuclear weapons."[104]

North Korea might well have needed the meeting to ascertain likely ROK and U.S. reaction to the report on the Rangoon bombing released by the government of Burma on November 2, 1983. The UNC senior member, Rear Admiral F. Warren Kelley, not only read into the record the entire text of the Burmese official report on the incident, but also presented additional data indicating that North Korea was responsible for the Rangoon bombing. Burma concluded, primarily from the confessions of captured North Korean nationals, captured equipment, and other evidence, that the explosion at the shrine was the work of DPRK saboteurs. The confession of North Korean Army Captain Kang Min Chul indicated the plot to murder President Chun during the October state visit to Burma had been hatched early in 1983 by Major General Kang Chang Su of the North Korean Army reconnaissance bureau.[105] Accordingly, Burma severed diplomatic relations with the DPRK and ordered the DPRK diplomatic mission to leave.[106]

In light of these developments, the UNC charged that the North Korean attempt to assassinate the ROK president and senior cabinet ministers had generated increased military tension on both sides and demanded North Korea cease its acts of terror and violence against the Republic of Korea.[107]

In a characteristic tactic of counteraccusation, the North Korean senior member, Major General Li Tae Ho, responded that "the real criminal of the Rangoon explosion is none other than Chun Doo Hwan himself." He repeated this propaganda theme throughout the meeting, interweaving it with charges that the United States incited tension on the peninsula in order to launch a nuclear war against North Korea. Seemingly unaware of his own hypocrisy, Li advocated that the armistice agreement be replaced with a peace treaty.[108]

8

★

Negotiating for Dialogue

A peculiar feature of political analysis on the Korean peninsula is debate over the *intentions* behind North Korea's unification proposals. Logic alone would suggest that North Korea desired to extend its system throughout Korea, and neither Kim Il Sung nor his followers saw a reason to hide this objective. Kim Il Sung wrote, "The ultimate objective of the Party is to build socialist and communist society, while its immediate objective is to carry out a people's democratic revolution against U.S. imperialism and fascist rule in South Korea, overthrowing the corrupt colonial and semi-feudal social system and setting up a people's democratic regime on its grave."[1] Although it has since been revised, the DPRK's 1972 constitution stated: "The Democratic People's Republic of Korea strives to achieve the complete victory of socialism in the northern half, drive out foreign forces on a nationwide scale, reunify the country peacefully on a democratic basis and attain complete national independence."[2]

The words "peacefully on a democratic basis" might seem reassuring were it not for the history of the North's aggression and the ideological foundations of Marxism. Both show that violence is considered a legitimate and, indeed, necessary method of extending communism. Lenin thought so: he said existence side by side with capitalist states for a protracted period was "unthinkable" and "collisions" were "inevitable."[3] Leninism is an interpretation of Marxist doctrine that posits violent revolution as a necessary stage in progress toward true communism. Kim Il Sung called Leninism the "powerful weapon for all revolutionary people," and proclaimed that "reality vividly proves the invincible vitality of Leninism."[4] Kim was also inspired by Mao Tse-tung, who said, "However much the reactionaries try to hold back the wheel of history, sooner or later revolution will take place and will inevitably triumph."[5] It is ironic that long after Lenin's heirs in Moscow sought "peaceful coexistence" with the West and Mao's heirs sought "rapprochement," Kim Il Sung adhered to a hardline position denying conciliation with the non-Communist world.

Kim Il Sung had signed an armistice with the West and pursued a decade of relatively peaceful development in the 1950s. The years of peace were in fact years of clandestine military buildup, but by the time of the Vietnam War, Kim appears to have become concerned that his approach might be viewed as revealing a lack of revolutionary fortitude. His biographer was accordingly compelled to explain his nonbelligerence in the following way:

> He considered that the prime duty of the Korean revolution was still to overthrow the U.S. imperialist aggressive forces and its allies, the landlords, the *comprador* capitalists, the pro-Japanese and pro-U.S. groups, the national traitors in south Korea, to liberate the south Korean people from their imperialist and feudalistic fetters, and thereby achieve national unification and complete national independence. To fulfill this revolutionary duty, he held, first the revolutionary base of the northern half, the strategic base of the Korean revolution, must be further strengthened politically, economically, and militarily.[6]

Kim defended himself against criticism that he relied on peaceful means to promote reunification:

> Our proposal about the peaceful reunification of the fatherland does neither rule out the struggles against the U.S. imperialists nor does it have anything in common with any kind of "compromise" with enemies of our nation and with the theory about the so-called "peaceful transition" of the social system.[7]

He theorized that eventual unification under communism would progress through stages, with the final stage being a violent clash. He hoped the people of the South would shoulder the major portion of the burden for the revolution against their leaders. "The South Korean people cannot expect to win genuine freedom and liberation," Kim asserted, "except by sweeping away U.S. imperialism and its stooges and seizing power by revolutionary and violent means."[8] Kim consistently viewed the removal of American troops as a necessary step in the process toward the Communist party's success in the South. "The peaceful unification of our country," he wrote, "can be materialized only after the U.S. imperialist aggressor army has been forced out of South Korea, and the South Korean people have overthrown the present puppet regime, and the progressive forces have come into power."[9]

Even at the table of the organization meant to supervise the armistice that Kim Il Sung had signed, his negotiator was authorized to threaten: "The entire Korean people, firmly rallied around Marshal Kim Il Sung, beloved leader of 40 million Koreans, will annihilate [U.S.] aggressors in this land and eventually realize the great cause of unification."[10]

Yet despite North Korea's efforts before 1950 to create a unified Communist state, despite the war it initiated to bring the South under its control, despite the tactics it pursued at the negotiating table to represent its military defeat as a victory over the West, despite its cunning in escaping armistice restrictions during its military buildup, and despite its violent efforts to infiltrate South Korea and bring down the government, there has always been a scholarly debate over the intentions behind the North's unification proposals.

The debate rages even though few objectives of any nation have ever been so consistently pursued and openly extolled as the North's struggle to bring South Korea under communism, with violence if that would bring success.

North Korea has viewed peace as an opportunity to build up strength "to meet the great revolutionary event in full readiness."[11] Before the ultimate violent stage of Kim's theoretical revolution, peaceful gestures, such as proposals for talks with the South, would help create an environment conducive to achievement of North Korea's long-range interests. Whether talks led to agreements the North found advantageous or failed when the North chose to exploit their termination, dialogue between North and South has served primarily as a means of promoting the North's goals. Dialogue has advanced few, if any, concrete steps toward unification, but it has served to aggravate political instability in the South, to excite Korean nationalistic zeal, to portray the Republic of Korea as incapable of advancing reunification, and to characterize the presence of American troops as the single most important obstacle to patriotic objectives.

North Korea has occasionally presented enticing proposals for unification that stir hopes and raise expectations. A pattern in this behavior, however, indicates that the proposals are motivated by interests other than unification. The North has made major proposals to take advantage of political instability and civil unrest in the South, from 1960 to 1962, and again in 1979 and 1980. It has rushed to conclude agreements with the South in order to reclaim control over the issue when international approaches toward unification were building momentum, especially in 1972 when the United States and China discussed their views on Korean unification during the Nixon-Chou talks. North Korea has also generated dialogue when it has needed to deflect international attention from acts of terror, following such attacks as the Panmunjom axe murders, the Rangoon bombing, and the downing of Korean Air Lines flight 858.

In each of those instances, the North's proposals were designed to take advantage of specific opportunities. There is a pattern not only of *when* North Korea pursued dialogue, but also *what* it proposed. During periods of political instability in the South, the North sought to portray itself as more genuinely democratic than the South, in an effort to attract support among South Korea's disenfranchised opposition. Its proposals therefore focused on convening "grand national assemblies" comprising thousands of participants, seemingly affording an opportunity for broad-based political participation. When its control over unification measures was challenged by the momentum behind international initiatives, the North portrayed itself as an emerging anticolonialist nation struggling to maintain its sovereignty. It rushed to sign on to unenforceable arrangements and debate inconclusively over protocols for peace talks. When the objective was to distract the world's attention from its acts of terror, the North portrayed itself as eager to resolve tensions, not from remorse but to escape accountability. It deflected attention from its crimes to its grievances, suggesting that the rationale for its acts of violence would end when national division ended and foreign troops withdrew.

The North pursued its diplomatic objectives in North-South dialogue skillfully. At various times, it seemed accommodating or unyielding, belligerent or peaceful, bombastic or pleading. But in every instance, the process of dialogue itself ended on terms dictated by

North Korea, in a stalemate or an unenforceable agreement, and in almost every standoff the issues would be brought to focus on only one: the North's precondition that American troops withdraw and foreign military assistance to the South cease.

The consistency with which U.S. troop withdrawal was used by North Korea as the deal-stopper in North-South dialogue shows: *first*, that the North's objective is not so much to proceed toward unification as it is to focus attention on its singular demand; *second*, that the North wishes to make the South vulnerable more than it wishes to make Korea unified. After all, dialogue could have made progress toward reunification under many of the arrangements that were discussed in North-South talks. The South was certainly flexible, but the North has repeatedly chosen to terminate the talks because the South would not agree to undermine its own security.

North Korea's focus on the withdrawal of foreign troops is not surprising, because its objective is to make the entire peninsula vulnerable to Communist methods of taking power. What is surprising is how frequently and how easily analysts forget the North's objectives and lull themselves into a false impression that the North's proposals might actually constitute steps toward peaceful reunification.

South Koreans have steadfastly rejected the system that controls Koreans in the North. In the years immediately following the negotiation of the armistice agreement, the Republic of Korea was the more openly belligerent of the two Koreas. President Syngman Rhee's announced policy objective was to liberate the North by force of arms. In a characteristic speech on the fifth anniversary of founding of the ROK, he said, "It is our wish and determination to march north at the earliest possible time to save our North Korean brethren from the sure death they are facing today."[12] Similarly, when he agreed to send a delegation to the political conference held in Geneva in 1954, Rhee issued the fatalistic statement, "We hope . . . that if and when the Geneva Conference has failed, the United States and our friends in the Free World will join us in employing other means to drive the enemy from our land."[13]

While President Rhee might have been cautious enough not to launch a war against the North, his rhetorical posture was to advocate precisely that. The United States government was compelled on many occasions to ask him to temper his remarks. He was frequently reminded that the South could not count on American aid if it initiated hostilities.[14]

Taking Advantage of Instability

In 1960, North Korea mistook the student demonstrations against Rhee's manipulation of the election process for the start of a Marxist revolution in the South. Kim Il Sung referred to it as "the initial victory of the South Korean people's struggle."[15] Student demonstrations during the "April 19 revolution" brought down President Rhee's government. They also ended Rhee's policy of "March North and Unify."[16]

Underestimating the insecurity most South Koreans felt during that period of political instability, the North launched a propaganda barrage blaming South Korea's economic troubles on the division of the nation, calling the presence of U.S. troops the major obstacle to reunification, and advocating extension of the Communist system to South Korea. Kim Il Sung appealed to the people of the South "to force the U.S. imperialist aggressor army out of South Korea."[17] A decade after U.S. forces had saved them from the North's invasion forces, however, the people of South Korea were not about to lower their guard, especially when weakened by domestic political instability. Despite, or perhaps because of, the turmoil surrounding the student protests, South Koreans voted conservatively in the national election of July 29, 1960.

The election brought to power Premier Chang Myon, Rhee's former vice president, who perceived that the North's unification gestures were "a propaganda maneuver aimed at infiltration and subversion, taking advantage of the period of political transition in our country."[18] Nevertheless, reunification was a popular aspiration, and the Chang government would give apparent consideration to specific North Korean proposals.

A mere two weeks after the election, sensing an opportunity to influence the South's politics, Kim Il Sung hit the fledgling government with a proposal for creating a confederation of North and South Korea. Kim's plan was not much different from the North's position in the Geneva conference in 1954. It envisioned unsupervised elections, sought equal voting strength for North and South in a national assembly despite the South's larger population, and demanded the withdrawal of foreign (particularly American) troops. It was an exciting idea, however, because it seemed to suggest that a distinct government in the South could coexist with one in the North. It also seemed to fit into the context of peaceful coexistence being espoused by the Soviet Union at the time, and therefore garnered some international credibility. The notion attracted considerable popular support in 1960, as it has since.

Kim Il Sung claimed his approach might accomplish socialist revolution in the South peacefully. In theory, if foreign influence were removed, economic cooperation would provide a basis for people in the South to comprehend "the supremacy of communism" and evoke a "yearning for participation in north Korean society."[19] Through a North-South economic committee, economic policy would promote unity of the Koreas; that is, implement Marxist economic policies in South Korea.

Kim Il Sung correctly noted that "the questions of the country's peaceful reunification and North-South negotiations" had become the topic of the day.[20] The Chang government was more than skeptical about the North's overtures, but accommodated popular interest in the North's proposals by announcing a policy of "Friendly Relations with the Neutralist Camp," and entertaining the idea of a collective security arrangement under a North East Asia Treaty Organization.[21]

Military officers, fearing Chang's steps might undermine South Korea's security, grew restive about South Korea's faltering economy and the potential for Communist penetration. On May 16, 1961, Major General Park Chung Hee seized control in a military coup d'état. The coup leaders issued a statement that had as its first point: "With anti-Communism as the first purpose of government, the anti-Communist posture, heretofore limited to form and as a verbal motto, will be reorganized and strengthened to prepare against foreign aggression."[22] Regarding the North's reunification proposals, Park wrote, "The advocacy of territorial unification with the society in a state of chaos, as it was under the Chang regime, is the way to national suicide."[23]

Passage of an anti-Communist national security law in July 1961 made criminals of those "sympathizing with domestic or international communism." "The first victims," according to Kim Hak Joon's comprehensive study of reunification policy, "were those who had advocated . . . north-south negotiation for unification or neutralization of Korea."[24] On these grounds, 3,098 South Korean citizens were arrested immediately following Park's accession to power.[25]

If Kim Il Sung genuinely sought to promote unification peacefully and believed that the North was a socialist paradise that would appeal to South Koreans, this would have been the time to set aside the question of foreign military assistance to South Korea. If he really believed, as he said on August 14, 1960, that "the South Korean people are in an indescribably wretched plight,"[26] he should logically have proposed confederation and waited for the popular groundswell to undercut the ROK's defense arrangements. Instead, by demanding removal of foreign troops as a precondition, he confirmed South Korean suspicions. His insistence that more positive North-South relations depended "on the condition that foreign aggressive forces are withdrawn from South Korea"[27] undermined support for his scheme among South Korea's war-hardened population. The North's approach revealed that the true intent behind its overtures was to render the people of the South powerless in the face of Communist tactics of terror and oppression.

Throughout the 1960s, the Park government sought to defer questions of reunification until the South could negotiate from a position of strength, focusing more immediately on South Korea's economic and political development. Ironically, almost as soon as the Park government renounced military means of reunification, the North embraced them.

Beginning in 1967, the North undertook the hostilities discussed in the previous chapter, including armed intrusions and attacks along the DMZ, infiltrations deep into the ROK, and assassination attempts against President Park himself. At Military Armistice Commission meetings during the crisis period, North Korean propaganda attacks were designed to discredit the U.S. presence and accuse the allies of planning to resume a new Korean war. The North sought to create war hysteria as a means of increasing control among its own population in the North and stimulating antipathy toward the American troop presence.

The North's violence during the 1960s may have discouraged some foreign investment in the South. Its efforts to inspire fear and uncertainty and to undermine political stability, however, proved counterproductive. The Park government's policy of cracking down on leftist dissidents and its call for increased military spending received wider popular support. In dialogue as well, the attack on the Blue House (presidential palace in Seoul), the seizure of the USS *Pueblo*, the Ulchin-Samchok commando raid, and other incidents made it impossible to talk of confederation as a means to unification. By the end of the decade, it was apparent that the North's violent tactics had failed and a new international atmosphere made continued belligerence unseemly. At that point, the North returned to its long-abandoned calls for peaceful reunification.

The North interpreted a 1969 shift in U.S. defense policy as an opportunity to facilitate the departure of American troops. The Nixon Doctrine, announced in Guam on July 25, 1969, emphasized that Asian countries should shoulder the burden of their own defense.[28] To that end, 20,000 American troops were removed from Korea and more were to be withdrawn when South Korean forces could take over their roles. Not wishing to undermine policies it thought might lead eventually to a complete U.S. withdrawal, North Korea halted armed infiltration and attacks across the demarcation line in the DMZ. Four U.S. soldiers were ambushed and killed by armed North Korean intruders in the DMZ on October 18, 1969, but afterward U.S. personnel casualties declined. In 1971, U.S. soldiers were withdrawn from the DMZ—except along the road to Panmunjom—and replaced by South Korean forces. A relatively peaceful period at the MAC held for the first two years of the 1970s.

At the same time, Washington sent signals of willingness to sponsor North-South dialogue, consistent with overtures being made to the People's Republic of China. In February 1970, the American ambassador to Seoul, William J. Porter, testified before the Senate Foreign Relations Committee that he had "requested and received authority to discuss with the [South] Koreans . . . where there might be areas in which dialogue [between North and South] could be conducted. . . . We made it clear that we think a dialogue is preferable to immobility on the subject."[29]

Recognizing American pressure, and understanding that some steps toward rapprochement between Washington and Beijing were under way, President Park took the initiative on August 15, 1970, to announce South Korea's willingness to negotiate with North Korea. His speech on the twenty-fifth anniversary of Korean liberation presented an "Idea for Peaceful Unification" that envisioned a peaceful competition between the two systems. In addition to calling for repudiation of the use of arms as a means to unification, Park proposed that the two sides "could remove the artificial barriers between them step by step and thereby reduce the pains, misfortune and inconveniences stemming from division."[30]

Like the proposals from the North, Park's presented conditions for reunification that he had no reason to believe the other side would accept. His preconditions included an end to North Korean military provocation and infiltration, renunciation of the goal of communizing all of Korea by force and overthrowing the ROK government by violence—and verification of both by the United Nations.[31] Park and other officials of his government took credit for having offered a gesture to the North, but made it clear they had no faith in the North's willingness to accept its terms.[32]

Three months later, at the Fifth Workers Party Congress, Kim Il Sung boasted "all of the people of North Korea know how to handle guns. The whole land has been fortified. . . . We can liberate South Korea on our own without any direct assistance from China and the Soviet Union."[33] This braggadocio seemed to confirm Park's low expectations.

Reclaiming Control over Unification Initiatives

A more comprehensive North Korean response came on April 12, 1971, when DPRK Foreign Minister Ho Dam proposed an eight-point program. It dusted off the decade-old notion of transitional confederation, to be accomplished through the following steps: (1) withdrawal of U.S. forces from Korea; (2) reduction of forces to 100,000 on both sides; (3) abrogation of the ROK defense arrangements with foreign powers; (4) election of a "unified central government" in votes conducted in North and South Korea "autonomously"; (5) removal of restrictions on Communist activities in the South; (6) confederation of North and South, with complete unification pursued gradually; (7) collaboration in the areas of economic, scientific, cultural, sports and arts, postal service, and visits by individuals; and (8) convocation of a North-South political conference.

Ho Dam added, "we will gladly negotiate the unification problems when a 'people's government' is founded in South Korea or 'patriotic new individuals' come into power there after the withdrawal of the American imperialists from South Korea."[34] North Korea felt compelled to dismiss President Park's "Idea for Peaceful Unification," and insult its author. But world events soon forced the North to take a more opportunistic view. The precondition of Park's removal was dropped after plans for President Nixon's visit to China were announced.[35] The antique proposal itself could have been ignored, except for the North's call on August 6 for talks at Panmunjom "at any time" and the Communist party's unprecedented willingness to meet representatives from South Korea's ruling party.

That willingness was seen as a signal that the North would discuss reuniting families separated by the war. Reunification, for all of its appeal and its consuming intractability, is not the only issue that draws North and South Korea to the negotiating table. In addition to dividing territory and politics, the Korean War had also divided families. The South Korean Red Cross had, since 1953, sought to determine the condition of approximately 10 million separated family members, arrange communications between loved ones, and organize reunions. Ho Dam's statement seemed to offer such an opening. The president of the South Korean Red Cross Society, Choi Doo Sun, was accordingly authorized to propose a meeting. He did so on August 12, and North Korea's Red Cross Society immediately agreed.

Initial meetings at Panmunjom on August 20 produced promising agreements on the venue for meetings, establishment of liaison offices, and installation of telephone links.[36] They led to working-level meetings that in turn yielded full-dress conferences. Meetings held in October and December made strides toward defining the process of contact between families and relatives. As it had done during negotiations on the armistice, the North pushed for wide access throughout South Korea yet sought to keep unwanted visitors out of North Korea.

These first-ever bilateral North-South discussions made good use of the Neutral Nations Supervisory Commission (NNSC) conference room at Panmunjom and other MAC assets. The UN Command (UNC) presence during these meetings was held to a minimum, however, to avoid disturbing the diplomatic atmosphere.

With public attention focused on the fast-moving Red Cross talks, the path seemed clear for discussions of a North-South political conference. On November 20, 1971, a member of the ROK National Red Cross, Chong Hong Jin, proposed a secret meeting with Kim Dok Hyon of the North Korean Red Cross. The two Red Cross delegates got the process started with reciprocal visits to Pyongyang and Seoul. The South hoped to allow the Red Cross negotiations to pursue strictly humanitarian issues, and therefore proposed a separate channel to satisfy the North's interest in political discussions.[37] The North, however, sought to use both channels for political purposes.

Even while the secret discussions were under way, Kim Il Sung condemned the South for avoiding discussions of political reunification in the Red Cross talks. "South Korea was using dilatory tactics," he told the *Yomiuri Shimbun*, "We will spur them and develop them into political talks." He also insisted that political talks could succeed only if U.S. troops withdrew from the peninsula. "To realize a peace pact between the North and South, it is essential for the U.S. forces to leave the South," he said. "South Korea often speaks of a 'threat of aggression' from the north. If a peace pact is signed and both the North and South reduce their respective arms, the alleged 'threat of aggression' will disappear."[38] Kim sought to hinder the Red Cross talks by insisting on political discussions, and to bind the political talks by insistence on the withdrawal of the troops defending the South's security. Progress seemed unlikely.

In February 1972, however, a dramatic shift in the relationship between China and the United States compelled the North Korean dictator to change his tactics. The Nixon-Chou talks resulted in the Shanghai communiqué, which seemed to usher in a new era in multilateral management of Northeast Asian security issues. The communiqué stated that "the United States will support efforts of the ROK to seek relaxation of tension and increased communication in the Korean peninsula" and that China "firmly supports the eight-point program for the peaceful reunification of Korea put forward by the Government of the Democratic People's Republic of Korea on April 12, 1971."[39] Both the United States and China had sought not to offend their ally's sensitivities with this almost inconsequential reaffirmation of standing policies. Yet both leaders of the Koreas were motivated to demonstrate their ability to bring Korean matters under their own control.

Higher level secret meetings were accordingly arranged in Pyongyang and Seoul. Director of the ROK Central Intelligence Agency Lee Hu Rak met Kim Il Sung in Pyongyang, May 2–5, 1972. In reciprocal exchange, Pak Song Chol, the vice premier of the DPRK, visited President Park Chung Hee in Seoul, May 29–June 1. These secret meetings led to the startling public announcement on July 4 of the "South-North Communiqué."

The Secret Talks

When South Korean CIA Director Lee Hu Rak visited Kim Il Sung in Pyongyang from May 2 to 5, the two talked about the need for tension reduction on the peninsula and steps that would precede national reunification. Kim described the distrust between North and South:

> We thought that the South Korean authorities were lackeys of U.S. imperialism and Japanese imperialism and would sell out our country. But you say that such will never be the

case, and request us over and over again to believe it. It may be possible to believe you and get rid of our past distrust. The South Korean authorities say they have had a misunderstanding that we were going to invade . . . and communize [the] South. . . . But we have no intention to do these.[40]

Kim's was a peculiarly one-sided formulation, but it sounded balanced and he further "conceded the attempted raid on *Chong Wa Dae* [the presidential mansion in Seoul]" offering what was recorded as a sincere apology.[41] When he found it useful to appear to promote Korean peace and unification, he disavowed the use of violence, and incidents along the line were, in fact, rare.

Demonstrating his concern over the Shanghai communiqué, Kim said to Lee, "nothing is more urgent than national reunification. If we should fail to reunify the country as soon as possible and should allow national division to drag on, our nation may become a plaything of great powers and be divided into two forever."[42] In the interest of regaining control over this issue, he was willing to defer troublesome details to subsequent negotiations.

Both Kim and Park appear to have considered it worthwhile to paper over serious issues in order to return the momentum of Korean issues to Korea's own leadership. As scholar B. K. Gills put it, "Under the guidance of Secretary of State Henry Kissinger, a period of U.S. diplomacy dominated by the dictates of realpolitik, rather than anti-Communist ideology, was commencing. South Korea grew wary of a U.S. proclivity to pursue its own interests first, and consult the opinions of its allies second."[43]

The first South-North secret talks produced agreement on two principles that modified previous unification proposals by avoiding troublesome details. The agreement reached in these secret sessions was that "unification shall be achieved through independent efforts without being subject to external imposition or interference" and "through peaceful means, and not through the use of force against each other."[44] These terms avoided specifications regarding autonomous voting that would have given the North's smaller population unreasonable advantage and replaced calls for removal of foreign forces with a general commitment to nonaggression. North Korea, clearly wanting an agreement, reserved its ability to insist on these preconditions at a later date.

Lee Hu Rak also found the North's temporizing tactic an advantageous opportunity to obtain three specific concessions. At his initiative, and over the objections of North Korea's negotiators, Kim Il Sung agreed the two sides would not: (1) slander or defame each other, (2) make unilateral unification proposals for propaganda purposes, or (3) use their militaries to harass the other side. Lee also drove home the point that the Red Cross talks should be handled exclusively as a humanitarian matter, divorced from political manipulation. Kim Il Sung proposed that to implement these objectives, reductions should be made in the militaries on both sides and a "South-North Coordinating Committee" should be established.[45]

The South's confidence in the secret sessions was due in part to the participation of Kim Il Sung's younger brother, Kim Young Joo, who at that time was considered Kim Il Sung's most likely successor. Yet from May 29 to June 1, 1972, North Korean Vice Premier Pak Sung Chul was sent in place of Kim Young Joo to meet with President Park in Seoul. Kim Young Joo, who had played a role in the Pyongyang sessions, was said to be ill and unable to participate.

The North Korean representative, Pak Sung Chul, accompanied by three aides, met twice with Lee Hu Rak and once with President Park. The points made in the Pyongyang discussions were confirmed, and the two sides reached agreement that a South-North Coordinating Committee (SNCC) would be established to carry out the objectives of the agreements, and would be cochaired by Lee Hu Rak and Kim Young Joo. In the delegation's meeting with President Park, Park emphasized that mutual understanding and trust would be enhanced by progress in the Red Cross sessions, an end to military provocation, and steps to promote "national homogeneity, transcending the difference in systems."[46]

The South clearly wanted progress on the question of reuniting family members, and would agree to an acceptable North-South declaration in the process; the North wanted an agreement that would restore its claim to having advanced a method of reunification, thereby deflecting mounting pressure from international, and perhaps even domestic, sources clamoring for advancement of long-sought Communist party objectives. The North got what it wanted.

At 10:00 A.M. on July 4, 1972, North and South Korea simultaneously announced that secret talks had been held and had resulted in the signing of the South-North joint communiqué. The terms of the communiqué were as follows:

1) The two sides have agreed to the following principles for unification of the fatherland:

First, unification shall be achieved through independent efforts without being subject to external imposition or interference.

Second, unification shall be achieved through peaceful means, and not through use of force against one another.

Third, a great national unity, as a homogeneous people, shall be sought first, transcending differences in ideas, ideologies, and systems.

2) In order to ease tensions and foster an atmosphere of mutual trust between the south and the north, the two sides have agreed not to defame and slander one another, not to take armed provocations against one another, whether on a large or small scale, and to take positive measures to prevent inadvertent military incidents.

3) The two sides, in order to restore severed national ties, promote mutual understanding and to expedite an independent peaceful unification, have agreed to carry out various exchanges in many areas.

4) The two sides have agreed to cooperate positively with one another to seek an early success of the South-North Red Cross Conference, which is currently in progress amidst the fervent expectations of the entire people of Korea.

5) The two sides, in order to prevent unexpected military incidents and to cope with problems arising in the relations between the south and the north directly, promptly and accurately, have agreed to install and operate a direct telephone line between Seoul and Pyongyang.

6) The two sides, firmly convinced that the aforementioned agreements correspond with the common aspirations of the entire people eager to see early unification of their fatherland, hereby solemnly pledge before the entire Korean people that they will faithfully carry out the agreements.

July 4, 1972
Upholding the desires of their respective superiors
Lee Hu Rak
Kim Young Joo[47]

Subsequent creation of the South-North Coordinating Committee to carry out the joint communiqué appeared to be a promising development. In an "agreed minute" concluded on November 4, 1972, the SNCC was given an elaborate organizational structure of two cochairmen, two vice chairmen, two executive members, and four other members; an executive council; five subcommittees—political, military, foreign affairs, economic, and cultural; and a joint secretariat operating out of Panmunjom. It had five functions, which were executive as well as deliberative:

- unifying the country independently and peacefully on the basis of the agreed principles for unification of the fatherland
- effecting a wide range of political exchanges among political parties, social organizations, and individuals
- facilitating economic, cultural, and social exchanges and cooperation
- relaxing tensions, preventing armed incidents, and reducing military confrontations
- enhancing the national pride as a single homogeneous nation by taking joint steps in overseas activities[48]

There were now two authorized umbrella structures for discussions between North and South: the higher level, official SNCC, and the Red Cross discussions (sometimes referred to as the South-North Red Cross Conference, or SNRCC). In the period of thirteen months following the joint communiqué, the two Koreas convened six South-North Coordinating Committee meetings, seven Red Cross plenary meetings, and many related subgroup meetings. Despite the electrifying momentum behind the communiqué and the serious attention given to the succeeding months of negotiation, however, both sets of talks failed. No one should have expected the North to give in on its long-term intractable demand, the removal of foreign troops, nor to unification at the expense of communism, but the initial stages appeared so promising as to raise expectations. Raising expectations was part of the North's strategy.

Phases of North Korean Negotiating Behavior

The signature of the two sides' leaders on the broad principles in the joint communiqué and the more specific directives of the agreed minute brought to completion a first phase in a pattern of North Korea's negotiations with the South. Two participants from the South's delegations, Lee Dong Bok and Song Jong Hwan, have written insightful analyses of what happened during the talks. Lee's and Song's writings echo some of the points Admiral Joy and Ambassador Dean observed two decades earlier about the North's approach to negotiations. They identified phases in the negotiations during which the North made grand initial gestures, then hardened its posture, and ultimately condemned its opponents for not accepting demands. The North reversed its positions to suit its needs, sometimes eagerly pursuing agreements, sometimes expressing a complete lack of interest in the same issues relating to the same text.

Lee Dong Bok perceived five negotiating stages—from the North's initial eagerness to conclude arrangements to the South's efforts to bring the North back to the table. He identified the five stages chronologically from November 1971 to the time of his writing in 1977, but the stages could also be characterized as: (1) getting to the table, (2) concluding an agreement, (3) disputing the agreement's terms, (4) disavowing the agreement, and (5) fixing the blame on South Korea for the collapse of negotiations.

Song Jong Hwan's studies simplified these gradations to three phases of North Korean behavior during the period of active negotiation itself, which he described as follows:

> In the first phase, the North Korean side induced its counterpart to negotiations and tried to reach "agreements in principle," the details of which could be worked out later. In the second phase, the North tried to secure advantageous detailed agreements by interpreting the above "agreements in principle" in arbitrary ways. In the last phase, in the case of disagreements, North Korea discontinued the talks unilaterally while blaming the failure of agreements on the South Korean side."[49]

The pattern Lee and Song described held true for both the SNCC and the Red Cross talks in the 1970s, and have appeared in numerous negotiations with North Korea before and since. Because the period of dialogue in the 1970s holds great significance for understanding the North's intentions behind recurrent proposals for "confederation," it is worth considerable attention.

Phase 1: Agreeing in Principle. In the opening stage, the North's negotiators were "very friendly to the South Korean delegation members."[50] "The first round in Pyongyang and the second round in Seoul were held in a festive mood," South Korean observers noted, "because of the emotions arising from the fact that for the first time since the territorial division, large delegations from the South and the North crossed the boundary line. Various congratulatory events prevailed over the conference itself."[51]

"During the first period every meeting produced an agreement," Song Jong Hwan observed, "The two sides came to speedy conclusions on such matters as agenda, venue, date, and other procedural matters."[52] Throughout this phase, Kim Il Sung showed a personal interest in the dialogue. When the South Korean delegations visited Pyongyang, Kim met with them and hosted a luncheon in their honor. Behind the scenes he was actively involved in supervising negotiations on the formation and operation of the SNCC. Last minute intervention by Kim Il Sung, Lee and Song noted, made it possible for the two sides to announce on November 4, 1972, that the agreed minute had been concluded. Kim Il Sung also intervened to order his negotiators to accept Lee Hu Rak's proposal that the two sides stop slandering each other.[53]

Nevertheless, the differences between North and South at these meetings were clear. From the start, the North's delegations acted as though they were conducting political rallies. Even at the Red Cross talks, which had a specific, nonpolitical, humanitarian objective, the North filled the sessions with political dogma. The first Red Cross meeting, held in Pyongyang, was staged like a convention of regional pro-Communist groups; congratulatory messages from trade unions that could not attend were read at the assemblies. At the second meeting in Seoul, the North's delegation broke into an organized chant, "Let's get rid of foreign influence." The North used the opportunity to deliver long speeches on the virtues of Kim Il Sung, and argued that unification under communism was the best humanitarian settlement.[54]

The North's tactic of representing itself as more truly democratic than the South emerged at this session in Seoul. "It tried to disguise its image of a closed society as well as its violent revolutionary line," Song noted, "by proposing principles of freedom and democracy and showing a positive attitude on peaceful unification."[55] The session concluded with the delegates agreeing to "adhere to the principles of democracy and freedom, the spirit of the South-North Joint Communiqué, brotherly love and the Red Cross humanitarianism in solving all problems envisaged in the agenda."[56]

In the separate SNCC talks, politics had been expected to play a larger role. At the first cochairmen's meeting of the SNCC, however, the North attempted to distort the meaning of the joint communiqué.

The North characterized it as requiring South Korea to abandon its anti-Communist policies, its reliance on the United Nations, and its own democratic form of government. On the basis of their misrepresentation of what the South had agreed to, the North Korean delegates argued that U.S. forces should withdraw and South Korea should dismantle its armed forces. Dismissing these misrepresentations, at the close of the meeting the South signed on to a limited joint statement that merely reaffirmed the spirit of the joint communiqué and announced plans for a second session.

The second cochairmen's meeting concluded the agreed minute setting out the functions of the SNCC. At that session, however, tensions grew as North Korea intensified attacks on the South's anti-Communist policies. Lee Hu Rak accordingly reminded the delegates that their purpose was to "transcend the difference in ideas and systems, not interfere in each other's policies."[57] Despite the intransigence shown by North Korea's delegation at the meeting, Kim Il Sung met with Lee Hu Rak, ordered his delegation to complete the agreed minute, and called for political, economic, and cultural "collaboration" between the two sides, defending the notion of mutual military reductions and applauding the "confederation" between North and South.[58] The South had reason to hope his interest might continue.

A third cochairmen's meeting in Seoul took final steps to appoint the membership of the SNCC and to prepare for the first plenary session, planned for November 30–December 1, 1972.[59]

Phase 2: Reinterpreting the Agreement. The cochairmen's sessions of the SNCC completed phase one. The second phase, in which the North reversed its approach and put obstacles in the path of negotiations, began to emerge from the first SNCC plenary session. To guarantee steady progress, the South proposed that the first projects undertaken should be nonpolitical and nonmilitary ones, where the likelihood of friction was minimal. The North, however, demanded consideration of military issues first, recommending the convening of a new forum—a special session of military representatives. North Korea further argued that the SNCC must simultaneously inaugurate all five subcommittees, arguing that since the joint communiqué had already been signed, "the South and North should trust each other."[60]

Once an agreement is concluded, the American and South Korean impulse is to set about implementing its terms. The agreed minute had envisioned an exciting new North-South institution to resolve the basic issues that divided Koreans. It was therefore with a great deal of excitement and high expectation that South Koreans approached implementation of the SNCC.

For North Korea, however, the task that follows conclusion of an agreement may be to guarantee that it is *not* implemented, or that a more advantageous arrangement is pursued. Even though the signatures on the agreed minute were barely dry, the North demanded that the SNCC be reorganized.

By the time of the second plenary session, held in Pyongyang on March 14, 1973, a change in the North's attitude had become clear. The first sign of the change, Lee Dong Bok observed, was that North Korea became increasingly reluctant to hold the SNCC plenary meetings on schedule. The second meeting was to have been held in Pyongyang sometime before the end of February, but North Korea postponed it until March 14–16.[61]

At midpoint between the time planned for the SNCC session in Pyongyang and the date the North actually agreed to hold the meeting, the North created an incident that would undermine the negotiations and give the impression that the United States was responsible for Korea's continuing division.

On February 27, the UNC had informed the North Korean side, in accordance with long-standing practice, that a South Korean work party would replace military demarcation line markers, a routine maintenance detail, in the central sector of the DMZ. On March 7, North Korean guards fired on that work party from a North Korean guard post. Attacking in broad daylight, the North Koreans killed one South Korean Army officer and one sergeant, and wounded a third soldier. The killings occurred while a South Korean delegation, transiting through Panmunjom, was traveling north to Pyongyang for the second SNCC plenary session.

The UNC called a Military Armistice Commission meeting, held on March 12, to protest the North Korean attack. At the MAC meeting, the North Koreans rejected the UNC proposal for a joint investigation of the incident, choosing to accuse the United States of "illegally occupying South Korea and blocking Korea's independent and peaceful reunification."[62] North Korea alleged that the South Korean work party had infiltrated deep into their portion of the DMZ to spy on their facilities and to conduct hostile acts "on the eve of north-south talks in Pyongyang."[63]

When the South's delegates arrived for the second SNCC plenary session in Pyongyang on March 14, the change in atmospherics was immediately noticed. North Korea did not supply the customary helicopters to ferry the delegates from Kaesong to Pyongyang. Furthermore, Kim Il Sung declined to meet them. "Without Kim Il Sung's personal participation," Lee Dong Bok noted, "the second meeting was destined from the outset to be merely a 'talk show.'"[64]

At the conference table, the North, having lost interest in trying to straighten out the functions of the SNCC, dismissed the South's efforts to develop implementing procedures. Contending that "unless the state of military confrontation between the two sides is removed first, no genuinely trustworthy dialogue can take place," the North's chief delegate Pak Sung Chul set out a five-point proposal dealing with military issues and demanded that his proposition be discussed before any other matters.[65] The five points included familiar features: limitations on South Korea's military size, weaponry, and operations; a demand for the withdrawal of American forces; and a call for a peace treaty to replace the armistice agreement.

North Korea also demanded that a new institution be established with responsibilities duplicating the functions of the SNCC. It called for a North-South Political Negotiation Conference "to resolve the problem of unification." Alternately calling it a "General National Congress" and a "Joint Meeting of Representatives of Political Parties and Social Organizations in the north and south of Korea," the North envisioned an assembly attended by an equal number of delegates from either side representing "all political parties, social organizations, and individuals of various classes." Its size alone would make it unwieldy; it was to have between 700 and 3,000 members. Such undemocratic systems of representation, based not on individual votes but on franchises awarded to societal sectors, are what scholars like John Fonte call "neomedieval corporatism." The North's proposal had precedents in Communist "national front" proposals before the Korean War, and in earlier North Korean unification proposals; it derived from the North Korean notion of convening an assembly that would give the North's population disproportionate power in a national assembly, creating an environment conducive to Communist predominance.

To drive home its propaganda theme that South Korea's government was not truly democratic, the North demanded that a reputed underground Communist network in South Korea be recognized as a legitimate political party, fully represented at the proposed assembly. Despite the practical difficulties of affording a public role to possibly fictitious covert operatives, advocates of political openness might readily suggest that the North's proposal should have been accepted. Note, however, that while the North called for opening the South's political process to Marxist parties, the North also argued that the unification process should be closed to anti-Communist parties. In a ploy reminiscent of the Communist party's 1946 attempt to control meetings on trusteeship by arguing that those opposed could not participate,[66] the North now argued that anti-Communist parties did not genuinely support true unification and therefore should be barred from participation.[67]

North Korea's policy regarding unification dialogue, consistent with its domestic policy, has been to grant political power only to like-minded people. The commitment to "transcend political divisions," so essential to the South's agreement to sign the joint communiqué, clearly meant something different to the North.

Taking a page from Admiral Joy's persistent effort to keep talks going by referring issues to subordinate levels, the South in March 1973 won the North's agreement to forming an executive council as a working-level steering group. The executive council had three rounds of meetings at Panmunjom. The meetings failed; the North used them as an opportunity to insist on a clause in operational regulations of the SNCC providing "representatives of political party social organizations and individuals may be invited as observers to the meetings of the SNCC." The South could not countenance yet another effort to dilute the executive effectiveness of the SNCC as an institution.

The Red Cross talks had made little progress after October 24, 1972, when North Korea proposed sending its agents throughout South Korea to explain how family reunions could be organized and to expound on the comparative benefits of life in the North.[68] At the sixth full-dress Red Cross meeting in Seoul, May 9–10, 1973, the North Korean Red Cross repeated its demands that the South abrogate its anti-Communist law and its national security law, and disband its anti-Communist agencies and organizations. It also demanded that the South guarantee "freedom of speech" and unrestricted rights of movement for people sent from the North to meet their separated families and relatives, provide facilities for their food and lodging, and take legal and administrative measures to respect the "inviolability of their safety and belongings."[69]

The North insisted that North Korean "expounders" should be sent south "to every *ri* or *dong*," the lowest administrative units, to engage in "publicity activities." These publicity activities were to include explaining how mistrust and misunderstanding between the South and the North could be removed, as well as providing information on the conditions of separated families. The North's proposal would have meant that some 36,000 Northern agents would travel into the South, while 4,300 could visit the North.[70] To the South, the North's demand for "free travel" by the separated families in the North and the South was not to search for families but rather to launch Communist political activities in every part of South Korean society.[71]

The chief South Korean Red Cross delegate, Lee Bom Sok, told the North Koreans that their "unreasonable and unrealistic" proposal demanding what they termed "prerequisites" was "outright interference in the internal affairs of the Republic of Korea." "For this very reason," he said, the South Korean Red Cross had itself avoided mentioning "the legal and social conditions now existing in North Korea."[72]

As South Korean delegates observed, the North was not only intruding into matters of the South's domestic policy, but was demanding that alterations in policy be made "as conditions for dialogue." "It is ironic," Song Jong Hwan observed, "that a country so resistant of outside influence would feel it could recommend settlement of military problems, improvement of legal conditions and social circumstances in South Korea, reorganization of the SNCC, and joint meetings of the political parties and social organizations in South and North Korea."[73] North Korea would not only risk, but also purposefully bring about, the end of this period of unification dialogue.

Phase 3: Blaming the Other Side for the Failure of the Talks. By the time of the third plenary meeting of the SNCC, held June 12–15, 1973, in Seoul, the North had unalterably hardened its approach, adhering to the demands it made at the second meeting, making any further discussions impossible. Lee Hu Rak pleaded with the North Koreans to show a more sincere attitude toward implementing regulations for the SNCC and the establishment of the joint secretariat mentioned in the agreed minute.

Finally, in an effort to revive North Korea's interest, the South proposed an extensive program of economic exchanges. On June 23, President Park Chung Hee issued a "Declaration for Peace and Unification" that might reasonably have been expected to re-ignite North Korea's interest in dialogue. The declaration reassured the North that the South continued to advocate peaceful unification as "the supreme task" and emphasized the South's continued regard for the joint communiqué, its commitment to noninterference and nonaggression, and its general pursuit of "peace and good neighborliness." In a major gesture to the North, the declaration also offered, "South Korea will not object to North Korea's dual admittance in the United Nations, provided that it does not hinder national unification; [and] even before North Korea's admittance into the United Nations, South Korea will not be opposed to its also being invited to attend the United Nations General Assembly's deliberations on the Korean question."[74]

The North, however, had decided the dialogue had outlived its usefulness. It refused to receive incoming calls over the South-North direct telephone line, so that additional meetings could not be scheduled.[75] The executive council was therefore suspended in June after three meetings. The working-level Red Cross talks had already been suspended indefinitely in March. At the seventh plenary session of the Red Cross delegations, held July 11–13, the South put forward a new proposal for groups from both sides to visit tombs in the South and North, but the North declined this overture as well.

Dismissing Park's offer of dual UN admission, Kim Il Sung declared that when Koreans were represented at the United Nations, it should be as a confederation "under the name of the Confederal Republic of Koryo." Kim's proposal, made at a mass rally in Pyongyang, had not been discussed between North and South and had no apparent connection to the continuing dialogue.[76] The high-handed way in which the proposal was made indicated that an historic period of dialogue between the Koreas had come to an end.

President Park's concession, offered freely, without demanding a North Korean concession in return, had been intended to breathe life into the faltering talks. Having already decided the talks should be terminated, however, Kim Il Sung was not to reverse his well-executed abandonment in an apparent response to a South Korean initiative. For North Korea, the South Korean offer was merely an advantage that could be stored away and put to use at an appropriate time. As Admiral Joy noticed two decades earlier, if concessions are made without insisting on an equal concession in return, "the Communists become more aggressive, demanding more, and conceding nothing."[77]

In a last-ditch effort, on August 15, President Park issued a clarification of his offer for dual UN membership, explaining that it would help to ease tensions, restore mutual trust, and advance the interests of all of Korea's people.

The North's final blow to the process came thirteen days later. On August 28, the North Korean cochairman of the SNCC broke into a regularly scheduled broadcast of Radio Pyongyang to declare a unilateral suspension of SNCC operations. He linked his Southern counterpart, Lee Hu Rak, with the kidnapping of South Korean opposition leader Kim Dae Jung.

On August 8, Kim Dae Jung, who had challenged President Park in the contested election of 1971, was kidnapped from a hotel room in Tokyo, causing considerable turmoil in South Korea and tension in relations with Japan. The intervention of United States forces rescued the opposition leader from being killed by his kidnappers.[78] North Korea saw the South's malicious act as an opportunity to shore up support among Park's opposition, and asserted, "We cannot sit together and discuss with Lee Hu Rak and other South Korean 'gangsters' important state affairs because they persecute a democratic personage calling for a peaceful unification."[79]

At the same time, North Korea signaled that President Park's June 23 "Foreign Policy for Peace and Unification" was an additional cause for complaint. Calling Park's offer of dual UN membership an "open manifestation of a two-Korea policy," the North asserted that it had "turned upside down the South-North joint communiqué."[80] The process North Korea began in March, a process of terminating the dialogue and blaming the South for its failure, was completed by late August.

Why had North Korea decided that the talks no longer served its interests? "By the end of 1972," Lee Dong Bok observed, "North Korea began to realize it had misjudged the situation." Rather than attracting a groundswell of support in the South, the North had made the ROK's citizens increasingly suspicious of the North's intentions. Furthermore, Lee surmised, visits by North Koreans to the South had "undermined two crucial ideological myths of North Korea—the 'absolute infallibility' of Kim Il Sung's words and the 'absolute superiority' of North Korea's self-styled *Juche* socialist economy and collectivized Communist political order."[81] Song agrees that at the end of 1972, "North Korea came to the conclusion that the existing dialogue had to be maneuvered by an all or nothing strategy into a dead end. Therefore, it stalemated the dialogue by demanding unacceptable proposals in 1973."[82]

A more cynical but well-substantiated view is that the North never intended to advance the cause of unification; it merely sought to restore the issue, which had become a matter of discussion led by others, to its own control. What the North accomplished during the period surrounding the joint communiqué was to deflate notions of "peaceful coexistence" that the Soviet Union had advocated, to isolate the Korean question from the rapprochement being pursued between Beijing and Washington, to seize from the ROK the initiative for advancing proposals, to portray the ROK as incapable of negotiating in its own right, and to demand withdrawal of American forces as its single most important precondition for continued dialogue. In short, the North Korean accomplishment was to frustrate the efforts of all who genuinely sought the reunification of Korea.

Although ten NSCC vice-chairmen's meetings were held at Panmunjom through March 1975, the discussions became mere recitations of the reorganization schemes the North had put forward in the earlier sessions. The vice-chairmen's meetings served as an additional forum for the South to convey worldwide revulsion at North Korea's attempt to assassinate President Park on August 15, 1974, and the November 1974 discovery of a North Korean invasion tunnel under the DMZ. The North's reaction was accordingly to call for suspension of those meetings. When the South refused the North's attempt to defer NSCC matters to lower level spokesmen's meetings, the North merely downgraded its representation in the vice-chairmen's meetings. Finally, North Korea indefinitely postponed the vice-chairmen's meeting scheduled for May 1975, and the vice-chairmen's meetings were thereby closed down.

The North's August 28, 1973, statement, on the eve of the eighth plenary session of the Red Cross conference, resulted in the cancellation of that session and ended the hope of progress in the humanitarian talks. Twenty-five working-level Red Cross talks were held over the next four years in a vain attempt to develop an agenda for an eighth plenary session until, on March 19, 1978, the North declared an indefinite suspension of the working-level talks. The North used as a pretext the argument that the annual joint U.S.-ROK military exercise *Team Spirit* caused "an artificial difficulty to the Red Cross talks." They thereby introduced a new precondition—cancellation of scheduled military exercises—that would be used to test Western eagerness for talks over the next two decades. With this step, "the last thread of inter-Korean dialogue" that had begun in 1972 was cut.[83]

North Korea shut down the various sessions of dialogue when

everything outside the negotiations seemed to be going its way. In 1975, many emerging third world countries had given formal diplomatic recognition to the DPRK at the expense of the ROK. North Korea's entrance into the Non-Aligned Movement (NAM) was unanimously approved by the organization and the ROK's application was rejected. A declaration adopted at the Lima, Peru, meeting of NAM foreign ministers called for withdrawal of foreign forces from South Korea and replacement of the armistice with a peace treaty.[84]

The collapse of the government of South Vietnam in late spring 1975 gave North Korea added incentive to sharpen its anti-U.S. and anti-ROK propaganda at MAC meetings. Renewed arrogance and bravado marked North Korean foreign policy pronouncements. Speaking at a dinner in Beijing on April 18, Kim Il Sung pledged, "Should revolution take place in South Korea, we, as one and the same nation, will not just look on with folded arms but would strongly support the South Korean people. . . . In this war, we would lose only the Military Demarcation Line."[85] Cautiously, China issued a statement that the DPRK was "the sole legitimate sovereign state of the Korean nation."[86] Some analysts believe that China dissuaded an overconfident North Korea from launching an attack on the South; the DPRK had made clandestine preparations for such an attack.[87]

Most significantly, North Korea benefited from the 1975 debate in the United Nations. The debate advanced the notion that each of the Koreas had a relatively equivalent claim to political legitimacy.

In November, the UN General Assembly adopted two contradictory resolutions, one meant to support the DPRK and one supportive of the ROK. The pro-DPRK resolution called for the parties to the armistice agreement to replace it with a peace agreement, dissolve the United Nations Command, and withdraw all foreign troops stationed in South Korea under the UN flag. The pro-ROK resolution urged the parties directly concerned with the Korean armistice agreement to initiate talks aimed at dissolving the UNC by January 1, 1976, provided that North Korea and China agree to a new four-way arrangement at Panmunjom. North and South Korea were expected to face each other across the table with the U.S. and Chinese representatives beside them.[88]

The more specific pro-ROK proposal mitigated the effect of the more general pro-DPRK proposal, so the DPRK strategy at the UN was less than a complete success. Nevertheless, the DPRK had succeeded in establishing new limits for the international debate: the international community had expressed its desire for the termination of the UN Command; the ROK could no longer cite the UN declarations of 1949 as recognizing its exclusive political legitimacy; the ROK government, heir to deeply held anticolonial convictions, was being portrayed as a colony itself and ridiculed by the emerging anticolonialist majority at the UN; and finally, pressure to conclude a permanent peace arrangement had been applied equally to all parties, despite the fact that it was the DPRK's refusal to accept the UN role that had stymied the peace conference in 1953.[89]

Moreover, the United States government had signed on to the goal of disbanding the United Nations Command, with the important qualification that four-way talks develop alternative means of maintaining the armistice. Ambassador John Scali's June 27 letter to the UN Secretary General, and Secretary of State Kissinger's speech before the UN General Assembly on September 22, initiated decades of U.S. support for four-way talks to resolve the question of Korea's unification.[90]

Responding negatively to the new U.S. approach, North Korea pressed harder for two-way talks between the DPRK and the United States. On October 10, 1975, Kim Il Sung reiterated his Koryo confederation proposal, but insisted that the peace agreement to replace the armistice would have to be signed between the DPRK and the United States.[91]

Neither U.S. insistence on four-way talks nor North Korea's insistence on U.S.-DPRK talks seemed to get at the actual circumstances underlying division. In fact, the standoff between the United States and the DPRK tends to obscure the most fundamental aspect of the problem: unification must be accomplished by the people of the North and South. Behind the American proposal for four-way talks is the recognition that the key parties are actually North and South Korea, with the United States and China serving as coordinators of the communities of nations whose interests and support they represent. North Korea, however, does not wish to accept the notion of legitimate competing interests on the peninsula; therefore it cannot accept that the South has a role, or that a community of nations supporting the South has a role. It had a similar problem in acknowledging a role for China, perhaps because it resents its dependence on China. From North Korea's perspective, two-way talks comport with the theoretical construct that the problem is one between an anticolonial state seeking to bring its entire territory under its sovereignty, and an external "imperialist" power pursuing a policy of divide and conquer.

North Korea's unprecedented if inconclusive success in the United Nations prompted it to assume a posture of highhandedness in its dealings with South Korea and to intensify its propaganda attacks at the MAC. Its attitude reached a peak on August 18, 1976, when North Korean guards committed the axe murders at Panmunjom. Thereafter, attempting to deal with the international revulsion the act inspired, North Korea quickly reversed its tactics. The Military Armistice Commission witnessed a peculiar quiet between meetings.

At the same time, a series of events demonstrated the momentum behind rapprochement between the major powers in Northeast Asia: the signing of the Sino-Japanese Peace and Friendship Treaty in August 1978; the normalization of relations between the United States and the People's Republic of China in January 1979; and improvements in the relationship between the ROK and the Soviet Union. None of these developments promoted DPRK objectives, but they contributed to shifts in American thinking regarding U.S. troop deployments in Asia. Kim Il Sung noted with optimism President Jimmy Carter's 1977 proposal to withdraw U.S. ground forces from South Korea.

While Kim Il Sung thought there was a chance that President Carter would pursue Kim's long-held objective of removing U.S. troops from the peninsula, North Korea maintained a low profile, refraining from confrontation with the UNC and the ROK. "We think that if the Carter administration withdraws the American troops from South Korea in accordance with its campaign pledges, renounces its unfriendly attitude, and changes its hostile policy towards our country," Kim Il Sung asserted, "we can establish good relations with it."[92]

The Carter administration's proposed troop withdrawal and its criticism of ROK human rights abuses caused friction in the U.S.-ROK alliance, however, and challenged more American interests than it advanced. When it was determined that American intelligence agencies had underestimated North Korean troop strength, the United States suspended plans for phased withdrawals of American troops and promised closer consultation with the ROK.[93] To strengthen the alliance, the United States and the ROK formed the Combined Forces Command in November 1978. If the UNC were disbanded, the bilateral command structure would still provide for Korea's security.

On January 19, 1979, ROK President Park proposed North-South dialogue "at any time, at any place, and at any level" to discuss "all problems pending between the two sides."[94] The only North Korean response came in the form of a statement from an organization identified as the "Democratic Front for the Reunification of the Fatherland." It proposed to convene, in September 1979, a "convocation of a whole-nation conference attended by the delegates of various political parties and social organizations in the south and north," another iteration of the North's "Grand National Assembly" idea.[95] In other words, the North was still fixed on funneling unification discussions toward an elaborate scheme for holding an unelected assembly that would be susceptible to the North's exploitation. An ROK spokesman despaired that in response to President Park's offer, "a mere social organization continues to make an impracticable demand, indulging in political propaganda."[96]

Soon after President Park's proposal, the ROK cochairman of the SNCC, which Seoul had continued to staff even while the organization was dormant, challenged the DPRK to fulfill the spirit of the joint communiqué. In reply, North Korea's "democratic front" on February 5 dismissed the legitimacy of the SNCC, an organization created through Kim Il Sung's personal intervention, by saying it had been "rendered irrational" and had lost its "raison d'être." Instead, North Korea wanted to talk of a "machinery for nationwide dialogue and conference."[97] Lee Dong Bok, spokesman for South Korea, defended the SNCC which, he pointed out, "offers an all-embracing forum of dialogue."[98] Were it not for the long history of North Korean Communist efforts to convene a nondemocratic assembly that would exclude disagreeing participants, one might think the Korean division had narrowed to a question of credentials of delegates to meetings.

There followed an interesting set of non-meetings that are called "anomalous contacts" by historians of North-South dialogue. Both sides could be described as having attended different meetings together. Pyongyang would not attend meetings under the terms of the SNCC; Seoul wanted to continue the dialogue toward fulfillment of the joint communiqué. In a spirit of compromise, South Korea sent its four SNCC members to convene an SNCC meeting at Panmunjom; simultaneously, Pyongyang sent a delegation of "democratic front" members to Panmunjom for a meeting with their Southern counterparts. Three such sessions of these coincidental gatherings were held in the Neutral Nations Supervisory Commission (NNSC) meeting room. These "anomalous contacts" resulted merely in airing the two sides' divergent proposals for resuming dialogue. Trying to use the same ploy to generate a higher working-level meeting that might prove more valuable, Seoul informed Pyongyang that it would send SNCC working-level delegates to Panmunjom on March 28 to the same meeting room. North Korean participation, however, failed to materialize. Alone at the table, the South Korean chief delegate, Dong Hoon, grumbled, "The SNCC, which is the product of a bilateral agreement, cannot be negated unilaterally."[99] Such legal niceties obviously mattered very little to North Korea; it would do as it pleased regardless of its 1972 commitment.

What pleased North Korea was that it undermined the Republic of Korea when its government was particularly vulnerable. In the spring of 1979, widespread opposition to Park Chung Hee's manipulation of the constitution, which had made him president for as many terms as he wished, generated protests across South Korea. Nearly two decades earlier, Rhee's overreaching effort to stifle political opposition and confine participation had brought down the founding father's government. As it did in 1960, the North thought the instability of 1979 might incite revolution in the South.

Times of domestic instability in the South are not the best opportunities for North-South dialogue. Yet when President Jimmy Carter visited South Korea on July 1, 1979, he persuaded Park Chung Hee to offer North Korea the opportunity for three-way talks. Park reluctantly agreed, believing that the North would reject the idea, and that he might win some leverage with President Carter.[100] During that visit Park had to persuade Carter to suspend plans for American troop withdrawals, and he chose not to fight on two fronts. The two presidents directed their foreign minister and secretary of state to communicate jointly with the foreign minister of North Korea, giving North Korea an opportunity to ridicule the South and insist on direct talks with the United States.[101]

On July 10, 1979, the DPRK minister of foreign affairs responded that the questions of withdrawal of U.S. forces from South Korea and replacement of the Korean armistice agreement with a peace agreement were matters to be resolved between the United States and North Korea, "who are the actual parties to the armistice agreement." North Korea imperiously allowed that South Korea might be permitted to observe the discussions. The North Korean minister of foreign affairs said that it would keep a door open for dialogue with the South Korean authorities, political parties, and social organizations and another door for a dialogue with the United States.[102] The reference to "authorities" rather than "officials" was a subtle insult undermining the status of the ROK government. The era of the joint communiqué, in which the two governments might deal with each other as equals, seemed long gone.

Recognizing widespread dissent against Park Chung Hee's suppression of his political opposition, and eager to convey the impression that a Marxist revolution in the South was under way, the North proceeded to infiltrate terrorist agents once again, as it had done in the 1960s. Between July 1979 and August 1983, seven infiltrations of North Korean vessels carrying commandos and four of ground forces who had crossed through the DMZ and the Han River estuary were discovered. Thirty-seven North Korean intruders and ten South Koreans were killed in exchanges of fire with the infiltrators; one North Korean and eight South Koreans were wounded.

On October 26, 1979, South Korea's political situation became more unstable when the head of the South Korean CIA, Kim Jae Kyu, assassinated President Park at a private dinner party. An interim government under Prime Minister Choi Kyu Hah was formed under martial law. In December, when Major General Chun Doo Hwan emerged as the leading power in the ROK Army, acting President Choi was reduced to a figurehead. Half a year later, South Korean protests against Chun Doo Hwan's martial law continued to inspire violent protests in a number of South Korean cities. In May, ROK Army units stormed Kwangju to retake control of that southwestern Korean city, which had been held for several days by protesters. American officials did not intervene to stop the violence, seeing the matter as a domestic one for South Korea to resolve itself. North Korea intensified its anti-U.S. propaganda by linking the United States with Chun Doo Hwan's oppressive measures.

As might be expected, North Korea took advantage of the South's period of political instability to generate talk of reunification. On January 12, 1980, it sent letters to eleven prominent political, military, and religious leaders across South Korea offering new opportunities for dialogue between the North and South, including a meeting of prime ministers. One letter from DPRK Premier Li Jong Ok was addressed to acting ROK Prime Minister Shin Hyon Hwak and was therefore taken as an official communication.

Prime Minister Shin agreed to holding working-level meetings in Panmunjom to work out the details for the proposed prime ministers' meeting. The North-South hotline, which had been unilaterally disconnected by North Korea, was put back into action. Preparatory meetings were held on ten occasions from February to August 1980, but broke down when the two sides could not agree on an agenda.

In keeping with the pattern noted by Lee and Song, the North Koreans moved from proposing, to disrupting, and then terminating the talks. The resumption of armed provocations initially signaled the shift in North Korea's approach, which was confirmed at the eighth round of contacts when the North feigned concern over the well-known fact that South Korea's prime minister was merely an acting prime minister. His position had not yet been confirmed by the National Assembly. At the tenth meeting, held on August 20, the North Korean delegation informed the South that it would be futile to continue working-level meetings until the "complicated situation in South Korea is stabilized."[103]

The North decided it would rather distance itself from the Chun regime than to negotiate with it. In other words, while the North initially exploited instability as an opportunity to push their objectives and probe conditions in the South, when they discovered another means to exploit the South's instability, they pursued that instead. Their objective was instability, not dialogue. The North Koreans refused to attend the eleventh meeting in Panmunjom on September 26, 1980, which would have been the first North-South meeting under Chun Doo Hwan's presidency, saying they would not deal with Chun's "military fascist clique."[104] They halted the dialogue and on October 10, 1980, at the sixth party congress, reiterated their fallback proposal for a Confederal Republic of Koryo.[105]

President Chun had concerns more serious than dealing with the broadsides from North Korea, and merely ignored the slurs. On January 12, 1981, he issued a policy statement saying:

> It is not my intention to argue over things past. To provide decisive momentum to creating mutual trust, . . . I invite President Kim Il Sung of north Korea to visit Seoul without any condition attached and free of any burden. I will ensure that his personal safety is fully guaranteed during his stay in Seoul. I will extend all possible cooperation to him if he wishes to travel to any place of his choice in order to take a first-hand look at the actual situation in Seoul, other cities, or rural areas. I also want to make it clear that I am prepared, at any time, to visit north Korea if he invites me on the same terms as I offer.[106]

South Korea reasoned that visits between the two leaders would further mutual trust and therefore diminish the chance of war through
miscalculation. On a more practical level, however, they knew that if
the two leaders exchanged visits, "contacts and dialogue of various
types would take place between the two sides in the course of translating the proposed visits into action, thereby providing a natural impetus to resuming the suspended inter-Korean dialogue."[107]

South Korea valued dialogue itself; North Korea sought other
benefits. In North Korea's reply of January 19, 1981, it demanded the
following preconditions:

- dismissal of the incumbent government and creation of a new regime sympathetic to communism
- freeing of political prisoners, including Kim Dae Jung (who later
  that year was permitted to seek asylum in the United States)
- abrogation of laws on anticommunism, and dissolution of anti-
  Communist offices and organizations
- disavowal of President Park's June 23, 1973, "Foreign Policy for
  Peace and Unification"
- pullout of U.S. forces in Korea.[108]

The government of President Chun Doo Hwan, however, would
not let the matter rest. North Korea would find itself the object of creative and often startling proposals from a persistent South Korean administration that kept pressure on the North to come to the table. In
President Chun's own words, "I want to make it clear that every possible effort has been and will continue to be made by the Republic of
Korea government to realize these proposals."[109]

When North Korea reissued a variation of its "Grand National
Assembly" idea, the Chun administration did not reject the much
worn idea but offered to convene meetings of high-level delegates to
hear the details of the proposal. Moving startlingly close to the North
Korean idea, President Chun issued a "Formula for National Reconciliation and Democratic Unification" on January 22, 1982, in which
he proposed convening a "Consultative Conference for National Reunification" that would draft a constitution of a unified "Democratic
Republic of Korea." Chun proposed that once the document was
drafted, it should be put into effect through "free, democratic referen-
dums held throughout the whole peninsula."[110] Until that time, certain measures would guarantee peace on the peninsula and form a

"basic agreement" which the South envisaged would be called the "Provisional Agreement on Basic Relations between South and North Korea."[111]

On February 1, the ROK proposed twenty pilot projects both governments could undertake cooperatively. These projects included highway construction, postal exchanges, family reunions, opening zones for tourism, free trade ports, joint fisheries, historical research studies, sports exchanges, North Korea's participation in the 1986 Asian Games and 1988 Olympiad, removal of military facilities in the DMZ, and arms control confidence-building measures.[112]

The South even made a gesture toward accepting the North's long-held antidemocratic view that delegates to a national assembly should be appointed from interest groups and trade unions rather than proportionately elected. It said representatives could be appointed from among government authorities, political parties, the Advisory Council on Peaceful Unification, and the Advisory Council on State Affairs. The North did not find this advantageous enough, however, and insisted on naming the South's fifty delegates itself.[113]

Keeping North Korea on the defensive, President Chun reissued the invitation to Kim Il Sung on June 5, adding:

> Should some unavoidable circumstance prevent President Kim from accepting my proposal or from inviting me to visit north Korea, I suggest that we meet each other at some other place for frank face-to-face talks. I leave the choice of venue to the north Korean authorities. It could be Panmunjom, or a third country, or any other place convenient to them.[114]

North Korea denounced the South Korean proposal, asserting that it was "aimed at some impure purpose," and on July 1, Kim Il Sung himself said he would not "have dialogue or contact of any kind with the incumbent South Korean government."[115] Whatever North Korea thought of Chun's proposals, however, it would be considerably more responsive after international disgust over the Rangoon bombing.

Deflecting International Disgust

Following the bombing that killed seventeen Koreans and four Burmese in Rangoon on October 9, 1983, North Korea was the object of international opprobrium. To deflect criticism, it once again emphasized an incentive to bring the South back to the table. Its tactic would seem to demonstrate a new level of willingness to negotiate unification, but it was actually an effort to redirect the world's attention to the North's grievances, primarily the presence of foreign troops. In hopes of eliciting a fast and favorable reaction, North Korea offered a proposal similar to the one offered by President Carter and President Park in 1979.

To signal Chinese endorsement and North Korean sincerity, North Korea enlisted China's help in floating the proposal. Chinese Premier Zhao Ziyang delivered North Korea's new offer for three-party talks to President Reagan when Zhao visited the White House on January 10, 1984.[116] North Korea might have thought that President Carter's three-way proposal was still on the table. The North might also have misread President Reagan's firm commitment in Seoul that there would be no talks with North Korea "without the full and equal participation of the Republic of Korea."[117] It seems not to have understood that the Reagan statement implied Seoul would have a leading role in matters of unification policy, not a secondary one. Reagan told Zhao that North-South bilateral negotiations would have to come first, and if the issue needed international attention afterward, then four-party discussions involving China and the United States would be appropriate.[118]

The Reagan administration's espousal of four-way talks, like the Clinton administration's a decade later, was not far different from the rationale behind Kissinger's original four-way proposal a decade earlier. It was defended by Assistant Secretary of State for Asian and Pacific Affairs Paul Wolfowitz before a Congressional hearing on June 15, 1984:

> On the Korean peninsula, the Chinese and we have different allies and therefore somewhat different perspectives on the key problems and their solutions, but we also acknowledge our common interests in seeking to reduce tensions and assure peace and stability. . . . The President made clear to the Chinese that our troops are in South Korea to defend our ally, and that the sole threat to peace and stability on the Korean peninsula emanates from the North as was evidenced in the Rangoon bombing atrocity last year. The Chinese expressed their support for North Korea's proposal for tripartite talks with the U.S. and South Korea. The President reiterated our strong preference—and that of our South Korean allies—for direct talks between North and South Korea or, if both Korean parties are willing, for quadripartite talks to involve the U.S. and China. The President

indicated that he hoped the Chinese might be helpful on the margins of any talks that get started, or participate in talks. At present, however, the Chinese have said that their participation in any formal talks would be difficult.[119]

The North Korean gambit would not be dropped easily. In an effort to appear democratic, the North Korean regime, through its legislative arm, the Supreme People's Assembly, repeated the three-way talks offer to the ROK directly. The ROK National Unification Board turned it down within a day, calling instead for bilateral talks.

For two months, the North considered what that quick negative reaction indicated, and might well have concluded that the Reagan administration was willing to back South Korea in an effort to drive a harder bargain. After two months' reflection, North Korea repeated its proposal for DPRK-U.S.-ROK tripartite talks and rejected the ROK proposal for North-South bilateral talks.

The North, however, tends to respect opponents' firm negotiating positions and adapts when its own interests are at risk. Its interests were at risk at that time not only because of the global reaction to the Rangoon bombing, but also because South Korea was making important economic and diplomatic gains. In 1981, the International Olympic Committee had announced that Seoul would host the 1988 Olympics. North Korea called the decision "the most vicious expression of a two-Korea policy."[120] The North sought either to cohost or to disrupt the international event.

In the years following the Rangoon bombing, the North pursued relatively businesslike negotiations before the International Olympic Committee, and appeared conciliatory toward Seoul as well. In April 1984, North Korea agreed to sports talks proposed by the ROK, hoping to send a single Korean team to the Los Angeles Olympics under the name of the Confederation of Koryo. The talks eventually broke down when demands from the South for an apology for the Rangoon bombing forced the embarrassed North Koreans to walk out of the sessions.[121] In a gesture of goodwill gratefully acknowledged by the South, the North sent a large quantity of relief goods—rice, clothing, medicine, and cement—to victims of South Korea's September 1984 floods. Precedent-setting North-South economic talks were convened in Panmunjom in November 1984. Although North Korea suspended all dialogue during the period of the joint U.S.-ROK military exercise *Team Spirit 1985*, the talks were resumed in May, and the two sides had an exchange of art troupes and family reunions in Seoul and Pyongyang, in addition to convening, at long last (in May 1985), the eighth session of full-dress Red Cross talks, in Seoul. Two more full-dress Red Cross sessions were held in 1985. In addition, two meetings of representatives from South Korea's National Assembly and North Korea's Supreme People's Assembly were convened to discuss an inter-Korean parliamentary meeting.[122]

While the flurry of sixteen exchanges and contacts over little more than a year was under way, President Chun instructed his National Security Planning Director Chang Se Dong to arrange North-South summit talks secretly through North Korean contacts in Panmunjom.[123] Ho Dam, secretary of the North Korean Workers party central committee secretariat, and Han Shi Hae, another member of the party central committee secretariat, traveled through Panmunjom to Seoul on September 4, 1985, to arrange the proposed summit.

The verbatim dialogue of these secret sessions, published in a South Korean monthly newsmagazine a decade later, provides interesting insights into the nature of North-South discussions.[124] The participants proceeded cautiously, testing each other for indications of new flexibility on old obstacles. Ho Dam began the discussion with exuberant flattery which Chang Se Dong deflected. Chang told Ho that whether the meeting was held would depend on the likelihood of making substantive progress along the lines of specific nonaggression terms or mutual exchanges and cooperation. Diplomatically taking his North Korean counterpart to task, he cautioned, "We should not persist in accepting a unilateral formula which is unacceptable to the other party, but examine all of the ideas submitted by both sides to adopt rational, efficient, and practical methods on the basis of the realistic situation in our divided country." He pointed out that South Koreans had learned to be circumspect about North Korean offers and that even as the two were meeting "a considerable percentage of our population suspects that the continuing Red Cross and economic talks might fall apart."

More interested in propaganda impact than substance, Ho Dam wanted to know whether the South envisioned "a joint announcement of a certain agreement, or our two leaders fixing their signatures to a written agreement before the announcement." He wanted something more useful to the regime's purposes than a nonaggression pact between two sovereign parties.

Unaware that his comments might be received adversely, Ho

Dam added, "The summit we are discussing here is not a conference of the heads of two different states; President Chun Doo Hwan is not going to a foreign country, but coming to Pyongyang to meet his brother, President Kim Il Sung." His South Korean counterpart could not let that suggestion stand for a moment. "Let us follow the international custom and rules," Chang Se Dong insisted, "because this is the first time for such a meeting in 40 years. . . . We can make it more informal and casual after the second and third time."

Chastened, Ho Dam explored possible provisions of a nonaggression agreement. "It should pledge a reduction of military forces and equipment," Ho reasoned. "Both the north and south are spending too much money for military expenditures, as a small nation. Why should we waste our national resources for huge military forces on both sides when we pledge that we would not invade each other? We can divert such large expenditures to the consumer sector to improve people's livelihood." Finally, picking up on Chang's earlier reference to the continuing talks, Ho enticed Chang by saying that following the summit, the economic talks and Red Cross talks might become successful.

Chang agreed that a number of issues could be worked out; then, in a test of the North Korean's patience and tenacity, raised a sore point:

> By the way, you may not be pleased with what I am going to say, but the incident which took place two years ago [the Rangoon bombing] was an event that I could not possibly forget especially because I was Chief, Presidential Security Force, at that time. I believe you were well aware of that serious event, and served as the Minister of Foreign Affairs in Pyongyang at that time. When Director Lee Hu Rak went to Pyongyang to work on the 1972 North-South Joint Communiqué, President Kim told him that the Blue House Raid was caused by a "careless extreme leftist element." The Rangoon Bombing is somewhat different from the Blue House Raid in that we suffered so many victims in a third country. Although President Chun wants to push for summit talks with President Kim regardless of past events, including the Rangoon Bombing, I have been thinking it would be very difficult for our people to overcome the tragic incident easily and trust your side.

Ho Dam had to rule out an apology, but could neither overstate nor undermine his own authority to foreclose the option. He fell back on North Korea's well-established propaganda line:

Frankly speaking, the Rangoon incident you brought up just now has really nothing to do with our side. This subject was brought up by my subordinates before I left Pyongyang, but my point was I am not going to Seoul to argue about the incident because it is not going to help our task to bring about the summit talks. There will be no end to such argument.

I thought, "We cannot possibly admit the responsibility for the incident, and it will be impossible for us to apologize for the incident. And if you demand we admit it and apologize for it we will not be able to make this summit happen."

So, when I was coming to Seoul I was thinking that this issue might be brought up, and if it were, I was going to say that we should not talk about the past. This incident will be clarified someday in the future, but there will be no end to discussion if we start to talk about it. Our position is that the history will tell the truth, and we hope our two sides do our best not to let such tragic incidents take place again. In fact, President Kim Il Sung has confidence in President Chun and wants to meet him with his mind wide open. How much more can we expect from him?

Such a response was expected, but Ho Dam had delivered it with patience, confidence, and courtesy. Perhaps with some respect for his artful counterpart, Chang responded, "I feel like I am meeting my old friend when I am talking to you. Our mission is to support our respective leaders, and I hope we can achieve our goal." Ho amicably replied, "The feeling is mutual." Chang then arranged the next day's meeting with President Chun.

At the Blue House, President Chun received the North Korean envoy with an expression of appreciation that Kim Il Sung had sent Ho to Seoul and gratitude for the North's earlier flood relief. After exchanging pleasantries, Ho produced the following letter:

> To: Republic of Korea President Chun Doo-hwan.
>   Seoul
>   Mr. President:
>   It is my genuine pleasure to dispatch Korea Workers Party Secretary Comrade Ho Dam to Seoul as my special envoy for the purpose of promoting necessary arrangements for your visit to Pyongyang in connection with your desire

to convene north-south summit talks, and I am sending my warm greetings to you on this occasion. Secretary Ho Dam is going to Seoul this time on my behalf to deliver my personal message to you and will consult with your people on the necessary arrangements for your visit to Pyongyang. I hope you will have confidence in him and have an extensive discussion with him in regards to various issues pertaining to summit talks. I sincerely wish my special envoy's visit to Seoul will result in great success and our meaningful summit talks in Pyongyang will be brought about. I wish you excellent health.

> Kim Il Sung
> President, Democratic People's Republic
> of Korea
> Pyongyang
> September 3, 1985

Ho launched into the "extensive discussion" Kim Il Sung referred to in the letter, pointing out how pleased Kim was with the progress that had been made in two-way talks at Panmunjom, and expressing Kim's fervent desire for unification in his lifetime. He extended appreciation to President Chun for having "an energetic and positive attitude toward national unification, unlike his predecessors." He said that Chun's "good deeds opened the tightly closed door to north-south dialogue." He gave Chun credit for already having generated the Red Cross talks, economic talks, and interparliamentary talks.

Ho Dam said Kim had asked him to emphasize that he was "especially impressed" that President Chun would travel to Pyongyang. "Your travel to Pyongyang after crossing the Military Demarcation Line," Ho said, "will make a great contribution to the entire nation that ardently desires unification and provide a new turning point for national unification."

President Chun recognized that an olive branch he had extended was being accepted, but he also knew that past dialogue had ended with the North's demand for the removal of military forces the South deemed necessary for its security. The former general told Ho he agreed with many of Kim's points, and earnestly hoped for progress through economic and humanitarian talks. But Chun was not shy about making the following firm statement defending the ROK's security:

We would be better off not to meet unless we can come up with some tangible results. It is a fact that North Korean military strength is superior to that of South Korea. For example, there was a report that the numerical strength of North Korean forces is about 770,000, but it was confirmed recently that it is about 880,000. This is about 1.2 to 1.3 times the South Korean military strength. . . . You have 3,520 tanks; 2.7 to 3 times more than we have. You have about 7,320 artillery pieces; 1.1 to 1.2 times more than we have. You have some 540 naval ships; 3.6 to 4 times more than we have. But we must take into consideration the military strength of the major powers surrounding us. . . . Therefore, even if North Korean strategists plan to finish a war [against South Korea] in a week, it would not work. They may have taken into consideration North Korea soldiers' devotion of duty, but such a war would result in complete ruin of the North Koreans. So, we must make certain that Korea does not become the starting point of a world war. In such a war, there will be no winner among Koreans.

The proposed summit meeting between Kim Il Sung and Chun Doo Hwan never occurred. The visit of Chun's envoys to Pyongyang was delayed a month and that made holding a summit before the end of the year difficult. The story of Ho's visit to Seoul leaked to the press, and the North was reportedly piqued at the breach of confidence. When Chang Se Dong, his assistant for secret negotiations, Park Chul Un, and three others visited Pyongyang, Kim Il Sung gave them a draft nonaggression pact and a demand that the U.S.-ROK military exercise *Team Spirit 1986* be cancelled. He could not have been surprised that the South would agree to neither. It is likely that Chun's firm response on the necessity of foreign troops disabused the North of any aspirations it may have had for propaganda exploitation of a quick agreement on broad principles.

With little likelihood of a summit, and with no progress toward North Korea's objectives in discussions with the International Olympic Committee, the North once again entered the phase of terminating the talks. On January 20, 1986, North Korea abruptly cut off all dialogue, focusing its ire on the joint U.S.-ROK military exercise *Team Spirit* that had been held annually since 1977—almost a full decade, with intermittent and generally low-key reaction from North Korea. In this instance, however, the North chose to label the routine exercise of allied forces a "nuclear war maneuver."[125]

Pyongyang decided it was time to go on the offensive again. North Korea forwarded to the United Nations Security Council a report concerning "Armistice Agreement violations by the UNC from July 1986 to June 1987 and North Korean initiatives to reduce tension on the Korean peninsula." In the report, North Korea claimed that the UNC had committed "ceaseless military provocation and hostilities" and "criminal acts" in violation of the armistice agreement on some 44,000 occasions during the period mentioned in the report. Of the 44,000 alleged violations levied against the UNC during the period more than 43,000 "violations" were referred to the MAC secretaries because they were either routine administrative issues or minor infractions such as not wearing the proper identification armbands. In fact, 24,789 allegations were charges that workers were not wearing proper armbands in the DMZ, and investigations revealed that most of these allegations were false. The number was designed to create the false impression that Seoul was an unsafe place to host the 1988 Olympic games.

In yet another effort to undermine the 1988 Olympics, two North Korean agents posing as Japanese tourists planted a time bomb in an overhead compartment on board Korean Air Lines flight 858. The agents disembarked in Abu Dhabi, and the plane continued on to Seoul. The bomb exploded in flight on November 29, 1987, killing the plane's 115 passengers. Through a strange twist of fate, the North Korean agents were unexpectedly detained in Bahrain where their forged travel documents came under scrutiny. When arrested, the two attempted to commit suicide, consistent with North Korean special operations training. The elderly male terrorist succumbed. A police woman, however, slapped the poison from the mouth of the twenty-five-year-old female terrorist, Kim Hyun Hui, and Kim lived to tell the story of North Korea's treachery. She explained how the attack had been ordered and directed by Kim Il Sung's son and successor, Kim Jong Il, in frustration over the North's unsuccessful attempt to block the holding of the Olympic games.[126]

In sharp contrast to North Korea's terrorism, South Korea demonstrated considerable national confidence and political maturity in the year 1988. In addition to the highly successful Seoul Olympics, South Korea conducted a clean and democratic election after which power transferred lawfully from Chun Doo Hwan to Roh Tae Woo at the end of Chun's constitutional term. On October 18, Roh became the first Korean head of state to address the United Nations General Assembly. The new president's speech at the UN mapped a "Road to Reconciliation and Unification," and initiated a rapid series of proposals for dialogue.

Six preparatory North-South contacts were held to lay the foundation for parliamentary talks and a North-South summit was planned. Having committed an act of terror in midair against innocent civilians, and having lost face to South Korea's success, the North returned to the table for dialogue. Once again it needed to refurbish its international image.

The decade closed with another constructive South Korean attempt to package "confederation" in a way that would preserve South Korea's independence and democracy, and guarantee both Koreas power commensurate with their de facto sovereignty. Roh's September 11, 1989, "Korean National Community Unification Formula" introduced the notion of "commonwealth," the name given to one of three phases of unification. Use of the term confuses Americans familiar with the term's application to certain states of the Union, Puerto Rico, and the Northern Mariana Islands; the Korean instance has more in common with Confucian notions of an ideal society. Roh's proposal, subsumed in President Kim Young Sam's July 6, 1993, unification policy as well, envisioned commonwealth as "a common sphere of national life to promote common prosperity and to restore national homogeneity."[127]

South Korean policy toward unification has since 1989 envisioned that after the phase of commonwealth, a unified assembly and government based on national elections would be established pursuant to a unified constitution. A council of ministers would discuss "ways to accelerate political dialogue, agree on military confidence building measures, the transformation of the current Armistice into a peace treaty and changing the DMZ into a Peace Zone." A council of representatives, to be composed of equal numbers of members of the legislatures in both the South and North, would draft a constitution for the unified republic. By layering these institutions, the onerous nonrepresentative and disproportionate advantages sought by the North for so many years in its "Grand National Assembly" might be avoided.[128]

A significant distinction later emerged between the South Korean government's approach and that of long-time opposition leader Kim Dae Jung, who was elected president in 1997. Kim and his followers "did not consider the increasing reconciliation and cooperation as necessary preconditions for the establishment of the Confederation," arguing "the Confederal Stage itself is one of reconciliation and cooperation."[129] In other words, they wanted to avoid lengthy periods of matchmaking between the two societies and move directly through levels of institutional stages, leaving the governing processes of North Korea intact longer, to develop at its own pace. The reason for this more accommodating attitude toward the North Korean regime was explained this way:

> The obvious reason for our difference is to alleviate the shock and confusion of integration, to make room for accommodating North Korea's unique situation and the sensibilities of North Korean residents, to recognize the autonomous nature of the Northern government, and to allow for a reasonable period of special assistance to northern Korea by the Federal Government.[130]

Although those specific structural steps have not yet been pursued, the South's initiatives have provided a conciliatory approach that both sides would find useful in the decade ahead. As a South Korean government publication on unification policy observes, the September 11, 1989, guidelines "were based on the recognition of the North as a partner in unification, rather than as an enemy in confrontation."[131] In the 1990s, dialogue between North and South yielded unprecedented success. After a series of six meetings between the South's Prime Minister Chung Won Shik and the North's Premier Yon Hyong Muk, the men signed two agreements that emerged out of the 1989 proposals: (1) the Agreement on Reconciliation, Nonaggression, and Exchanges and Cooperation between the South and North, and (2) the Joint Declaration of the Denuclearization of the Korean peninsula. Both entered into force on February 19, 1992, after having been endorsed by Presidents Roh Tae Woo and Kim Il Sung.

The agreements, however, did not come about because the South was more confident and conciliatory; the South's attitude had never been a barrier to progress in the dialogue. Like most favorable changes in North Korea's negotiating positions, the agreements of the early 1990s came about only after North Korea recognized that its alternatives were considerably less attractive.

In the 1980s, North Korea's Marxist allies had begun to see that their own interests were more closely connected to the South's burgeoning economy and diplomatic openness than to the North's unproductive reclusiveness. After a series of summit meetings and diplomatic exchanges, the Soviet Union formally recognized South Korea on January 1, 1991. Pyongyang then watched the process repeated between South Korea and its long-standing ally China until China granted diplomatic recognition to the ROK in 1992. In spite of Kim Il Sung's condemnation of cross-recognition for almost two decades, North Korea had no choice but to acknowledge its allies' diplomatic priorities. It was also forced to accept cross-recognition at the United Nations when it became clear that China would no longer enforce Pyongyang's objection. North Korea took a seat in the United Nations simultaneously with South Korea on September 17, 1991.

Having agreed to the UN Charter's provision disavowing the use of force against another UN member, negotiating similar terms in a South-North agreement was a logical step. Although the North had consistently demanded a peace agreement with the United States first, it reversed this approach in 1992 and signed a nonaggression pact with South Korea. The North perceived that its new approach increased the pressure it could apply for a peace treaty with the United States. Two days after the South-North agreement went into effect, Kim Il Sung argued, "There no longer exists the need for foreign troops to remain on the peninsula. There can also be no excuse for the presence of foreign bases."[132]

In the 1990s, the United States and South Korea accommodated the North's stated desire for negotiations toward a peace treaty, insisting, however, on four-way negotiations, and dismissing as always the North's precondition for the withdrawal of American troops from the Korean peninsula. Despite South Korea's rhetoric of conciliation, it continued to meet the challenge of defense against the North's increasingly powerful army, and vigorously resisted any effort to unify the peninsula under communism.

As the failure of communism reached Eastern Europe and the Soviet Union, North Korea discovered there was a price for its defiant form of isolationist tyranny. Even as it succumbed to the same economic consequences that characterized the failure of Communist policies elsewhere, North Korea adhered to hardline Stalinism and resisted reform. It decried the weaknesses of other socialist systems around the world, and continued to proclaim its own self-reliance. But reality mocked the North's propaganda. Years of negative growth rates, inadequate harvests, and low production rates yielded widespread devastation across the North as its economy collapsed and its people faced famine. In the 1990s, the world recognized that North Korea's brand of communism had been, in fact, heavily dependent on external support.

By the 1990s, history itself had rendered unification of the peninsula under Communist rule impossible. The question became not whether communism would be extended throughout the peninsula, but whether it could find a means to survive in the northern half. The regime would once again turn to negotiations as a means to strengthen its grip on power.

9

Leveraging Uncertainty

Through years of selective revelation and deception, North Korea raised justifiable concern that it had undertaken a program to develop nuclear weapons. By 1993, substantial evidence indicated that North Korea might already have extracted enough plutonium from its nuclear power reactors for construction of a few nuclear bombs. Although it had many opportunities to open its nuclear facilities to international inspectors and to clarify its intentions, at critical points North Korea chose to cultivate uncertainty instead. It permitted enough exposure of its program to generate concern, but denied the inspections that could yield conclusive evidence. Kim Il Sung himself repeatedly denied that a nuclear weapons program existed, but, hiding behind a screen of national sovereignty and convenient concepts of face, refused to permit the inspections that would validate his words. He chose to keep the world worrying.

That a rogue regime suffering increasing political isolation and imminent economic collapse might devote its dwindling resources to nuclear weapons was indeed a serious concern. It raised the possibility of war and, more likely, extortion: the regime could ensure its continued existence as well as its continued oppression of the people of North Korea by threatening nuclear catastrophe if its demands for survival were not met. As international fears grew, the United States had little choice but to deal with the crisis North Korea had generated. America's global leadership brings with it worldwide responsibilities, including a commitment to the nonproliferation of weapons of mass destruction. These interests and responsibilities go well beyond the U.S. role as an ally of South Korea, although they do not necessarily conflict with it.

As North Korea could have predicted, the United States found it necessary to coordinate an international effort to determine the nature of North Korea's program and deal with its potential danger to global peace and security. North Korea was as aware of American emphasis on halting nuclear proliferation as it was of American focus on Vietnam at the time of the attack on the USS *Pueblo* in 1968. In a time-tested strategy, the North hit at interests that would justify direct negotiation between Washington and Pyongyang and that could put the United States at odds with South Korea and thereby reduce allied deterrence.

Difficulties between the United States and South Korea over the nuclear issue could predictably arise whether the United States sought a military solution that risked the lives of South Koreans in a war or whether it pursued a conciliatory approach that might strengthen the North and leave its dangerous leverage intact. The North Korean nuclear crisis was cleverly devised. It was also well implemented.

At the start of North Korea's investment in nuclear technology, its international reputation was already so suspect that its erstwhile friends and nuclear mentors proceeded with caution. In the 1960s, after the Soviet Union had trained North Korean scientists for a decade, it provided a small experimental reactor and subjected the reactor to International Atomic Energy Agency (IAEA) inspection. The Soviets took care to remind the Kim regime publicly that the reactor was for civilian, not military, purposes.[1] Mao Tse-tung reportedly turned down a request from Kim Il Sung for nuclear assistance in the mid-1960s and again in 1974.[2] After providing some assistance in the 1980s, China reportedly decided to withdraw its nuclear technicians and halt transfers of nuclear technology by 1987.[3] East German sources said years later that they had reservations regarding the North's nuclear program after discussions with Pyongyang in 1981.[4] Simultaneously with its requests for aid, North Korea undertook an indigenous nuclear program, to which it did not give its Communist allies access, and which it did not submit to international inspection.

After considerable Soviet efforts to persuade it to do so, North Korea signed the nuclear Non-Proliferation Treaty (NPT) in 1985, a step that many claim was taken to obtain light-water nuclear power reactors from the Soviet Union. Although the Soviet Union did not provide the reactors, the North had entered into an international agreement pledging not to obtain nuclear weapons and not to use reprocessed fuel from nuclear reactors for weapons production. Under the terms of the treaty, signatories were to negotiate a subsequent "safeguards agreement" that would go into such matters as inspections and other measures for "verification of the fulfillment of its obligations under this Treaty."[5]

North Korea's signing of the NPT is too often discussed as though it were a contract conditioned on provision of reactors from the Soviet Union. Failure to obtain a desired diplomatic result, however, is no excuse for a nation to disavow standing treaty commitments. Obtaining Soviet reactors was not the only benefit North Korea stood to gain by signing the treaty. The North signed in the period following the Rangoon bombing, when it sought to improve its international image and hoped to have a role in hosting the Olympic games. Its signature was a reassuring signal of responsible nuclear behavior. Signing the treaty opened up the possibility of technical assistance; treaty signatories are "entitled to participate in the fullest possible exchange of equipment, materials, and scientific and technological information for the peaceful uses of nuclear energy."[6] Treaty inspections under the safeguards agreement would promote safety as well as guarantee compliance. Inspections accordingly offered benefits a responsible regime might want for its people, providing a level of assurance that the best available advice was being exploited in a safe and scientifically sound nuclear program. The North had signed the NPT of its own free will, seeing the step as conducive to its national interests.

North Korea did not, however, rush to comply with the NPT's requirement that a safeguards agreement permitting inspections be concluded within 180 days. There was reportedly a mistake in the IAEA's processing of the necessary forms,[7] but North Korea did not bother to correct the organization's oversight. North Korea was not unfamiliar with the safeguards process. From 1977 on it had observed a safeguards agreement for the Soviet research reactor,[8] the only reactor operating at the time North Korea signed the NPT. North Korea could have extended that safeguards agreement to the reactor it brought on line in 1986, but it did not. Instead, North Korea ignored the requirement for a safeguards agreement, and got away with it for many years. It eventually fulfilled its obligation to conclude a new safeguards agreement only in exchange for substantial additional concessions.

Even as the North was taking the reassuring step of signing the NPT, committing itself exclusively to peaceful uses of nuclear technology, Washington's intelligence agencies were poring over evidence that suggested the North had embarked on a nuclear program aimed at weapons development. In the early 1980s, satellite imagery had revealed the stages of construction of a nuclear reactor at Yongbyon, sixty miles north of Pyongyang.[9] The reactor, later identified by North Korea as having an electrical output of five megawatts, appeared to be a uranium-fueled, graphite-moderated reactor capable of producing plutonium for use in nuclear weapons. No electrical transmission wires were connected to the reactor until 1992, immediately before an IAEA inspection.[10] Adding to these concerns, satellites above North Korea revealed a series of what appeared to be craters created by an explosive technique associated with nuclear weapons.[11]

North Korea has made strategic deception a matter of military doctrine and a fine art. Many of its defensive operations during the Korean War and its plans for invasion in the decades afterward were conducted underground. Yet in the years following the North's signature of the NPT, North Korea openly constructed a huge "unroofed" facility, exposing to American satellite reconnaissance "a long series of thick-walled cells in the typical configuration for separation of plutonium."[12]

Reprocessing is the means to extract plutonium, a toxic material that can be used either in making nuclear weapons or for fuel in advanced and, for the North Koreans, prohibitively expensive, breeder reactors for electricity generation. Because building a reprocessing facility is expensive, it is difficult to rationalize building one without intending to extract plutonium. A country that wanted to reprocess plutonium for nuclear weapons, however, would be expected to do so clandestinely, if only to protect the facility from a preemptive bombing strike like Israel's 1981 raid on the Iraqi nuclear facility at Osirak. North Korea, however, seemed to be constructing what appeared to be a reprocessing facility, and was doing so openly.

Built within view of airplanes taking off from Pyongyang,[13] this possible reprocessing plant and a second graphite reactor were later described by North Korea as a radiochemical laboratory and a fifty-megawatt electric generating plant. Despite its purported use for generating electricity, however, this facility, like the North's two smaller reactors, did not have a power grid adequate to deliver its electricity to the North Korean countryside.[14] The reactor appeared to have the capability of producing enough plutonium for ten to twelve bombs per year. When completed, the reprocessing plant was estimated to have a capability of producing 200 kilograms per year—enough for forty bombs annually.[15]

As intelligence analysts concluded that North Korea had the potential for developing a large nuclear arsenal, policymakers began to debate how to deal with an ostensibly civilian but potentially military nuclear development program. Throughout the Reagan and Bush administrations, and during the first two years of the Clinton administration, the answer was to increase multilateral pressure on North Korea to conform with internationally accepted standards of behavior, maintain firm military deterrence, and strengthen U.S. relationships with allies. There were costs, but there were also indications that the strategy worked. The Reagan administration had urged the Soviet Union to pressure North Korea to sign the nuclear nonproliferation treaty, and it had done so. In the wake of the collapse of Eastern European and Soviet communism, and after President Bush's September 1991 announcement of a worldwide withdrawal of tactical nuclear weapons, North and South Korea signed an agreement on the denuclearization of the Korean peninsula, in addition to the basic agreement on South-North relations. In 1991, it seemed that progress was being made.

In dealing with North Korea, however, the appearance of progress is not necessarily evidence of progress. The "Joint Declaration of the Denuclearization of the Korean Peninsula" is a short, six-paragraph agreement that might have caused previous negotiators with North Korea considerable anxiety. At the time of the signing, all of the phase one characteristics noticed in South-North dialogue during the 1980s were apparent. There was considerable fanfare and excitement as both North and South agreed not to "test, manufacture, produce, receive, possess, store, deploy or use nuclear weapons," and to "use nuclear energy solely for peaceful purposes." Both sides agreed they would "not possess nuclear reprocessing and uranium enrichment facilities," and would verify "denuclearization of the Korean peninsula" through mutual inspections. Trying to implement the much heralded agreement would, unfortunately, pass through the familiar second and third stages of reinterpretation and disavowal within the next year.

As Admiral Joy had pointed out four decades earlier, North Korea could be expected to "strive to retain a veto on all machinery of enforcement of agreements."[16] The denuclearization agreement stated that inspections would be permitted of "objects selected by the other side and *agreed upon between the two sides*, in accordance with procedures and methods to be determined by the South-North Joint Nuclear Control Commission." That provision requiring mutual agreement would effectively bar enforcement, just as similar provisions of the armistice agreement had in the 1950s.

Admiral Joy had advised that it was necessary to negotiate a mechanism for guaranteeing compliance before negotiating a pledge itself. That advice, however, is not so easy to follow. The North naturally resists and its negotiating opponents have little choice but to set aside Joy's advice. Like Joy's own armistice negotiations, the 1972 South-North communiqué, and the nonproliferation treaty, the denuclearization declaration deferred implementing procedures. It stated South and North Korea would "establish and operate a South-North Joint Nuclear Control Commission within one month of the effectuation of this joint declaration."[17] Lee Dong Bok, who had been involved in the frustrating effort to implement the 1972 agreement, would find himself in a similar position two decades later when, in the capacity of special assistant to South Korean Prime Minister Chung Won Shik, he tried to persuade North Korea to agree to nuclear inspections by the Joint Nuclear Control Commission.[18]

As an inducement to facilitate the mutual inspections North Korea had agreed to, South Korea cancelled for 1992 the U.S.-ROK military exercise that North Korea complained about—*Team Spirit*. The North did not reciprocate by permitting the desired inspections, but South Korea nevertheless considered the cancellation of *Team Spirit 1992* appropriate in the atmosphere of forward movement. The North was signing up to commitments, even if it was not implementing them, and this seemed positive.

In retrospect, however, the cancellation of *Team Spirit* calls to mind another warning from Admiral Joy: Do not offer a concession "to gain nothing more than apparent and illusory progress in the negotiations."[19] After the South cancelled *Team Spirit 1992*, the North's interest in subsequent dealings with the South lessened, and South-North dialogue entered the deep sleep identified in the 1980s as "phase three." Even though the North did not live up to its part of the bargain and permit North-South inspections, it complained vociferously when exercise *Team Spirit* was scheduled the following year.

While the South attempted to persuade the North to permit the mutual inspections it had just signed on to in the denuclearization agreement, the United States attempted to persuade the North to meet its 1985 commitment to conclude a safeguards agreement permitting international inspections. As Secretary of State Baker recalled succinctly in his memoirs, "Our diplomatic strategy was designed to build international pressure against North Korea to force them to live up to their agreement to sign a safeguards agreement permitting inspections."[20]

The first step was to develop a consensus among concerned nations about the nature of the threat. North Korea's neighbors—China, Russia, Japan—might have been expected to have the best intelligence on the North's programs and had the most at stake, but they were the most confident that North Korea's infant program was benign.[21] The United States accordingly organized briefings to share intelligence, first with its allies and eventually with the International Atomic Energy Agency. No images could provide proof of North Korea's intentions or capabilities, or fill in gaps about hidden activities, but the overall picture was troubling.

There were also differences of opinion within the United States government. Nonproliferation experts inclined toward the worst case scenario, arguing that North Korea might already have extracted enough plutonium to make a few bombs. On the other hand, some Asia experts familiar with North Korea argued that there was not enough information to conclude that North Korea had extracted plutonium, and even less to conclude that it had the technical capability to use reprocessed plutonium in constructing a nuclear device.[22]

On questions as serious as nuclear nonproliferation, however, lack of certainty is almost as great a call to action as conclusive evidence. Unable to prove whether North Korea was making nuclear weapons, the Bush administration sought to entice North Korea to demonstrate its compliance with the NPT. To persuade North Korea to fulfill its treaty obligations, the Bush administration interested North Korea with a number of long-stated objectives of the North Korean regime: the establishment of direct contact with the United States and significant changes in U.S. force posture on the Korean peninsula, including the removal of nuclear weapons as well as reductions in American troops.

On January 21, 1992, the third highest ranking official of the State Department, Under Secretary of State Arnold Kanter, met with North Korean officials in New York. Although counselor-level meetings had been initiated with North Korean representatives in Beijing in 1988, this was the first session at so high a level. The meeting was undertaken not only with South Korean consent, but also with South

Korean advice. The American under secretary met with individuals the South believed were among the rising powers in Pyongyang.[23] Kanter used the opportunity to drive home the seriousness with which the Bush administration viewed nonproliferation, and advised North Korea that its deepening economic difficulties could be resolved only with greater openness, particularly on the matter of nuclear inspections.[24] North Korea accordingly found it advantageous to sign the safeguards agreement on January 30, 1992, complying at long last with the pledge it had made when it signed the NPT in 1985.

North Korea had been clever enough to devise a policy of revealing an apparent reprocessing plant while denying any interest in reprocessing. Well before the Kanter meeting, the North knew that international concerns could be used for leverage. In exchange for a promise to permit outside inspections of their facilities, which they should have wanted for safety reasons anyway, they had already obtained cancellation of an important military exercise, the removal of U.S. nuclear weapons from the Korean peninsula, an agreement with the South that the North could defy, and direct high-level contacts with the United States.

The North's conclusion of a safeguards agreement was nevertheless a significant American policy achievement. In a departure from standard North Korean negotiation of inspection procedures it could veto, the safeguards agreement seemed to open North Korea for inspections it could not block. The North was able to delay inspections for a few months—until after the Supreme People's Assembly ratified the agreement. But even before the North's assembly took action, the IAEA declared its intention to conduct inspections. Ratification on April 9, 1992, accordingly indicated the North's clear understanding that inspections would proceed, and on May 4 North Korea took the initial step of submitting a list of its nuclear facilities to the IAEA.

On May 12, IAEA Director General Hans Blix made his first orientation visit to North Korea's nuclear sites and was given access to all the sites he requested to see. In addition to the two reactors at Yongbyon, he visited the suspected reprocessing facility, which the North Koreans insisted on calling a radiochemical laboratory, and the newest addition to the North Korean program—a 200-megawatt reactor at Taechon, about five miles north of Yongbyon. Thus began a period of revelation in the North's handling of international attention.

The Bush administration had reason to be pleased with the steps toward progress. By the time of President Bush's 1992 Asian strategy report, the positive North Korean attitude had given rise to cautious optimism. "Few would have predicted two years ago that South Korea and the Soviet Union would normalize relations, that Beijing would open an official commercial office in Seoul, that both South and North Korea would be in the United Nations, and that North and South Korea would have signed a nonaggression pact and an agreement to forswear the possession and development of nuclear weapons," the report noted. The report also cautioned that "North Korea has not yet implemented these agreements, has still not allowed effective bilateral monitoring and inspection of its nuclear program, and has continued to build up its massive, oversized conventional forces." Nevertheless, the environment was hopeful. "As progress in tension reduction continues," the report concluded, "further adjustments [in the U.S. troop presence] would be made."[25]

Tensions, however, increased after the IAEA conducted its initial on-site inspections. On their own initiative, the North Koreans revealed that they had once extracted a small amount of plutonium, and gave it to the inspectors as proof.[26] The world no longer could doubt that North Koreans had the capability to extract plutonium. And, during the inspection, the large facility North Korea called a radiochemical research laboratory was discovered to be what intelligence agencies had suggested: a reprocessing facility at the midpoint of construction. The world could no longer doubt that North Korea would someday be capable of extracting large amounts of plutonium from reprocessed reactor fuel. The IAEA concluded that day would come in the mid-1990s.

At the time of the inspection, the plant was neither fully constructed nor fully equipped. "If it were in operation and complete, then certainly, in our terminology, we would call it a reprocessing plant," IAEA Director General Blix commented.[27] Because the facility was incomplete, however, North Korea seemed to be within a hair's breadth of its commitment under the denuclearization agreement not to possess reprocessing facilities.

North Korea acknowledged that the facility could become a reprocessing plant, and claimed it had been built for potential use in extracting plutonium if North Korea "should choose to use plutonium to fuel a breeder reactor."[28] Such a use would violate the South-North denuclearization agreement, but construction had started before that agreement was in force. Reprocessing for electrical generation would not, if subject to appropriate safeguards, violate the NPT. Why the economically strapped regime would divert scarce national resources to construct facilities to preserve an option to pursue even more onerous expenditures in the future was, however, puzzling. Since North Korea has plentiful supplies of natural uranium, a breeder reactor would be an unnecessary expense. The IAEA observed it was not economically sound to build that kind of reprocessing plant for generation of electricity, and it was also highly unusual to do so without first constructing a smaller pilot project.[29]

Even though North Korea devoted tremendous resources to national development projects of questionable value in the 1980s,[30] this plant's existence tended to give credence to those who argued North Korea had built the facility to manufacture nuclear weapons and had probably hidden other facilities as well. The not-yet-operable reprocessing facility accordingly remained a critical factor in raising international concern over North Korea's intentions, even after the IAEA inspections.

North Korea claimed at this point that three ounces of plutonium, some of which it had given to the IAEA, was the only plutonium that it had extracted from its nuclear reactors, in a single reprocessing effort in 1990.[31] Such assertions can be tested by the IAEA through isotopic analysis. Tests on samples taken from the indigenous five-megawatt reactor revealed to the IAEA that contrary to North Korea's assertions, there had been not one but three different episodes of plutonium extraction. The IAEA concluded that more plutonium had been extracted than North Korea admitted, but could not discern how much. To make matters worse, the plutonium the North Koreans provided did not match samples obtained from the reactors. The North Koreans, who at that time were stonewalling the bilateral inspections called for in the denuclearization agreement, seemed also to be unable or unwilling to provide answers to IAEA inquiries about the discrepancies.

In Washington, the hopes that had accompanied the initiation of inspections gave way in the fall of 1992 to severe disappointment. The Bush administration had sticks as well as carrots, and did not hesitate to use them to encourage North Korea to be more forthcoming. In October, the United States and South Korea resumed planning for *Team Spirit 1993*, the U.S.-ROK military exercise that had been cancelled the previous year. Facing an adversary that seemed likely to have hidden enough plutonium for a few nuclear weapons, and seemed to have lied about it, allied troops needed to learn to operate together. Although the North had not reciprocated when the exercise was cancelled the previous year, the allies thought the North might be more forthcoming in exchange for a second cancellation.

A more significant enticement, however, was a potential reduction in the level of American troops on the peninsula. In the previous year's atmosphere of improved relations with North Korea, the United States Army had proposed to withdraw 6,500 of its personnel from South Korea. The move, considered in full consultation with South Korea, had been approved at the Pentagon and was about to be executed when the IAEA's inspections uncovered the troublesome discrepancies. Whether the North had meant to create concern or to deceive the IAEA—or could not account for the plutonium for other reasons—Secretary of Defense Dick Cheney concluded that the time was not right for a major reduction in American troop strength on the peninsula. In November, he suspended the withdrawal of troops, citing uncertainties regarding the North's nuclear threat.[32]

In the seemingly amiable atmosphere of early 1992, North Korea had come close to achieving its long-stated goal of reducing the American military presence on the peninsula. Its relationship with the United States and with South Korea held the potential for highly beneficial advances. From its new seat at the United Nations, North Korea had unprecedented opportunities for diplomatic progress, and its willingness to permit IAEA inspections earlier in the year had purchased a new regard for North Korea in the international community. All of these apparent achievements were tossed aside in late 1992. Instead of providing truthful information that IAEA inspections would substantiate, or possibly admitting past mishandling or improper disposal of nuclear materials, North Korea chose to aggravate international fears.

Some suggest that North Korea was surprised by the IAEA's capabilities and genuinely embarrassed by the revelation of the discrepancies. This interpretation posits that subsequent resistance to inspections was somehow understandable, perhaps even justified. But the conclusions of the IAEA were determined by what North Korea consciously provided; it could have chosen not to provide the sample, and could have chosen to explain what the IAEA discovered. North Korea's own actions determined that the discrepancy would remain unexplained.

When IAEA inspectors arrived in Yongbyon in November, they asked to visit two sites that were believed to be storage areas for nuclear waste. Inspection of those sites might provide information on the disposition of unaccounted for plutonium. The first site the IAEA sought to explore was a suspected in-ground nuclear waste site, adjacent to an earlier waste site used for waste from the Soviet reactor. U.S. satellites had observed North Korean workers burying and camouflaging that site.[33] The second was a basement in a building that U.S. intelligence sources knew had been connected through underground passages to the reprocessing facility. North Koreans had taken steps to cover the connecting passages and mask the external appearance of the building, hiding the existence of the basement.[34] North Korean officials at the plant were initially disposed to providing the requested access, relying on the regime's earlier guidance. The scientists abruptly changed their minds, however, after receiving new instructions from Pyongyang, and disallowed the IAEA inspection.[35]

The inspectors were told that the building they wanted to see— and had visited a few months earlier—was a military site and exempt from inspection. The claim was irrelevant, because the IAEA had full authority under the safeguards agreement to inspect any nuclear facility to guarantee it was not being used for military purposes. Discovering military uses of plutonium is, after all, what the safeguards agreement is all about.

In its dealings with the IAEA, North Korea was beginning to display a pattern of negotiating behavior that had been characterized as phase two behavior in the history of North-South dialogue. It had entered into an agreement, and was now reinterpreting it. Within months, it would pursue phase three and seek to terminate its adherence to the agreement, blaming others for its decision. This pattern is so well established in North Korean negotiating behavior that it is difficult not to conclude that by late 1992 the North had determined the strategy it would implement over the next two years. It would create an ever-increasing level of crisis until the crisis was resolved to the North's advantage.

Before the North created a situation requiring international attention, however, it had to be sure that the international community could not insist the issue be resolved between the two Koreas themselves. To dispose of that option, North Korea had to bring the talks with the South to an end. The announcement of plans for *Team Spirit 1993* provided an opportunity like that the North had used in 1978, 1985, and 1986 to break off talks with the South. Using its familiar tactic of reversal, the North claimed that *Team Spirit* was intended to "put the brakes on North-South relations and drive the North-South dialogue to a crisis."[36] It then took the actions it claimed were caused by the United States and South Korea.

North Korea called off the meetings of North-South joint commissions scheduled for the month of November as well as the ninth session of the prime ministers' talks scheduled for December 21, 1992, in Seoul. As it had done in a similar tactical situation in the mid-1970s, it called off all the talks but the one the other side's attention was most focused on. In the 1970s, it had been the Red Cross talks on family reunions. In 1992, it was the stalled discussion of the Joint Nuclear Control Commission. With attention focused exclusively on the remaining aspect of North-South dialogue, the North brought the talks to an impasse in the JNCC's last meeting on January 25, 1993. For North Korea, it was more important to terminate the talks than to cancel the exercise *Team Spirit*. Although South Korea and the United States were willing to bargain for a cancellation of *Team Spirit*, the North would not agree to resume talks and inspections in exchange.[37]

When the IAEA pressed for access to the suspected nuclear waste sites in January, Pyongyang had honed its legal argument against inspections a little more sharply than the scientists had been able to articulate in November. North Korea said that permitting inspections of nonnuclear military facilities might jeopardize its "supreme national interests."[38] Although the safeguards agreement has no such provision, the NPT allows a nation to withdraw from the treaty under certain conditions jeopardizing its "supreme interests," a phrase that generally means the nation's security. Article X section 1 of the treaty provides that

> . . . each Party shall in exercising its national sovereignty have the right to withdraw from the Treaty if it decides that extraordinary events, related to the subject matter of this Treaty, have jeopardized the supreme interests of its country. It shall give notice of such withdrawal to all other Parties to the Treaty and to the United Nations Security Council three months in advance. Such notice shall include a statement of the extraordinary events it regards as having jeopardized its supreme interests."[39]

Presumably such extraordinary events might be a clear and present danger of nuclear attack, in which circumstances a nation might reasonably find it necessary to deter the attack by threatening a nuclear response. North Korea, however, applied the withdrawal provision to a demand for inspection, not a threat of attack. It hastened to argue that the exercise *Team Spirit* constituted a nuclear threat, but that was disingenuous.

Saying that its supreme national interests would be threatened by an inspection of the Yongbyon sites raised concern because if military sites are within a nuclear complex, the nuclear facility houses a military function. The assertion was tantamount to saying that the Yongbyon facility housed a nuclear weapons development program in noncompliance with the NPT. North Korea had reversed its posture of trying to demonstrate it had only a peaceful nuclear program and instead implied it might have a military one, but dared others to prove it.[40]

A decisively deteriorated situation greeted the new American president and his administration as they turned their attention to the predicament in Korea. It was not, however, theirs alone to solve. In the initial months of the Clinton administration, the North Korean nuclear issue was being pursued primarily by an international organization—the IAEA—with a nation the incoming administration might understandably prefer to ignore. The IAEA was eager to take the lead on the issue. It had been embarrassed by revelations of the extent of Iraq's nuclear program, and had a new sense of purpose. A year earlier, its board of governors had affirmed the IAEA's right to conduct special inspections whenever it suspected safeguards violations. Special inspections could by definition be conducted over the objections of suspected proliferators.[41] The IAEA wanted to put teeth in its inspections, and North Korea was to become the object and, it could also be argued, the beneficiary of the IAEA's new zeal.

On February 9, 1993, the IAEA demanded a special inspection of the two suspected nuclear waste sites near Yongbyon. North Korea dismissed the demand, saying it had no obligation to open up military facilities for special inspection, and suggesting that it would withdraw from the nonproliferation treaty rather than submit military facilities to special inspections. North Korean Ambassador Ri Chul argued, "If we accept the request to inspect ordinary military sites, at the end we will have to reveal all of our military facilities."[42] In fact, North Korea remained under a 1953 obligation to reveal its military facilities. In Article I of the armistice agreement, North Korea agreed to allow "complete freedom of movement" to investigatory agents of the Military Armistice Commission to determine whether North Korea was engaged in a military buildup.[43] Through the process explained in chapter 6, however, North Korea had eviscerated that inspection regime. Forty years later it could assert that its military sites were off limits, and no one would contest the assertion.

To demonstrate reason to believe the facilities were likely nuclear waste sites, the United States presented satellite imagery of the facilities in various stages of construction to the IAEA's board meeting on February 22. In spite of the protests of North Koreans present at the briefing, the evidence was so persuasive that the IAEA board, on February 25, decided to give North Korea one month to open the sites to inspection, after which the IAEA threatened it would take the matter to the UN Security Council.[44] The next day, IAEA Director General Hans Blix cabled Pyongyang, proposing a March 16 inspection of the sites in Yongbyon, and also informed the Security Council of his action.[45]

Keep in mind that the issue centered on the IAEA's request to inspect two suspected nuclear *waste* sites. Storage sites for reactor byproducts and spent reactor fuel might provide answers to the whereabouts of unaccounted for plutonium. If nuclear waste was found to have been stored improperly, the inspection would be a first step in addressing a serious public health risk. If the inspection verified the North Korean claim that the areas were not used for nuclear storage or that nuclear waste was being handled safely, the North Koreans would have scored a victory, and the world might be able to account for the missing nuclear material.

A responsible regime concerned with the safety of its people and desiring to adhere to its treaty commitments would have permitted the inspections to proceed. Neither sovereignty nor face precludes a state from deciding to act in consonance with domestic and international obligations. But North Korea, wanting more than that approach would yield, preferred to take a more difficult course. "If any special inspections or sanctions are enforced on us, and if the sacred lands of our fatherland are trampled underfoot by big countries, this will be a dangerous fuse that will drive all lands, including the North and the South, into the crushing calamities of war."[46] Rather than pursuing international reassurance or domestic safety, North Korea threatened war.

Having decided to block inspections, North Korea also had the power to let the standoff rest at that point. North Korea could have refused to permit IAEA access to the two sites, and international pressure might predictably have increased. The Security Council, at the request of the IAEA, could in turn have been expected to take action to impose sanctions to force North Korea to open the sites. North Korea, already cut off from most of the world's trade, having been put on a cash basis by its two trading partners that remained relevant (Russia and China), and having lost much of its subsidies from sympathetic organizations in Japan, might have endured the sanctions and continued to hobble along. That less than desirable outcome might have resulted had the North decided to block inspection of two nuclear waste sites while threatening to withdraw from the NPT. But North Korea knew it could achieve more than that scenario would yield.

In the already tense situation, North Korea chose to ratchet up tensions—striking hard at an interest critical to the United States and the international community. On March 12, 1993, North Korea became the first (and thus far only) signatory to announce its intention to withdraw from the NPT. In much the same way it distracted attention from its 1968 commando attack on the South Korean presidential palace by seizing the USS *Pueblo*, it now distracted attention from the demand for inspections by focusing on withdrawal from the treaty. North Korea invoked its Article X prerogative, initiating the required period of advance notification. The three-month clock started to tick.

Fragile as it is, the nonproliferation treaty is the foundation of the international community's efforts to account for and thereby restrain the spread of nuclear material suitable for weapons. Its brittle architecture rests on signatory nations' good faith and their willingness to submit to inspections in exchange for obtaining nuclear technology. In an international system of sovereign states there is little alternative short of military action that can constrain the spread of nuclear weaponry. North Korea's announced withdrawal, based as it was on resistance to inspection, did nothing less than challenge the validity of the best efforts the international community had undertaken for four decades to stop nuclear proliferation. Its action stood to establish a precedent that any nation suspected of noncompliance could avoid inspection merely by withdrawing from its treaty obligations. If the North Korean understanding of rights under the treaty held, the treaty would have been transformed into a system for the dissemination of nuclear technology with no countervailing restraint on that technology's use for weaponry.

Many reasons have been advanced for North Korea's decision to withdraw. Explanations have cited North Korean umbrage over having lost face during the inspections; their profound sense of national paranoia; power plays between soft-line and hard-line factions in Pyongyang; succession politics as Kim Il Sung transferred power to Kim Jong Il; angry reactions to Russian reinterpretation of the USSR-DPRK defense treaty; and even, giving credit to an expression of exasperation from Kim Il Sung, that for North Korea to prove it did not have a nuclear weapons system was like proving a negative and therefore impossible. Some analysts, who view the North's stated reasons for its action as precisely indicative of its motives, argue that *Team Spirit* and IAEA cooperation with American intelligence left North Korea no alternative. But the North did have choices, and its highly centralized decisionmaking process made those choices consciously, with its own objectives in mind.

The North Koreans may well have sought to form the crisis around issues that reflect their interpretation of world events, but precedents for the style of brinkmanship they pursued abound in their negotiating record. The eventual solution to the crisis further suggests that their moves constituted a risky but effective negotiating strategy to gain tangible benefits having little to do with the nonproliferation treaty itself. Those benefits included direct political (if not diplomatic) relations with the United States and an end to the major allied military exercise that addressed the military threat from North Korea.

What is difficult to know, however, is whether they purposefully sought to undermine the international nonproliferation apparatus in the process or whether they used it as a vessel of convenience, primarily to get the other benefits. Although they signed a statement at the end of the crisis promising to work to "advance the goals" of the treaty, they had done much to undermine it.

The IAEA predictably took countermeasures to assert its right to inspections and to enforce compliance among signatory states. On March 18, its board of governors, convened hastily after the North Korean announcement, adopted a resolution expressing "concern" over North Korea's withdrawal. After additional efforts to persuade North Korea to permit the inspections and to rescind its withdrawal failed, the IAEA on April 1 found North Korea to be in noncompliance with the NPT. The IAEA board of governors notified the Security Council that it was "not able to verify that there has been no diversion of nuclear materials required to be safeguarded under the terms of the IAEA-DPRK safeguards agreement to nuclear weapons or other nuclear explosive devices."[47] On May 11, 1993, the UN Security Council, noting the IAEA's findings, adopted a resolution calling upon North Korea to reconsider its announcement of March 12 and to honor its obligations to comply with the safeguards agreement. The Security Council resolution threatened further action if necessary.

The moves were answered with a barrage of belligerence from North Korea. On April 25, 1993, North Korean People's Army Marshal Choe Kwang warned that the DPRK would be compelled to take "effective countermeasures against any sanctions in self-defense."[48] North Korea reacted angrily to the Security Council's May 11 resolution, saying if the UN pursued sanctions that would be construed as a "declaration of war."

The tactic of responding to international demands with war threats was directed by Kim Il Sung himself. To make sure that the world understood the message, Kim declared, "If anyone is imprudent enough to impose sanctions on us, we will respond with a 'just counterattack.'"[49] North Korea readied its population for war. At the same time, North Korea said that the only way war could be averted would be through direct DPRK-U.S. talks.[50]

While the Security Council's ability to approve condemnatory resolutions and its power to enforce global economic sanctions inspire assiduous compliance among many of the world's proud nations, its ability to influence North Korea is decidedly limited. For North Korea, the Security Council is a forum that affords certain benefits. Its limited ability to counter belligerence, and its susceptibility to viewing threats with grave concern, bolster North Korea's defiant stance and further its objective of creating a crisis atmosphere. Faced with war threats, the international organization tends to look to the world's strongest military power, the United States, for crisis resolution. The Security Council's reliance on American leadership in turn tends to serve North Korean efforts to portray it as a puppet of America. Just as this tactic has caused friction between South Korea and the United States, it has also created tension between UN agencies and the United States. Finally, because China holds a permanent seat on the Security Council, the institution offers North Korea an additional advantage. North Korea has been able to count on China both to draw in the United States and to restrain its options. China predictably urges the United States to pursue exclusively peaceful resolution of the crises its ally North Korea causes. Such peaceful resolutions are never merely diplomatic; they generally involve an exchange of tangible benefits. Having an issue brought before the Security Council can therefore become a rewarding opportunity for North Korea.

North Korea pursued a two-pronged approach, creating the crisis and proposing its resolution. On April 5, Pyongyang's news media charged that the Security Council resolution was "illegal" and insisted that DPRK-U.S. bilateral talks would be the only way to resolve the nuclear issue.[51] Washington opposed talks, pointing out there was nothing to talk about; North Korea knew its obligations and should carry them out.[52]

As often happens, however, China used its position in the Security Council to encourage American accommodation. Surprisingly, China discovered that in this instance South Korea was also willing to support bilateral U.S.-DPRK talks, as long as they were limited exclusively to nuclear matters. South Korean Foreign Minister Han Sung Joo met with Chinese Foreign Minister Qian Qichen in Bangkok and offered to support the two-way talks if China would not veto a UN Security Council resolution calling on North Korea to adhere to the NPT and to permit inspections.[53] The United States finally acquiesced, as Michael Mazarr points out in his comprehensive study *North Korea and the Bomb*, "to demonstrate to Beijing that diplomacy was being given a fair chance."[54] On April 22, the United States agreed to U.S.-DPRK talks, a move the Chinese Ministry of Foreign Affairs welcomed. In the first week of May, North Korea permitted IAEA teams to replace batteries and film in cameras in Yongbyon facilities, and preparatory meetings for the U.S.-DPRK talks commenced in Beijing,[55] giving rise to cautious hope.

When the U.S.-DPRK talks were finally convened in New York, there was indeed little to talk about. North Korean First Vice Foreign Minister Kang Sok Ju met U.S. Assistant Secretary for Politico-Military Affairs Robert Gallucci at the U.S. Mission to the United Nations for four sessions beginning on June 2, 1993. Progress in the bilateral talks was extremely slow, but that may have been preordained. On June 10, after the third meeting failed to produce an agreement, Kang made the peculiar comment that the issue would be decided on the following Friday, June 11.[56] On that date, with one day remaining in the treaty's mandatory three-month notification period, Kang announced that his country would "unilaterally and temporarily suspend its withdrawal" from the treaty, and a joint statement was issued by the two sides.

Radio Pyongyang reported the full text of the "Joint Statement of the DPRK and the United States of America":

> The DPRK and the United States of America have reached an agreement on the following principles: (1) They ensure that they shall not use armed forces, including nuclear

weapons, nor threaten each other with such armed forces. (2) They ensure the de-nuclearization, peace and security of the Korean peninsula, including a guarantee of impartiality of fullscope nuclear safeguards. (3) They will mutually respect the sovereignty of the other side and will not interfere in the other side's domestic affairs. . . . (4) They support the peaceful reunification of Korea. According to these principles, the Governments of the DPRK and the United Sates agreed to continue dialogue based on equality and fairness. In connection with this, the DPRK Government has decided unilaterally and temporarily suspended, as long as it considers necessary, the effectuation of its withdrawal from the Nuclear Non-Proliferation Treaty.[57]

No outstanding issue was resolved in the negotiations; the United States did not yield new ground or offer incentives, and North Korea did not change its position on inspections. The meliorative result seemed to have been achieved merely in exchange for direct bilateral talks themselves. As First Vice Foreign Minister Kang commented in a press conference following the North Korean concession, "The talks were not a commercial dealing for giving and taking something over the issue of our withdrawal from the NPT, but were a political course dealing with policies."[58]

The North had for decades sought a direct political relationship with the United States, and in this crisis it had accomplished much toward that objective. Although the United States had insisted it would engage only in discussions of nuclear nonproliferation, side discussions by Korean specialists at the State Department[59] and the final communiqué clearly delved into wider issues. In addition to language that implied a form of political recognition and granted security assurances, the United States agreed to a formal channel for future U.S.-DPRK discussions, through DPRK offices at the UN in New York.[60] A subtle shift had occurred in U.S. reasoning. Official statements no longer said U.S.-DPRK talks would be restricted to the nuclear matter; they said instead that whatever was discussed between the United States and the DPRK, the question of a peace settlement on the Korean peninsula would be discussed only with the full participation of South Korea.[61] That was not the formula Seoul had supported.

Like the private negotiations over the release of the *Pueblo* crew, this negotiation spawned an element of distrust in the U.S.-ROK alliance. South Korea knew the North had obtained a long-sought objective. It had established a channel for direct talks with the United States, without giving anything in return. From the U.S. perspective, however, the time for such links had long since arrived. The U.S.-DPRK relationship had changed dramatically beginning in 1988,[62] when the counselor-level talks were started in Beijing, and in 1992, when Under Secretary of State Kanter met Kim Yong Sun in New York. The lower level negotiations of 1993 seemed merely to be an incremental step beyond the earlier precedents. While North Korea had given nothing away, the same could be said for the United States. The United States had applied language already signed onto in other agreements, such as the UN Charter, to this agreement, and did not see the statement as setting new ground. From the American perspective, North Korea seemed to have blinked, but Washington was officially circumspect. As Washington-based North Korea watchers Kongdan Oh and Ralph Hassig pointed out, "The U.S. side did little boasting about the agreement, calling it merely 'a step in the right direction.'"[63]

The joint statement did not seem to justify South Korea's disappointment or North Korea's pleasure.

There is an ominous possibility that North Korea achieved a much darker objective on June 11, 1993. Antonio F. Perez, a former State Department attorney, has observed:

> Because the DPRK suspended its notice of withdrawal only a day before it would have become irrevocable, there remains the somewhat theoretical question whether, if the DPRK were to revoke its suspension of its notice of withdrawal, that action would result in its withdrawal on the very next day.[64]

Kongdan Oh and Ralph Hassig may have been the first to notice that Pyongyang added a word in the joint statement's Korean-language version that did not appear in initial English-language versions:

> In the communiqué, Washington and Pyongyang agreed to continue their dialogue, and "in this respect the government of the DPRK has decided unilaterally ["and temporarily" in the Korean-language version] to suspend the effectuation of the withdrawal from the NPT as long as it considers it necessary.[65]

Even without the addition of "and temporarily," however, the statement demonstrates that North Korea took great care to insist on terms like "suspension" and to include the phrase "as long as it considers it necessary." These repetitive points of emphasis suggest that the North cynically constructed a legalistic subterfuge so that it might one day threaten it had a right to withdraw from the NPT with one day's notice. Although North Korea can seldom be expected to abide by the legal terms of the agreements it signs, it often makes legalistic arguments to enhance its position.

At the height of some future crisis, North Korea might attempt to inspire panic by asserting it could transform its ostensibly peaceful nuclear program into a military one overnight. If there were reason to believe that North Korea had used the intervening time to improve its delivery systems—the missiles that could carry nuclear warheads— and to maintain a clandestine nuclear program, the North's threat would have to be taken very seriously.

Nevertheless, as a consequence of the DPRK's June 11 suspension of its withdrawal, the integrity of the nonproliferation treaty appeared to have been preserved. No signatory had been permitted to withdraw from the treaty after having extracted its benefits. None of North Korea's legal arguments had been accorded precedence. The North's assertion that it could limit inspections to nonmilitary sites was not accepted, nor was its more general assumption that withdrawal from the NPT would have removed North Korea from the purview of IAEA inspectors.[66] North Korea would argue that its temporary suspension of its withdrawal allowed it to continue to deny special inspections on the basis of the "partiality" of the IAEA. That position as well would meet with disdain from the international community. Nevertheless, the matter became the central point in an intensifying crisis that North Korea managed toward a crescendo in the spring of 1994—mirroring North Korea's tactical handling of the crisis it had nurtured in the spring of 1993.

Uncharacteristically, North Korea boldly revealed its next negotiating objective during the second round of negotiations with the United States, held in Geneva, July 14 to 19, 1993. During the six days of negotiations, North Korea delivered its terms for the resolution of the crisis it had created. North Korean delegation chief Kang Sok Ju argued that it had developed nuclear power capabilities not for any sinister purpose but merely to generate electric power. He said it had long sought nuclear technology less susceptible to use for the extraction of nuclear materials that could be used in weapons. If the international community would provide light-water reactors to North Korea, he argued, the world's unfounded fears about North Korea's program could be set aside. North Korea would forgo its existing nuclear program if it were provided with light-water reactors.

Kang could point to some evidence of the North's previous interest in light-water reactors. As early as 1992, North Korea had asked the International Atomic Energy Agency for assistance in light-water reactor technology. The IAEA had dismissed the expensive idea, recognizing that cash-strapped North Korea had more reasonable ways to generate electric power. Even though LWRs are described as "proliferation-resistant," hydroelectric generators and other means of nonnuclear generation, in addition to being cheaper, would have established more clearly North Korea's intention not to proliferate. At any rate, the international agency was not in the business of dispensing free electric generation equipment. Similarly, when North Korea's Deputy Premier Kim Dal Hyon held a secret meeting in Seoul in July of 1992, he had also suggested South Korea should cooperate in a light-water reactor project north of the DMZ, but neither the idea itself nor the notion of North-South cooperation seemed justified, given the North's refusal to carry out its commitments under the South-North agreements.[67]

Nevertheless, when, on July 15, 1993, Kang proposed that the DPRK could exchange its nuclear development program for light-water reactors provided by the international community, some members of the American negotiating team thought the suggestion held promise, if not merit.[68] At the close of the negotiating round, Assistant Secretary Gallucci carefully agreed that the United States would support the introduction of LWRs to North Korea and explore with the DPRK ways in which that could be accomplished, as part of a full resolution of the nuclear issues.

The July 1993 round adjourned without the North's agreement on special inspections. A U.S. statement accordingly cautioned that there would be no third round until "serious discussions" were under way between North and South Korea and between North Korea and the IAEA. The United States position was to build pressure on North Korea to accept IAEA inspections, ensure the continuity of safeguards, forgo reprocessing, and permit IAEA observation of any effort to refuel its reactors. The North seems to have concluded that this approach was suitable for its own purposes; it would have to endure a great deal of pressure to obtain the prize it sought.

In May and August, North Korea permitted IAEA inspectors limited access to the nuclear facilities to check seals and replace film and batteries in cameras that the IAEA had installed during the 1992 inspections. These opportunities were welcomed by the IAEA because they permitted it to ascertain whether basic safeguards had been violated. Such opportunities did not provide information on earlier nuclear activities, or an accounting of the unaccounted for plutonium, but they gave some insights into the North's continuing program at the acknowledged nuclear sites.

While providing the North with an opportunity to appear responsive from time to time, these limited openings to the IAEA also provided an opportunity to aggravate tensions when that tactic served North Korea's purposes. North Korea is adept at finding subtle ways to denigrate its opponents and emphasize who exercises control over an issue. Those matters, so significant in the North's techniques of domestic control, can also be applied to foreign policy. In August, for example, North Korea forced IAEA inspectors to conduct their activities in the dark, using only flashlights.[69] The IAEA's report on the visit contained the following measured comment: "The overall degree of access granted is still insufficient for the agency to discharge its responsibilities."[70]

Because of North Korean intransigence on inspections, the United States refused to participate in a third round of negotiations planned for the fall of 1993. In November, the IAEA reported to the United Nations that it was unable to verify North Korea's compliance with its safeguards responsibilities, that North Korea's noncompliance was "widening."[71] The UN General Assembly, by a margin of 140 to 1, voted to approve a resolution calling on North Korea to comply with IAEA demands. North Korea, however, chose not to comply. On December 2, Director General Blix told the IAEA board of governors that because of the North's refusal to permit inspections, the IAEA "cannot provide any meaningful assurance" that the DPRK was not producing new plutonium. North Korea deflected such criticism by proposing a "package solution" with the United States, and offering to permit the IAEA to change batteries and film once again, but limiting the scope of inspections it would allow. "There must be unrestricted access to all declared sites," the IAEA responded; "restrictions on the two facilities are not negotiable."[72]

Despite the IAEA's hard line, the United States and the DPRK reached a "tentative understanding" on December 29, 1993, that would give the IAEA access to the North's declared nuclear facilities except for the two nuclear waste sites.[73] American support for the new opening permitted a series of negotiations to begin between the IAEA and North Korea. By February 15, 1994, when the IAEA would likely report to the UN that North Korean safeguards had completely broken down, North Korea agreed to a checklist for IAEA inspections. Ten days later, the United States and North Korea issued "agreed conclusions" which specified, among other things, that the inspections would proceed as North Korea and the IAEA had agreed. For its part, the United States agreed to a new round of talks to start in March, after inspections had commenced.

The North did not live up to its part of the agreement. Although IAEA inspectors were given entry visas and permitted to begin inspections at Yongbyon, they were blocked from entering parts of the reprocessing plant and barred from taking samples and conducting isotopic scans in the reprocessing facility—points that North Korea had specifically agreed to allow in the checklist of February 15.

Even though the inspectors were hampered, they were given new cause for concern. North Korea had resumed construction on the second reprocessing line in the facility and completed new connections between the two reprocessing lines. Furthermore, if the advances in reprocessing construction were not enough to heighten concern, North Korea had taken a more obviously alarming step—the seal on the entrance to a "hot cell" in the reprocessing facility, secured by the IAEA a year earlier, had been severed. The long-sought inspections aggravated rather than allayed international fears, likely as North Korea desired.

As is often the case, North Korea punctuated an act of defiance with a rhetorical blast. At a working-level meeting in Panmunjom, North Korean representative Park Yong Su concluded a heated exchange with a direct personal threat to Song Young Dae, his South Korean counterpart: "Seoul is not far from here. If a war breaks out, it will be a sea of fire. Mr. Song, it will probably be difficult for you to survive."[74]

Predictably, the United States, faced with North Korea's bold act of bad faith and incendiary rhetoric, cancelled the promised round of high-level negotiations on the inspections and sought action in the UN Security Council. On March 21, the IAEA once again reported to the Security Council that it could not ascertain whether North Korea's nuclear materials were being diverted for weapons.

The action taken by the UN Security Council in early April was characteristically stern but ineffective; the Security Council asked North Korea to allow the IAEA to complete its inspections. A year after North Korea had created the crisis over its withdrawal from the

NPT, the full inspections had still not been allowed to proceed, and there appeared to be no end to the delay. This sequence of events played out by the North Koreans gave them additional time—time for advancing their nuclear program, perhaps, and time that was inexorably proceeding toward an event mandated by deteriorating fuel rods in one of their nuclear reactors.

In mid-May 1994, North Korea took an action that would forever obscure the history of its nuclear program and make it impossible for the world to feel secure that North Korea had not developed a few nuclear bombs. It began to remove spent fuel rods from its five-megawatt reactor. This action clearly violated the DPRK-IAEA safeguards agreement. Always willing to set the scene to serve its advantage, North Korea made a point of inviting IAEA inspectors to witness the process. Little of scientific merit could be obtained by merely observing the process, however; and North Korea would not permit the IAEA to conduct an isotopic analysis of the fuel rods. Human eyes would witness only the position of impotence to which IAEA inspectors had been relegated. The North's invitation, the IAEA responded, "does not constitute the basis for sending an inspection team to the DPRK."[75]

While the manipulation of the March inspections had caused the United States to cancel the third round of talks, the "serious violation" of the safeguards agreement in May caused the opposite reaction. The United States called for the scheduling of the third round, with a number of unspecified economic and political enticements on the table. It was now North Korea's turn to demur. North Korea first agreed to meet with the IAEA to discuss methods of preserving the fuel rods, but then rejected the IAEA's proposal for monitoring the refueling.

The seriousness with which the world's preternaturally tolerant diplomatic leaders viewed the North's undeniable challenge to UN, IAEA, and U.S. interests caused due alarm in New York, Geneva, and Washington. On May 30, the UN Security Council held an emergency meeting to hear "the IAEA's assessment that if the discharge operation at the five-megawatt reactor continues at the same rate, the IAEA's opportunity to select, segregate, and secure fuel rods for later measurements in accordance with IAEA standards will be lost within days."[76] The president of the Security Council called on North Korea "to proceed with the discharge operations at the five-megawatt reactor in a manner which preserves the technical possibility of fuel measurement, in accordance with IAEA's requirements."[77] That warning notwithstanding, on June 2, IAEA Director General Blix informed the

Security Council that North Korea had removed all but 1,800 of the 8,000 fuel rods in the reactor and that by mixing them up, had made it impossible to reconstruct the operating history of the reactor. The North Koreans had made it impossible to determine how much plutonium they had produced.

Recognizing that North Korea had blatantly violated its agreements with the IAEA, IAEA members voted on June 10 to halt the flow of technical assistance to the noncompliant IAEA member. North Korea reacted by withdrawing from the IAEA on June 13. Saying that his country would neither allow inspections nor be bound by IAEA rules and resolutions, North Korea's Foreign Minister Kim Young Nam threatened to expel the two IAEA inspectors who had remained in North Korea. In Washington, Assistant Secretary Gallucci registered American consternation by dropping the call for a third round of talks and seeking further action in the Security Council.[78] Specifically, the United States announced it would pursue global economic sanctions against North Korea, and the North responded that such sanctions would be an act of war.

The North's threat came as no surprise to American policymakers. A policy based on international pressure necessarily requires the resolve to proceed with punitive measures. Economic sanctions might naturally lead to war. Those who had designed policy were painfully aware of its potential consequences. Planners in the Pentagon had assessed the likely course of conflict and had developed estimates of the costs.[79] The North's clear strategic advantages of proximity to the South's major population centers, its huge artillery arsenal, its troop strength in excess of a million men in arms and its progress in long-range missile development were taken into account as were its debilitated economy, poor war production and resupply capabilities, and malnourished population, signs of which had been seen even in its ground forces.[80] As Assistant Secretary of Defense Edward L. Warner later explained to Congressional subcommittees, "We were prepared to add over 10,000 military personnel, additional aircraft and other military equipment in order to enhance our military capabilities as we moved toward sanctions."[81]

The United States did not seek war; the objective of American policy was to force compliance with international agreements the North Koreans themselves had signed. The patience exhibited over the preceding three years and the substantial volume of United Nations resolutions calling upon the North Koreans to fulfill their obligations showed that North Korea had been the cause and not the victim of whatever hostilities might occur. If war were required, the United States was prepared. Given the U.S. experience in *Desert Storm*, and advantages that allied forces had over North Korea's military capabilities—including an increasingly competent South Korean military force—a war in Korea would have been costly, but it would also have been decisive. Both the justification for war and its likely outcome were clear in 1994.

No matter how isolated Pyongyang is, Kim Il Sung understood the predicament in which he had placed his society. The North Korean leader was risking what President Clinton had referred to a year earlier as "the end of their country."[82] This was a tremendous risk for meager objectives: a defiant show of "face" and generating equipment. As odd as this may seem, making fearsome threats for minimal demands is a strategy that perpetually strengthens tyranny. By using high-pressure tactics but restricting demands to concessions the rest of the world can afford to make, when the alternative appeared to be war, Kim Il Sung guaranteed his success.

In that sense, there was nothing unreasonable about the strategy he was pursuing. He had defined for the United States a choice: war or accommodation. From Kim's perspective, war would have meant the regime's end; accommodation would lead to a mutually reliant relationship that would tend to guarantee the North's indefinite survival. His was a dangerous stratagem involving high stakes and firm resolve, but to the aging despot it must have seemed an acceptable use of his powers and a valid means to enhance and preserve his legacy.

To pursue such a negotiating strategy requires tremendous control over domestic factors that in other countries would have undermined national resolve. North Korea had that control. Even among the many other cruel and efficient totalitarian regimes of the twentieth century, few had achieved the degree of control necessary to follow such an unswervingly perilous course. Kim Il Sung knew he possessed the control essential to carrying out his plan; no voice would emerge within his own society to decry the strategy he had dictated.

And he knew that the opposing side in the negotiations was constructed differently. He understood the character of democracy. Starting from the fact that many voices would emerge and be heard in a public debate, he could be confident that some of the voices would argue for peace at a known cost rather than war at an unknown cost. He knew that if a means could be found, the United States would be inclined to pursue peace rather than war, accommodation rather than protracted confrontation. In spite of the risks, Kim Il Sung could feel relatively confident he would eventually win a settlement on acceptable terms.

A practical problem, however, was to find an agent of peaceful accommodation, one powerful enough to argue persuasively that the United States should accommodate the North Korean view. Kim Il Sung had been building pressure, and he needed a way to release that pressure. Someone had to clear the path toward resolution.

For its part, the Clinton administration was content to keep the pressure on, and to keep discussions in official channels, through the DPRK office in New York. It nevertheless welcomed an offer from two senators—Sam Nunn (D-Ga.) and Richard Lugar (R-Ind.)—to visit Pyongyang to explain the severity of North Korea's predicament. Although the United States Congress operates independently of the executive branch, it is an official part of the government and has a role in foreign policy outcomes. Many congressional voices had been sharper in condemning North Korea's refusal to submit to inspections and had called for sanctions months earlier than the president.

Nunn and Lugar, powerful senators from the two major American political parties, were well respected for their reasoned and informed foreign policy positions. They could be expected to deliver a stern message to the North Korean dictator. On February 23 they had called for a series of graduated economic sanctions. Their report had concluded that if the presence of nuclear weapons in North Korea were confirmed, "the re-introduction of short-range nuclear weapons on South Korean territory, as a visible deterrent to a North Korean first-use of nuclear weapons, would clearly have to be considered."[83] By June 16, their colleagues in the Senate passed a resolution 93–3 urging President Clinton to take action to prepare U.S. troops "to deter and, if necessary, repel an attack from North Korea."[84]

Understanding the angry sentiment building in the Congress, the two senators requested North Korea's approval for a visit to Pyongyang. Believing the North Koreans would approve the visit, on May 23 the administration briefed the senators on the diplomatic state of play. With their bags packed, and ready for a midday departure from Andrews Air Force Base, Senators Nunn and Lugar were informed on May 25 that Kim Il Sung would not be able to meet with them because of scheduling conflicts. The trip was cancelled.[85]

Another American's invitation, however, remained valid. President Jimmy Carter had also become concerned about the way the standoff was shaping up. His dealings with North Korea, notably his 1976 pledge to remove American troops from the peninsula, had given him a certain standing within North Korea. The Carter Center's International Negotiation Network, described by the center's 1994 annual report as "an informal group of leaders who, upon request, help resolve conflicts," had been following the situation closely. "North Korean President Kim Il Sung had invited President and Mrs. Carter to his country several times since 1991," according to the Carter Center, and "in the face of heightening tensions, that invitation was reaffirmed."[86] Carter called President Clinton to explore the possibility of a visit and decided to accept the invitation "to alleviate the crisis and avoid another Korean war."[87] When President Clinton sent Assistant Secretary Gallucci to brief Carter on June 5, Carter noted with concern "the seriousness of the situation and the apparent lack of an avenue of communication with the top leader of North Korea."[88] Kim Il Sung agreed that the former president could visit from June 15 to 18.

In Kim Il Sung's villa outside of Pyongyang, Kim thanked Carter for accepting his invitation and listened politely while Carter described the diplomatic state of play. Carter then heard the North Korean dictator's proposal for resolving the crisis North Korea itself had created. Kim Il Sung made two requests according to Carter's account of the meeting:

> One was that the U.S. support their acquisition of lightwater reactor technology, realizing that the funding and equipment could not come directly from America. . . . This is something we want the North Koreans to have, because the enriched fuel will have to be acquired from foreign sources, and the production of weapons grade plutonium is not so easy as in their old graphite moderated reactor that can use refined uranium directly from their own mines. His second request was that the U.S. guarantee that there will be no nuclear attack against his country. He wanted the third round of U.S.-NK talks to be resumed to resolve all the outstanding nuclear issues. He was willing to freeze their nuclear program during the talks, and to consider a permanent freeze if their aged reactors could be replaced with modern and safer ones.[89]

Before Carter left Pyongyang, he also obtained the North Korean leader's consent to joint investigations of American war remains buried in the Korean countryside, a North-South summit meeting, and a reversal of the expulsion order for the two IAEA inspectors who had remained in Pyongyang.

After the meetings with Kim Il Sung, former President Carter met with Vice Foreign Minister Kang Sok Ju, the negotiator who had originally outlined the freeze-for-LWRs proposal in July of 1993. This gave Kang the chance to rewrite the history of the crisis and refine North Korea's propaganda posture to suit North Korea's new objectives. Kang portrayed North Korea as a victim, threatened adverse consequences if Carter's agreements did not win support in Washington, and laid down markers for how the history of the difficulties over the preceding few months should be explained. As Carter reported the session:

> Vice Minister Kang informed me that when I arrived they had already decided to expel the inspectors and disconnect surveillance equipment as a response to the abusive sanctions language announced by UN Ambassador Madeleine Albright and Bob Gallucci. Also, he said, "All the people in this country and our military are gearing up now to respond to those sanctions. If the sanctions pass, all the work you have done here will go down the drain." He said they are convinced that the spent fuel rods can still be assessed by the IAEA, and are willing to be flexible if this conviction is proven wrong. He maintained that noted physicists in Europe and the United States agreed with their position. We discussed a number of other points of a somewhat technical nature. I saw no reason to argue with him on these points, but just to protect the agreement I had reached with his president.[90]

The Carter formula for resolution of the issue did not immediately meet with Washington's approval, but it provided a basis for the resumption of talks and eventually provided a foundation for an accord between North Korea and the United States.

When former President Carter stopped in Seoul on his return from Pyongyang, he told President Kim Young Sam that Kim Il Sung had proposed a North-South summit. The South Korean president recognized the proposal for a summit as a constructive but not a new development. He responded that he would meet with the North Korean president "at any time, any place, and with no conditions," echoing the statements of his predecessors, President Park on January 19, 1979, and Chun Doo Hwan on January 12, 1981. Working-level contacts immediately set about making arrangements and, on June 28, a declaration announcing the summit for July 25–27 was signed at Panmunjom by ROK Deputy Prime Minister and Unification Minister Lee Hong Koo and the DPRK's Supreme People's Assembly Reunification Policy Committee Chairman Kim Yong Sun.[91] Thirteen days later, because of the death of Kim Il Sung on July 8, the planned talks were indefinitely postponed.[92]

The hope of progress in South-North relations was set aside when North Korea made an issue over South Korea's decision not to express condolences on the death of Kim Il Sung. It served North Korea's interest to take umbrage; as ever, the North used a difference as a reason to deal directly with the United States. The United States and North Korea held meetings in September and October to address four basic aspects of the proposed settlement: the means of supplying light-water reactors, the disposition of spent fuel, methods for meeting interim energy requirements of the DPRK with conventional facilities, and improvements in the bilateral relationship, including the creation of liaison offices. By October 21, the skeletal formula that Carter had discussed was fleshed out, and, after President Clinton sent a letter to Kim Jong Il reassuring the "Supreme Leader" of North Korea that he would honor the proposal, the negotiators in Geneva announced the "agreed framework" to resolve the nuclear issue.

According to the State Department's summary, the October 21 agreement had the following terms:

- North Korea agreed to freeze its existing nuclear program under enhanced IAEA safeguards.
- Both sides agreed to cooperate to replace the DPRK's graphite-moderated reactors for related facilities with light-water reactor power plants.
- The two sides agreed to move toward full normalization of political and economic relations.
- Both sides agreed to work together for peace and security on a nuclear-free Korean peninsula.
- Both sides agreed to work together to strengthen the international nuclear nonproliferation regime.[93]

The agreement was in many ways a first in the history of negotiations with North Korea. It differed from previous arrangements in three ingenious ways.

First, it offered tangible inducements that were clearly attractive to the regime and could be expected to influence its behavior. Earlier Western dealings with North Korea had attempted to compel or constrain North Korean behavior through moral suasion, something to which North Korea was peculiarly inured. As Admiral Joy cautioned three decades earlier, "An agreement is binding on Communists only if it operates to the advantage of their purposes."[94] He stated this maxim with a certain resigned pessimism. The agreed framework, however, was actually designed to provide them with advantages, and therefore had some prospect of winning North Korea's adherence.

A few analysts of the nuclear crisis criticized the administration for not having proffered enticing benefits earlier in the crisis. "By remaining wedded to its own form of incrementalism," Michael J. Mazarr wrote, the United States had actually helped North Korea "in prolonging the nuclear dispute."[95] Many analysts, including Bush administration officials Arnold Kanter and Bob Manning, thought the administration should have shown North Korea "what's in it for them" as early as November 6, 1993.[96] By early June 1994, Heritage Foundation scholar Daryl Plunk also advocated incentives for North Korean compliance with IAEA inspections and implementation of the North-South denuclearization agreement.[97]

Second, the attainment of the benefits North Korea desired was explicitly tied to North Korea's performance. After four decades of dealings with North Korea, Western analysts had observed North Korea's tactic of avoiding, undermining, and finally circumventing enforcement provisions. Admiral Joy had first cautioned that "Communist refusal to accept effective inspection and supervision of any international agreement to disarm" was a portent of "premeditated violations of agreements."[98] He and later South Korean negotiators concluded that enforcement mechanisms should be negotiated before other aspects of an agreement. Addressing this concern, Secretary of Defense William J. Perry commented that in the agreed framework, "We did not believe we should base our security on what they told us they would do but only on what, in fact, step by step, they did."[99]

Ambassador at Large Gallucci[100] devised a schedule of phased delivery of benefits contingent upon North Korean compliance with its pledges. The light-water reactors would not be provided until North Korea had frozen its program, permitted inspections, and taken other actions to comply with international concerns. "The most significant benefits for North Korea will come several years from now, after we have had an opportunity to judge its performance and its intentions,"

Secretary of State Warren Christopher pointed out. "The most important benefit they will receive, the sensitive nuclear component for the light-water reactors, will not be provided until North Korea fully complies with safeguard obligations, which includes accounting for its past activities."[101]

The Clinton administration saw this approach as advantageous in two ways: first, it compelled North Korean compliance and, second, it reduced American costs in the event North Korea failed to live up to its commitments. "Since the burden of up front performance falls on the North," Ambassador Gallucci explained, "if the agreement breaks down before the LWRs are complete, we will still be ahead of the game."[102]

Secretary Christopher emphasized the point in this way:

> . . . the framework accord is structured so that we are not disadvantaged in any significant way if North Korea reneges on any of its commitments at any time. If the North backs out of the deal in the next several years, for example, it will have gained very little except modest amounts of heavy oil and some technical help in insuring the safe storage of the spent fuel. Should the North renege when it is required to submit to the International Agency's special inspections, Pyongyang will be left with only empty shells of two light water reactors. Even if this happens, we will still have benefited because the North's entire nuclear program will have been frozen for the intervening years.[103]

The Clinton administration made it clear that if the agreed framework broke down, it expected to return to the conditions that held in May 1994. As Under Secretary of Defense Walter B. Slocombe stated, "If they don't perform, we can and, in my view, we must go back to sanctions, military enhancements, and international pressure."[104]

Third, implementation of the agreement was based in large part on international consensus regarding North Korea's intentions and performance. Under the framework's terms, the light-water reactors were to be provided by an international consortium, the Korean Peninsula Energy Development Organization (KEDO). As Secretary Christopher explained, "It is KEDO that will ensure the provision of light-water reactors to North Korea, the heavy fuel oil shipments, the safe storage of the spent fuel and its eventual shipment out of North Korea."[105] What this means in practical terms is that the light-water reactors will be provided only when lengthy and difficult diplomatic efforts have

persuaded legislatures in a number of capitals that North Korea's behavior warrants the advantages the agreement proposes.

International pressure has proved to affect North Korean behavior—a nonaligned coalition helped persuade North Korea and China to
conclude the armistice, U.S.-China rapprochement in 1972 prompted
the South-North communiqué, and international revulsion against
North Korean terrorism ten years later paved the way for a proposal for
three-way talks. In the agreed framework, international consensus is
essential to funding the plan of action, and that consensus will be destroyed if North Korea behaves as badly as it has in the past.

In addition to the restraining quality of the coalition-dependent
approach, there is also a revelatory aspect. At the core of the nuclear
crisis, and of the fundamental tensions that generally exist between
North Korea and all other nations, is North Korea's tight lid of secrecy.
It has become commonplace for analysts to call this phenomenon North
Korea's "lack of transparency" and say it is a result of "xenophobia"
and "paranoia." Official secrecy on the scale of North Korea's, however, is based on more complex motivations, including the requirements of domestic oppression as well as a fear of external influence.
Greater exposure of North Korea is therefore valuable both for the West
and for the people of North Korea. The coalition implementing the
agreed framework necessarily brings more foreigners into contact with
North Korean society and casts some light on the regime's operations.
As Principal Deputy Assistant Secretary of State Charles Kartman en-
visions the impact of this process:

> . . . as the LWR project progresses, North Korea's contact
> with the world and with the ROK will rapidly increase. Most
> specialists working on the project will be ROK citizens and
> South Korea's national power company—KEPCO—is the
> prime contractor. Already, it has facilitated North-South
> contact through almost constant KEDO-DPRK negotiations
> at KEDO headquarters in New York and through the regu-
> lar visits of South Koreans, under KEDO sponsorship, to the
> North to prepare for the reactor project.[106]

The high price tag for the light-water reactors—initially 4 billion, but now more than 5 billion dollars—was felt to be justified by
the termination of the North's troubling and dangerous investment in
plutonium enrichment, the avoidance of war, the affirmation of international efforts to control proliferation, and the potential to bring
North Korea into the family of nations and to facilitate its relations

with South Korea. Because these benefits promoted peace and stability on the peninsula, it was of little importance whether North Korea had pushed the United States and its allies into the agreement through threats, blackmail, or deceit. The significant point was that the North would immediately shut down and eventually dismantle its graphite-moderated reactor program, comply with its obligations under the NPT and the IAEA safeguards agreement, prevent the reprocessing of spent fuel, and remove properly canned spent fuel from North Korea. Those valuable objectives had presumably been achieved.

The administration's analysis might be profoundly wise and still generate controversy. An advantage of a free society is that open debate informs and alerts decisionmakers to potential pitfalls negotiators might not have perceived, or might have believed they could not pursue within their negotiating environment. Negotiating environments change. As North Korea has demonstrated better than any other nation, the signing of an agreement is not the culmination of the process of negotiating; it is merely another step in a longer process. The agreed framework is so constructed that while it is being implemented, pointing out potential adverse implications may well serve to further American interests.

Criticism of the agreed framework generally falls into three categories: concern over the possibility of a clandestine and undetected military buildup; concern that North Korea may use the terms of the agreement to "blackmail" the United States at various stages of implementation; and concern regarding the impact the agreed framework will have on allied relationships, particularly the relationship between the United States and South Korea.

A coherent and most alarming assessment of the agreed framework has been developed by Carl Ford, a former official of the Bush administration with long tenure in the Central Intelligence Agency and experience dealing with the nuclear crisis as deputy assistant secretary for Asian and Pacific Affairs at the Pentagon. Ford gives the agreed framework credit because it may "greatly limit the amount of weapons-grade plutonium Pyongyang could produce in the future, and make the production of large numbers of nuclear weapons impossible."[107] If this is its only result, says Ford, "the bargain would be well worth the costs stipulated in the agreement." But he believes a fundamental premise of the agreement is mistaken. He thinks that North Korea has no intention of giving up its nuclear weapons program.

Ford reasons the North may have decided to scale back the size of its nuclear weapons program, but not to terminate it. He observes that the original plans at Yongbyon could have produced hundreds of nuclear weapons, but as North Korea "understood the vulnerability of its physical plant, particularly after Desert Storm, it seems likely that Pyongyang could have decided on a much smaller number."[108]

A smaller number, perhaps, but Ford doubts that means a total departure from the North's nuclear policy. He finds it unlikely that at the point in North Korea's history when nuclear weapons would be especially valuable, "the leadership made a decision to give it all up for two light-water reactors and a few boat loads of heavy fuel oil."[109]

This is how Ford explains North Korea's strategic motivations:

> Since the 1950s North Korea has had to calculate that once a military conflict erupted with the South, regardless of how it might have started, it would inevitably lead to the regime's destruction. Unless its forces could overrun the South quickly—something it clearly understood was beyond its means—the combined power of the ROK, the U.S., and others would eventually march North, and not stop until they had crushed all resistance. The Communist regime would cease to exist. Although the North possesses considerable tactical advantage in a quick strike into the narrow area between the DMZ and Seoul, and would likely achieve a number of early successes, such an action would immediately invite an air war on the North of unprecedented size and scope. Unable to sustain its advantage against such fire power, and with no real defense against the pounding it would take in its rear areas as well as in the main battle zone, Pyongyang would have to be suicidal to consider such a major military adventure. . . . More and better conventional forces certainly will not solve its problems. The only thing that could change the strategic equation significantly would be weapons of mass destruction. Adding nuclear or chemical weapons to its arsenal could provide a much needed measure of deterrence against air strikes and land invasions. Threats to use such weapons, if credible, would greatly complicate the plans of UN forces, and possibly limit their operations.[110]

In short, to achieve either of North Korea's strategic objectives— reunification of the peninsula under Communist rule and survival of the regime, North Korea knows it cannot rely on conventional weapons. It must have a credible ability to threaten to use nuclear weapons. Here Ford's scenario dovetails with the ominous prediction from the former State Department lawyer, Antonio Perez, who noticed that North Korea might have positioned itself to provide a twenty-four-hour notice that it would not longer abide by the nonproliferation treaty.

Ford concludes that North Korea's motivation for signing the agreed framework was to buy time, hoping to survive and, optimistically, to regain its competitive edge. "Pyongyang may fail," Ford admits, but if it were to succeed, "it could dramatically alter the strategic equation." He supports this view with an observation that even though Pyongyang's economic troubles have required cutbacks in training, and a slowdown in the pace of military modernization, strategic programs, such as ballistic missiles, have been spared major reductions.[111]

The ominous import of Ford's analysis is disturbingly difficult to refute. "What seems for some the safest and less risky option today," he cautions, "could turn out in the end to be the most dangerous of all—a war, but one which the regime in North Korea could well survive."[112] If that war were to begin with a nuclear demonstration and end in a nuclear standoff, the consequences would indeed be far graver than a war would have been in May of 1994.

Carl Ford is not alone in fearing the consequences of a hidden military buildup as North Korea purports to comply with the agreed framework. Larry Niksch of the Congressional Research Service cautions Capitol Hill analysts, "The freeze will not prevent North Korea from producing a few nuclear weapons if . . . it has enough plutonium, sufficient technology to manufacture them, and hidden facilities."[113] Reports of hidden underground nuclear facilities have not abated since the signing of the agreed framework. One article in Seoul's *Chosun Ilbo* newspaper went so far as to suggest that an underground site in Ha'gap has been targeted by allied military planners because it is believed to be a plutonium handling facility.[114]

Seven months after that story appeared, U.S. intelligence agencies admitted they were concerned that a huge underground nuclear facility was under construction.[115] Even if North Korea were content with the level of plutonium it produced before the freeze, some analysts suggest it would now be devoting its energies to constructing bombs and delivery systems. "The agreement itself does not directly restrict any of the North's weapons fabrication or missile development activities," Carl Ford points out; "it does not specifically require the North to stop its nuclear weapons research and development, or restrict in any way its missile programs."[116] Leonard S. Spector, director of the Nuclear Nonproliferation Project of Carnegie Endowment for International Peace, told a congressional panel that the North Koreans "could advance the missile program while they are sitting on perhaps a bomb or two worth of plutonium . . . [and] at some later stage they could call the deal off, and start reprocessing at that point, and be much further along."[117] Observing that there is a difference between terminating a program and freezing it, South Korean negotiator Lee Dong Bok characterized the agreed framework as "an agreement to administer sleeping pills to North Korea's nuclear weapons capabilities."[118]

Victor Gilinsky, an engineer with a doctorate in physics, and a former director of the RAND Corporation's physical sciences department, was appointed by Presidents Ford and Carter to serve on the Nuclear Regulatory Commission. "The worst aspect of the agreement," he has written, "is that it has left the United States subject to continued blackmail."[119] He points out that by leaving the facilities intact, instead of demanding their destruction, the agreed framework gives North Korea the chance to threaten to reactivate its program. During the negotiations in Geneva, Pentagon officials sought provisions requiring immediate destruction of the North's facilities, but U.S. negotiators believed North Korea would walk away from a deal that demanded up-front destruction of their facilities. They were probably right.

Gilinsky, like Ford, believes that a delaying tactic underlies North Korea's motivation. Drawing on his engineering background, Gilinsky concludes that obtaining light-water reactors for electric power generation was not in fact North Korea's objective:

> Large nuclear reactors are an exceptionally poor choice for generating electricity in North Korea. . . . Their electrical grid of less than ten thousand megawatts is too small and unreliable to absorb individual units of one thousand megawatts. Moreover, grid unreliability poses safety problems for nuclear reactors, which may need outside electrical power sources to maintain cooling in the event of a sudden shutdown, since the emergency diesel generators are not especially dependable. Providing the necessary grid infrastructure is likely to add $1 billion or so to the original project cost estimates. Altogether, the host of practical and political problems in transferring nuclear technology to North Korea ensures that, of all the ways of supplying North Korea's electrical needs, nuclear power will take by far the *longest time* to bring on line.[120]

He concludes that "the North Koreans must have chosen this course because completing the electric-generating project was not their top priority."[121] Other types of electric generating equipment would have been delivered quickly, and North Korea would accordingly have had to come into compliance with international standards and destroyed their nuclear facilities earlier. This was not what they desired:

> The North Koreans may not necessarily be motivated to per-
> form their part of the bargain in the way the United States
> has assumed. They may not be counting on the LWRs any-
> time soon or perhaps at all. What they wanted most, they
> got: direct negotiations with the United States while keep-
> ing their nuclear weapons option in mothballs as security
> for U.S. performance.[122]

Former National Security Adviser Richard V. Allen describes the impact of the agreed framework on U.S.-ROK relations as its "core problem." The agreed framework has created a new relationship between the United States and North Korea that causes strains in the bilateral alliance between the United States and South Korea, despite provisions that call for North-South dialogue.

Lee Dong Bok, an expert on North Korean negotiating behavior cited throughout this book, explained the troubling phenomenon:

> While promising "to engage in North-South dialogue,"
> North Korea says that it would do so "as this Agreed Frame-
> work will help create an atmosphere that promotes such dia-
> logue." Spoken succinctly, where there is no atmosphere,
> there is no dialogue. In other words, what North Korea says
> in the Agreed Framework is merely that it is prepared to
> engage in North-South dialogue only on conditions of its
> own.[123]

Lee points out that this technique of postponing determining factors is a frequent North Korean negotiating tactic. He argues that "after decades of North-South dialogue, a compromise had finally been reached" in the agreements of 1992, and the United States should have insisted that North Korea live up to those agreements. "But in the agreed framework," Lee regrets, "the North was permitted to pursue dialogue only on Northern terms, in total disregard of all past inter-Korean agreements."[124]

As Allen sees it, the agreed framework allowed North Korea "to escape its commitment to productive dialogue with South Korea." Soon after the agreed framework was signed, Allen warned:

North Korea, after declaring the armistice agreement to be invalid in April 1994, now insists that the settlement of the nuclear issue would include a peace agreement, and that it be a bilateral treaty with Washington and not a treaty with Seoul. In this way the patient and very clever North Korean negotiators seek millimeter by millimeter to link the nuclear agreed framework with other long-sought political objectives, chief among them the isolation of Seoul by successful end runs directly to Washington.[125]

To achieve the goals of the agreed framework, North Korea had entered into a complex set of interconnected political relationships with countries it had derogated in the past. This was clearly what North Korea had desired, and had sought at great risk during the nuclear negotiations. Developing a political relationship with former enemies, winning their commitment to peace, and raiding their treasuries for an expensive project that benefited the regime seemed undeniably advantageous.

Many analysts, in fact, have suggested North Korea won everything it wanted. As the agreement's supporters have said, North Korea obtained tangible physical benefits. As the agreement's detractors have pointed out, North Korea retained its ability to threaten and blackmail during future crises. The benefits that accrued to North Korea seemed to justify the way the agreement was announced in Pyongyang—it was heralded as a supreme national achievement. The agreement seems in many ways to have demonstrated the skill of North Korea's negotiators; they had finally secured a level of international recognition that their predecessors had sought at the negotiating table for decades.

As Richard Allen predicted, the North Koreans would turn their attention to negotiation of a peace treaty as their next, seemingly ultimate, objective at the negotiating table. Presumably such an agreement would establish the regime's legitimacy and guarantee its security. Neither legitimacy nor security, however, can be based on external factors. Both must be established domestically before they can be recognized internationally.

Whether the connections to the rest of the world that North Korea had attained through the negotiations on nuclear matters would promote the long-term survival of the regime or facilitate its demise remained to be seen. It is possible that in the final decade of the twentieth century, no amount of negotiating skill could have saved the North Korean regime.

10

★

Dealing with the Truth

The words "crazy," "irrational," "erratic," and "bizarre" are too often used to describe North Korea's negotiating behavior. None of them accurately characterizes the generally effective, cleverly devised, skillfully implemented negotiating strategy pursued by this small, poor, and relatively powerless country.

The word "unpredictable" is also used, with greater validity, but more often in frustration than from an understanding of the North's strategy. Doubtless North Korea's maneuvers are often unanticipated. The incidents it creates to initiate negotiations frequently employ shock, and the brinkmanship it follows to bring negotiations to closure generally relies on an element of surprise.

Few nations, however, have so regularly practiced negotiation as their principal foreign policy instrument, so repeatedly used a familiar set of negotiating tactics, and so doggedly pursued a set of fundamental negotiating objectives. Despite the prevalent characterizations of its negotiating style, North Korea has been extraordinarily consistent. It has also been surprisingly successful. Although it brings little to the table, it has succeeded in focusing the world's attention on its demands, and in many cases has won substantial concessions. North Korea has wrested from the negotiating process advantages that have repeatedly brought it back from the edge of apparent defeat.

North Korea has failed to achieve its stated long-term goals— revolution in the South, reunification of the peninsula under socialism, withdrawal of foreign forces—but these elusive goals themselves are used as an element of negotiating strategy. North Korea has tenaciously adhered to this set of inflexible and unrealistic demands as a device for blocking progress, backing out of agreements, and restructuring the arrangements for negotiations.

Because it negotiates from a position of relative weakness, North Korea's success must be measured not only by the concessions it has obtained but also by the compromises it has avoided. It has generally derived advantages from the negotiating process itself, not from entering into formal agreements. Hence it values process over result, and focuses on controlling the process.

North Korea initiates negotiation by appearing to be open to fundamental changes in its policies, uses its willingness to participate to demand benefits and concessions, and terminates discussions when it has gained maximum advantage. It manages negotiations so that its adversaries experience stages of optimism, disillusionment, and disappointment. Adversaries' disappointment, in turn, paves the way for creating an illusion of fresh cooperation in the initial stage of the next negotiation. Whatever talks are under way when the reader considers these words, one of these cyclic stages will apply. And whatever stage applies will be replaced as the negotiating process proceeds. The cycle can be expected to continue as long as the current regime holds power.

In the years immediately following negotiation of the agreed framework, the Clinton administration optimistically trumpeted changes in North Korea's approach to negotiations with the West. "North Korea has begun to move, ever so slowly, in the direction of greater contact and openness with the outside world," Secretary of State Madeleine Albright observed in a 1997 speech at the United States Naval Academy. From her perspective, this warranted a change in dealing with the North: "While maintaining our firm policy of deterrence, we will also continue to make clear the benefits of cooperation."[1]

In his book on the agreed framework, Leon Sigal quoted U.S. negotiator Thomas Hubbard: "Kang really worked hard to convince us that this was a major change in North Korea's approach to the world. He told us it had Kim Jong Il's blessing and was designed to open up North Korea."[2] In a similar vein, Kim Jong U of North Korea's External Economic Commission was quoted as saying, "We have opened the doors, and we will open them wider."[3] There was evidence that North

Korea recognized benefits would accrue if the regime improved relations with the United States and other potential economic partners. The perception arose that North Korea might be willing to be paid to behave.

It seems to make sense that North Korea's desperate circumstances would motivate it to rectify its international behavior. Admiral Joy observed, "the Communists can be compelled to negotiate seriously for the alleviation of the basic issues between their world and ours," but he concluded that happened "only through the imminent threat of application of our military power."[4] Today, American officials tend to think that the pressure from economic and political collapse will bring change without a resort to military pressure against North Korea. One of the administration's leading experts on Korean issues, Ambassador Charles Kartman, observed, "dire prospects are pressing the North Korean leadership to review its traditional isolation, a development we, the ROK, and others want to encourage."[5] Similarly, Madeleine Albright, on her first visit to Korea as secretary of state, said the prospects for peace on the Korean peninsula depended "basically on how much the North Koreans are hurting."[6]

The Assumption That Communist Collapse Is Inevitable

Twenty years before the Berlin Wall fell, long before most in the free world would have predicted the collapse of communism, South Korean President Park Chung Hee wrote, " . . . liberalization will eventually affect North Korea. The liberalizing trend in the Communist world is, I believe, so great a force that it cannot be held in check by any one dictator, however powerful he may be."[7] Today, although North Korea disputes it, the rest of the world believes North Korea will fall as inexorably as the rest of the Communist world has fallen.

There are sound reasons to conclude that any political system based on coercion will eventually fail. Accurate information is essential to sound political decisionmaking, but the Soviet system distorted the truth. In his book about the fall of Soviet communism, Michael Ledeen pointed out "the leaders in the Kremlin often had very bad information about some very important subjects . . . [because] intelligence services lied to and otherwise misinformed their superiors."[8] Officially sanctioned falsification to satisfy the ideological postulations of dictators may yet cause the collapse of North Korea, even if outside pressure or popular revolution do not.

The Soviet Union also fell, however, because it could not compete with its rivals. Economist Nicholas Eberstadt has observed that in response to the West's deterrent strategy and technological superiority, Soviet military planners like Marshal Ogarkov demanded a "scientific-technical revolution" to advance their own military technology. That effort demanded hard cash valued in the international marketplace, something the Soviet system was ill equipped to generate.[9]

As a consequence of the Soviet Union's attempt to maintain its global reach and competitive standing, the Soviet bloc's subsidies for smaller Marxist states, which drained precious resources, were necessarily curtailed. North Korea was particularly vulnerable. It had been dependent on massive Soviet-bloc subsidies from the start. Economists Albina Birman and Marc Rubin have explained that the North Korean economic marvel was not so marvelous after all; industrial goods and raw materials had been transferred to North Korea "practically free of charge" during the years of North Korean industrial mobilization. The subsidies were rationalized on the Marxist notion that compensation in products manufactured by North Korea's state factories would reimburse the expense of their construction.[10] For political reasons, however, the value produced was squandered on the regime's monumental self-aggrandizement and its expensive apparatus of oppression.

At the close of the twentieth century, it is a generally accepted theorem that Communist systems naturally collapse of their own weighty incompetence. American and South Korean policymakers' confidence in North Korea's collapse is founded on a kind of post-cold-war determinism—the view that communism cannot succeed—and North Korea must therefore eventually adopt new ideological underpinnings.

Signs of Collapse

North Korea might well be sobered by the likelihood of its own collapse.

As the Soviet bloc suffered economic failure, North Korea's subsidized economy suffered as well. North Korea's trade volume almost halved in three years, from $5.42 billion in 1988, to $2.72 billion in 1991.[11] Oil imports from Russia dropped from 440,000 to 40,000 tons from 1990 to 1991, tightening the North's energy use so much that it caused a reduction in the North Korean regime's sacrosanct military exercises.[12] North Korea's gross national product (GNP) declined by 4 percent in 1990 and similar figures in subsequent years. By mid-decade, its overall external debt surpassed $7.86 billion.[13]

Reports of famine emerged in 1996, after a five-year period in which food supplies averaged less than half of the population's estimated needs.[14] On April 28, 1997, Reuters reported that some peasants delayed burying their dead, for fear the bodies would be dug up and eaten by starving neighbors.[15] American newspapers reported Chinese truck drivers' concern for the starving children they saw while transporting goods across the border into North Korea.[16]

Few eyewitnesses can attest to the human costs of North Korea's economic devastation. Most Western observers are permitted to visit only carefully selected areas, and North Koreans are understandably circumspect about making critical comments.

One outspoken witness to North Korea's desperate straits, however, is Hwang Jang Yeop, the former North Korean Workers Party secretary who defected to Seoul in February 1997. Hwang, who attained power while Kim Il Sung was alive and trained Kim Jong Il in North Korea's Marxist ideology, puts the blame for North Korea's failing economy squarely on the younger Kim's shoulders. He described North Korea's economic failure in an extensive interview in November 1997, explaining that the North Korean dictator believes it is within his power to create a "personal economy" governing his personal assets, a "party economy" that sets foreign exchange rates as Kim dictates, and a "military economy" that employs about 500,000 at military factories.

The system of military-run industries is reputed to be one of the most efficient aspects of the North's economy. Hwang claims, however, that one military factory received no food rations for nine to ten months and, as a result, 2,000 educated engineers at the plant starved to death. He argues that Kim's economic policies have succeeded only in creating a new business in China: North Koreans sabotage their factories and sell dismantled factory equipment to the Chinese in exchange for flour and corn.[17] Desperate North Koreans have even sawed off parts of Kim Il Sung's bronze statues for sale across the border.[18]

Kim Jong Il might claim that the situation became grave only in the period after his father died, and before he was given the full authority he needed to correct the economy. He portrayed himself as trying to alleviate North Korea's hardships in the following speech in December 1996:

> I could see food-begging people lining the streets. The country is awash with food-begging roamers. They fill trains and railroad stations. In such famine circumstances, however, neither Party secretaries nor other Party cadres in provinces, cities, or counties show their noses on the scene. They are only lecturing in conference rooms. The mass media are blaring out the "Painful March" campaign, but the Party officials do not care a bit. They seem to take the campaign for an observance of perseverance, doing nothing.[19]

Kim Jong Il must be clever about where the blame is ascribed for the system's failures. Hardships and confusion may have been to his advantage during the hiatus in power so that his own accession would be welcomed and more secure. Even if he profited from indecision during the period 1994–1997, however, he cannot so easily resolve North Korea's systemic problems now that he holds power. He will not advocate the regime-toppling changes that must occur to meet the needs of the people of North Korea.

In any society, such severe conditions take a political toll. A former American ambassador to Korea and China, James R. Lilley, quotes visitors to North Korea as saying that North Koreans have become "mutually suspicious, uncertain about their roles in the system."[20] According to a study by South Korea's Integrated Defense Headquarters (IDH), North Korea's devastated economy caused an increase in the number of drifters and beggars from 13,000 in 1996 to 230,000 in 1997. IDH concludes that this itinerant population of vagabonds might well become a potential focus of opposition to the Kim Jong Il regime.[21]

Hwang Jang Yeop says that when ideological offenders are on their way to be executed they no longer succumb to pressure to renounce their beliefs. He concludes "the minds of the general public are slowly deserting the system in favor of reform."[22] Other defectors and visitors have described how North Koreans dismantle and reconstruct state-issued radios to receive outside stations. Despite appearances, neither the regime nor the West can assume that the population of North Korea is docile, loyal, or patient.

A telling sign of political collapse is the flow of defectors from North Korea. High-level defectors, diplomats and party members like

Hwang, attract global attention, but there is an increasing flow of ordinary working people who are willing to risk their lives for nothing more than a chance to move their families away from North Korea. In December of 1996, a sixty-one-year-old stroke victim led sixteen others, including five children and a pregnant woman, across 2,000 miles of unfamiliar Chinese territory to Hong Kong.[23] Chinese sources in border towns tell of the constant outflow, often assist the escapees, and express sympathy for those who are apprehended by North Korean authorities and forced to return. "The North Korean police put a metal wire through the noses of some people who escape, like a brand that marks them out," a Chinese witness told a Western news agency, "We can hear the screams of children when they put the metal wire through their noses, because they do it as soon as they cross into North Korea."[24]

North Korea's regime can deal with its disenchanted people only through ever-increasing measures of oppression. To demonstrate weakness might cause a spontaneous rebellion. But increasing oppression cannot extend Kim Jong Il's regime indefinitely.

Some of the defectors in late 1998 came from the North Korean military's rank-and-file. The West assumes that North Korea's military is motivated by a desire to preserve its privileged status. But the North's soldiers are second-class citizens compared to the party elite; the training they endure is excessively cruel and the state ideology they uphold is based on a lie—that the regime serves the people. In the event of widespread rebellion, it is not at all clear that the military would engage in the wholesale slaughter of their starving countrymen.

Believing that the collapse of North Korean communism was as certain as the collapse of communism elsewhere, the Clinton administration envisioned a system of economic interdependence to draw North Korea out of isolation. Until the phrase was discarded after a spate of airplane jokes, administration officials advocated what they called a "soft landing" for North Korea's regime. The policy was premised on the notion that a catastrophic collapse of the North Korean regime was more dangerous than its slow demise and that dependence on American handouts would lead to changes in North Korea's behavior.

The Clinton administration, proud of the agreed framework and its broader vision of engagement with North Korea, hopes it has ushered in a new, more responsive relationship between North Korea and the international community. If that is the case, the achievement should be applauded; if it is not, such delusions could prove terribly dangerous and should be dispelled. The administration's analysis might well be logical, but the North Korean regime might perceive that there are different ways to win its objectives.

The notion that the calamity faced by North Korea determines its approach to negotiations with the West deserves rigorous scrutiny. It is therefore necessary to analyze in depth what happened after the Clinton administration signed the agreed framework with North Korea.

Signs of Improved Behavior

North Korea's initial performance under the agreed framework was taken as an early indication of a changed international approach. Just weeks after the agreed framework was signed, American and North Korean nuclear experts agreed to provisions for the safe storage of spent nuclear fuel from the five-megawatt experimental nuclear power plant. Two weeks later, the IAEA declared that North Korea had complied with the agreed framework in freezing its nuclear program. "The IAEA visited the nuclear facilities in Yongbyon and Taejon," it said, "and confirmed that these facilities were not in operation and that construction work has stopped."[25]

Administration officials readily acknowledged the progress made by North Korea. In remarks at the National Defense University, Under Secretary of Defense for Policy Walter B. Slocombe said:

> Because the actions are so striking an improvement over past North Korean secrecy, it's worth pointing out that North Korea has permitted IAEA inspectors to remain permanently at Yongbyon with access to the reactor construction site at Taechon to implement the freeze, and verify and monitor, on a daily basis, that the freeze remains in effect. In addition, the North has permitted a U.S. technical team to visit the Yongbyon complex to do surveys of measures necessary to stabilize the spent fuel so it can be stored until removed from North Korea, as required by the agreement. Removal will start when the first nuclear components for the LWRs begin to be delivered. Obviously, continued vigilance will be necessary, and we expect some more or less serious bumps in the road during implementation. But the critical first step of compliance for the DPRK has been accomplished—a verified freeze on the North Korean nuclear program.[26]

In January 1995, consistent with the tenor of these developments and the terms of the agreed framework, the United States delivered the first tranche of 50,000 metric tons of heavy residual fuel oil to North Korea and eased economic sanctions against North Korea by authorizing "U. S. companies to provide direct telecommunications services between the U. S. and DPRK, to allow the import of magnesite from the DPRK, to reduce the restrictions on financial transactions not involving the DPRK government or its entities, and to authorize the licensing of U.S. business transactions that further KEDO's construction of light-water reactors in the DPRK."[27]

Despite the American show of good faith, however, progress on implementation of the agreed framework was delayed for the first half of 1995 by North Korea's complaint that the light-water reactors to be supplied should not be of *South Korean* design. In a February 23, 1995, hearing, the powerful chairman of the Subcommittee on Asia and the Pacific, Douglas Bereuter (R-Neb.), reflected the exasperation of many in the capital over "North Korea's current adamant stance about receiving South Korean reactors."[28] To overcome North Korea's objection and advise the North Koreans that they jeopardized political support for the agreed framework, U.S. officials met with North Korean diplomats in Kuala Lumpur, Malaysia. The talks lasted three weeks.

Finally, on June 12, 1995, North Korea agreed to defer to the Korean Peninsula Energy Development Organization (KEDO) on matters such as the selection of the model for the LWRs and the contractor to carry out the project. KEDO then selected the South Korean–designed light-water reactors and a South Korean firm. South Korea and Japan provided the funds for the light-water reactor project and both were determined that South Korean reactors would be purchased. As Robert M. Gallucci stated at a hearing in Washington before the talks, "There simply is no alternative to the South Korean reactor."[29] U.S. negotiators stood their ground; to do otherwise would have unraveled the tightly interwoven arrangements under the agreed framework. To preserve the agreed framework, North Korea set aside its objection.

There were other difficulties as well in the first year of the agreed framework. At the time, they seemed to call the new relationship into question, but after their resolution they seemed to confirm the administration's hopes regarding the North's post-agreed-framework foreign policy approach.

On December 17, 1994, during routine training near the DMZ, Warrant Officers David Hilemon and Bobby Hall inadvertently flew an unarmed U.S. Army helicopter four miles into North Korean air-space. North Korean anti-aircraft guns shot the helicopter down, killing Hilemon. Hall escaped from the wreckage and was captured by North Korean soldiers who tied him to a tree, kicked him, threw stones at him, and forced him to pose for a photograph with his hands in the air.

Readers will recognize the historical precedent for this treatment, but Warrant Officer Hall was not prepared for it. After he was moved to Pyongyang, North Korean interrogators lectured him about an event they considered highly important but he had never heard of before—the 1968 seizure of the USS *Pueblo*. They explained that the *Pueblo* crew had spent a year in captivity and had been released only after they provided a written confession. Hall was forced to write many drafts of a confession and signed a final one on December 27, back-dating it to Christmas Day on the North Koreans' demand.[30]

The incident occurred while Congressman Bill Richardson (later appointed U.S. ambassador to the UN) was visiting North Korea on a fact-finding mission. After two days of being kept waiting and two days of difficult negotiations with Vice Foreign Minister Song, Richardson formed the impression that there were differences between the North Korean military and the Ministry of Foreign Affairs over how to handle the incident. Richardson and Song reached an understanding that the congressman could leave North Korea with Hilemon's body, but the Foreign Ministry needed a few more days to resolve the matter of Hall's release in discussions with North Korea's military.

As it turned out, North Korean interagency discussions took longer than expected. An "official letter of regret" signed by the commander in chief of the UN Command, General Gary Luck, was accepted by North Korea but it did not clear the way for Hall's release."[31] Hall was not released until the North Korean military had an opportunity to press for bilateral U.S.-DPRK military talks. The United States did not accede to the North Korean request, but it did send Principal Deputy Assistant Secretary of State Thomas C. Hubbard to Pyongyang. He became the highest ranking American official ever to have visited the North Korean capital on official business. Hubbard agreed to a statement of "sincere regret for this incident," and pledged to meet "in an appropriate forum" to prevent such incidents in the future.[32]

North Korea took this to mean replacing the Military Armistice Commission with an "appropriate forum." Even that reading conveyed nothing new, however; the terms of the armistice agreement called for its replacement with a political settlement. Hall was released on December 30, 1994. Hubbard concluded, "What we have seen, I believe, in our negotiations in Geneva, as well as in the helicopter incident, is a [North Korean] policymaking process that seems to work. And in the final analysis, it seems to bring logical decisions."[33] The world was nudged a bit closer toward peace talks with North Korea but not toward the resolution of the key issues.

Encouraged, North Korea intensified its long-standing argument that the Military Armistice Commission should be dissolved and replaced. North Korea had always characterized its dealings with the MAC as a matter between an indigenous command and foreign forces with no right to remain on the peninsula. Its attempts to extinguish the MAC were premised on the North's demand that a peace treaty was long overdue. Unfortunately, dissolving the MAC could be easy; negotiating a peace treaty or finding an effective institution to carry on the MAC's duties had always been the more difficult challenge, as history had more than adequately shown.

On March 25, 1991, UNCMAC had named a South Korean, Major General Hwang Won Tak, as its senior member of the Military Armistice Commission and North Korea had taken offense. Unable to make reality fit its propaganda, the North argued that a South Korean could not be named to represent the UNC because the Republic of Korea had not signed the armistice agreement. It may be hard to believe that North Korea could presume to require the opposing command to adhere to an organizational structure that it formed in war forty years earlier, but presumption has often benefited the North. Moreover, North Korea has seldom missed an opportunity to determine who its interlocutors will be.

Three years later, on April 28, 1994, North Korea recalled all of its MAC personnel and announced that it would not recognize UNC-MAC as its counterpart or participate in MAC meetings. North Korean representatives nevertheless attended meetings until July 5, 1995, which they announced was to be their final MAC meeting. They delivered a letter from Lieutenant General Ri Chan Bok, proposing that a bilateral U.S.-DPRK peace mechanism replace the armistice.[34] Even in the era of the agreed framework, however, the North's effort to discredit and terminate the MAC did not lessen the need for both sides to maintain it. Events soon proved that the North would return to the MAC when it suited them.

North Korean military representatives were quick to request

meetings in late September and October 1996, after learning some details of a botched infiltration mission from South Korean news accounts. The submarine infiltration had resulted in the murder/suicide of eleven crew members and the escape of as many as fifteen commandos into the South Korean countryside. In the weeks that followed, thirteen of the commandos were killed in various towns, in shoot-outs with South Korean soldiers. One was captured and interrogated.[35] Another may have found his way back to North Korea, but South Korean authorities concluded the submarine probably held a total of twenty-five. The commandos, well-trained infiltrators, succeeded in killing five soldiers and four civilians as they fled across South Korea.

At the MAC meetings, North Korean officers demanded the return of the submarine and the crew, and threatened to retaliate "a hundredfold or a thousandfold" over the deaths of the North Korean commandos, eleven of whom had taken their own lives.[36] This was not the first time North Korea threatened drastic action against the ROK or UNC, but it was the first time they did so while attending meetings of an institution they had claimed to terminate years earlier.

The submarine infiltration naturally provoked South Korean anger, slowed progress on implementation of the agreed framework, and risked its termination.[37] Although slow to do so, North Korea eventually realized that its interests lay with moving beyond the incident. In late December, it issued the following apologetic statement:

> The spokesman of the Ministry of Foreign Affairs of the DPRK is authorized to express deep regret for the submarine incident in the coastal waters of Kangnung, South Korea, in September 1996, that caused the tragic loss of human life.
>
> The DPRK will make efforts to ensure that such an incident will not recur and will work with others for durable peace and stability on the Korean peninsula.[38]

South Korean public reaction to the statement was generally negative, along the lines of the *Hankook Ilbo's* comment that "the North never meant to apologize. The statement is just a scheme to advance relations with the United States and Japan."[39] Even North Korean efforts to seek better relations are seen as a step forward. Acting Assistant Secretary Kartman commented that "persistent diplomacy by the U.S., in close consultation with the ROK, resulted in the unprecedented statement of regret made by the DPRK last December and laid the groundwork for a resumption of our efforts to improve the situation on the Peninsula." He concluded, "If North Korea clearly calculates its own interests and opts for greater cooperation, including with the ROK, we can make significant progress."[40]

A few days before Kim Jong Il's accession to power as general secretary of the North Korean Workers Party, there was an incident that delayed work on the light-water reactor project for a week. After South Korean construction workers moved out of a guest house to new dormitories, they left behind a crumpled newspaper, North Korea's *Rodong Shinmun*, which featured a picture of Kim Jong Il. North Korean authorities took the discarded newspaper as an affront to the man they had always called the Dear Leader. They removed North Korean workers from the site and confined the South Koreans to house arrest in their dormitory. Demanding an apology, North Korea threatened it could not guarantee the safety of the South Koreans.

Coming as it did at the time of Kim Jong Il's nomination, the incident was susceptible to a number of troubling interpretations. If coordinated at the highest levels, it might have indicated Kim's interest in cancelling the LWR project, perhaps even disavowing the agreed framework. If taken on the initiative of lower level authorities, the action could have represented an effort to provide Kim Jong Il with an opportunity to exploit. Perhaps it was nothing more than an overzealous official's way to demonstrate his affection for the Dear Leader or his assiduous implementation of routine orders about mistreating official photographs. For all the West knew, Kim's detractors were setting up an incident as a test of whether Kim Jong Il had his father's fortitude to take advantage of an opportunity for confrontation, or his stamina to demand respect for his image.

Whatever the motivation behind the incident, it met with a firm answer from South Korea. Protesting the treatment of its construction workers, the South demanded they be allowed to move freely about the site, invoking the agreement North Korea had concluded with the Korean Peninsula Energy Development Organization. The South also made it clear that it would not offer an apology and dismissed North Korean umbrage by pointing out that "it is not at all unusual for a South Korean to throw away a newspaper after use."[41] The North dropped its complaint, and work resumed two days before Kim's accession to power, perhaps indicating that Kim Jong Il valued the agreed framework and chose to see its work proceed.

In an incident a week after Kim Jong Il took control of the party, two South Korean farmers were abducted at gunpoint by North Korean soldiers near the village of Taesong-dong, not far from Panmunjom. Hong Song Sun, age sixty-seven, and her son Kim Yong Bok, age forty-one, were gathering acorns when they were surrounded by soldiers and taken into captivity on October 16, 1997.

If that incident was an attempt by the army to present Kim Jong Il with an opportunity to exploit confrontation and demand negotiation along the lines of incidents that occurred in his father's reign, it did not proceed in the familiar pattern. Instead, the incident led to talks that seemed identical to the colonel-level sessions that MAC secretaries had held for decades. Colonel Thomas Riley for the UN Command and Colonel Yu Sang Yol for the Korean People's Army even formed a joint observer team, the investigative mechanism established by the armistice agreement, the first to be convened since 1976. Despite the fact that North Korea declared the MAC to have been terminated as of April 28, 1994, it attended a MAC meeting on October 16, 1997. At that meeting, the North asserted that the two acorn-gatherers had crossed the military demarcation line, were on the Northern side when they were apprehended, and would be released "in due course."[42]

After the joint observer team performed its investigation on October 21, the two detainees agreed, "It seems we accidentally crossed the Military Demarcation Line in an area that is not clearly marked." The UNC spokesman, Kim Young Kyu, said, "We accepted the farmers' statement to secure their safe and timely release."[43]

The abduction presented an opportunity that North Korea might well have used to pressure the United States, embarrass South Korea, or manipulate Southern politics. The United States had at that time postponed the next preparatory session of the four-way talks, and North Korea might have pressed to have the talks accelerated. A South Korean presidential campaign was under way at the time, and North Korea might have used the situation to increase pressure on the sitting party's candidate. But these familiar North Korean tactics were not pursued this time. Indeed, one South Korean analyst observed, "Kim Jong Il, who recently assumed the top post of the North Korean Workers party, did not want to appear to be a rigid Communist leader."[44]

To that end, there were changes in the way North Korea handled its dealings with the United States. In light of such indications, the United States set about addressing the major challenge that has remained unresolved since the end of the Korean War: the negotiation of a peace treaty to settle tensions on the Korean peninsula.

Four-Party Talks

As earlier chapters have explained, the armistice agreement brought about a truce, not a peace. By its own terms, it deferred political issues to a subsequent peace conference. One was held in 1954, but it merely reaffirmed the basic sources of tension. Since then, North Korea demanded direct bilateral peace negotiations with the United States. Although there were times when both sides considered three-way talks, the most balanced arrangement, supported by the United States since 1976, was for negotiations involving the four nations directly concerned.

On April 16, 1996, President Clinton and South Korean President Kim Young Sam proposed to convene a four-party meeting of representatives of South Korea, North Korea, the United States, and the People's Republic of China *without preconditions*. The meeting, they said, was aimed "at replacing the current military armistice agreement with a permanent peace." "In framing this proposal," the U.S. State Department announced, "the U.S. and South Korea took the DPRK's expressed concerns into account. The main difference between this proposal and North Korean proposals is that the DPRK wishes to negotiate only with the U.S. This is not feasible, as the establishment of a permanent peace is primarily the responsibility of the Korean people—North and South."[45]

North Korea might be expected to balk at discussing a peace settlement with South Korea at the negotiating table, but the U.S. administration hoped its new approach to external dealings would overcome that objection. As Acting Assistant Secretary Kartman said in a February hearing:

> The North's overall awareness of their own weakness seems to have driven them to seek a new arrangement. They appear to put great emphasis on improving relations with the United States as the key element. We have, of course, declined to do this in a strictly bilateral way; we insist that it must be done in concert with our ally on the Peninsula, the ROK. This is why we made relatively little progress in the political area. Now, however, the North Koreans may be acknowledging that they have to enter into a process in which the ROK is at least an equal partner with the United States.[46]

To explain the proposed four-party process, the United States and South Korea invited North Korea to attend a briefing in New York set for March 5, 1997. North Korea had reasons to welcome the invitation. In keeping with its perception that a concession or, in this case, an invitation, from the West represents weakness that can be exploited, however, North Korea assumed that the United States and South Korea would negotiate specific levels of food assistance to entice North Korea to attend the briefing. Thus began a confusing display of public posturing in which North Korea tried to tie its reluctant participation to allied generosity, while the allies emphasized that they would be generous but denied that their contributions were linked to the four-party talks.

The United States and South Korea argued that food assistance would be based on an assessment of the appropriate response to a humanitarian need, not the result of negotiation. In South Korean Foreign Minister Yoo's words, "We are not going to provide food aid just because they say, 'We'll come to the talks if you give us food.'"[47] Nevertheless, on February 15, the United States announced a decision to provide additional food assistance worth $15 million. Kartman explained that the gesture was in keeping with "the long-standing American tradition of offering assistance to needy people regardless of the political views of their leaders."[48]

For its part, North Korea attended the briefing in March and, after a few months' reflection, decided to participate in the four-party process. In Hong Kong for the turnover of the British Crown Colony to the People's Republic of China, Secretary of State Albright announced that the DPRK had accepted the proposal "for four-party peace negotiations." In this setting calling to mind China's emerging relationship with the United States and its increasing power, Albright emphasized, "The successful conclusion of a peace agreement would bring lasting peace and stability to the Korean Peninsula and contribute greatly to the peace and stability of the entire region." Preparatory talks were scheduled for August 5 in New York to decide the date, venue, agenda, and procedures for the talks.[49]

The preparatory talks in August set a date for an additional preparatory meeting in September, with a plenary to follow six weeks later. There was agreement on a location—Geneva—and composition of the delegations—senior officials under the direction of foreign ministers. The United States would chair the first meeting, and the chairmanship would then rotate by random drawing to the other three. At the State Department press briefing where these results were announced, Spokesman James Rubin remarked, tongue in cheek, "People who follow this issue tell me that they consider that substantial agreement."[50]

It certainly seemed like substantial progress, but the hurdle over the agenda was even more familiar to students of North Korean negotiating behavior.

"There was not agreement on the agenda," Rubin said, "and there was significant difference over whether the agenda should be general or whether the agenda should be specific." Had he been there, Admiral Joy might have cracked a smile. Rubin may not have been conscious that he was echoing Admiral Joy's words when he explained, "The DPRK agenda items—including discussion of the withdrawal of U.S. troops—would, in our view, prejudge the results of the plenary talks before the negotiations began."[51] In 1951 and again forty-six years later, North Korea proposed as an agenda item "withdrawal of foreign forces." At either time, U.S. acceptance of this agenda proposal would have given North Korea a most desired objective before peace talks even commenced.

From Rubin's perspective, the straightforward American approach could be explained plainly: "We do not want the negotiations to be bogged down with issues that are nonstarters, like U.S. withdrawal of troops from the Korean Peninsula or a U.S.-DPRK separate agreement."[52] For North Korea, however, such issues are not nonstarters; they are kept in reserve for use as terminators. The North had no need to exploit an impasse at this point, however; advantages were still to be gained by discussing *preparations* for the talks.

The North Koreans knew the United States could not agree to the withdrawal of U.S. forces. Because those forces do not in any way impinge on the ability of North Korea to conduct its affairs within its own territory, the only consequence of removal is to make the South more vulnerable. The reasons for North Korea to emphasize force withdrawal, however, are considerably more complex. The reasons include preserving the option to walk away from the negotiations—thus creating a specter of war that enhances the domestic power of the DPRK military, justifies purges against those presumed to be disloyal, and silences those who would counsel alternative policy approaches. When the "foreign forces" issue emerges from the background to the foreground of negotiations, renewed preparations for war, heightened domestic repression, strident new demands, and threats to terminate the talks follow.

Hoping to avoid giving the North Koreans a means to disengage from the talks, the United States modified its stance somewhat to accommodate North Korean sensitivities. In spite of Rubin's earlier dismissal of U.S. troop withdrawal, the United States went to considerable length to appear flexible on the issue after the second preparatory session:

> . . . we're not saying that these issues of concern to the North Koreans cannot be addressed in the four-party talks. They will be free to raise their concerns and their issues, and that's what the negotiation is all about. What we will not do, though—and on this, again, the question is the North Korean side understanding the firmness of our position—but what we will not do is place the specific items as specific agenda items. Rather, under a general rubric, we believe that all sides will be free to raise whatever issues of concern they wish to.[53]

After working-level talks in New York on November 10, and a third session of preparatory talks on November 21, 1997, the first plenary session of the four-party talks was finally convened in Geneva, December 9–10. That session was described as "cordial and productive" and settled the protocol for future meetings, particularly the rotation of chairing the meetings. The United States proposed to chair an intersessional consultation at a lower level in Beijing, but North Korea was unenthusiastic. Assistant Secretary of State Stanley Roth was pleased with the progress at the first plenary session, but wisely refused to give a timetable for subsequent talks.[54] He was under no illusion that success was at hand. State Department spokesmen aptly termed the negotiating process "a marathon and not a sprint."[55]

Negotiations do not occur in a vacuum and many seemingly unconnected developments began to slow the momentum behind the talks.

Most significantly, South Korea followed Southeast Asia into a deep and largely unanticipated financial crisis. In exchange for financial reforms, the International Monetary Fund provided a bail-out, including credits equivalent to $21 billion, on December 5.[56] Within the next year, $50 billion would be made available to South Korea from international financial institutions.

North Korea might have viewed such massive aid as a demonstration of the benefits of being a member in good standing of the international community. It is also possible, however, that it concluded it had set its sights too low by accepting the light-water reactors as compensation for its nuclear freeze.

In South Korea, the election in December 1997 of former opposition leader Kim Dae Jung as president, the inaugural festivities on February 28, 1998, and the period of governmental transition also distracted attention from the four-party talks for many weeks. North and South exchanged subtle signals while the Kim administration unveiled its approach to dialogue. The new South Korean administration supported the four-party talks, but was also willing to pursue direct talks between the two Koreas simultaneously. President Kim Dae Jung proposed an exchange of special envoys and offered to meet with Kim Jong Il directly.

In February and March, 1998, reports of unusual military activity in Pyongyang and political turmoil—street fighting between field officers of the North Korean Army and Kim Jong Il's personal guard, and an assassination attempt on Kim Jong Il—emerged from North Korea.[57] Although admitting that streets had been closed to traffic, and office buildings, including the party headquarters, had been taken over by North Korea's military, South Korean government sources dispelled the reports by explaining that that was merely part of the North's annual winter mobilization drill.[58] In Pyongyang, Vice Foreign Minister Yi In Kyu called a press conference to explain, "The current state of wartime mobilization not only applies to regular armed forces, but also to all sectors of the national economy and social life which will operate with wartime mechanisms."[59]

But the events were not routine. There was a reshuffling of the Workers Party hierarchy and a purge of the youth organization during the winter mobilization. In April, a high-ranking general was arrested on allegations of having plotted the assassination of Kim Jong Il the previous summer; the general was subsequently executed.[60] Some of those responsible for dealing with external business interests disappeared, including Kim Jong U, the North Korean official who had said North Korea was "opening a door."[61] A few months later it was reported that he had been executed.[62]

Pyongyang unquestionably had a growing number of political problems with which to deal. The third secretary in North Korea's diplomatic mission to the Rome headquarters of the UN Food and Agriculture Organization (FAO), Kim Dong Su, defected on February 6, 1998, adding his name to that of North Korea's ambassador to Cairo, Jang Sung Gil, his brother Jang Sung Ho, a trade official in Paris, and, of course, Hwang Jang Yeop, all of whom had defected within the previous year.[63] Although of lesser rank and stature, a military defection must also have troubled the North Korean regime. On February 3, Captain Byon Yong Kwan, an army officer in charge of psychological warfare along the DMZ, changed sides and asked for asylum in the South.[64]

The Breakdown of the Four-Party Talks

In this uncertain environment, North Korea refused to participate in the intersessional meeting to be chaired by the United States in Beijing, and it was cancelled. Nevertheless, the United States pressed ahead. On March 2, 1998, the State Department announced that bilateral U.S.-DPRK meetings would be held on March 13 in Berlin, where North Korea has a large diplomatic mission, and preliminary four-party talks in Geneva the next day, preceding the plenary session. The United States, always hopeful the four-party talks would lead smoothly toward the eventual inter-Korean resolution of issues, welcomed North-South talks.

The lines between the four-way talks, which North Korea called "a plot to promote two-way talks," and North-South dialogue itself, were blurred. As a senior American official explained to a perplexed reporter:

> . . . you're asking me to erect very thick walls between each of these things—the bilateral U.S.–North Korean talks; the four-party talks; the inter-Korean dialogue. And in fact, these thick walls don't exist, because in Geneva at four-party talks, it's very possible for the U.S. and North Korea to meet; it's very possible for the two Korean sides to meet. In fact, when this is really working, I expect those sorts of things to happen.[65]

Unfortunately, the Berlin meeting ended without perceptible progress, and the standstill in Berlin was followed by a standoff in Geneva.

The United States saw the agenda boiling down to two issues: develop ways to reduce tensions on the Korean peninsula and replace the armistice with a permanent peace treaty.[66] These issues were intentionally broad in order to get the negotiating process started. All that could be hoped for were small, incremental steps toward reducing tensions. Despite these limited hopes, however, the week in Geneva bogged down in frustrating discussions of procedural mechanisms. Much of the work focused on whether to set up two subcommittees on confidence-building measures or just one.

The effort centered on distinguishing which issues belonged in four-way talks and which issues were appropriately deferred to North-South dialogue. From the allies' perspective, both the four-party talks and the inter-Korean talks needed to focus on building trust and confidence. The South Korean representative to the talks, Deputy Foreign Minister Song Young Shik, said the political and economic aspects of confidence-building measures would be emphasized in North-South talks, while military issues would be discussed in the framework of the four-party talks.[67] In the four-party talks, American officials noted as examples that reestablishing a hotline telephone between North and South could be a four-party topic; refraining from name calling and slander could be a North-South confidence-building measure.[68] The talks were all to promote peace—to build confidence on the peninsula, to generate North-South discussions, and eventually to lay the foundation for a peace treaty. Peace first, then a treaty. If North Korean negotiating behavior had genuinely changed, either out of a new sense of constructive purpose or in an effort to alleviate North Korea's suffering, that approach might have been embraced.

By the time the Geneva talks were under way, however, the differences between the allied approach and North Korea's was apparent. As a United States official observed:

> There is a tremendous gap between the North Korean position—which is wanting to begin with a negotiation over U.S. troop withdrawal, preceded by a U.S.-North Korean peace treaty—versus the position of the other three parties—which is that we really should begin this process by trying to take some practical steps to build up some confidence and establish the basis for greater dialogue.[69]

The North Koreans insisted that the only matters for discussion were negotiating a peace treaty and withdrawing U.S. troops. To this a U.S. public affairs spokesman sternly replied that the presence of U.S. forces in Korea "is, and will be, determined by the U.S. and the Republic of Korea on the basis of our mutual security alliance. It is not a subject for negotiation with any other nation."[70]

The North Koreans complained that "the U.S. side brought forward matters which have nothing to do with the purpose of the talks . . .

justifying foreign interference in the internal affairs of the Korean nation by mixing inter-Korean dialogue with the 'four-way talks' and internationalizing the Korean issue."[71] Speaking in Geneva, North Korea's chief delegate Kim Kye Gwan commented, "How can an agreement be reached easily when enemies are sitting together?"[72] After these comments, it was difficult for the Clinton administration to maintain that North Korea was a desperate nation that had improved its international diplomatic behavior.

The breakdown of talks, although undoubtedly temporary, brought the return of many familiar North Korean tactics. North Korea vehemently complained about American behavior, charged American noncompliance with agreements, portrayed itself as a victim, and issued threats. It prepared for war, and exhorted its starving people to defend the regime with their lives. It also hinted that additional material concessions might bring it back to the negotiating table.

The Breakdown of the Agreed Framework

On March 31, North Korean newspapers charged the United States with "acting irresponsibly over delaying the purchase of oil and the construction of the two 1,000-megawatt light-water nuclear reactors." The deadline for the supply of heavy fuel oil was still many months away, and construction was proceeding on a reasonable schedule, but North Korea's news agency (KCNA) threatened that the United States "would have to pay" for delays. The North Korean complaint clearly indicated something more than what was stated, and the threat to resume its nuclear program followed: "The DPRK cannot continuously sacrifice its independent nuclear industry with an eye on the LWRs, not knowing when they will be supplied." Even though the light-water reactor project had been delayed by such matters as North Korea's objection to South Korean–manufactured systems, and the crumpled picture of Kim Jong Il, the North Korean press complained that the United States had delayed the project "under this or that pretext, three years since it was adopted."[73]

North Korea also delivered an old-style propaganda diatribe against the United States: "Wantonly violating the framework agreement, their deeds are not proper behaviors in view of both the elementary norms of international relations and the political and moral honor of the United States styling itself as a big power," the news agency clamored. "If the U.S. side continues to delay implementing the framework agreement under groundless pretexts and conditions, it will have to be held wholly responsible for all consequences to be entailed by its perfidious misdeeds."[74]

In Washington, State Department spokesman James Foley calmly stated that the United States "fully expects that by the end of this year we will have provided the amount of heavy fuel that we have pledged to provide" and pointed out that the United States had already contributed approximately $86 million to KEDO for heavy fuel oil and administrative expenses, and $27 million for the canning of spent fuel rods.

At the start of this rhetorical offensive, hints emerged that North Korea no longer was satisfied with light-water reactors for generating electric power. There was a profound DPRK policy shift on electric energy production techniques. On March 27, President Li Jong Ok, Party Central Committee Secretary Han Song Ryong, and Deputy Premier Hong Song Nam called North Korea's electrical workers to a two-day conference in Pyongyang to win their support of the "Great General" Kim Jong Il's effort to build more small and medium-sized power stations "suitable to local geographical conditions."[75] On April 2, Hong Song Nam credited "the respected and beloved general" with a policy advocating "small- and medium-sized power plants" that were "not to simply guarantee lighting, but to realize the Communist electrification."

Oddly echoing a number of pragmatic Western analysts, North Korean officials questioned whether light-water reactors were an appropriate method of solving the North's electric power problems. Just two weeks after the four-party talks were brought to a standstill, Kim Jong Il was said to favor "small and medium-sized power plants at every corner of the country" to enable "people to cook and heat houses using electricity and use TV sets and other cultural appliances to their hearts' content."[76] This new emphasis could be read as an indication that North Korea sought more practical means of electric production—to be obtained through negotiation with the West. But first North Korea needed to undo the agreed framework.

On April 24, North Korean verbal attacks became particularly shrill. Even though the U.S.-ROK military exercise *Team Spirit* was not held in 1998, and U.S.-ROK military activities had been relaxed to avoid provoking the North Koreans, complaints against routine U.S. military activities poured out of Pyongyang. North Korea claimed that the United States was "planning to stage large-scale military training in areas around the Korean peninsula." *Rodong Shinmun* reported, "the South Korean puppet army, U.S. troops in South Korea, and U.S. forces on the U.S. mainland and in the Pacific region, will participate in this training."[77] The motives ascribed to U.S.-ROK activities echoed the kinds of charges leveled by Korea in its darkest hours of anti-Americanism:

> The United States is further accelerating its preparations for an aggressive war in order to realize its Asian strategy under the preposterous pretext of coping with someone else's threats. . . . The United States should discard its dominationist outlook and war mentality. As history shows, what is in store for the warmongers is only death and destruction. The United States is well advised not to forget the lesson of history.[78]

Other old tactics were also retrieved from North Korea's attic. On April 29, 1998, Kim Jong Il published a letter on reunification in which he described "machinations of the U.S. Imperialists and their stooges" for a "separate government" in South Korea. "The Foreign Forces which do not like Korea's reunification," Kim wrote, "are now fanning the confrontation between the North and South in an attempt to fish in troubled waters; the imperialists are intensifying their plot of dominating everywhere. . . . The United States is pursuing as ever its ambition to keep our nation divided forever and rule it . . . instigating the South Korean authorities to confrontation against their fellow countrymen, continuing to keep their troops in South Korea and ceaselessly stepping up war exercises and military buildup."[79]

On May 8, North Korea's foreign ministry officially announced the termination of its compliance with the agreed framework. "All facts show that the DPRK has gone farther in implementing the agreement whereas the U.S. side is not sincerely fulfilling its obligation," the Foreign Ministry statement said, concluding that "the DPRK should no longer lend an ear to the empty promises of the U.S. side, but open and readjust the frozen nuclear facilities and do everything our own way."[80]

North Korea recognizes that an announcement of its intent to terminate an agreement does not necessarily mean that the agreement is invalid. In the absence of clear evidence that North Korea has violated the agreement, the United States can be expected to argue that it remains in effect. The United States will continue to carry out its obligations, many of which benefit North Korea, and it will exhort the North Koreans to do the same. The North Koreans accordingly find themselves in the enhanced posture of benefiting from the other side's compliance while eschewing any responsibility to comply themselves. They also find it advantageous to have the other side imploring them to honor the agreement, thus allowing them to extract concessions for merely returning to an agreement they have already made.

At that point, however, North Korea was not willing to be cajoled to returning to the negotiating table. It had entered the phase of disavowal and had set about unraveling the agreement to create a crisis that would demand a new negotiated settlement.

North Korean Military Advancement under the Agreed Framework

Contrary to the Clinton administration's view that North Korean behavior had improved as a result of the agreed framework, North Korea had actually undertaken to develop a more threatening military posture. Rather than focusing on the development of nuclear weapons, this program focused on the means of their delivery—missiles.

North Korea developed an extensive network for the proliferation of its missile technology. In October 1996, it planned to test a new missile before an audience of Middle Eastern arms buyers but reportedly cancelled the tests after American pressure.[81] Even without the demonstrations, it was able to sell missile technology to Pakistan and Iran. Pakistan put the North Korean technology to use in its launch of the *Ghauri* missile, a *No-dong* derivative, on April 6. Security analysts believe that test launch tipped the scales in India's decision to test nuclear weapons a month later. Iran used the North Korean technology in its launch of a *Shahab 3* missile, a *Taepo-dong* derivative, on July 21, 1998. The *Shahab 3* has a range of 1,300 kilometers, allowing it to "strike all of Israel, all of Saudi Arabia, most of Turkey, and a tip of Russia . . . [and] put at risk all US forces in the region."[82] After the tests, Iran and Pakistan returned important test data to North Korea that was useful in North Korea's own missile program.[83]

The degree to which this technical exchange enhanced North Korea's capabilities was revealed at the time of the fiftieth anniversary of the founding of the North Korean Workers Party. On August 31, North Korea launched a three-stage *Taepo-dong 1* missile 1,380 kilometers across Japan and into the Pacific Ocean.[84] The official North Korean news service reported:

At the emotion-filled time of greeting the 50th anniversary of the National Day, our scientists and technicians succeeded in launching the first artificial satellite with a multistage carrier rocket. This is a historic event and a jubilee of all the people which eloquently demonstrates the inexhaustible potentials and the level of tremendous development of our republic which has advanced along the road of prosperity under the guidance of Kim Jong Il.[85]

The test launch ushered in Kim Jong Il's ascension to power. At the tenth Supreme People's Assembly, Kim Jong Il had the party declare his father was an irreplaceable figure in Korean history and no one would ever again attain Kim Il Sung's title of President of North Korea. On September 5, with all due filial piety, Kim Jong Il instead accepted the role of chairman of the National Defense Committee. Kim Yong Nam, Kim's second in command, explained, "The NDC chairmanship is the highest post of the state with which to organize and lead the work of defending the state system of the socialist country and the destinies of the people and strengthening and increasing the defense capabilities of the country and the state power as a whole through command over all the political, military, and economic forces of the country."[86] In other words, his power was unquestioned.

Despite North Korea's claim that the missile launch was a peaceful exercise in space exploration, the launch was an intentionally threatening act. It revealed with absolute clarity that North Korea had attained a new capability to threaten every part of the territory of two American allies—Japan and South Korea—as well as the 100,000 American troops stationed there. No warnings were provided to commercial fishermen in the area of the splashdown and no diplomatic warnings were provided to Japan. The North Korean regime had apparently decided that lulling the West into a false sense of security was no longer as advantageous as threatening it.

The North's development of multistage missiles was an impressive achievement for North Korean technology. It was particularly threatening because North Korea can arm such missiles with conventional, chemical, biological, or even nuclear warheads. Asia's fragile confidence in America's ability to ensure security, which keeps South Korea from developing long-range missiles and Japan, Taiwan, and South Korea from developing nuclear capabilities, was called into question. Indeed, America's own security was challenged. Because it provided evidence of the technical capability to launch multistage rocketry with boosters, the test also demonstrated that North Korea's capability to deploy intercontinental ballistic missiles was not far behind. For many years North Korea has been developing a *Taepo-dong 2* missile with a range of 3,000 to 4,000 kilometers that could reach the western United States.

If opponents of the agreed framework were right and North Korea had maintained a clandestine nuclear capability after signing the agreed framework, North Korea's missile advances meant regional powers now faced a new nuclear threat. Unfortunately, a few weeks before the missile launch, American intelligence had reason to suspect North Korea was constructing a huge underground nuclear complex in violation of the agreed framework. Just two weeks before the rocket launch, the *New York Times* reported that "spy satellites have extensively photographed a huge work site 25 miles northeast of Yongbyon." Sources told the *Times* that "thousands of North Korean workers are swarming around the new site, burrowing into the mountainside." Clinton administration officials "believed that the North intended to build a new reactor and reprocessing center" under the mountain.[87]

North Korea had used the four-way talks as it had used every previous negotiation: to extract concessions that filled gaps in its economic performance, to provide a pretext for domestic political purges and increased political oppression, and to build up its military capabilities. This was the same, tested strategy that North Korea had pursued time and again. It used this strategy to take territory during the armistice talks, to build up its military in defiance of armistice constraints, to gain international recognition through terrorist attacks, to intervene in South Korea's politics while promoting dialogue, to win concessions by denying inspections, and, in this most recent instance, to perfect its weaponry while it pursued peace talks.

Whose Side Is Time On?

A self-serving, corrupt government that cannot provide the basic needs of its people seems doomed to failure. Yet when a regime controls the means of distribution, any benefit received from the outside can actually enhance the regime's political oppression. The regime will determine that food supplies, health services, and commercial investments are provided to those who are loyal and withheld from those who are not. On September 29, 1998, the charitable organization Doctors Without Borders withdrew its aid workers from North Korea because it observed the regime "feeding children from families loyal to the regime while neglecting others."[88] As Hwang Jang Yeop explained, "North

Korea controls the entire country and people with food distribution. In other words, food distribution is a means of control."[89] External assistance not only buys the regime time, it also enhances its leverage over its own people.

External assistance also permits the regime to redirect its people's labor and resources from addressing desperate economic problems to strengthening military capabilities. Just as the North Korean regime can subvert the world's humanitarian impulses to reinforce its oppressive domestic policies, it can also take advantage of the world's confidence in security arrangements to gain time and resources to develop new military technology. As deplorable as it may seem, North Korea's national objective is not to ensure its people's survival, it is to ensure the regime's survival. In this regard, weaponry is a more important investment than agriculture.

North Korea sees the benefits of outside assistance more clearly than American policymakers do. It has learned through more than fifty years of negotiations to accept any concession from friend or foe. It certainly has no problem with replacing a subsidy from Moscow with one from Washington. Having very effectively maintained its political independence while extracting support from the world's most merciless Communist dictatorships, it can confidently accept aid from humane Western democracies.

North Korea, not surprisingly, never subscribed to the notion that its collapse was inevitable. The developments of late summer, 1998, suggested that instead of tottering on the verge of collapse, North Korea had actually gained strength. After the agreed framework was signed, the Clinton administration was confident that North Korea's collapse would occur before a war. Years later, that premise is not so clear.

While American policymakers believe collapse is inevitable, the policy of intervening to cushion collapse may yet prove it is not. The danger in providing aid to North Korea is that the United States will bear responsibility for prolonging the regime's survival. In economic, political, security, and moral terms, shouldering the burden of helping the North Korean regime survive is a dubious objective for American foreign policy.

Understanding North Korea's Negotiating Strategy

What does it mean when a nation that appears to be on the verge of collapse invests in threatening military capabilities rather than its people's needs? It means that, contrary to the theory that collapse promotes cooperation, North Korea perceives that impending collapse compels increasingly threatening behavior.

For the United States and South Korea, the negotiations under way with North Korea—the four-party talks—have been motivated by a sincere interest in peace on the peninsula and by charitable sentiments toward the subjects of a cruel and belligerent regime. The talks were seen as the fruition of a process that had been under way for almost five decades.

For North Korea, however, the four-way talks were merely the next step in its strategy of negotiating for survival.

The North has made steady progress through fifty years of negotiation. At the close of the Korean War, North Korea was worse off than it is today. It was recognized only by its ideological sponsors, condemned by the international community for instigating a war, and devastated as a result of its own aggression. Today, North Korea has obtained political recognition, security assurances, and significant economic assistance from its former enemies. Its negotiating strategy has brought the regime back from the point of collapse time and again during the intervening years.

North Korea's situation today is indeed grim, but such circumstances are not unfamiliar for the regime. In fact, it is only the regime's tenuous hold on power that impels it to negotiate at all. The regime uses negotiations exclusively to ensure its survival, extend its power, and enhance its control. Whatever peripheral benefits it may acquire, North Korea consistently uses negotiations to pressure its adversaries to disarm, obtain advantages that compensate for the regime's economic failure, and reinforce the regime's oppressive domestic political measures.

North Korea's negotiating strategy is unique because it is defined by the character of the North Korean regime it serves and is derived from the unique circumstances and worldview of that regime. It differs from other nations' negotiating strategies because it must address the regime's own systemic problems: its tenuous hold on its people's loyalty, its dissolute national economic policy that cannot meet its people's needs, and its antagonistic approach to other nations.

At least one American negotiator recommended in all seriousness that the way to deal with North Korea is simply to refuse to negotiate.[90] Such an approach would leave North Korea to confront its own failings, and therefore holds a great deal of logical appeal. The desire to achieve a resolution of troublesome issues is, however, a constant influence on Western nations and their negotiators. The hope of resolving the intractable issues on the peninsula has always attracted the attention of well-motivated, dedicated diplomats who genuinely seek peace and stability. Furthermore, North Korea has often forced the West to enter into negotiations—by capturing hapless citizens or military personnel and holding them as ransom, by conducting military adventures below the threshold that would start a war, or by promising a new era of progress.

Fear of war is one reason the West negotiates with North Korea.[91] Because North Korea is perceived as irrational and unpredictable, and because the consequences of war would be severe, there will always be people in the West who fear that negotiation is the only alternative to war. North Korea has a different view: negotiation is war by other means. The process of negotiation is cleverly managed by North Korea to postpone war while it strengthens its military ability and pressures the West to disarm. The danger for the West is that war may in fact be inevitable, but it will come only at a time of North Korea's choosing, when North Korea has perfected its weaponry and can be confident of surviving the conflict.

The genuine alternative to war with North Korea is now, and always has been, credible deterrence. North Korea will not consciously incite a regime-terminating war any more than it will pursue regime-threatening reforms. In every instance when Western resolve was credible, North Korea retreated. On the verge of conflict, North Korea hastened to offer alternatives in order to ensure the regime's survival.

Similarly, the alternative to North Korean management of the negotiating process is Western management of the process. There are very few tactics in North Korea's repertoire that the West could not use at least as effectively. Self-restraint, not allied weakness, keeps South Korea from infiltrating the North, demanding negotiations on its own terms, and undermining the incompetent regime in the North.

The West negotiates from a position of strength, but neglects to bring its strength to bear. It chooses not to pressure North Korea with its superior military power, agreeing instead not to threaten. It holds economic power that North Korea cannot compete with, but gives the regime economic aid. It can afford not to negotiate, but instead of making North Korea sue for peace, the West implores North Korea to participate in talks in which the West has virtually nothing at stake. In every negotiation, the West holds tactical and strategic leverage it will not employ.

As North Korea accurately understands, management of key aspects of the process of negotiation is difficult for the West. In democracies, foreign policy is a matter for public debate. Because democracies listen to many voices, rigid discipline in the face of North Korean brinkmanship is elusive, if not impossible. Despite the consistency of North Korea's long-term negotiating record, there will always be those who interpret North Korean actions sympathetically. There are also those who view North Korea's weaknesses as destabilizing rather than advantageous. A number of analysts will rationalize that actions of the North Korean regime can be ascribed to the same motivations as those of other nations. Furthermore, there will always be some who bargain for peace even when they suspect they are only delaying confrontation. Resolve is hard to muster when it appears money can buy peace and concessions can save lives.

The above factors will always influence the debate over policy toward North Korea. They are factors that have always influenced interactions between free people and tyranny. But misconceptions about North Korea's character can be corrected. After almost fifty years of negotiation, patterns have emerged from the negotiating record that provide a body of knowledge on how North Korea negotiates. Although North Korea pursues a deceptive strategy, there is no reason for the West to continue to be deceived.

Yet today, as at every other time since the beginning of the armistice talks, underlying misconceptions of the opposing sides determine the course of the negotiating process and undermine its success. Underlying North Korea's approach to negotiating are a number of demands that it will neither dispose of nor attain: disarming its rivals, extending its power over South Korea, and adhering to discredited economic precepts. North Korea deludes itself with a number of false assumptions: that its enemies pose the greatest threat to the regime's survival, that acquiring other nations' riches can make its economy work, and that the regime's success can be assured by enforcing absolute discipline over its citizenry.

American negotiators have their own unreasonable expectations: that the North Korean regime will compromise on long-standing objectives, reform in order to meet the needs of its people, and adhere to the spirit of the arrangements it negotiates. Even in the fifth decade of North Korea's totalitarian oppression, Western negotiators tend to assume that North Korea's government is one that seeks to serve its people. The Western approach to solving North Korea's problems is also based on false assumptions: that North Korea enters into negotiations to resolve difficulties, redress its grievances, and better its people's plight.

In the closing years of the twentieth century, these misconceptions have combined to produce a curious spectacle: the world's strongest democracies are attempting to cajole an unwilling tyrant to negotiate an accommodation extending his regime's survival or at least cushioning its collapse.

Today, North Korea's negotiating objectives are as much at odds with the rest of the world as they have been at every point since the founding of North Korea. The United States seeks an accommodation in order to avoid the violence it fears might accompany North Korea's decline. North Korea, to the contrary, seeks to deny accommodation, and uses both collapse and the threat of war as leverage in what is merely the latest, not in its view the last, round of talks between the regime and the world North Korea resents.

After North Korea has completed its latest round of strident demands, harsh accusations, and belligerent threats, the atmosphere will undoubtedly, one day, improve. Perhaps an underground facility will be inspected and found empty; perhaps missiles will not be deployed; perhaps new arrangements will purport to limit the North's threatening capabilities. There will almost certainly come a time when it will appear that an accommodation can be reached, and the cycle of negotiation with North Korea will begin anew. At that point, it is certain North Korea will want something in exchange for its commitment to participate in further talks. What is uncertain is whether the West will have the resolve to deny what the regime requires.

Notes

In the text, we have chosen one uniform transliteration for each Korean name. In the Notes, names appear as published in the sources.

CHAPTER 1: UNDERSTANDING NORTH KOREA'S NEGOTIATING STRATEGY

1. In the war, 229,000 South Korean troops and 38,000 United Nations troops were killed; 717,000 South Korean troops and 115,000 UN troops were wounded; 43,000 South Korean soldiers and 500 UN troops were listed as missing; an additional 245,000 South Korean civilians were killed, 230,000 injured, and 330,000 missing according to the December 31, 1988, edition of *A White Paper on South-North Dialogue in Korea* (Seoul: National Unification Board, 1988), p. 20.

2. Max Hastings, *The Korean War* (New York: Simon and Schuster, 1987), p. 329.

3. Benjamin Franklin, from *Historical Review of Pennsylvania*, cited in *Bartlett's Familiar Quotations*, digital version.

4. "Three Million Victims in 50 Years of North Korean Communism," *Chosun Ilbo*, Seoul, November 7, 1997.

5. Dr. Song Young-dae in a lecture to the Hyundai Economic Research, cited in *Korea Times*, "Over 500 North Koreans Executed in Public Last Year: North Korea Expert," April 2, 1997.

6. The United Nations estimated 4.7 million faced starvation in 1997, according to Steven Mufson, "Koreas Agree on Food Aid to the North," *Washington Post*, May 27, 1997, p. 1. See also Stephanie Nebehay, Reuters News Agency,

"5 Million N. Koreans Seen Facing Starvation," *Washington Times*, June 21, 1997, p. A6.

7. Kenneth Todd Young, *Negotiating with the Chinese Communists: The United States Experience, 1953–1967* (New York: McGraw-Hill, 1968), p. 301.

8. Matthew B. Ridgway, *The Korean War* (Garden City, N.Y.: Doubleday & Company, 1967), p. 197.

9. C. Turner Joy, *How Communists Negotiate* (New York: Macmillan Company, 1955), p. 26. Hereafter cited as Joy.

10. Arthur H. Dean, "What It's Like Negotiating with the Chinese," in *New York Times Magazine*, October 30, 1964, p. 47. Hereafter cited as Dean.

11. William H. Vatcher, *Panmunjom: The Story of the Korean Military Armistice Negotiations* (New York: Frederick A. Praeger, 1958), p. 31, quoting from Colonel Andrew J. Kinney, USAF: "Secrets from the Truce Tent," *This Week*, August 31, 1952, p. 7.

12. Joy, p. 14.

13. Dean, p. 54. See also Korean Briefing Meeting, December 21, 1953, in *Foreign Relations of the United States*, 1952–1954, vol. 15, part 2, p. 1667.

14. William H. Vatcher, *Panmunjom: The Story of the Korean Military Armistice Negotiations* (New York: Frederick A. Praeger, 1958), pp. 49–50. Hereafter cited as Vatcher.

15. Proceedings of the 100th MAC Meeting, April 27, 1959.

16. Park Yong Su statement as reported by Don Oberdorfer, *The Two Koreas: A Contemporary History* (Reading, Mass.: Addison Wesley, 1997), p. 304. "Annihilating Blow Will Be Given," Korean Central News Agency, Pyongyang, December 3, 1998.

17. Song Jong-Hwan, "How the North Korean Communists Negotiate: A Case Study of the South-North Korean Dialogue of the Early 1970s," in *Korea and World Affairs*, vol. 8, no. 3 (fall 1984), p. 617.

18. Herbert Goldhamer, *The 1951 Korean Armistice Conference: A Personal Memoir* (Santa Monica, Calif.: RAND, 1994), pp. 58–71. Hereafter cited as Goldhamer.

19. Goldhamer, p. 67

20. Joy, p. 39.

21. Ibid., p. 40.

22. Fred C. Iklé, *How Nations Negotiate* (New York: Harper and Row, 1964), pp. 250–51.

23. Vatcher, p. 60.

24. Lucien W. Pye, "Understanding Chinese Negotiating Behavior: The Roles of Nationalism and Pragmatism," in Kim R. Holmes and James J. Przystup, *Between Diplomacy and Deterrence: Strategies for U. S. Relations with China* (Washington: Heritage Foundation, 1997), pp. 213–14, 238.

25. Goldhamer, pp. 72–73.

26. Goldhamer, p. 72.

27. Goldhamer, p. 61.

28. Vatcher, p. 67.

29. Song Jong-Hwan, "How the North Korean Communists Negotiate: A Case Study of the South-North Korean Dialogue of the Early 1970s," in *Korea and World Affairs*, vol. 8, no. 3 (fall 1984), p. 617.

30. Official North Korean publication entitled *Chosun-Mal-Dae-Sajon* (Pyongyang: The Social Science Printing House, March 20, 1992).

31. Chuck Downs interview with Donald W. Boose Jr., January 8, 1998.

32. Lee Dong Bok, "Dealing with North Korea: The Case of the Agreed Framework," text of a presentation delivered at "Beyond the Nuclear Crisis: The Prospects for Korean Peace," a conference sponsored by the American Enterprise Institute and the Nonproliferation Policy Center, Washington, D.C., March 13, 1995, p. 5.

33. December 31, 1988, edition of *A White Paper on South-North Dialogue in Korea* (Seoul: National Unification Board, 1988), p. 23, quoting North Korean Workers Party documents.

34. The description of Kaesong and the dialogue between Kinney and Chang appear in Vatcher, pp. 26–27.

35. Nicholas Eberstadt, *Korea Approaches Reunification* (Armonk, N.Y.: M. E. Sharpe for the National Bureau of Asian Research, 1995), p. 132.

36. See Shu Guang Zhang, *Deterrence and Strategic Culture: Chinese-American Confrontations, 1949–1958* (Ithaca: Cornell University Press, 1992), p. 279.

37. Chas. W. Freeman, Jr., *The Diplomat's Dictionary* (Washington: National Defense University Press, 1994), p. 113.

CHAPTER 2: SECURING KOREAN DEMOCRACY

1. Richard Whelan, *Drawing the Line* (Boston: Little, Brown and Company, 1990), pp. 24–28. Hereafter cited as Whelan.

2. T. R. Fehrenbach, *The Fight for Korea: From the War of 1950 to the Pueblo Incident* (New York: Grosset and Dunlap, 1969), p. 38. Hereafter cited as Fehrenbach.

3. Kim Joungwon, *Divided Korea: The Politics of Development, 1945–1972* (Cambridge, Mass.: Harvard University Press, 1975), p. 86. Hereafter cited as Kim Joungwon. For the assertion that Kim Il Sung was among those sent in by the Russians, see William H. Vatcher, *Panmunjom: The Story of the Korean Military Armistice Negotiations* (New York: Frederick A. Praeger, 1958), p. 146, n. 16. Hereafter cited as Vatcher.

4. Whelan, p. 29, quoting *Foreign Relations of the United States*, 1945, vol. 6, p. 1039.

5. A comprehensive study of the decisions reached on the division of surrender responsibilities between American and Soviet forces is available in Donald W. Boose, Jr., "Portentous Sideshow: The Korean Occupation Decision," in *Parameters*, U.S. Army War College Quarterly, vol. 25, no. 4 (Winter 1995–96), pp. 112–29.

6. Whelan, p. 29.

7. Kim Joungwon, pp. 30–33.

8. U.S. officials had become aware of the research facility in the spring of 1945. Robert K. Wilcox, *Japan's Secret War* (New York: Marlowe and Company, 1995), pp. 150–51.

9. Hodge appointed Major General Archibald V. Arnold, commanding general of the Seventh Division, to head the United States Army Military Government in Korea. See Major Robert K. Sawyer, *Military Advisors in Korea: KMAG in Peace and War* (Washington: Department of the Army, Office of the Chief of Military History, Department of the Army, 1962), p. 7.

10. Kim Joungwon, p. 66.

11. Whelan, p. 44, citing *Foreign Relations of the United States*, 1947, vol. 6, pp. 817–18. The South Korean Interim Legislative Assembly would thereby have been excluded from power; on January 20, 1947, it had passed a resolution opposing trusteeship.

12. Whelan, p. 45.

13. For a comprehensive discussion, see Kim Joungwon, p. 81.

14. United Nations General Assembly action referred to in: United Nations Security Council, *Resolutions and Decisions of the Security Council, 1950* (New York: United Nations, 1965), p. 4. See also *A White Paper on South-North Dialogue in Korea* (Seoul: National Unification Board of the Republic of Korea, 1988), pp. 16–17.

15. Fehrenbach, p. 54.

16. Kim Joungwon, pp. 34, 39–40.

17. Ibid., p. 86, and chap. 3, "Consolidation of Power in North Korea, 1945–1948."

18. There is no longer a historical question regarding Kim's initiative to use force to reunify the peninsula. It has been made clear by documents released by Beijing and Moscow. See Chen Jian, *China's Road to the Korean War* (New York: Columbia University Press, 1994), chap. 3, especially pp. 85–90.

19. Sources generally agree that 90,000 troops participated in the North's invasion, but the size of the buildup before the invasion is estimated at various levels. South Korean Minister of Defense Sihn Sung Mo claimed in a press conference on May 10, 1950, that the North had amassed forces of 185,000 along the 38th parallel. Whelan, p. 106.

20. A full description of the peace offensive appears in William B. Breuer, *Shadow Warriors: The Covert War in Korea* (New York: John Wiley and Sons, 1996), pp. 26–32. Hereafter cited as Breuer. See also *A White Paper on South-North Dialogue in Korea* (Seoul: National Unification Board of the Republic of Korea, 1988), p. 18.

21. Fehrenbach, pp. 59–60.

22. Resolution of June 25, 1950, in United Nations Security Council, 82 (1950) in *Resolutions and Decisions of the Security Council, 1950* (New York: United Nations, 1965), pp. 4–5.

23. Remarks by Secretary of State Dean Acheson at the National Press Club, Washington, January 12, 1950, entitled "Crisis in Asia—An Examination of U.S.

Policy" in *Department of State Bulletin*, vol. 22, no. 551, January 23, 1950, pp. 111–18.

24. C. Turner Joy, *How Communists Negotiate* (New York: Macmillan Company, 1955), p. 67.

25. Resolution of June 27, 1950, 83 (1950) in *Resolutions and Decisions of the Security Council, 1950* (New York: United Nations, 1965), p. 5.

26. Breuer, pp. 50–51, and Fehrenbach, p. 69.

27. Resolution of July 7, 1950, 84 (1950) in *Resolutions and Decisions of the Security Council, 1950* (New York: United Nations, 1965), pp. 5–6.

28. Headquarters, United Nations Command, "Command Historical Summary," compiled by the Command History Office, Unit #15237, 1996, p. 18. Hereafter cited as "Command Historical Summary."

29. The sixteen allied nations to contribute troops to the United Nations Command were: Australia, Belgium, Canada, Colombia, Ethiopia, France, Greece, Netherlands, New Zealand, Philippines, Republic of Korea, South Africa, Thailand, Turkey, the United States, and the United Kingdom.

30. "Command Historical Summary," p. 18, quoting James I. Matray, ed., *Historical Dictionary of the Korean War* (New York: Greenwood Press, 1991), pp. 498–501.

31. Breuer, pp. 87–88 regarding the Kimpo airport; and pp. 47–48 and 86 on the tribunals.

32. Robert Leckie, *Conflict: The History of the Korean War, 1950–53* (New York: G. P. Putnam's Sons, 1962), pp. 152–53.

33. Ibid.

34. Ibid., p. 130.

35. Ibid., p. 162.

36. MacArthur told Truman this at a meeting on Wake Island. See ibid., p. 165.

37. Chen Jian, *China's Road to the Korean War* (New York: Columbia University Press, 1994), pp. 143–46.

38. Ibid., pp. 158–60.

39. Ibid., pp. 180–81; Whelan, p. 212; and Leckie, pp. 154–69. For a discussion of missed signals and military preparations in North Korea before the invasion, see also Suk Bok Lee, *The Impact of U.S. Forces in Korea* (Washington: National Defense University Press, 1987), pp. 35–43.

40. Fehrenbach, p. 84.

41. "Command Historical Summary," p. 19.

42. Vatcher, p. 18, and Fehrenbach, p. 94.

CHAPTER 3: SEEKING THE TRUCE

1. "Memorandum Concerning the Sections Dealing with Korea from NSC 48/5, Dated May 17, 1951," Foreign Relations of the United States (hereafter cited as FRUS), 1951, vol. 7, pp. 440–41.

2. Robert Leckie, *Conflict: The History of the Korean War, 1950–53* (New York: G. P. Putnam's Sons, 1969), pp. 291–92. Hereafter cited as Leckie.

3. Leckie, p. 292. See also David Rees, *Korea: The Limited War* (New York: St. Martin's Press, 1964), p. 257.

4. Leckie, p. 293, quoting Matthew B. Ridgway, *Soldier: The Memoirs of Matthew B. Ridgway* (New York: Harper and Brothers, 1956), pp. 219–20.

5. Syngman Rhee statement, issued June 30, 1951, summarized in Fehrenbach, *The Fight for Korea: From the War of 1950 to the Pueblo Incident* (New York: Grosset and Dunlap, 1969), p. 97.

6. William Stueck, *The Korean War: An International History* (Princeton, N.J.: Princeton University Press, 1995), p. 207. Hereafter cited as Stueck.

7. Kennan meeting with Malik, May 31, 1951, in *FRUS*, 1951, vol. 7, p. 485.

8. Memorandum of Conversation by Assistant Secretary for UN Affairs Hickerson, May 31, 1951, *FRUS*, 1951, vol. 7, p. 482.

9. Walter G. Hermes, Truce Tent and Fighting Front (Washington: United States Army, Office of the Chief of Military History, 1988) p. 19, citing Memo, Gen. Ridgway for General and Flag Officer Members of the UN Delegation, July 6, 1951, in UN Command/Far East Command files.

10. Stueck, pp. 119–212.

11. Leckie, p. 293.

12. Ibid., p. 294.

13. Amb. Kirk to Sec State, June 27, 1951, *FRUS*, 1951, vol. 7, p. 561

14. Amb. Kirk to Sec State, June 25, 1951, *FRUS*, 1951, vol. 7, p. 552.

15. Maclean claimed "it was he who got the Chinese deeply involved in the war and kept the Russians out of it." John Miller, "Maclean Coup in Korea War," from the London *Sunday Telegraph*, March 27, 1963. Reprinted in an extension of remarks by Rep. Larry McDonald, in *Congressional Record*, June 29, 1983, p. E3253.

16. Amb. Kirk to Sec State, June 27, 1951, *FRUS*, 1951, vol. 7, p. 561.

17. George F. Kennan to the Deputy Under Secretary of State (Matthews), June 5, 1951, *FRUS*, 1951, vol. 7, p. 509.

18. Alfred D. Wilhelm Jr., *The Chinese at the Negotiating Table* (Washington: National Defense University Press, 1994), pp. 124–25.

19. The meeting was attended by General Omar Bradley, chairman of the Joint Chiefs of Staff; General Hoyt S. Vandenberg, chief of staff of the Air Force; General J. Lawton Collins, chief of staff of the army; Admiral McCormick, vice chief of naval operations; General Bolte, deputy chief of staff for plans of the U.S. Army; Vice Admiral Davis, USN; Major General White, USAF; Major General Taylor; Dean Rusk, Assistant Secretary of State; and U. Alexis Johnson.

20. Memorandum of conversation by the director of the office of Northeast Asian Affairs, June 28, 1951, *FRUS*, 1951, vol. 7, p. 567.

21. Ibid.

22. Ibid., pp. 567–68.

23. Ibid.

24. Ibid.

25. Memorandum of conversation by the director of the office of Northeast Asian Affairs, June 29, 1951, *FRUS*, 1951, vol. 7, p. 597.

26. Memorandum of conversation by the director of the office of Northeast Asian Affairs, meeting with the Joint Chiefs of Staff, June 29, 1951, *FRUS*, 1951, vol. 7, pp. 586–87, no. 3. This version of the text is consistent with Leckie, p. 294, and Stueck, p. 209.

27. Commander in Chief, Far East (CINC-FE) to JCS, July 2, 1951, *FRUS*, 1951, vol. 7, p. 609.

CHAPTER 4: BEGINNING AT KAESONG

1. Matthew B. Ridgway, *The Korean War* (Garden City, N.Y.: Doubleday and Company, 1967), p. 198. Hereafter cited as Ridgway.

2. C. Turner Joy, *How Communists Negotiate* (New York: The Macmillan Company, 1955), p. 2. Hereafter cited as Joy.

3. Ki-baik Lee (translated by Edward W. Wagner with Edward J. Shultz), *A New History of Korea* (Cambridge, Mass.: Harvard University Press, 1984), pp. 228–29.

4. Kaesong is one of the few North Korean cities with a known tradition of anti–Kim Il Sung resistance. Defector Koh told the author that he was warned not to walk the city's streets as a young man because, as the son of the leader of the Communist party there, he was a target for attack. He also claimed that because of popular resistance, much of the population of Kaesong was relocated to North Korea's severe and isolated northeastern provinces. Similar points are also made in Internet articles posted by visitors to Kaesong. See, for example, Out There News Service (with *Associated Press*), "Flickers of Unrest Dog the North," at www.megastories.com., no date.

5. Joy recorded Kinney's account; Murray's account is in William H. Vatcher, *Panmunjom: The Story of the Korean Military Armistice Negotiations* (New York: Frederick A. Praeger, 1958), p. 26. Hereafter cited as Vatcher. The location is identified in David Rees, *Korea: The Limited War* (New York: St. Martin's Press, 1964), p. 289. Hereafter cited as Rees. Numerous Western sources refer to Nae Bong Jang as "a teahouse," probably because, with its graceful tile roof, it is a fine example of Korean traditional architecture. It was actually a private residence. The meeting room itself was the *sarang bang*, the parlor for receiving guests. The circumstances of the death of Mr. Yi Hee Cho are not known outside of North Korea, but it is believed he died in 1951. The author is indebted to Mr. Yi's grandson, Mr. Kwang-Won Rhim, for providing this information, which has also been recorded in Hak-Joon Kim's *50 Years of History of North Korea*, p. 161.

6. The Italianate mansion had been a hotel/spa that specialized in ginseng baths, and had a restaurant popular with the local gentry, according to Mr. Kwang-Won Rhim, who lived in Kaesong as a child.

7. Vatcher, pp. 26–27.

8. Commander in Chief, UN Command, to JCS, message, July 1, 1951, in *Foreign Relations of the United States,* 1951, vol. 7, pp. 607–08. Hereafter cited as *FRUS.*

9. There are numerous, generally consistent accounts of the problem of the chairs. Alfred Wilhelm, in his book *The Chinese at the Negotiating Table* (Washington: National Defense University Press, 1994), p. 234, n. 43, cites the 1835 precedent which was in turn cited in Maurice Collis, "The Victory of the Chairs," in *Foreign Mud* (London: Faber and Faber, Ltd., 1946), pp. 144–54.

10. Joy, pp. 3–4.

11. Memorandum of Conversation by Frank P. Lockhart of the Bureau of Far Eastern Affairs, July 3, 1951, in *FRUS,* 1951, vol. 7, p. 616.

12. Ibid.

13. Exchange of messages between Ridgway and Kim Il Sung and Peng Teh Huai, *FRUS,* 1951, vol. 7, p. 624.

14. Joy, pp. 2–3.

15. JCS to Ridgway, *FRUS,* 1951, vol. 7, p. 639.

16. Ridgway to JCS, *FRUS,* 1951, vol. 7, p. 639, n. 1.

17. Joy, pp. 16–17; Vatcher, p. 77; Rees, pp. 342, 356.

18. William Lindsay White, *The Captives of Korea* (New York: Charles Scribner's Sons, 1957), pp. 160, 168, 177, 250, 273–74; Rees, pp. 342, 356; Leckie, p. 352.

19. Alan Winnington and Wilfred Burchett, *Plain Perfidy* (London: Britain-China Friendship Association, 1954) and *Koje Unscreened* (London: Britain-China Friendship Association, undated, probably 1954).

20. Leckie, p. 300.

21. Vatcher, p. 29, and Ridgway, pp. 198–99.

22. Walter G. Hermes, *Truce Tent and Fighting Front* (Washington: United States Army, Office of the Chief of Military History, 1988), p. 21. Hereafter cited as Hermes. He cites Col. J. C. Murray, "The Korea Truce Talks: First Phase," United States Naval Institute *Proceedings,* vol. 79, no. 9 (September 1953), p. 982.

23. Joy, pp. 4–5.

24. CINCUNC to JCS, July 10, 1951, *FRUS,* 1951, vol 7, p. 651.

25. Ibid.

26. Vatcher, p. 35.

27. Ibid., p. 35.

28. Joy, p. 8.

29. See, e.g., JCS to Ridgway, June 30, 1951: "Great care should be used, in putting forward a negotiating position, not to allow talks to break down except in case of failure to accept our minimum terms." *FRUS,* 1951, vol. 7, p. 598, and JCS to Ridgway, July 21, 1951, *FRUS,* 1951, vol. 7, p. 716.

30. CINCUNC to JCS, July 10, 1951, *FRUS*, 1951, vol. 7, p. 651.

31. Ibid.

32. Ridgway message to Kim Il Sung and Peng Teh Huai, July 3, 1951, *FRUS*, 1951, vol. 7, p. 616.

33. Message from Kim Il Sung and Peng Teh Huai to Ridgway, translated in message from Ridgway to JCS, July 15, 1951, *FRUS*, 1951, vol. 7, pp. 682–84. See also Hermes, p. 40.

34. Joy, p. 31.

35. Joy, pp. 31–32.

36. Wilhelm, *The Chinese at the Negotiating Table* (Washington: National Defense University Press, 1994), pp. 126–27.

37. Joy, p. 32.

38. Ridgway, p. 199.

39. Joy, p. 32.

40. Joy, pp. 32–33.

41. Ridgway, p. 199.

42. Vatcher, p. 59.

43. Ibid.

44. Ibid.

45. Hermes, p. 42, n. 28: Report of Investigation, subject: Summary of Protest 19 August 1951, Communist Patrol Ambushed, Communist Truck Attacked, in FEC 387.2, Korean Armistice Papers, Reports of Investigation.

46. Vatcher, p. 65, provides portions of the protest by Kim Il Sung and Peng Teh Huai.

47. Ibid., p. 60.

48. Hermes, p. 42, n. 29, "Report of Investigation, subject: Summary of Protest and Replies . . . Bombing of Kaesong," no date, in FEC 387.2, Korean Armistice Papers, Reports of Investigation.

49. Joy, p. 36.

50. Vatcher, p. 70.

51. Suk-bok Lee, *The Impact of US Forces on Korea* (Washington: National Defense University Press, 1987), pp. 53–54.

52. Memorandum of Teletype Conference, prepared in the Department of the Army, June 28, 1951, *FRUS*, 1951, vol. 7, p. 584.

53. Wilhelm, p. 126.

54. Ridgway, p. 198. He made the same point in his message to Kim Il Sung and Peng Teh Huai of July 13, 1951. See *FRUS*, 1951, vol. 7, p. 671.

55. E.g., Goldhamer and Joy.

56. Stueck, p. 412, n. 29.

57. CINCUNC to JCS, July 2, 1951, *FRUS*, 1951, vol. 7, p. 611.

58. Briefing of Ambassadors on Korea, State Department Memorandum dated July 3, 1951, *FRUS*, 1951, vol. 7, p. 617.

59. Ibid.

60. Emphasis as it appeared in the original. This quotation appears here

exactly as in the original, showing slight changes from the truncated version that was published in the Attachment to the Johnson notes on the meeting in *FRUS*, 1951, vol. 7, pp. 569–71. A look at the original document clarifies that the note referring to Kaesong was in fact typed into the original and not added later.

61. The State Department's Korea team took a very hard line on proceeding to open the talks. See the dissenting views set out in the Korea desk's memo, drawn up while Rusk and Johnson were meeting at the Pentagon, in: "Memorandum by the Officer in Charge of Korean Affairs (Emmons) to the Director of the Office of Northeast Asian Affairs (Johnson)," June 28, 1951. *FRUS*, 1951, vol. 7, pp. 571–72.

62. No reference to Kaesong appears in other JCS discussions of potential locations for the talks. See *Memorandum of Teletype Conference*, June 28, 1951, *FRUS*, 1951, vol. 7, pp. 583–86.

63. E.g., The British Embassy to the Department of State, undated, *FRUS*, 1951, vol. 7, pp. 497–98; Memorandum of Conversation between Rusk and British Ambassador Sir Oliver Franks, June 4, 1951, *FRUS*, 1951, vol. 7, pp. 500–03; Secretary of State to Certain Diplomatic Offices, June 8, 1951, in *FRUS*, 1951, vol. 7, pp. 524–26; Briefing of Ambassadors on Korea, June 19, 1951, pp. 531–34; and Briefing of Ambassadors on Korea, June 27, 1951, in *FRUS*, 1951, vol. 7, pp. 557–60. Given the sensitivity of the issues involved, it seems peculiar that the UK was represented in these meetings at a relatively low level, generally by a first secretary or counselor. As a general rule, the lower the level of participant, the wider the distribution of his reports. There is no doubt, however, that from 1949 to May 25, 1951, information regarding Korea transmitted through official UK channels was seen by the Foreign Office's American desk, then headed by Maclean.

64. William B. Breuer, *Shadow Warriors: The Covert War in Korea* (New York: John Wiley and Sons, 1996), pp. 98–104. Hereafter cited as Breuer. See also Vice Admiral A. E. Jarrell (Ret.), U.S. Naval Institute *Proceedings*, Annapolis, January 1974.

65. Bruce Page, David Leitch, and Philip Knightley, *The Philby Conspiracy* (New York: Doubleday, 1968), p. 197, and Breuer, p. 149.

66. Chapman Pincher, *Too Secret Too Long* (New York: St. Martin's Press, 1984), pp. 178–79. Hereafter cited as Pincher.

67. William Manchester, as cited in Anthony Cave Brown, *Treason in the Blood* (New York: Houghton and Mifflin, 1994), p. 569.

68. Pincher, p. 176, citing Roy Medvedev, *Washington Post*, 19 June 1983.

69. Breuer, p. 151.

70. John Miller, "Maclean Coup in Korea War," from the *London Sunday Telegraph*, March 27, 1963. Reprinted in an extension of remarks by Rep. Larry McDonald, in *Congressional Record*, June 29, 1983, p. E3253. With Soviet assistance, Maclean fled from his position in London to Moscow around May 25, 1951, having learned that security officials were closing in on him; Burgess disappeared from Washington at the same time. The dual "defections" cast doubt

on Philby in Washington, but he continued to operate in Washington until June 12, 1951, and continued to serve in the British foreign service until 1963, the year Burgess died in Moscow and Philby escaped to Moscow.

CHAPTER 5: NEGOTIATING THE ARMISTICE

1. Arthur H. Dean, "What It's Like Negotiating with the Chinese," in the *New York Times Magazine*, October 30, 1964, p. 44.

2. See, for example, U. Alexis Johnson's critical comments on the lack of experience and flexibility of military negotiators in Alfred Wilhelm, *The Chinese at the Negotiating Table*, p. 109, hereafter cited as Wilhelm. William Stueck's criticism that the UNC negotiators "underestimated their successes, failed to understand that their own overzealousness had been the source of embarrassment, not erratic signals from Washington, which had consistently cautioned against adopting rigid positions, and ignored the fact that the initial arrangements for talks had compromised UNC bargaining power," appears in Stueck, *The Korean War: An International History* (Princeton, N.J.: Princeton University Press, 1995), p. 207; hereafter cited as Stueck. See also the criticism leveled against Joy, Ridgway, Burke, and Hodes by Herbert Goldhamer in *The 1951 Korean Armistice Conference: A Personal Memoir* (Santa Monica, Calif.: RAND, 1994), p. 121. Hereafter cited as Goldhamer.

3. William H. Vatcher, *Panmunjom: The Story of the Korean Military Armistice Negotiations* (New York: Frederick A. Praeger, 1958), p. 113. Hereafter cited as Vatcher.

4. Joint Chiefs of Staff to Commander in Chief, United Nations Command, June 30, 1951, *Foreign Relations of the United States*, 1951, vol. 7, pp. 598–600. According to Vatcher, the seventeen allied nations with forces in Korea met in July and adopted similar terms to be presented to the Communists. Vatcher, p. 27.

5. Joint Chiefs of Staff to Commander in Chief, United Nations Command, June 30, 1951, *FRUS*, 1951, vol. 7, p. 598.

6. Ibid.

7. Ibid.

8. C. Turner Joy, *How Communists Negotiate* (New York: Macmillan Company, 1955), p. 18.

9. Ibid., pp. 18–19. Hereafter cited as Joy.

10. Vatcher, p. 43.

11. Stueck, pp. 223 and 233.

12. Vatcher, p. 47; Stueck, p. 227.

13. Vatcher, pp. 46–47.

14. Dean Acheson, *The Korean War* (New York : W. W. Norton and Company, 1971), p. 118, citing *Hearings on the Military Situation in the Far East*, pp. 1729–30, 1782.

15. Joint Chiefs of Staff to Commander in Chief, United Nations Command, June 30, 1951, *FRUS*, 1951, vol. 7, p. 598.

16. As support for this assertion, note that Joy's Diaries, which detail the back-and-forth with Nam Il on this topic, make no mention at all of the argument Washington proposed. They, do, however, emphasize his arguments about a commander's obligation to the security of his forces. See Allan E. Goodman, ed., *Negotiating While Fighting: The Diary of Admiral C. Turner Joy at the Korean Armistice Conference* (Stanford, Calif.: Hoover Institution, 1978), pp. 23–24; and Goldhamer, pp. 67–74.

17. Vatcher, p. 52

18. Ibid., pp. 52–53.

19. Ibid., p. 53.

20. Ibid., pp. 53–54. In spite of its apparent utility, the tactic was criticized by Goldhamer, who noticed that unlike the Communist side, the UNC side permitted its liaison officers to grant concessions more easily than their superiors. See Goldhamer, p. 92.

21. Vatcher, p. 56.

22. Ibid., p. 81. Ridgway felt strongly that the truce talks should not permit the Communists to turn what had been "no-man's land" around Kaesong into Communist territory. See CINCFE to JCS, November 1, 1951, *FRUS*, 1951, vol. 7, p. 1081.

23. Stueck, pp. 238–41.

24. Memorandum on the Substance of Discussions at a Department of State–JCS Meeting, November 12, 1951, in *FRUS*, 1951, vol. 7, pp. 1122–23.

25. CINCFE to JCS, November 1, 1951, *FRUS*, 1951, vol. 7, p. 1079.

26. CINCFE to JCS, November 3, 1951, *FRUS*, 1951, vol. 7, p. 1086.

27. Vatcher, p. 81.

28. Ibid., p. 82.

29. Ibid.

30. Ibid., p. 83.

31. Ibid., p. 84.

32. CINCFE to JCS, November 13, 1951, in *FRUS*, 1951, vol. 7, p. 1129.

33. JCS to Ridgway, November 13, 1951, in *FRUS*, 1951, vol. 7, p. 1126.

34. Joy, p. 118.

35. Ibid., p. 131.

36. Vatcher, p. 86.

37. Joy, p. 28.

38. Memorandum on the Substance of Discussions at a Department of State–JCS Meeting, November 12, 1951, in *FRUS*, 1951, vol. 7, pp. 1122–24 and JCS to Ridgway, November 13, 1951, in *FRUS*, 1951, vol. 7, p. 1126.

39. Stueck, p. 242, citing U. S. Department of the Army, *United States Army in the Korean War*, 3 vols, (Washington: Government Printing Office, 1962–1972), vol. 2, p. 177.

40. JCS to Ridgway, November 13, 1951 in *FRUS*, 1951, vol. 7, p. 1126.

41. Vatcher, p. 86.

42. Stueck, pp. 247–48. On the Mao cables, Stueck cites Zhang draft manuscript, pp. 218–21; the references seem to point to pages pp. 221–22 of Zhang Shu Guang, *Mao's Military Romanticism: China and the Korean War, 1950–1953* (Lawrence, Kans.: Kansas University Press, 1995).

43. Leckie, p. 317.

44. Joy, p. 129.

45. Ibid.

46. Stueck, p. 253 citing Jianguo Yilai, Mao Zedong Wengao, *Mao Zedong's Manuscripts Since the Founding of the PRC*, vols. 1–3, (Beijing: Central Document Publishing House, 1987) vol. 2, p. 642.

47. Joint Chiefs of Staff to Commander in Chief, United Nations Command, June 30, 1951, *FRUS*, 1951, vol. 7, pp. 598–600.

48. Joy, p. 129.

49. Vatcher, p. 41.

50. Ibid., p. 42.

51. See Leckie, p. 322, and Vatcher, pp. 50–51, 53.

52. Joy, p. 21.

53. Alfred D. Wilhelm Jr., *The Chinese at the Negotiating Table* (Washington: National Defense University Press, 1994), pp. 136–38; Stueck, p. 243.

54. Vatcher, p. 42.

55. Joy, p. 135.

56. Ibid., pp. 135–136.

57. Joint Chiefs of Staff to Commander in Chief, United Nations Command, June 30, 1951, *FRUS*, 1951, vol. 7, pp. 598–600.

58. Briefing of Foreign Government Representatives, October 26, 1951, in *FRUS*, 1951, vol. 7, p. 1064.

59. CINCFE to JCS November 13, 1951, *FRUS*, 1951,vol. 7, p. 1130.

60. Vatcher, p. 91.

61. Ibid., p. 92.

62. Ibid., pp. 92–93.

63. Ibid., p. 93.

64. Ibid., p. 97. The wording is almost identical to the Ridgway message to JCS proposing the statement, in *FRUS*, 1951, vol. 7, p. 1126.

65. U.S. Ambassador in the Soviet Union to the Secretary of State, June 27, 1951, in *FRUS*, 1951, vol. 7, p. 561.

66. Vatcher, pp. 93–94.

67. Joy, p. 99.

68. Ibid., pp. 74–75.

69. The JCS instructions had said that the armistice agreement "shall require the commanders concerned to cease the introduction into Korea of any reinforcing air, ground or naval units or personnel during the armistice. This shall

not be interpreted as precluding the exchange of units or individual personnel on a man-for-man basis." Joint Chiefs of Staff to Commander in Chief, United Nations Command, June 30, 1951, *FRUS*, 1951, vol. 7, p. 598.

70. Vatcher, p. 92.

71. Joy, p. 66.

72. Ibid., p. 65.

73. Ibid., p. 67.

74. Ibid.

75. See Allan E. Goodman, ed., *Negotiating While Fighting: The Diary of Admiral C. Turner Joy at the Korean Armistice Conference* (Stanford, California: Hoover Institution, 1978), p. 225.

76. Vatcher, p. 109.

77. Memorandum of conversation by the director of the office of Northeast Asian Affairs, June 28, 1951, *FRUS*, 1951, vol. 7, p. 567.

78. Joy, pp. 89–90.

79. Ibid., p. 90.

80. Ibid., p. 91.

81. Ibid., pp. 74–75.

82. CINCFE to JCS, November 24, 1951, in *FRUS*, 1951, vol. 7, p. 1175.

83. Joy, p. 123.

84. Ibid.

85. Ibid., p. 73.

86. Vatcher, p. 111.

87. Ibid., p. 112.

88. Joy, p. 72.

89. Ibid., p. 160.

90. Joint Chiefs of Staff to Commander in Chief, United Nations Command, June 30, 1951, *FRUS*, 1951, vol. 7, pp. 598–600.

91. Stueck, p. 253, n. 135.

92. Vatcher, p. 122 and William Lindsay White, *The Captive of Korea* (New York: Charles Scribner's Sons, 1957), p. 30. Hereafter cited as White.

93. Vatcher, p. 120.

94. Ibid., p. 122.

95. Ibid., p. 123.

96. Ibid.

97. Ibid.

98. For a thorough discussion of the treatment of captives in North Korea see White. See also *Treatment of British Prisoners of War in Korea* (London: Ministry of Defence, 1955).

99. Alan Winnington and Wilfred Burchett, *Plain Perfidy: The Plot to Wreck Korean Peace* (London: Britain-China Friendship Association, 1954) and *Koje Unscreened* (London: Britain-China Friendship Association, undated, probably 1954). The author is indebted to Herbert Romerstein, who brought these books to his attention.

100. Vatcher, p. 126.

101. Hermes, p. 139.

102. Ibid., p. 141.

103. Vatcher, p. 127.

104. Ridgway to JCS, December 24, 1951, *FRUS*, 1951, vol. 7, p. 1432.

105. Vatcher, p. 129.

106. White, p. 42.

107. Winnington and Burchett, *Plain Perfidy*, p. 8.

108. Article 118 of the Geneva Convention Relative to the Treatment of Prisoners of War, August 12, 1949, TIAS 3364; 6 UST 3406.

109. Vatcher, p. 116, Hermes, p. 147. Article 4 of the Geneva Convention Relative to the Treatment of Prisoners of War, August 12, 1949, TIAS 3364; 6 UST 3320-21.

110. Article 7 of the Geneva Convention Relative to the Treatment of Prisoners of War, August 12, 1949, TIAS 3364; 6 UST 3324.

111. Joy, p. 133.

112. Vatcher, p. 133.

113. Joy, p. 152.

114. Ridgway to JCS, *FRUS*, 1952, vol. 15, pp. 66, 92.

115. Hermes, p. 136 and Stueck, p. 244, especially n. 68.

116. Vatcher, p. 135.

117. Memorandum for the Record, February 4, 1952, *FRUS*, 1952–1954, vol. 15, pt. 1, p. 33.

118. Ibid.

119. Memorandum for the Record, February 8, 1952, *FRUS*, 1952–1954, vol. 15, pt. 1, p. 41

120. Memorandum for the Record, February 4, 1952, *FRUS*, 1952–1954, vol. 15, pt. 1, p. 34.

121. Draft Memorandum by the Secretary of State and the Secretary of Defense for the President, February 4, 1952, *FRUS*, 1952–1954, vol. 15, pt. 1, p. 35.

122. Stueck and Cumings quote this version, which appears as Memorandum by the Secretary of State, February 8, 1952, vol. 15, pt. 1, pp. 44–45.

123. Vatcher, p. 140.

124. Ibid., 141.

125. Ibid.

126. Ibid.

127. Leckie, pp. 332–33.

128. Hermes, p. 171.

129. Vatcher, pp. 144–145.

130. Hermes, p. 171.

131. Ibid., p. 174.

132. Vatcher, p. 250.

133. "Statement by the President on General Ridgway's Korean Armistice

Proposal," May 7, 1952, in *Public Papers of the Presidents of the United States: Harry S. Truman, 1952–1953* (Washington: GPO, 1966), p. 321.

134. Stueck, p. 262, Hermes, p. 236, and Vatcher, p. 146.

135. Hermes, p. 245.

136. Ibid., p. 247.

137. Ibid.

138. Ibid., p. 252.

139. Iibd., p. 253.

140. Ibid., 259.

141. Ibid.

142. Ibid., 264.

143. Ibid.

144. Ibid., 265.

145. Whelan, pp. 358–61.

146. Hermes, pp. 402–03; Stueck, pp. 298–307.

147. Stueck, p. 326.

148. Richard Whelan, *Drawing the Line* (Boston: Little, Brown and Company, 1990), p. 354. Hereafter cited as Whelan.

149. Hermes, p. 413.

150. Ibid.

151. Ibid., p. 412.

152. Whelan, p. 354.

153. Hermes, pp. 425–28.

154. Ibid., p. 429.

155. Ibid., p. 430.

156. Whelan, p. 366. Rhee's letter to Clark explaining the action is in *FRUS*, 1952–1954, vol. 15, pt. 2, pp. 1197–99.

157. CINFE Clark to JCS, June 19, 1953, *FRUS*, 1952–1954, vol. 15, pt. 2, p. 1211.

158. Ambassador Briggs to Department of State, June 19, 1953, in *FRUS*, vol. 15, pt. 2, pp. 1221–23.

159. JCS to CINCFE Clark, July 15, 1953, *FRUS*, vol. 15, pt. 2, p. 1382.

160. Hermes, p. 483.

161. Agreement between Commander in Chief, United Nations Command, and Supreme Commander, Korean People's Army, and Commander of the Chinese People's Volunteers, Concerning a Military Armistice in Korea, July 27, 1953, 4 UST. 234, TIAS 2782.

CHAPTER 6: IMPLEMENTING THE ARMISTICE

1. Article IV of the Armistice Agreement, paragraph 60.

2. President Rhee to President Eisenhower, July 27, 1953, *Foreign Rela-*

tions of the United States, 1952–1954, vol. 15, pt. 2, p. 1444. Hereafter cited as *FRUS*.

3. Dean message to Department of State, October 24, 1953, *FRUS*, 1952–1954, vol. 15, pt. 2, p. 1561.

4. Korean Briefing Meeting, December 21, 1953, *FRUS*, 1952–1954, vol. 15, pt. 2, p. 1667.

5. Kenneth Todd Young, *Negotiating with the Chinese Communists: The United States Experience, 1953–1967* (New York: McGraw-Hill, 1968), p. 25. Hereafter cited as Young.

6. Arthur H. Dean, "What It's Like Negotiating with the Chinese," in *New York Times Magazine*, October 30, 1964, p. 47. Hereafter cited as Dean.

7. Ibid., p. 49.

8. Dean message to the Department of State, November 1, 1953, in *FRUS*, vol. 15, pt. 2, p. 1578.

9. Dean, p. 49.

10. Ibid., p. 52.

11. Ibid., p. 54. See also Korean Briefing Meeting, December 21, 1953, *FRUS*, vol. 15, pt. 2, p. 1667.

12. Dean message to the Department of State, December 12, 1953, *FRUS*, vol. 15, pt. 2, p. 1656.

13. Dean, p. 59.

14. Young, p. 3.

15. Signed October 1, 1953, the Seoul-Washington security pact entered into force on November 17, 1954, after the United States Senate had insisted on provisions clarifying that the United States would come to the defense of the ROK only in the event of an external armed attack on the South, not in the event of ROK initiation of an attack on the North.

16. Young message to the Department of State, January 23, 1954, *FRUS*, vol. 15, pt. 2, p. 1731.

17. "The Record on Korean Unification, 1943–1960," Department of State Publication 7084, p. 158.

18. "Declaration by the Sixteen," June 15, 1954, in *FRUS*, 1952–1954, vol. 16, pp. 385–87.

19. Armistice Agreement, paragraphs 19–35.

20. The agreement required that three members must be of general or flag rank, while two could be colonels or equivalent rank.

21. A Navy captain was the first MAC secretary, and four additional Navy captains served as MAC secretaries through March 17, 1958, but the position has been filled by Army colonels since then. Headquarters United Nations Command, "Command Historical Summary, January 1, 1995–December 31, 1995," pp. 26–27.

22. Subsequent Agreement, tab N-2, approved at the 9th MAC meeting, August 8, 1953.

23. North Korean MAC Secretary's message of February 8, 1955, calling for the 53rd MAC meeting, held on February 9, 1955.

24. UNCMAC Secretary's message of February 17, 1955, calling for the 55th MAC meeting, held on February 21, 1955.

25. Unless otherwise noted, the term "MAC meeting" in this chapter refers to a plenary session.

26. The October 30, 1954, "Subsequent Armistice Agreement."

27. Proceedings of the 9th MAC meeting, August 8, 1953, p. 4; and Proceedings of the 97th MAC Secretaries meeting, December 23, 1953, pp. 11–12.

28. "North Korean Statement of Apology" issued by the spokesman of the North Korean Foreign Ministry on December 29, 1996: "The spokesman of the Ministry of Foreign Affairs of the DPRK is authorized to express deep regret for the submarine incident in the coastal waters of Kangnung, South Korea, in September 1996, that caused the tragic loss of human life. The DPRK will make efforts to ensure that such an incident will not recur and will work with others for durable peace and stability on the Korean peninsula." Printed in *Korea Focus on Current Topics* (Seoul: Korea Foundation, 1997), vol. 5, no. 1, p. 109.

29. C. Turner Joy, *How Communists Negotiate* (New York: The Macmillan Company, 1955), p. 80. Hereafter cited as Joy.

30. Ibid., p. 62.

31. Of fifty-two JOT meetings convened to investigate incidents reported to have occurred in the DMZ prior to the JOT meeting of April 6–7, 1967, the North Koreans proposed forty-five and the UNC proposed seven. The North Koreans called twenty-two JOT meetings to investigate alleged South Korean espionage infiltration to the north across the line; and the UNC denied them all. Since the signing of the armistice in 1953, the UNC admitted 117 armistice agreement violations, incuding ninety inadvertent aerial overflights, four inadvertent naval intrusions, and twenty-three ground violations such as accidental crossing of the MDL (military demarcation line) and accidental firing of weapons in the DMZ.

32. Proceedings of the meeting of Joint Observer Team Number Two, Military Demarcation Line Marker no. 0109, April 7, 1967, pp. 1–20.

33. Armistice Agreement, Article II, paragraphs 36–50.

34. Armistice Agreement, Article II, paragraph 13 (d).

35. Proceedings of the 105th NNSC meeting, February 17, 1954.

36. Letter from Swiss/Swedish NNSC members to MAC, May 7, 1954.

37. Proceedings of the 107th NNSC plenary session, February 23, 1954.

38. Proceedings of the 68th MAC meeting, February 14, 1956, p. 11.

39. Proceedings of the 87th NNSC plenary session, January 15, 1954.

40. JCS to Secretary of Defense Wilson, June 11, 1954, in *FRUS*, 1952–1954, vol. 15, pt. 2, p. 1807.

41. Proceedings of the 107th NNSC Plenary Session, February 23, 1954.

42. E.g., Secretary of State to the Embassy in Korea, November 8, 1954, in

FRUS, 1952–1954, vol. 15, pt. 2, pp. 1910–11, and Second Progress Report by the Operations Coordinating Board to the NSC on NSC 170/1, December 29, 1954, in *FRUS*, 1952–1954, vol. 16, pt. 2, p. 1946.

43. Ambassador Briggs to the Department of State, *FRUS*, 1952–1954, vol. 15, pt. 2, pp. 1871–72.

44. UNCMAC-SA, "History of the NNSC" (unclassified), August 1, 1979.

45. UNCMAC-SA, "Overview of NNSC" (unclassified), July 2, 1992.

46. Hak Joon Kim, *Unification Policies of South and North Korea, 1945–1991: A Comparative Study* (Seoul: Seoul National University Press, 1978), third edition, p. 188.

47. Proceedings of the 70th MAC Meeting, May 31, 1956, pp. 7–8.

48. Proceedings of the 75th MAC Meeting, June 21, 1957, pp. 1–3.

49. Walter G. Hermes, *Truce Tent and Fighting Front* (Washington: Department of the Army, Office of the Chief of Military History, 1988), p. 46, citing Message, UNC 309, CINCUNC to CINCFE, September 19, 1951.

50. For the first three cases in which UNC pilots were forced down in North Korea, North Korea returned aircraft or wreckage along with the pilots. The North stopped returning wreckage in 1958 when it chose not to return the wreckage of a U.S. Air Force F-86 that was shot down in North Korea on March 6.

51. Proceedings of the 174th MAC Secretaries Meeting, March 17, 1958, p. 2.

52. Proceedings of the 157th MAC meeting, October 5, 1962, pp. 10–12.

53. Kim Il Sung letter to CINCUNC, February 17, 1964, delivered through Joint Duty Officers Meeting at Panmunjom, February 17, 1964, UNCMAC Headquarters Historical File.

54. Text of Receipt for Captains Stutts and Voltz, returned through the MAC on May 16, 1964, in Proceedings of the 174th MAC Secretaries Meeting, March 17, 1958.

55. Proceedings of the 309th MAC Meeting, December 5, 1970, pp. 1–3.

56. Proceedings of the 316th MAC Meeting, June 2, 1971, pp. 30–31.

57. UNCMAC-SA Study on Negotiations for the Return of Military Personnel, July 14, 1977, pp. 3–4.

58. Ibid.

59. Personal recollection of James M. Lee from conversations, April 1968–January 1969.

CHAPTER 7: MANAGING THE YEARS OF CRISIS

1. Proceedings of the 239th MAC Meeting, January 21, 1967, pp. 5–10.

2. Ibid., pp. 2–4.

3. Proceedings of the 257th MAC Meeting, November 7, 1967, p. 7.

4. T. R. Fehrenbach, *The Fight for Korea: From the War of 1950 to the*

Pueblo Incident (New York: Grosset and Dunlap, 1969), p. 11. Hereafter cited as Fehrenbach.

5. Proceedings of the 261st MAC Meeting, January 24, 1968, pp. 2–9.

6. Joint Duty Officer files Summary of Messages, January 22, 1968. Hereafter cited as JDO.

7. Rear Admiral Daniel V. Gallery, USN Ret., *The Pueblo Incident* (Garden City, N.Y.: Doubleday & Company, 1970).

8. Ibid., p. 10.

9. *Pacific Stars & Stripes*, February 6, 1968.

10. *Pacific Stars & Stripes*, AP radiophoto, January 28, 1968.

11. Proceedings of the 261st Military Armistice Commission (MAC) Meeting, January 24, 1968, pp. 2–3.

12. Foreign Broadcast Information Service (hereafter cited as FBIS), Pyongyang KCNA international service in English, December 17, 1967.

13. Proceedings of the 261st Military Armistice Commission Meeting, January 24, 1968, pp. 10–11.

14. Ibid., pp. 11–14.

15. Ibid., pp. 10–11, 24.

16. When, in December 1968, the UNC senior member signed a "letter of apology" prepared by North Korea, it differed little from this initial North Korean demand.

17. Proceedings of the 261st Military Armistice Commission Meeting, January 24, 1968, pp. 10–11, 24.

18. FBIS, Pyongyang News Broadcast in English, January 25, 1968.

19. Rear Admiral Daniel V. Gallery, USN, Ret., *The Pueblo Incident* (Garden City, N.Y.: Doubleday & Company, 1970), p. 2.

20. *Time*, February 2, 1968, pp. 9–13.

21. *Japan Times*, January 29, 1968.

22. *Pacific Stars & Stripes*, January 29, 1968.

23. *Time*, February 2, 1968, pp. 9–12.

24. Recollection of Mr. James M. Lee, who attended the private meetings (February 2, 1968–December 23, 1968) for the return of the *Pueblo* crew members.

25. Unclassified UNCMAC Senior Member's letter to KPA/CPV MAC Senior Member, January 29, 1968.

26. FBIS, Pyongyang KCNA international service in English, January 31, 1968.

27. Robert J. McCloskey, quoted in *Japan Times*, February 4, 1968.

28. FBIS, Pyongyang domestic radio service in Korean, February 4, 1968.

29. FBIS, Pyongyang KCNA international service in English, February 8, 1968.

30. *Chosun Ilbo*, February 5, 1968.

31. Bum-shik Shin, press secretary to the ROK president, press conference, February 9, 1968, in *Korea Herald*, February 10, 1968.

32. FBIS, Pyongyang KCNA Radio Pyongyang News Broadcast, January 25, 1968.

33. Proceedings of the 262nd MAC Meeting, February 14, 1968, pp. 2–6.

34. Ibid., pp. 7–9.

35. Ibid., pp. 23–27.

36. FBIS, Pyongyang domestic service in Korean, March 10, 1968, "U.S. Apology Called for Concerning *Pueblo*." The *Pueblo* crew members, after their release from North Korea, explained that Pyongyang had coerced them to write their "confessions" and letters.

37. FBIS, Pyongyang KCNA international service in English, March 22, 1968.

38. Proceedings of the 265th MAC Meeting, March 25, 1968, pp. 14–18.

39. Proceedings of the 266th MAC Meeting, April 18, 1968, pp. 7–11.

40. Ibid.

41. Ibid.

42. Ibid., pp. 12–22.

43. Proceedings of the 270th MAC Meeting, May 17, 1968, pp. 2–6; 272nd MAC Meeting, July 8, 1968; 274th MAC Meeting, July 25, 1968, pp. 10–30; 275th MAC Meeting, August 5, 1968, pp. 7–15; 276th MAC Meeting, September 5, 1968, pp. 17–23; 277th MAC Meeting, September 5, 1968, pp. 2–6, 7–15; and 278th MAC Meeting, September 14, 1968, pp. 2–9, 31–50.

44. Proceedings of the 271st MAC Meeting, June 26, 1968, pp. 8–13, 16–23.

45. Proceedings of the 277th MAC Meeting, September 5, 1968, pp. 2–6.

46. Proceedings of the 280th MAC Meeting, October 16, 1968, pp. 2–6.

47. Ibid., pp. 6–15.

48. Proceedings of the 281st MAC Meeting, November 5, 1968, pp. 5–9.

49. Ibid., pp. 18–25.

50. Ibid., pp. 44–45.

51. Proceedings of the 282nd MAC Meeting, December 10, 1968, pp. 2–11.

52. Ibid., pp. 19–25.

53. At the press conference on December 23, 1968, upon the release of the *Pueblo* crew, Major General Woodward, UNCMAC senior member, provided to the press the complete text of both the U.S. government "repudiation" statement and the "letter of apology." *Korea Times*, December 24, 1968: "Signed Only to Free Crew: Woodward" includes the complete text of both documents, and Woodward explained the proposal to the press.

54. "North Korean Document Signed by U.S. at Panmunjom," in *Department of State Bulletin*, vol. 60, no. 1541, January 6, 1969, pp. 2–3.

55. FBIS, "Pueblo Crew 'Expulsion' Follows U.S. Apology," Pyongyang KCNA international service in English, December 23, 1968.

56. State Department press release 281, dated December 22, 1968, on Secretary Rusk's remarks. *Department of State Bulletin*, vol. 60, no. 1541, January 6, 1969.

57. Ibid.; President Johnson's statement read by his press secretary, December 22, 1968.

58. Photostat of the "Document of Apology" signed by Major General Woodward and doctored by North Korea, with the receipt clause removed or covered up, has been displayed in and out of the MAC conference room a number of times.

59. Proceedings of the 284th MAC Meeting, January 28, 1969, pp. 9–12.

60. Proceedings of the 290th MAC Meeting, April 18, 1969, pp. 2–6.

61. Ibid.

62. Ibid., pp. 6–7.

63. Ibid., and *Korea Times*, April 19, 1969.

64. *Korea Times*, April 23, 1969.

65. FBIS, "Statement of the DPRK," KCNA Pyongyang domestic service, April 23, 1969.

66. Ibid.

67. Proceedings of the 291st MAC Meeting, August 14, 1969, pp. 3–10, 15–17.

68. Ibid., pp. 10–12.

69. Proceedings of the 292nd MAC Meeting, August 19, 1969, pp. 2–7.

70. Ibid., pp. 7–9.

71. Unclassified CINCUNC Message to JCS, August 30, 1969.

72. North Korea dropped the "O"; "OH" designated an *unarmed* observation helicopter.

73. JDO, Summary of Messages, September 2, 1969.

74. Unclassified CINCUNC Message to JCS, September 5, 1969.

75. Proceedings of the 296th MAC Meeting, October 23, 1969.

76. Ibid.

77. JDO, Summary of Messages, August 19, 1976.

78. Ibid.

79. Proceedings of the 379th MAC Meeting, August 19, 1976, pp. 2–5.

80. Ibid.

81. Ibid., pp. 6–10.

82. Recollections of James M. Lee, who attended General Stilwell's Command group meeting, August 18, 1976.

83. UNC/USFK/EUSA Public Affairs Division Report, Seoul, Korea, October 6, 1976.

84. JDO, Summary of Messages, August 21, 1976.

85. Unclassified JDO/USASG-JSA Operations Log, August 18–22, 1976.

86. Proceedings of the 380th MAC Meeting, August 25, 1976.

87. Unclassified CINCUNC to JCS Message, August 1976.

88. Proceedings of the 380th MAC Meeting, August 25, 1976, p. 2.

89. Ibid., pp. 2–4.

90. Ibid., pp. 6–7.

91. Ibid., pp. 5–6.

92. Tokyo *Mainichi Shimbun*, November 27, 1976.

93. FBIS, Pyongyang domestic service in Korean, July 14, 1977.

94. Proceedings of the 385th MAC Meeting, July 16, 1977, pp. 2–5.

95. FBIS, Pyongyang KCNA in English, July 15, 1977.

96. Proceedings of the 407th MAC Meeting, September 1, 1981, pp. 2–3.

97. Proceeding of the 385th MAC Meeting, July 16, 1977, pp. 2–5.

98. Ibid., pp. 4–6.

99. Joseph S. Bermudez, Jr., *Terrorism: The North Korean Connection* (New York: Taylor and Francis, 1990), p. 45, and "Seoul Condemns Bombing as Plot by North Korea," *New York Times*, October 11, 1983, p. A1.

100. UNCMAC unclassified Memorandum for the Record, "Next (422nd) MAC Meeting," October 23, 1983.

101. Ibid.

102. Proceedings of the 422nd MAC Meeting, October 31, 1983, p. 6.

103. *Washington Post*, May 2, 1983.

104. Proceedings of the 423rd MAC Meeting, December 23, 1983, pp. 2–10.

105. Ibid., pp. 3–4.

106. Ibid., p. 3.

107. Ibid., pp. 2–10.

108. Ibid., pp. 17–24.

CHAPTER 8: NEGOTIATING FOR DIALOGUE

1. Kim Il Sung, *For the Independent, Peaceful Reunification of Korea* (New York: International Publishers, 1975), p. 132.

2. Foreign Broadcast Information Service (hereafter FBIS), "KCNA Issues Text of DPRK 'Socialist Constitution,'" Pyongyang KCNA in English, December 27, 1972.

3. Song Jong-Hwan, "How the North Korean Communists Negotiate: A Case Study of the South-North Korean Dialogue of the Early 1970s," in *Korea and World Affairs*, vol. 8, no. 3, fall 1984, p. 621, citing V. I. Lenin, *Selected Works*. Hereafter cited as Song.

4. Kim Il Sung on the occasion of the Centenary of the Birth of V. I. Lenin, April 16, 1970, in Li Yuk-sa, ed., *Juche! The Speeches and Writings of Kim Il Sung* (New York: Grossman, 1972), p. 210. Hereafter cited as *Juche*.

5. Song, p. 625, citing *Peking Review*, vol. 9, no. 44 (October 28, 1966), p. 7.

6. Bong Baik, *Kim Il Sung Biography* (Tokyo: Miraisha, 1969), vol. 2, p. 423, cited in Hakjoon Kim, *Unification Policies of South and North Korea, 1945–1991: A Comparative Study* (Seoul: Seoul National University Press, 1978), third edition, p. 168. Hereafter cited as Hak Joon Kim.

7. Kim Il Sung, September 7, 1968, cited in Song, p. 630.

8. *Kim Il Sung Biography*, vol. 3, pp. 464–68 cited in Hak Joon Kim, p. 250.

9. Kim Il Sung on the occasion of the Centenary of the Birth of V. I. Lenin, April 16, 1970, in *Juche*, p. 223.

10. UNCMAC-SA Memorandum for the Record "Thrust of Communist Propaganda at MAC Meetings," August 31, 1970, p. 3.

11. Kim Il Sung, *For the Independent, Peaceful Reunification of Korea* (New York: International Publishers, 1975), p. 133.

12. Hak Joon Kim, p. 169, citing Peter V. Curl (ed.) *Documents on American Foreign Relations, 1953* (New York: Harper, 1954), pp. 298–302.

13. *New York Times*, April 19, 1954, cited in Hak Joon Kim, p. 170.

14. See Richard Whelan, *Drawing the Line* (Boston: Little, Brown and Company, 1990), pp. 363–70. Hereafter cited as Whelan. Also, William Stueck, *The Korean War: An International History* (Princeton, N.J.: Princeton University Press, 1995), pp. 330–39. Hereafter cited as Stueck. The definitive clarification of this point may have been that provided by Secretary of State Dulles before the United States Congress. See U.S. Senate hearings, "Mutual Defense Treaty with Korea," 83rd Congress, 2nd session, January 13 and 14, 1954, p. 4.

15. *Juche*, p. 61.

16. Hak Joon Kim, pp. 196–97, and B. K. Gills, *Korea Versus Korea: A Case of Contested Legitimacy* (New York: Routledge, 1996), p. 147. Hereafter cited as Gills.

17. FBIS, April 22, 1960, quoted in Hak Joon Kim, p. 201

18. Chang Government spokesman on November 24, 1960. FBIS, *Daily Report*, November 25, 1960, cited in Hak Joon Kim, p. 207.

19. Hak Joon Kim, p. 215.

20. Kim Il Sung, *For the Independent, Peaceful Reunification of Korea* (New York: International Publishers, 1975), p. 60.

21. Gills, pp. 147–48.

22. Hak Joon Kim, p. 223, citing Park Chung Hee, *The Country, The Revolution and I* (Seoul: Hollym Corporation, 1962), p. 59.

23. Hak Joon Kim, p. 224, citing Park Chung Hee, *The Country, The Revolution and I* (Seoul: Hollym Corporation, 1962), p. 192.

24. Hak Joon Kim, p. 224.

25. Ibid., citing government sources quoted in *Dong-A Ilbo*, July 17, 1961.

26. Kim Il Sung, *For the Independent, Peaceful Reunification of Korea* (New York: International Publishers, 1975), p. 63.

27. Hak Joon Kim, p. 243.

28. "The Nixon Doctrine," in *Public Papers of the Presidents of the United States: Richard Nixon, 1971* (Washington: Government Printing Office, 1972), pp. 222–28.

29. Hak Joon Kim, pp. 278–79, citing U.S. Congress, Hearings before the Subcommittee on United States Security Agreements and Commitments Abroad of the Committee on Foreign Relations, Senate, 91st Congress, 2d session, part 6 (Washington: U.S. Government Printing Office, 1970), pp. 1680–81.

30. December 31, 1988, Edition of *A White Paper on South-North Dialogue in Korea* (Seoul: National Unification Board, 1988), p. 34. Hereafter cited as White Paper.

31. Hak Joon Kim, p. 299.

32. Ibid., pp. 300–02, citing among other sources, Chung Hee Park, *To Build A Nation* (Washington: Acropolis Books, 1971), pp. 166–67.

33. White Paper, p. 34.

34. Hak Joon Kim, pp. 303–04, note 165.

35. Ibid., p. 304.

36. Ibid., p. 305.

37. White Paper, pp. 56–57.

38. *Yomiuri Shimbun*, Tokyo, January 11, 1972, morning edition, p. 1.

39. The Shanghai Communiqué, February 28, 1972, in *Public Papers of the Presidents of the United States: Richard Nixon, 1972* (Washington: Government Printing Office, 1974), pp. 376–79.

40. "Great Leader Comrade Kim Il Sung's conversation with the South Korean Delegates to the High-level Talks, May 3 and November 3, 1972," from the North Korean Workers Party newspaper, *Rodong Sinmun*, July 4, 1982.

41. White Paper, p. 59

42. "Great Leader Comrade Kim Il Sung's conversation with the South Korean Delegates to the High-level Talks, May 3 and November 3, 1972," from the North Korean Workers Party newspaper, *Rodong Sinmun*, July 4, 1982.

43. Gills, p. 155.

44. White Paper, p. 59.

45. Song, pp. 637–38.

46. White Paper, p. 60.

47. Text of the South-North Joint Communiqué of July 4, 1972, minus the prefatory announcement of the secret talks, as printed in White Paper, pp. 54–56. At the same time, the two sides made public a detailed nine-point agreement governing the management of the telephone link, which had been in use since April 28, 1972 (precisely one month after the U.S.-PRC Shanghai Communiqué). In a pattern of behavior that would be seen again in the negotiations of supporting arrangements for KEDO operations in North Korea, it detailed seemingly inconsequential matters of responsibility for operation and repairs of the communication line; it specified total autonomy in handling the link on each side and pledged confidentiality would be respected by both sides.

48. White Paper, pertinent parts of sections 2 a-e "The functions of the SNCC" of *Agreed Minute on Formation and Operation of South-North Coordinating Committee*, pp. 63–64.

49. Song, p. 634.

50. Ibid., p. 614.

51. White Paper, p. 76.

52. Song, p. 636.

53. White Paper, pp. 58–60; and Song, p. 637.

54. White Paper, p. 77.

55. Song, p. 637.

56. White Paper, p. 85.

57. Ibid., p. 68.

58. Ibid., p. 69.

59. Ibid., pp. 69–70.

60. Ibid., p. 71.

61. Lee Dong Bok, "South-North Coordinating Committee of Korea: An Analytical Review of How It Was Originally Designed to Function and How It Has Failed to Function As Originally Planned," in Hak Joon Kim, *The Unification Policy of South and North Korea*, (Seoul: Seoul National University Press, 1977), p. 313. Hereafter cited as Lee.

62. Message from CINCUNC to JCS, unclassified, March 12, 1973.

63. Proceedings of the 337th MAC Meeting, March 12, 1973, p. 4.

64. Lee, p. 313.

65. White Paper, pp. 72–73.

66. Kim Joungwon, *Divided Korea: The Politics of Development, 1945–1972* (Cambridge: Harvard University Press, 1975), pp. 65–66.

67. Lee, p. 315.

68. Song, p. 643.

69. White Paper, pp. 78–79.

70. Song, p. 643.

71. White Paper, p. 80.

72. Ibid.

73. Song, p. 655.

74. Hak Joon Kim, pp. 353–54.

75. White Paper, p. 103.

76. Hak Joon Kim, p. 355, and Kim Il Sung, *For the Independent, Peaceful Reunification of Korea* (New York: International Publishers, 1975), pp. 201–07.

77. C. Turner Joy, *How Communists Negotiate* (New York: Macmillan & Company, 1955), p. 119. Hereafter cited as Joy.

78. Kim Dae Jung, *Prison Writings* (Berkeley: University of California Press, 1987), p. x, states: "1973: Kim Dae Jung is abducted from his hotel in Tokyo by KCIA agents and removed by boat to the Sea of Japan, where the agents prepare to kill him by weighting him and throwing him overboard. American aircraft spot the KCIA boat and keep it under surveillance, preventing the assassination."

79. White Paper, p. 101.

80. Ibid.

81. Lee, p. 320.

82. Song, p. 639; Lee, p. 315.

83. White Paper, p. 116.

84. See Gills, pp. 134–36.

85. FBIS, Text of Kim Il Sung Speech at 18 April Peking Banquet, Peking KCNA April 18, 1975; also, Hak Joon Kim, p. 361.

86. Gills, p. 135, citing *Pyongyang Times*, April 26, 1975.

87. Hak Joon Kim, pp. 360–61. In 1983, Deng Xiaoping told Secretary of Defense Caspar Weinberger that North Korea would never invade the South for two reasons. Deng said that South Korean forces were superior and that North Korea knew there would be no support from China. See Caspar W. Weinberger, *Fighting for Peace: Seven Critical Years in the Pentagon* (New York: Warner Books, 1990), p. 275.

88. Record of the UN General Assembly, 30th Session, Doc. No. A/10327.

89. See Gills, p. 174.

90. Letter from John Scali, Permanent Representative of the U.S. to the UN, June 27, 1975; UN General Assembly, 30th Session, doc. no. S/11737. Also, Secretary of State Kissinger's speech to the 30th UN General Assembly, September 22, 1975, cited in Hak Joon Kim, pp. 371–72.

91. FBIS, text of Kim Il Sung speech, Pyongyang KCNA in English, October 10, 1975.

92. *Pyongyang Times*, July 23, 1977, as cited in Hak Joon Kim, p. 379.

93. For a fuller discussion of the Carter reversal on the withdrawal of troops, see Joe Wood and Philip Zelikow, "Persuading a President: Jimmy Carter and American Troops in Korea," (Cambridge, Mass.: Kennedy School of Government, Harvard College, 1996) Case program C18-96-1319.0, and Don Oberdorfer, *The Two Koreas: A Contemporary History* (Reading, Mass.: Addison Wesley, 1997), chapter 4, pp. 84–108. Hereafter cited as Oberdorfer.

94. White Paper, p. 118.

95. Ibid., p. 121.

96. Ibid.

97. Ibid., p. 123.

98. Ibid., p. 124.

99. Ibid., p. 132.

100. Oberdorfer, p. 105.

101. *South-North Dialogue in Korea* (Seoul: National Unification Board, 1979), no. 22, October 79, p. 23.

102. FBIS, Pyongyang KCNA international service in English, July 10, 1979.

103. 1982 edition of *A White Paper on South-North Dialogue in Korea* (Seoul: National Unification Board, 1982), pp. 136–50.

104. FBIS, KCNA, "DPRK Prime Minister's Statement" in Pyongyang domestic service, September 24, 1980.

105. White Paper, p. 155.

106. Ibid., p. 166.

107. Ibid.

108. Ibid., p. 167.

109. Ibid., p. 176.

110. Ibid.

111. Ibid., p. 180.

112. Ibid., pp. 170–72.

113. Ibid., p. 172.

114. Ibid., p. 168.

115. Ibid., p. 169.

116. Hak Joon Kim, p. 412.

117. *Korea Herald*, November 12, 1983, as cited in Hak Joon Kim, p. 411. Oberdorfer, p. 146, quotes Ho Dam as saying that North Korea had proposed trilateral talks "in full consideration of the long-maintained demand of the United States." Of course, it was not a "long-maintained demand"; it was an idiosyncratic one-time proposal by President Carter in July 1979, reluctantly supported by President Park.

118. Hak Joon Kim, p. 413.

119. Hearing of the House of Representatives Foreign Affairs Subcommittee on Asian and Pacific Affairs, June 15, 1984. *Source Material, Korea and World Affairs*, vol. 8, no. 4 (Winter 1984), pp. 944–48.

120. White Paper, p. 307.

121. Hak Joon Kim, p. 417.

122. White Paper, p. 188.

123. Even earlier, on December 26, 1984, Chun Doo Hwan had sent Channing Liem to meet with Kim Il Sung in Pyongyang to discuss a North-South summit. This secret meeting was loosely supervised by the KCIA. See Oberdorfer, p. 149.

124. The summary of the secret talks between Chang Se-dong and Ho Dam was published in the November 1996 issue of *Wolgan Chosun*, a monthly magazine published by the *Chosun Ilbo* in Seoul. The dialogue appears here as transtated by James M. Lee.

125. White Paper, p. 328.

126. A full account is provided in Oberdorfer, pp. 182–86. A U.S. government publication gives the number of passengers killed as 135. U.S. policy analysts viewed the bombing as an ominous change from North Korea's attacks on prominent political personages and military to civilians, but in fact civilians had been killed in numerous North Korean incursions, notably the Ulchin-Samchok raid of 1968. See Andrea Matles Savada, editor, *North Korea: A Country Study* (Washington: Federal Research Division, Library of Congress, June 1993), p. 262.

127. Hak Joon Kim, p. 464, and (for the Kim Young Sam policy) Office of South-North Dialogue, National Unification Board, *South-North Dialogue in Korea No. 58, October 1993* (Seoul: National Unification Board, 1993), p. 8.

128. Hak Joon Kim, pp. 464–65.

129. Rhee Tong-chin (translator), *Kim Dae Jung's "Three Stage" Approach to Korean Reunification* (Los Angeles: University of Southern California, 1997), p. 44.

130. Ibid., p. 45.

131. Ministry of National Unification, *Peace and Cooperation, A White Paper on Korean Unification, 1996* (Seoul: Ministry of National Unification, 1996), p. 20.

132. Kang Sang-yun article in *Korea Herald*, February 21, 1992.

CHAPTER 9: LEVERAGING UNCERTAINTY

1. Don Oberdorfer, *The Two Koreas: A Contemporary History* (Reading, Mass.: Addison-Wesley, 1997), p. 252. Hereafter cited as Oberdorfer.

2. Oberdorfer, pp. 252–53.

3. Michael J. Mazarr, *North Korea and the Bomb: A Case Study in Nonproliferation* (New York: St. Martin's, 1997), p. 44. Hereafter cited as Mazarr.

4. Oberdorfer, p. 253.

5. NPT, Article III, section 1. NPT refers to the Treaty on the Non-Proliferation of Nuclear Weapons signed at Washington, London, and Moscow, July 1, 1968. It entered into force in the United States on March 5, 1970.

6. NPT, Article IV, section 2. In 1992, for example, the IAEA planned to spend $300,000 in technical assistance for North Korea. See Mazarr, p. 82.

7. Oberdorfer, p. 254.

8. Agreement of July 20, 1977, between the IAEA and the DPRK for the Application of Safeguards in Respect of a Research Reactor Facility, IAEA Document INFCIRC/252, November 14, 1977.

9. Oberdorfer, pp. 249–51. All references to information obtained through intelligence sources are from unclassified, secondary, published accounts.

10. North Korea's Known Nuclear Infrastructure, Internet: www. Wideopen. igc.org/nci/nkib6.htm

11. Mazarr, p. 45; Oberdorfer, pp. 250–51.

12. Oberdorfer, p. 251.

13. Ibid., p. 255.

14. Victor Gilinsky, "Nuclear Blackmail: The 1994 US-DPRK Agreed Framework on North Korea's Nuclear Program," *Essays in Public Policy* (Stanford, Calif.: Hoover Institution, 1997), p. 4.

15. Secretary of Defense William J. Perry; Internet www. Wideopen.igc.org/nci/nkib6.htm

16. C. Turner Joy, *How Communists Negotiate* (New York: Macmillan Company, 1955), p. 74. Hereafter cited as Joy.

17. Text of Joint Declaration of the Denuclearization of the Korean Peninsula, Young Whan Kihl, *Korea and the World* (Boulder, Colo.: Westview Press, 1994), appendix C, pp. 347–48.

18. National Unification Board, "South-North Dialogue in Korea," no. 56, October 1992, p. 15.

19. Joy, p. 129.

20. James A. Baker, *The Politics of Diplomacy* (New York: Putnam, 1995), p. 595, quoted in Oberdorfer, p. 256.

21. The Russians who were in a position to know the North Korean program well were especially dismissive of its capabilities for producing nuclear weapons. See Mazarr, pp. 46–47.

22. Oberdorfer, pp. 249–51.

23. Oberdorfer, p. 265.

24. Mazarr, p. 70, appears to have particularly well-informed sources for his description of this meeting.

25. Presidential report prepared by the Office of the Assistant Secretary of Defense for International Security Affairs, "A Strategic Framework for the Asian Pacific Rim" (Washington: Department of Defense, 1992), pp. 5, 19.

26. Oberdorfer, p. 269.

27. Kongdan Oh and Ralph Hassig, "North Korea's Nuclear Program," in Young Whan Kihl, *Korea and the World* (Boulder, Colorado: Westview Press, 1994), p. 237. Hereafter cited as Oh and Hassig.

28. Ibid.

29. Ibid., and Oberdorfer, p. 269.

30. Nicholas Eberstadt, *Korea Approaches Reunification* (Armonk, N.Y.: M. E. Sharpe for the National Bureau of Asian Research, 1995), p. 25.

31. Oberdorfer, p. 269.

32. See Mazarr, p. 63

33. Mazarr, p. 63, and Leon V. Sigal, *Disarming Strangers: Nuclear Diplomacy with North Korea* (Princeton, N.J.: Princeton University Press, 1998), p. 43.

34. Mazarr, pp. 94–95 provides an unclassified description of the two sites and explains why they came under suspicion.

35. Oberdorfer, p. 275.

36. Oberdorfer, p. 273. The source of the North Korean statement is not provided.

37. Mazarr, p. 67; Oh and Hassig, p. 238.

38. Statement of the DPRK Declaring Withdrawal from the NPT, March 12, 1993.

39. NPT, Article X (1).

40. All the while, however, North Korea claimed it had only a peaceful nuclear program. Oberdorfer writes that in a December 1992 meeting with Congressman Stephen Solarz, whom many believed would be appointed to a high-level foreign policy position in the incoming Clinton administration, Kim Il Sung said forcefully, "We have no nuclear reprocessing facilities." Oberdorfer, p. 264.

41. Antonio F. Perez, "Survival of Rights under the Nuclear Non-Proliferation Treaty: Withdrawal and the Continuing Right of International Atomic Energy Agency Safeguards," in *Virginia Journal of International Law Association*, Summer 1994, 34 Va. J. Int'l L. 749.

42. DPRK Ambassador to UN agencies in Geneva, as cited in Mazarr, p. 96, n. 79.

43. Armistice Agreement, Article I, section 11.

44. Oberdorfer, p. 277; Oh and Hassig, p. 239.

45. Oberdorfer, p. 279.

46. "We Should Not Fall Prey to the Big Powers," *Rodong Sinmun* commentary of February 21, 1993, as translated in FBIS-EAS, February 22, 1993, pp. 11–13 and quoted in Mazarr, p. 99. See also the translation by North Korean News, March 1, 1993, pp. 3–4, as cited in Oh and Hassig, p. 239.

47. "Statement of IAEA Director General regarding DPRK at informal briefing of UN Security Council, April 1993," issued by the IAEA in New York, April 6, 1993.

48. FBIS, Pyongyang Korean Central Broadcasting Network in Korean, April 25, 1993.

49. FBIS, Pyongyang Korean Central Broadcasting Network in Korean, May 12, 1993.

50. Ibid.

51. UPI wire report cited in Mazarr, p. 116.

52. Mazarr, p. 116.

53. Oberdorfer, p. 283.

54. Mazarr, p. 117.

55. Ibid.

56. AP wire cited in Mazarr, p. 121.

57. FBIS: Pyongyang Korean Central Broadcasting Network in Korean, June 12, 1993.

58. Ibid.

59. Oberdorfer, pp. 283–86.

60. Ibid., p.286.

61. U.S. State Department web page on North Korea.

62. As the U.S. State Department has described it, these changes in U.S.-DPRK relations were as follows:

> Recognizing that the North's isolation is an inherently destabilizing factor in the Northeast Asia region and an impediment to the peaceful reunification of Korea, the United States encourages the DPRK to adopt policies that will help bring it more fully into the world community. To advance this goal—and in support of South Korean President Roh Tae Woo's 1988 reunification initiatives—the U.S. Government on October 31, 1988, announced the following steps regarding relations with the DPRK:
>
> —Authorized U.S. diplomats to hold substantive discussions with DPRK officials in neutral settings;
>
> —Encouraged unofficial, nongovernmental visits from the DPRK in academics, sports, culture, and other areas;
>
> —Facilitated the travel of U.S. citizens to the DPRK by permitting travel services for exchanges and group travel on a case-by-case basis; and
>
> —Permitted certain commercial exports to the DPRK of goods that meet basic human needs (food, clothing, medical supplies, etc.) on a case-by-case basis.

As a result, there have been cultural, academic, and diplomatic exchanges between the two countries. From January 1989 to May 1993, U.S. and North Korean officials met thirty-three times in Beijing, China.

63. Oh and Hassig, p. 240.

64. Perez, p. 751, n. 9.

65. Oh and Hassig, p. 240.

66. Regrettably, North Korea's view that withdrawal from the NPT would have automatically permitted it to avoid inspections is given too much currency in scholarly summaries of the nuclear issues. The notion is dismissed by scholars of international law. See Perez, p. 751, and United States General Accounting Office Report, "Nuclear Nonproliferation: Implications of the U.S.-North Korean Agreement on Nuclear Issues" (Washington: Government Printing Office, October 1996), p. 33, n. 10. Hereafter cited as GAO.

67. Oberdorfer, p. 290.

68. Ibid.

69. GAO, p. 27.

70. David R. McCann, editor, *Korea Briefing: Toward Reunification* (Armonk, N.Y.: M. E. Sharpe for the Asia Society, 1997), pp. 145–46. Hereafter cited as *Briefing*.

71. Ibid., p. 149

72. Ibid., p. 152.

73. GAO, pp. 28–29; *Briefing* says January 5.

74. Park Yong Su statement as reported by Oberdorfer, p. 304.

75. *Briefing*, p. 160.

76. Ibid.

77. GAO, p. 32

78. *Briefing*, p. 161

79. Oberdorfer, p. 315. See also the testimony of Edward L. Warner III, assistant secretary of defense for strategy and requirements, in "North Korean Military and Nuclear Proliferation Threat: Evaluation of the U.S.-DPRK Agreed Framework," Joint Hearing before the Subcommittees on International Economic Policy and Trade and Asia and the Pacific of the Committee on International Relations, House of Representatives, February 23, 1995 (Washington: GPO, 1995), pp. 15–19.

80. Oberdorfer, p. 314.

81. "North Korean Military and Nuclear Proliferation Threat: Evaluation of the U.S.-DPRK Agreed Framework," Joint Hearing before the Subcommittees on International Economic Policy and Trade and Asia and the Pacific of the Committee on International Relations, House of Representatives, February 23, 1995 (Washington: GPO, 1995), p. 18.

82. Gwen Ifill, "In Korea, Chilling Reminders of Cold War," *New York Times*, July 18, 1993, pt. 4, p. 1.

83. "Nunn, Lugar Urge Stronger Policy on North Korea." Congressional Report, February 24, 1994.

84. Dole, McCain, et al., amendment to S. 2201 (FAA Authorization Act), *Congressional Record*, vol. 140, part 9, June 16, 1994, pp. 13278–92.

85. Oberdorfer, p. 317, and interviews with staff who had planned to travel with the senators.

86. "Waging Peace Around the World," the Annual Report of the Carter Center, Atlanta, Georgia, 1994.

87. "Report of Our Trip to Korea, June 1994," provided through the courtesy of the Carter Center, Atlanta, Georgia, p. 1.

88. Carter trip report, p. 1.

89. Ibid., p. 3.

90. Ibid., p. 4.

91. *Briefing*, p. 163.

92. Ibid., p. 164.

93. State Department press release, October 21, 1994.

94. Joy, p. 134.

95. Mazarr, p. 122.

96. Kanter and Manning presented their views at a Carnegie Endowment for International Peace symposium on "The United States and North Korea: What Next?" November 16, 1993. The session is discussed in Leon V. Sigal, *Disarming Strangers: Nuclear Diplomacy with North Korea* (Princeton, N.J.: Princeton University Press, 1998), p. 85.

97. Daryl M. Plunk, "Defusing North Korea's Nuclear Threat," in *Backgrounder* (Washington: Heritage Foundation, 1994), no. 224, June 3, 1994.

98. Joy, p. 62.

99. Testimony of Secretary of Defense William J. Perry in "North Korea Nuclear Agreement," Hearings before the Committee on Foreign Relations, United States Senate, January 24 and 25, 1995 (Washington, GPO, 1995), p. 16.

100. Robert L. Gallucci served as assistant secretary of state for politico-military affairs from July 1992 to August 1994. On August 29, 1994, he was appointed ambassador at large.

101. Testimony of Secretary of State Christopher in "North Korea Nuclear Agreement," Hearings before the Committee on Foreign Relations, United States Senate, January 24 and 25, 1995 (Washington: GPO, 1995), p. 7.

102. "North Korean Military and Nuclear Proliferation Threat: Evaluation of the U.S.-DPRK Agreed Framework," Joint Hearing before the Subcommittees on International Economic Policy and Trade and Asia and the Pacific of the Committee on International Relations, House of Representatives, February 23, 1995 (Washington: GPO, 1995), p. 11.

103. Testimony of Secretary of State Christopher in "North Korea Nuclear Agreement," Hearings before the Committee on Foreign Relations, United States Senate, January 24 and 25, 1995 (Washington: GPO, 1995), p. 7.

104. Walter B. Slocombe, "The Agreed Framework and the Democratic People's Republic of Korea," National Defense University, Washington D.C., INSS paper no. 23, March 1995, p. 4.

105. Testimony of Secretary of State Christopher in "North Korea Nuclear

Agreement," Hearings before the Committee on Foreign Relations, United States Senate, January 24 and 25, 1995 (Washington: GPO, 1995), p. 13.

106. "Engaging the Hermit Kingdom: U. S. Policy Toward North Korea, Hearing before the Subcommittee on Asia and the Pacific of the Committee on International Relations, U.S. House of Representatives, February 26, 1997 (Washington: GPO, 1997), p. 41.

107. Carl W. Ford, Jr., "A Peace Regime on the Korean Peninsula: Problems and Prospects" in *New Discourses on a Peace Regime in Northeast Asia and Korea: Contending Views and New Alternatives;* International Forum Proceedings, November 22–23, 1996 (Seoul: Research Institute for International Affairs, 1996), pp. 17–35. Hereafter cited as Ford.

108. Ford, pp. 17–35.

109. Ibid., pp. 24–25.

110. Ibid., pp. 30–31.

111. Ibid., pp. 29–30.

112. Ibid., p. 32.

113. Larry A. Niksch, Congressional Research Service Memorandum, "US-North Korea: Agreed Framework and Other Aspects of US-North Korean Relations," January 9, 1995.

114. "NK May Be Building Underground Nuclear Facility" *Chosun Ilbo,* digital edition, January 17, 1998.

115. David E. Sanger, "North Korea Site an A-Bomb Plant, U.S. Agencies Say." *New York Times,* August 17, 1998, p. 1.

116. Ford, pp. 23–24.

117. Leonard S. Spector statement in "North Korean Military and Nuclear Proliferation Threat: Evaluation of the US-DPRK Agreed Framework," Joint Hearing before the Subcommittees on International Economic Policy and Trade and Asia and the Pacific of the Committee on International Relations, House of Representatives, February 23, 1995 (Washington: GPO, 1995), p. 48.

118. Lee Dong-bok, "Dealing with North Korea: The Case of the Agreed Framework," text of a presentation delivered at "Beyond the Nuclear Crisis: The Prospects for Korean Peace," a conference sponsored by the American Enterprise Institute and the Nonproliferation Policy Center, Washington, D.C., March 13, 1995, p. 11.

119. Victor Gilinsky, "Nuclear Blackmail: The 1994 US-DPRK Agreed Framework on North Korea's Nuclear Program," *Essays in Public Policy,* no. 76 (Stanford, Calif.: Hoover Institution, 1997), p. 1. Hereafter cited as Gilinsky.

120. Ibid., p. 12.

121. Ibid., p. 13. See also, Victor Gilinsky and Henry Sokolski, "A Silver Lining to Asia's Financial Cloud," *Washington Post,* January 19, 1998, p. A25, and James R. Lilley, "The Nuclear White Elephant," *Newsweek,* international edition, March 5, 1998.

122. Gilinsky, p. 13.

123. Lee Dong-bok, "Dealing with North Korea: The Case of the Agreed

Framework," text of a presentation delivered at "Beyond the Nuclear Crisis: The Prospects for Korean Peace," a conference sponsored by the American Enterprise Institute and the Nonproliferation Policy Center, Washington, D.C., March 13, 1995, p. 7.

124. Ibid., p. 8.

125. Richard V. Allen before the Senate Foreign Relations Committee, "North Korea Nuclear Agreement," Hearings before the Committee on Foreign Relations, United States Senate, January 24–25, 1995 (Washington: GPO, 1995), p. 64.

CHAPTER 10: DEALING WITH THE TRUTH

1. Madeleine K. Albright, "American Principle and Purpose in East Asia," April 15, 1997, in *U. S. State Department Dispatch*, March/April 1997, p. 23.

2. Leon V. Sigal, *Disarming Strangers: Nuclear Diplomacy with North Korea* (Princeton, N.J.: Princeton University Press, 1998), p. 68.

3. David W. Jones, "N. Korean official, in U.S., calls for closer ties, food aid," *Washington Times*, April 28, 1996, p. A7, and Andrew Higgins, "N. Korea aims not easy to discern," *Washington Times*, October 4, 1996, p. A19.

4. C. Turner Joy, *How Communists Negotiate* (New York: Macmillan, 1955), p. 175.

5. "Engaging the Hermit Kingdom: U.S. Policy Toward North Korea," Hearing before the Subcommittee on Asia and the Pacific of the Committee on International Relations, U.S. House of Representatives, February 26, 1997 (Washington: GPO, 1997), p. 44.

6. "Peace Is up to North Korea, Albright Tells Front Line Troops," *New York Times*, February 23, 1997, section 1, p. 10.

7. Park Chung Hee, *To Build A Nation* (Washington: Acropolis Books, 1971), p. 166.

8. Michael Ledeen, *Freedom Betrayed* (Washington: AEI Press, 1996), p. 54.

9. Nicholas Eberstadt, "North Korea's Reunification Policy in Korea and World Affairs," vol. 20, no. 3, fall 1996, p. 423.

10. Albina Birman and Marc Rubin, "The Importance of Socialist Trade in North Korean Economic Development, 1948–1993," paper prepared for the International Programs Center, Population Division, U.S. Bureau of the Census, April 11, 1995, p. 4.

11. B. K. Gills, *Korea versus Korea: A Case of Contested Legitimacy* (Routledge, New York: 1996), pp. 230–31. Hereafter cited as Gills.

12. Unclassified U.S. Defense Intelligence publication, "North Korea: Pursuing Economic Reforms?" November 4, 1997.

13. Gills, pp. 230–31.

14. Nayan Chanda et al., "On Borrowed Time," *Far Eastern Economic Review*, June 26, 1997, p. 26.

15. "Cannibalism Fears in Hungry North Korea," Reuters, Beijing, April 28, 1997.

16. Steven Mufson, "Tales of Starvation Emerge from North Korea," *Washington Post*, April 17, 1997, p. A1; Sonny Efron, "Suffering in Silence: Travelers from North Korea Recount Horrors," *Los Angeles Times* World Report, May 3, 1997, p. 3.

17. "2,000 North Engineers Starve to Death: Hwang Jang Yeop," digital edition of the *Chosun Ilbo*, Seoul, November 12, 1997; and FBIS transcribed text, Hong Kong Agence France-Presse (AFP) in English, Shanghai, "DPRK Workers Sabotaging Production," March 18, 1998.

18. "Leg of Kim Il-Sung Bronze Statue Found Sawed Off," *Korea Times*, digital edition, April 15, 1997.

19. Remarks of Kim Jong-Il December 7, 1996, on the 50th anniversary of the founding of Kim Il Sung University, published first in the *Monthly Chosun*, April 1997, and later in *Naewoo Press*, "Vantage Point," vol. 20, no. 4, April 1997, pp. 40–41.

20. "Engaging the Hermit Kingdom: U.S. Policy Toward North Korea, Hearing before the Subcommittee on Asia and the Pacific of the Committee on International Relations, U.S. House of Representatives, February 26, 1997 (Washington: GPO, 1997), p. 21.

21. "Anti-Kim Jong-il Forces Likely to Surface in North Korea: Report," *Korea Herald*, Seoul, January 22, 1998.

22. "Defector Says Conditions in North Could Spark Revolt," *Korea Herald*, Seoul, November 14, 1997; and Seoul, "2,000 North Engineers Starve to Death: Hwang Jang Yeop," digital edition of the *Chosun Ilbo*, November 12, 1997.

23. See also Chuck Downs, "Tiny Cracks in the Walls of a Stronghold," *Washington Post*, January 13, 1997, p. A17.

24. "Cannibalism Fears in Hungry North Korea," Reuters, Beijing, April 28, 1997.

25. David R. McCann, editor, *Korea Briefing: Toward Reunification* (Armonk, N.Y.: M. E. Sharpe for the Asia Society, 1997), p. 169.

26. Walter B. Slocombe, "The Agreed Framework and the Democratic People's Republic of Korea," (Washington: National Defense University, 1995), INSS paper no. 23, March 1995, p. 3.

27. Charles Kartman statement in "Engaging the Hermit Kingdom: U.S. Policy Toward North Korea," Hearing before the Subcommittee on Asia and the Pacific of the Committee on International Relations, U.S. House of Representatives, February 26, 1997 (Washington: GPO, 1997), p. 43.

28. Opening statement of Rep. Douglas Bereuter, Chairman, Subcommittee on Asia and the Pacific, Joint hearing before the Subcommittees on International Economic Policy and Trade and Asia and the Pacific of the Committee on International Relations, U.S. House of Representatives, February 23, 1995, in "North

Korean Military and Nuclear Proliferation Threat: Evaluation of the U.S.-DPRK Agreed Framework," (Washington: GPO, 1995), p. 3.

29. Ibid., p. 12.

30. Major Scott R. Morris, "America's Most Recent Prisoner of War: The Warrant Officer Bobby Hall Incident," *Army Lawyer*, September 1996, p. 4. (Hereafter cited as Morris.)

31. CINCUNC to the Supreme Commander of the KPA, December 24, 1994, cited in Morris., p. 5.

32. Morris, p. 6, citing Willis Winter, "Events Reveal Pyongyang Power Plays," *Washington Times*, December 30, 1994, p. A1.

33. Joint hearing before the Subcommittees on International Economic Policy and Trade and Asia and the Pacific of the Committee on International Relations, U.S. House of Representatives, February 23, 1995, in "North Korean Military and Nuclear Proliferation Threat: Evaluation of the US-DPRK Agreed Framework," (Washington: GPO, 1995), p. 23.

34. Headquarters United Nations Command, "Command Historical Summary, January 1, 1995–December 31, 1995," pp. 34–36.

35. "North Korea to Meet UN Command over Submarine," *Singapore Straits Times*, October 2, 1996, Internet edition; "North Korea Sends Mixed Signals as South Returns Bodies," CNN News, December 30, 1996; and Carroll Bogert and Jeffrey Bartholet, "A Few Cracks in the Ice," *Newsweek*, January 13, 1997.

36. "N. Korea warns of 'serious consequences' over sub," *Web News*, October 2, 1996.

37. Kevin Sullivan, "Bodies of S. Koreans Found Near Beached Sub," *Washington Post*, October 10, 1996, p. A46.

38. Statement issued December 29, 1996, printed in *Korea Focus on Current Topics*, January–February 1997, vol. 5, no. 1, p. 109.

39. Media reaction summarized by USIA and distributed by Northeast Asia Peace and Security Network Special Report, Berkeley, California, January 9, 1997.

40. Charles Kartman, acting assistant secretary for East Asian and Pacific Affairs, before the House International Relations Committee, February 26, 1997. State Department website, "Testimony on North Korea," p. 6.

41. Kim Ji-Soo, "Work at North Korea Reactor Site Suspended for Five Days over Crumpled Newspaper Incident," *Korea Herald*, Internet edition, October 6, 1997.

42. "UNC Makes Little Progress in Having Farmers Released," *Korea Times*, Internet edition, October 18, 1997.

43. Lee Sung-yul, "North Korea Releases Two Abducted Farmers," *Korea Herald*, Internet edition, October 22, 1997.

44. Ibid.

45. Statement of President Clinton and President Kim Young Sam, April 16, 1996, available on the State Department Web page.

46. Charles Kartman testimony, "Engaging the Hermit Kingdom: U.S. Policy

Toward North Korea," Hearing before the Subcommittee on Asia and the Pacific of the Committee on International Relations, U.S. House of Representatives, February 26, 1997 (Washington: GPO, 1997), p. 13.

47. Minister of Foreign Affairs Yoo Chong-ha at press conference, February 22, 1997.

48. Charles Kartman testimony, "Engaging the Hermit Kingdom: U.S. Policy Toward North Korea," Hearing before the Subcommittee on Asia and the Pacific of the Committee on International Relations, U. S. House of Representatives, February 26, 1997 (Washington: GPO, 1997), p. 7.

49. Secretary of State Albright, June 30, 1997, State Department Web page.

50. State Department Daily Press Briefing, August 8, 1997.

51. Ibid., and Joy, p. 28.

52. State Department Daily Press Briefing, August 8, 1997.

53. State Department Daily Press Briefing, September 22, 1997, p. 3.

54. Reuters, "New Round Set for Historic Korea Talks," Geneva, December 10, 1997.

55. State Department Daily Press Briefing, December 10, 1997; available on the State Department Web site.

56. IMF Press Release, "IMF Approves SDR 15.5 Billion Stand-by Credit for Korea." The text was released by the United States Information Agency on December 5, 1997.

57. "Rumors on DPRK Coup d'état Alarm Government," Seoul, *Joongang Ilbo,* March 7, 1998.

58. Kim Tang, "North Korea's Alarming Movements", Seoul, *Sisa Journal,* March 26, 1998, pp. 10–11; and Seoul, "Minister Kang Plays Down North Korea Crisis Rumors," *Korea Herald,* Internet edition, March 28, 1998. In this article, Kang is quoted as describing the comparative benefits of thermal, instead of nuclear, electric generating capabilities.

59. FBIS translated text, Xinhua News Service, Pyongyang, March 13, 1998.

60. FBIS translated text, Yu Kun-kol, "Large-scale Personnel Reshuffle" in *Today's North Korea, Seoul Shinmun,* Seoul, February 9, 1998; and FBIS translated text, "DPRK Officials Involved in 'North Korea Wind' Executed," Seoul, KBS-1 Radio Network in Korean, March 19, 1998.

61. "Hong Kong Paper Reports that DPRK May Be Under Martial Law," The *Sankei Shimbun,* Hong Kong, March 27, 1998, and "North Korean Trade Officials Reportedly Missing," Reuters, Hong Kong, March 26, 1998.

62. Park Jong-hoon, "Kim Jong-Woo [sic] Executed in NK," digital *Chosun Ilbo,* September 22, 1998, citing a Japanese Kyodo News Agency report.

63. Kim Kyung-ho, staff reporter, "North Korean Defector Arrives in Seoul from Rome," *Korea Herald,* Internet edition, Seoul, February 7, 1998.

64. "North Korean Officer Defector Found to be a Psy War Specialist," digital *Chosun Ilbo,* February 4, 1998.

65. State Department background briefing on the four-party talks, March 2, 1998, distributed by Northeast Asia Peace and Security Network.

66. State Department Daily Press Briefing, March 2, 1998.

67. "Talks 'Major Test' of DPRK's Will to Accept ROK Overtures,"*Korea Herald*, Internet edition, Seoul, March 14, 1998; and Kim Kyung-ho, staff reporter, "Seoul Plans to Push for S-N Contact During 4-Way Talks," March 5, 1998.

68. State Department background briefing on the four-party talks, March 2, 1998, distributed by Northeast Asia Peace and Security Network.

69. Ibid.

70. FBIS transcribed text, "KCNA Denounces US for 'Deadlocked' Talks," KCNA in English, Pyongyang, March 30, 1998.

71. Ibid.

72. FBIS transcribed text, "No Possibility of Progress with Enemies," Agence France Presse (North European Service), Geneva, March 20, 1998.

73. FBIS transcribed text, "US Perfidious Behavior," KCNA, Pyongyang, March 30, 1998.

74. Ibid.

75. "Workers in Electric Power Sector Hold Two-day Meeting," *Naewoo Press*, Seoul, April 1998.

76. FBIS translated text, "Hong Song-nam Addresses Electricity Sector," Pyongyang Korean Central Television Network in Korean, April 2, 1998.

77. FBIS translated text, "They Should Not Act Recklessly and Rashly," *Nodong Shinmun*, April 24, 1998.

78. Ibid.

79. FBIS transcribed text, "Comrade Kim Chong-il Publishes Work on Reunification," KCNA, Pyongyang, April 29, 1998.

80. "North Korea Threatens to Reactivate Its Suspect Nuclear Program," *Korea Times*, May 8, 1998.

81. See the State Department press briefing of October 22, 1996, and daily reports during October 1996 distributed by Northeast Asia Peace and Security Network.

82. Jane's Information Group, IWR *Daily Update*, vol. 5, no. 140, July 23, 1998.

83. Duncan Lennox, "ICBM Threat to the West," *Jane's Defence Weekly*, August 5, 1998.

84. Lee Sung-yul, "Pyongyang's Test-Fire Alerts Neighbors; Military Sources Say Taepo-Dong 1 Missile Could Reach Hong Kong, Taiwan," *Korea Herald* digital edition, September 1, 1998.

85. Speech by Kim Yong Nam at the 10th Supreme People's Assembly, as reported by KCNA, Pyongyang, September 5, 1998, "Kim Jong Il's election as NDC Chairman Proposed."

86. Ibid.

87. David E. Sanger, "North Korea Site an A-Bomb Plant, U.S. Agencies Say," *New York Times*, August 17, 1998, p. 1.

88. John Pomfret, "Aid Group Pulls Out of N. Korea," *Washington Post*, September 30, 1998, p. A22.

89. Hwang Jang Yeop at press conference in Seoul, July 10, 1997.

90. Lieutenant General William K. Harrison, Jr., USA, in 1951; and William J. Taylor, "The Best Strategy Is to Do Nothing," *Los Angeles Times*, September 2, 1998, p. A11.

91. At a speech before the UN General Assembly on September 22, 1998, North Korea's Assistant Minister of Foreign Affairs, Choi Soo Hun, raised the possibility of a new Korean War before the turn of the century. Lee Chul-min, "North Korea Hints at Possibility of Future War," digital *Chosun Ilbo*, September 29, 1998.

Index

About the Author

Chuck Downs, whose career in defense and national security issues spans two decades, wrote *Over the Line: North Korea's Negotiating Strategy* while serving as associate director of Asian Studies at the American Enterprise Institute. From 1991 to 1996, Mr. Downs was deputy director for Regional Affairs and Congressional Relations in the Pentagon's East Asia policy office. He attended the Department of State's Senior Seminar of the Foreign Service Institute from 1990 to 1991, after holding a number of senior positions in the International Security Affairs division in the Department of Defense. In the early 1980s, he worked on territorial and international issues for the Department of the Interior.

In 1997, after a two-year detail to the American Enterprise Institute, Mr. Downs returned to the Pentagon, where he helped build the multinational coalition on Iraq and worked on South Asian security issues.

During his extensive national security experience with the Reagan, Bush, and Clinton administrations, he was awarded the Defense Civilian Service and Meritorious Service medals.

He has published numerous articles and books on foreign policy and defense issues, including, in particular, Asian security and defense matters. He graduated with honors in political science from Williams College in 1972.

DATE DUE